The Complete Guide
to Your Own Business

The Complete Guide to Your Own Business

CURTIS E. TATE, JR.
University of Georgia

LEON C. MEGGINSON
Louisiana State University

CHARLES R. SCOTT, JR.
University of Alabama

LYLE R. TRUEBLOOD
The University of Tulsa

 **DOW JONES-IRWIN**   Homewood, Illinois   60430

First Printing, August 1977

ISBN 0-87094-144-5
Library of Congress Catalog Card No. 77–6166
Printed in the United States of America

Preface

"Doing our own thing" and searching for a sense of meaning, identity, creativity, and achievement are important to all of us.

One of the best ways of accomplishing these things is to become the owner of a business. Yet, the management of all types of economic activity is becoming increasingly more complex and difficult because of the problems and pressures involved. This is especially true of independent businesses, as shown by the fact that about 930 out of every 1,000 new businesses started in the United States will eventually fail. The failure rate is a shocking 93 percent!

Because of this reality, the purpose of this book is to improve your opportunity for successfully "doing your own thing." This does not mean that you will be successful after you have read and studied the material, but it should help improve your chances of succeeding.

Our objectives in developing this book have been to:

1. Tell you how to own your own business.
2. Show you how to avoid some of the mistakes in conceiving, initiating, organizing, and operating an independent business that have been economically fatal to others.
3. Teach you how to get the most from the limited economic and human resources you are able to muster for your business.
4. Guide you in managing and operating your own business.

You will note that we make frequent reference to THE DOW JONES-IRWIN BUSINESS PAPERS. This is a separate publication which contains 75 different checklists and forms to use in managing your business.

Owning and operating a business is a very practical job. It involves desire, hard work, and an independent mind. We commend you for these uncommon traits. You will also need some luck: We wish you the very best of that common element.

July 1977   Curtis E. Tate, Jr.
                                                  Leon C. Megginson
                                                  Charles R. Scott, Jr.
                                                  Lyle R. Trueblood

Contents

You As an Independent Businessman

Independently owned businesses now account for about one half of all this country's business activities. Thus such businesses perform an important function in our economic system. We begin this book by showing the unique challenges involved in managing one of them.

If you are considering entering an independent business, the first thing you should decide is whether owning and managing such a business is the "right" thing for you to do. The material in Part One should help you make that decision.

If you are already an independent business executive, this material will permit you to take a hard look at where you are and where you are going. (To simplify our presentation and avoid needless repetition, we will assume that you are entering an independent business for the first time.)

The role of independent business in our economy and the challenges it affords are taken up in Chapter 1. Then, Chapter 2 considers the characteristics, attitudes, and objectives of owner-managers of independent businesses

You, as one of those owner-managers, will enter business for yourself because you want financial profits and certain nonmonetary benefits. To achieve these objectives, you must give up the benefits you get through working for someone else, and you must assume the risks of ownership. These ideas are covered in Chapter 3.

chapter 1

The Challenge of Owning
an Independent Business

In managing a business, a person must often make decisions after he[1] weighs the advantages and disadvantages of various alternatives. You should also use this approach when you decide whether to become the owner of a business or whether you should work for someone else. This chapter is designed to help you evaluate the advantages and disadvantages of becoming the owner of an independent business.

INDEPENDENT BUSINESS AND BIG BUSINESS

In distinguishing between big business and independent or small business, some of the criteria used are relative size, type of customers, financial strength, and number of employees. For example, in the Small Business Act of 1953, Congress defined a small business as one which "is independently owned and operated and which is not dominant in its field of operation."

Distinction according to Size

The definitions of an independent business vary all the way from that of the office of the secretary of the treasury (a firm with "receipts of less than $1,000,000,") to our own ("an organization with a name, a place of operations, an owner, and one or more workers other than the owner"). According to the first definition, there were more than 14.5 million independent businesses in the United States in 1969.[2] According to the second, there were around 5.7 million independent businesses in 1971.[3] The Small Business Administration says there were over 8 million independent

---

[1] The common pronouns *he, him,* and *his* are used in this book to refer to persons of both sexes.

[2] Small Business Administration, *Annual Report,* vol. 2 (Washington, D.C.: U.S. Government Printing Office, 1972), p. 28.

[3] National Foundation of Independent Business reports.

3

businesses.[4] That number included "invisible" businesses, such as people working out of their own homes.

According to Dun & Bradstreet, there are about 2,250,000 businesses in this country. Well over half are worth less than $50,000. Only 5 percent are worth more than $200,000 (see Figure 1–1).

According to the definition used in this book—an organization with a name, a place of operations, an owner, and one or more workers other than the owner—independent businesses make up about 95 percent of all U.S. business units. These firms account for around 37 percent of our gross national product; 99 percent of firms and 85 percent of sales in construction; 96 percent of firms and 72 percent of sales in retail trade; 94 percent of firms and 70 percent of sales in wholesale trade; and 94 percent of firms and 30 percent of sales in manufacturing.

FIGURE 1–1
Distribution of Business Firms by Worth, 1972

Source: W. H. Kuehn, *The Pitfalls in Managing a Small Business* (New York: Dun & Bradstreet, 1973), p. 3.

Distinction according to Intentions

The *intentions* of owners and managers of independent firms tend to be different from those of managers of large enterprises.

The intentions of managers of large businesses can probably be summarized as the desire for job security; for place, power, and prestige; and for high income.

While these same motives might impel someone to become the owner of an independent business, a vast difference can be summarized by the word *independence*. This distinction was made by a recent graduate of a large university when he explained to one of us why so few college graduates want to go into business for themselves.

I believe that at least part of the answer is that the new graduates just don't know where to start and what to expect in the business world. With this lack of knowledge, they just don't have the "guts" to try it on their own. . . . I always said that if I were going to make anyone rich, it was going to be myself. (Unfortunately, it has not worked out that way—yet.) Even with this burning desire to be my own boss, I was very hesitant and almost afraid to go into business for myself. However, I'm still glad I did.

[4] Small Business Administration, *Annual Report*, vol. 1 (Washington, D.C.: U.S. Government Printing Office, 1972), p. 2.

This letter illustrates the goal of freedom from interference or control by "superiors." Managers of independent businesses want autonomy in exercising their initiative and ambition.

The independent business has many advantages over its larger competitors. It is usually in closer touch with its customers, employees, and suppliers. It tends to have better employee relations. It can do a more individualized job for customers and thus attracts customers on the basis of specialty product, quality, and personal services rather than on the impersonal factors of price or mass production. Due to the small percentage that goes for overhead and non-revenue-producing activities, some activities can be performed more efficiently by independent organizations.

The independent enterprise is often a source of new materials, processes, ideas, services, and products that larger firms are reluctant to provide. The big company, because it is not as flexible as a smaller firm, is usually committed by its investment in tools, inventory, and personnel to producing the same product in larger quantities or for longer periods of time.

Smaller companies keep the bigger concerns "on their toes." By introducing new products, methods, services, and so forth, independent businesses help check the development of monopolies. Therefore, independent businesses encourage competition, if not in price, at least in design and efficiency.

Independent businesses usually have a more intimate knowledge of their communities, and therefore take more interest in them. Another advantage of independent businesses is that they *produce people as well as goods and services.* They enable their people to achieve a more well-rounded development than these people could achieve in larger organizations. This development is accomplished by providing a greater variety of learning experiences in work activities. People have greater freedom in making decisions and in performing a greater variety of activities. This freedom lends zest and interest to their work. In addition, it trains people to become better leaders and to use their talents and energies most effectively.

It has been said that the independent business is a manifestation of one of the basic American freedoms, namely, risk taking—with its rewards and punishments. Americans are to enter or leave a business at will, to start small and grow big, to expand or contract, and to succeed or fail. This freedom is the basis of our economic system. However, certain legal and other requirements must be met before one can start or close a firm. The manager may have responsibilities to customers, employees, investors, and/or the community which prevent leaving at will.

The independent business is flexible. Therefore, it can switch its production readily to meet changing market conditions and can adapt itself quickly to changing demands within its field and capacity. It can even change fields. It is a center of experiments and innovations. Many products originate in independent businesses. This is especially true in the electronic computer field.

DISADVANTAGES OF AN INDEPENDENT BUSINESS

The discussions of the disadvantages of independent business usually boil down to three things: inadequate management ability, inadequate financing (including "unfair" taxation), and poor competitive position. One study showed the pitfalls facing independent business managers and what can be done about them (see Figure 1-2).

FIGURE 1-2
Pitfalls Facing Small Businessmen

Pitfalls

1. Lack of experience.
2. Lack of money.
3. The wrong location.
4. Inventory mismanagement.
5. Too much capital going into fixed assets.
6. Poor credit-granting practices.
7. Taking too much out for yourself.
8. Unplanned expansion.
9. Having the wrong attitudes.

What Can Be Done about These Pitfalls?

1. Recognize limitations.
2. Planning.
3. Record keeping.
4. Watch the balance sheet—not just the profits.
5. Investigate.
6. Suppliers and banks.
7. Learning.
8. Professional assistance.
9. Watch your health.

Source: W. H. Kuehn, *The Pitfalls in Managing a Small Business* (New York: Dun & Bradstreet, 1973).

The problems of managing independent businesses have multiplied during recent years. During World War II, the Korean War, and the Vietnam War, many new businesses showed unusual profits. However, as the "seller's market" ended each time and a "buyer's market" developed, the problems of confronting them began to multiply.

During these periods, many independent business managers *relied on one-person management.* They seldom selected effective subordinates. If they did, they failed to give them enough authority and responsibility. Often family members who were not capable were given positions of authority.

Managers of independent businesses *cannot be specialized* in one area. They must make their own decisions and are forced to live with those decisions. Because of the independent business's limited resources, it cannot afford costly mistakes; but because the independent organization is so small, it cannot afford to hire assistance to help prevent managers from making mistakes. Lack of sufficient time to give attention to the various managerial functions accounts for the vast majority of failures among independent businesses.

A related limitation of independent businesses is the *shortage of working capital.* This leads to the inability to keep up with larger competitors in facilities, equipment, tools, and methods. Efforts have been made to overcome this difficulty by making loans available to small businesses and by obtaining favorable tax laws to assist them.

Another disadvantage is the *lack of coordination between production and marketing.* It is important for an independent business to keep a balance between (1) having too few products so that sales are lost, and (2) diversifying too fast. This means that there should be a balance between the advantages of diversification and the advantages of product specialization.

Some other disadvantages are—a lack of proper recordkeeping; a lack of effective selling techniques—especially market research, specialty advertising, and personal selling; too rapid and unplanned expansion; and the increasing complexity of internal management as the organization grows in size. These disadvantages are covered throughout this book. However, some of the problems associated with growth will be discussed here.

The problem of growth appears to be a built-in dilemma facing many independent businesses. First, if the owners are inefficient and if their initiative or abilities are insufficient, their organizations flounder and eventually become "business failures."

Second, if the owners are mediocre, their organizations do not grow and are constantly plagued with the problems associated with smallness.

Third, if the owners are efficient and capable, they run the risk of losing the very things they seek from their business firms. The organizations succeed and grow, and this means that the owners lose some of the autonomy and control they seek. If nothing else, the owners must now please a larger number of people, including customers, the public, and employees. They also have the problem of controlling other people, of doing the very thing they resented in others. All too often, owner-managers are not equipped to control other people well, and they begin to have interpersonal problems in their firms. If the firms become large enough and require outside capital for further success and growth, the owners may lose autonomy and control.

Historically, the ownership and management of independent businesses have tended to follow the growth pattern shown in Figure 1–3. In

THE PROBLEM OF GROWTH

the first stage, the owner manages the company and performs all the work himself. In the second stage, the owner hires one or more employees to help perform the manual and mental activities. In the third stage, the owner hires a manager to run the business. Thus, the company takes on the form, characteristics, and many of the problems of a big business.

FIGURE 1–3
Stages in the Development of an Independent Business

First Stage--One-person operation, where owner does all the activities.

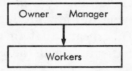

Second Stage--Separation of management and nonmanagement functions; hired subordinates to do some of the manual and/or mental activities while owner manages.

Owner – Manager

↓

Workers

Third Stage--Separation of ownership and management functions; owner begins to relinquish the responsibilities for the day-to-day running of the business activities to a professional manager.

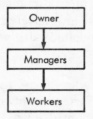

Source: Adapted from L. C. Megginson, *Providing Management Talent for Small Business* (Small Business Management Research Reports; Baton Rouge: College of Business Administration, Louisiana State University, 1961), p. 7.

THE PROBLEM OF "FAILURE"

The threat of failure is ever present for independent businesses. Voluntary discontinuances may result from such factors as ill-health, changes in family situations, and the apparent advantages of working for someone else. Other discontinuances are the result of inability to make the business "go." Things just don't work out as planned. These are "failures."

There are two types of failures. One ends up in court with some kind of loss to the creditors. There are relatively few of these failures. In fact, there were only 10,326 such failures in 1971 and 9,566 in 1972.[5] The underlying causes of these "formal failures" for 1972 are shown in Figure 1–4.

[5] *The Business Failure Record, 1972* (New York: Business Economics Department, Dun & Bradstreet, 1973), p. 3.

FIGURE 1-4
Causes of 9,566 Business Failures in 1972

Overall Causes	Underlying Causes
Neglect due to	Bad habits, poor health, marital difficulties, etc.
Fraud due to	Misleading name, false financial statement, premeditated overbuy, irregular disposal of assets, etc.
Lack of experience in the line, lack of managerial experience, unbalanced experience, incompetence due to	Inadequate sales, heavy operating expenses, receivables difficulties, inventory difficulties, excess fixed assets, poor location, competitive weakness, etc.
Disaster due to	Fire, flood, burglary, employee fraud, strike, etc.

Source: *The Business Failure Record, 1972* (New York: Business Economics Department, Dun & Bradstreet, 1973), pp. 11–12.

What are the characteristics of the firms which suffer this type of failure? Retailers and service establishments tend to fail earlier than other types of businesses, while manufacturers, construction firms, and wholesalers fail later. This is shown in Table 1-1.

TABLE 1-1
Formal Business Failures Classified by Year and Size of Liability

Year	Under $5,000	$5,000 to $25,000	$25,000 to $100,000	$100,000 to $1 million	Over $1 million
1970	4.0	29.7	40.9	22.8	2.6
1971	3.8	27.2	42.7	23.5	2.8
1972	4.1	26.1	43.4	23.4	3.0

Source: *The Business Failure Record, 1972* (New York: Business Economics Department, Dun & Bradstreet, 1973), p. 6.

The other kind of failure is more important numerically, and probably emotionally as well. This involves situations where individuals have put their savings—or income—into a business only to see losses wipe out their investment. Creditors don't suffer, for the owner has put up the funds to pay off the debts. The owner is the one who packs up, closes the door, and says, "That's it! I'll never try starting a business of my own again."

The Service Corps of Retired Executives (SCORE) estimates that around 400,000 small firms go out of business each year in the United States, and 100,000 of these fail in the first year of existence.[6] The causes of failure, in descending order, are: (1) lack of business records, (2) lack of business experience, (3) insufficient stock turnover, (4) accounts receivable, (5) inventory shrinkage, (6) poor inventory control, (7) lack of finances, (8) improper markup, and (9) lack of sales.

---

[6] "Failing Businesses," *Parade*, September 8, 1974, p. 24.

chapter 2

What Are Your Objectives?

After presenting the challenges of owning and operating an independent business, we would like to explore the role you could play as the owner of such a business.

YOUR PERSONAL OBJECTIVES

A person's occupation is more than just a set of skills and functions; it is a way of life. It largely determines the environment in which the person lives; it selects, and often strengthens, the traits that he uses most frequently. It usually carries a status in the community, and it provides the person's social roles and patterns for living. Since it largely determines with what sorts of people the person spends much of his life, it greatly influences value judgments and ethical standards. Occupational preference and personality traits are also usually related. Consequently, your ultimate objective in choosing your occupation should be the satisfaction of your individual needs.

Human Motives in General

Many efforts have been made to classify and explain human needs. The more popular efforts are summarized here.

Maslow's Needs Hierarchy. Abraham Maslow, a psychologist, said that human needs could be grouped together in a hierarchy, from the bottom up.[1] As one need is satisfied, the next higher need comes into play. The needs are:

5. Self-fulfillment.
4. Ego.
3. Social.

2. Safety.
1. Physiological.

---

[1] Douglas McGregor, *The Human Side of Enterprise* (New York: McGraw-Hill Book Co., 1960), pp. 36–39.

10

Herzberg's Motivators and Maintenance Factors. Frederick Herzberg, another psychologist, said two sets of factors are present in every job situation.[2] One set of factors is necessary to *maintain a good working relationship,* but these factors *do not motivate the individual to produce at a higher level.* They are:

1. Supervision
2. Company policies and administration.
3. Employee benefits.
4. Job security.
5. Working conditions
6. Salary.
7. Relationships with others.

The other factors *motivate people to produce at a high level.* They are:

1. Achievement.
2. Recognition.
3. Responsibility.
4. Creative and challenging work.
5. Advancement.

Motives of Independent Business Owners

As the owner of an independent business, you can fulfill all of these needs through managing your own firm. How you do this depends upon the knowledge, skills, and personality traits you bring to your business. Your personal objectives express the type of life you wish to lead.

A great deal depends on the type of person you are and your dedication to your business. Owning your own business can be very rewarding in the following ways:

1. You can make a great deal of money, including certain expense account benefits.
2. You can perform a satisfying service to your community.
3. You can obtain prestige in your community.
4. You can find many new challenges and new experiences.
5. You can be proud of what you have built.

There is a certain satisfaction in managing something you have built that does not come from directing a business that others have built. But before you decide upon this course, other questions must be answered—if you are to succeed. Ambition, desire, capital, and willingness are not enough. You still need:

1. Technical and managerial know-how.
2. Preparation.
3. Experience.
4. Ability.
5. Perserverance.
6. Willingness to work.
7. Personality.
8. Judgment.
9. Competitive spirit.
10. Health.

---

[2] Frederick Herzberg et al., *The Motivation to Work*, rev. ed. (New York: John Wiley and Sons, 1959).

Now, one last time, before you consider risking your money, time, and effort to become an entreprenueur, ask yourself the following questions:

1. Am I willing to make the personal and family sacrifices?
2. What is my objective—to make a lot of money or to perform a useful service?
3. Do I have the patience and tenacity required?
4. Do I have the skills and knowledge so that I can collect the resources needed; can I convert those resources so that customers will want them; and can I organize and direct the activities needed to succeed?
5. How much of me do I want to put into the business?
6. How much money do I need to get started, and where do I get it?

THE OBJECTIVES OF AN INDEPENDENT BUSINESS

Since the most valid distinction between independent and big business is based on the *intentions, aims, goals,* or *objectives* of the owner-manager and the firm itself, these factors deserve considerable attention on your part at the very beginning. One of the most important functions you—as the owner-manager—will perform is setting these objectives. The *objectives are the ends toward which all the activities of your organization will be aimed.* They determine the "character" of your firm.

The objectives of the organization itself and those of its owner, managers, and employees are not necessarily the same. We will now look at some organizational objectives which should be considered along with the personal objectives which have just been discussed.

As for the business itself, there are at least two sets of objectives—the *overall objectives of the organization* and the *subsidiary goals* of the individual parts of the organization. The overall objectives give unity of direction to the organization and provide standards by which the actions of members of the firm can be measured. Each part of the firm will then set its objectives in order to contribute to the overall objectives.

Among the *overall objectives* that are important for you to consider are:

1. Service.
2. Profit.
3. Social.
4. Growth.

The Service Objective

The overall objective of any business organization must be to perform a useful *service* for society by producing goods or services and distributing them to the public. A private organization is expected to receive a profit for its operations. In a free-enterprise economy, profit is considered to be in the public interest. Even in a profit-oriented organization, however, the primary objective is service to the public in the form of producing goods or services at a cost which will ensure a "fair" price to the consumer and "adequate" profits to the owners. Thus, the person who aspires to operate an independent business must make service his primary objective. If the enterprise ceases to give service, people will not accept it and it will go out of business.

When you make decisions concerning the products and customers of the type of business you desire to establish or enter, you will be considering the service objective.

The *profit motive* is not always understood, so a word of explanation may be needed. Profits are the reward for taking risks—such as investing your funds in an untried business and trying to anticipate the needs and wants of the public—and they are required if any private business is to survive. Profits are needed to create new jobs, acquire new facilities, and develop new products or services. Profits come into existence through satisfying the demand for a product or service efficiently and effectively.

In summary, profits compensate you for your acceptance of business risks and for your performance of an economic service. They are needed to assure the continuity of your business.

Your firm also has *social objectives* for people in the community other than customers—employees, suppliers, the government, and the community itself. All of these groups should be served effectively. Therefore, you—as owner—have a social responsibility. You occupy a trusteeship position and should act to protect the interests of your customers, employees, suppliers, and the general public. Your personal moral code should have a sound basis if you are to act fairly and honestly in your relationships with all of these groups.

You should select a *growth* objective for your firm early in your business career. Some questions you need to answer in setting this objective are:

1. Do I seek mere survival?
2. Do I seek a rate of profit which is "satisfactory," considering my efforts and investment?
3. Do I seek to maximize profits?
4. Will I be satisfied to remain small?
5. Do I want to grow and challenge larger firms?

Walter Barnett is a local contractor specializing in commercial construction. He has had many offers to expand locally, regionally, and even statewide. He has consistently chosen to remain small, bid on the jobs he wants, have few labor problems, earn a comfortable living, and "enjoy life." He appears to be achieving these objectives.[3]

---

[3] The names in these incidents and illustrations are disguised, although the events are real.

Subsidiary Objectives

The primary function of the independent business manager is to direct the activities of the organization toward attaining its overall objectives. Subsidiary objectives should be set for each functional unit of the organization (such as production, marketing, finance, personnel, and research) to provide guidelines in meeting the overall objectives. In addition, the tasks of all employees must be directed toward the organization's overall objectives.

This process is not simple, for each level of objectives may consist of several related objectives. In a practical business situation, the attainment of two or more objectives on any given level is often achieved only at the expense of other objectives on the same level or between levels. Consequently, conflict sometimes arises among objectives. This conflict must be resolved or minimized if productivity and profitability are to be achieved.

THE MESHING OF OBJECTIVES

A survey of 97 small, owner-managed firms in the San Antonio area revealed a correlation between profitability, customer satisfaction, manager satisfaction, and psychic rewards.[4] It also showed that the chances of success are greatly increased when the objectives of the business—service at a profit—are meshed with owners' personal objectives.

An integration of objectives can be accomplished if the emphasis is directed toward *optimizing objectives* and *minimizing company and personal conflicts.* Communication plays an important part in the process. The close interpersonal relationships between owners of independent businesses and their subordinates, customers, and others speed up communication and make integration easier.

The independent organization offers a sense of belonging that is missing in larger groups. It has an *espirt de corps* that cannot be duplicated in a large company. According to the sales manager of a small distribution company:

> There is a sense of belonging that is hard to find in a big company. Also, in a small company, the job carries with it a position which gives the person a sense of prestige that he would lose if he went to a larger company.

Exhibit 1 in *The Dow Jones-Irwin Business Papers* is a checklist you can use to help you determine the objectives of your firm.

---

[4] Hál B. Pickle and Brian S. Rungeling, "Empirical Investigation of Entrepreneurial Goals and Customer Satisfaction," *Journal of Business,* vol. 46, no. 2 (April 1973), pp. 268–73.

chapter 3

Do You Have What It Takes?

In Chapter 1, some of the characteristics, advantages, and disadvantages of independent business enterprises were pointed out. Personal and business objectives were examined in Chapter 2. Now you will look at some characteristics of successful independent business managers, some personal requirements for success in an independent business, and an introspective personal analysis you can make to see whether you have the characteristics needed for success in managing an independent firm.

As one studies the careers of people who failed as independent business managers, one becomes acutely aware that all too often the failure resulted from one or more of the following weaknesses:

1. Too much was left to chance.
2. Crucial obstacles went unnoticed through ignorance.
3. The amounts of time and physical effort demanded were not recognized and planned for.
4. The amount of capital required for a particular business was not determined or was grossly underestimated.
5. Too many vital decisions were made by "hunch" or through intuition, without adequate background and experience upon which to base them.

The skills, abilities, and personal characteristics of owner-managers exert a more powerful influence on the fortunes of independent companies than on larger firms. Whether or not you have the necessary characteristics should weigh heavily in determining whether or not you enter an independent firm. Also, the methods and procedures you adopt in an independent firm should be designed to offset any personal deficiencies you may have and to build upon your strengths.

There are at least seven common characteristics of owners of independent enterprises:

COMMON CHARACTERISTICS OF SUCCESSFUL INDEPENDENT BUSINESS MANAGERS

1. A great sense of independence.
2. A strong sense of enterprise.
3. Dominated as much by personal and family considerations as by professional choices.
4. Enter small business more by chance than design.
5. Jealously guard their time.
6. Limited formal education.
7. Expect quick results.

These are the characteristics we have found to be present most frequently in owner-managers of independent firms.

A Great Sense of Independence

Successful managers of independent businesses have *a highly developed sense of independence* and *a strong desire to be independent of outside control,* whether this control is financial, governmental, or any other type. They enjoy the feeling of freedom which comes from being "captain" of their own fate.

Robert Smith worked his way through college sweeping floors in a lighting fixture store. He believed that success depended upon "never working for a company that you can't own" and upon building a firm of moderate size that "you can control completely." At age 23, he borrowed $75,000, purchased some metalworking equipment, and set up shop producing and selling modern lighting fixtures. Seven years later he was selling several million dollars worth of lamps each year.

A Strong Sense of Enterprise

The managers of independent businesses have a strong sense of enterprise which gives them a desire to use their ideas, abilities, ambitions, aspirations, and initiatives to the greatest degree possible. They are able to conceive new ideas, plan them, see them carried out, and profit from the results. In larger organizations different specialists usually do different phases of the work.

Another aspect of enterprise which is almost always present in independent businessmen is their drive for achievement and their willingness to work long, hard hours to reach their goal.

Dick Crowe, who worked his way through college doing odd jobs, bought a Weight Watchers franchise. He is totally committed to the firm, works long hours, and doesn't "know how to enjoy myself. I can't relax, for my mind is always working, thinking, calculating."

Strong Personal and Family Considerations

Independent business managers are probably dominated as much by personal and family considerations as by the profit-making motive. Quite frequently, our students tell us they are returning home to start a business

16

because that is what their family expects them to do. Even more frequent is the comment that they are going back to run the family business rather than go somewhere else and work for another company.

Many people have gravitated by chance into a position of ownership or management of an independent firm. This is especially true when the person has grown up in the business and then one day finds himself in the positions of having to take it over. These are the owners or managers who quite frequently ask for assistance in the form of management training and development. This type of individual differs sharply from the type of individual who comes to college with the ambition to become a professional manager and gears his whole program toward that end.

Acquire Businesses by Chance

Time is very valuable, because of the many hours that must be dedicated to an independent business. The position of an independent business manager is very different from that of the manager of a large corporation who is expected to devote time to "public relations" and to have someone else perform his duties while he is away. The independent business manager must still perform all the duties even if he engages in outside activities. He is very jealous of his time and becomes irritable if someone infringes upon it.

Guard Their Time

> Dudley Moore has an insurance agency. Although he is active in his church, he accepts only those positions where his expertise is really needed. Also, he is usually the last one to arrive at a committee meeting—only after the chitchat is over—and he leaves as soon as the business activities are over.

Independent business managers are apt to have only limited formal education. But they tend to supplement this through reading, "picking the brains" of others, and taking extension and correspondence courses.

Limited Formal Education

Independent business managers expect quick results from an investment of either time or capital. They seek a quick turnover of a relatively small investment rather than engaging in the long-range planning which is common in large businesses.

Expect Quick Results

In general, independent business managers are unreconstructed rebels who wish to remain free from the conformity required in the larger organizations. They are rugged individualists who are willing to take risks and who have the determination and perseverance to capitalize upon those risks.

REQUIREMENTS FOR SUCCESS IN AN INDEPENDENT BUSINESS

Although it is impossible to determine or state *all* the requirements for success in an independent business, we do know that the following are important:

1. A sensitivity to internal and external changes affecting the business.
2. The ability to react quickly to those changes.
3. Accurate and useful operating and marketing information.
4. The effective, but humane, use of human resources.
5. Obtaining sufficient investment capital at a reasonable price.
6. The effective handling of government laws, rules, and regulations.

Adaptability to Change

An important characteristic of independent business enterprises is their vulnerability to technological and environmental changes. Because the businesses are small, such changes have a great impact upon their operations and profitability. Yet independent businesses can have an advantage over larger firms in this respect, for they can react faster to change because they have fewer people making decisions. It is extremely important that you *be sensitive to the changes taking place inside and outside your firm and that you be ready to react quickly to those changes.*

Accurate Operating and Marketing Information

Gathering *accurate and useful information concerning the operations of your business and its market* is also extremely important. You must keep informed—on a regular and frequent basis—of the financial position and market position of the business. You must know how to analyze this information and how to develop plans to maintain or improve your position.

Effective Use of Human Resources

The *effective, but humane, use of human resources* is very important to an independent business enterprise, because its owner-managers have a more personal association with their employees. Your workers can be an economical source of information and ideas and their productivity can be greatly increased if you allow them to share ideas with you—and if you are *willing to recognize and reward their contribution.*

Sufficient Investment Capital

One of the most difficult problems facing independent business managers is *obtaining sufficient investment capital—at a reasonable price.* This requires that you plow back more of the profits into your business. You must delay your desire for immediate dividends in favor of the best long-run interest of the business. You must develop a strong credit rating and pay your debts promptly.

You need to be able to *handle "red tape" effectively,* for the day when independent business firms enjoyed an exemption from governmental legislation and regulation has passed. It is now even argued that independent businesses are taxed disproportionately higher than larger businesses. Recent civil rights, occupational safety and health, and environmental legislation no longer exempts independent business establishments, but frequently adds tremendously to their costs of operation.

Effective Handling of Government Regulations

Now that you have seen some of the characteristics of successful independent business managers, as well as the personal requirements needed for success in an independent firm, you should be particularly interested in whether you possess a sufficient number of those characteristics and requirements to be successful. The following personal evaluation should help you decide this important question.

PERSONAL ANALYSIS

Your management philosophy will provide a basis for decision making in your company. In order to manage your firm effectively, you need an ethical value system and some basic principles that you believe in and can use as guidelines. Among the more important questions related to your ethical value system are the following:

What Is Your Philosophy of Life?

1. What are your true motives?
2. What are your real objectives?
3. What psychological and social relations do you consider necessary for success?
4. What general economic atmosphere do you prefer to operate in?

Advantages of Such a Philosophy. To begin with, let us state that everyone has a philosophy, whether it is conscious or unconscious, whether it is well-defined or ill-defined. However, having and using a conscious and well-formed philosophy of management will give you many major advantages. Such a philosophy should:

1. *Help you win effective support and followers.* People will know what you stand for and why you act as you do and will therefore have more confidence in your actions.
2. *Provide guidelines for you and provide a foundation for your managerial thinking and decision making.* Your management philosophy should be especially useful in coping with rapidly changing conditions to which there are no tailor-made solutions.
3. *Supply a framework within which you can improve your thinking abilities.*

Types of Philosophies. There is an infinite variety of philosophies. However, we will discuss only the following:

1. Rugged individualism versus a group-centered philosophy.
2. An activities-oriented philosophy versus a results-oriented philosophy.

Characteristics associated with these philosophies vary, but in general the *rugged individualist* is a highly self-reliant decisionmaker. Most of the strong-willed, powerful industrialists of the late 1800s and early 1900s—such as Henry Ford—were rugged individualists. On the other hand, many present-day managers believe that the group should be considered in all managerial decisions. These *group-centered* individuals use committees extensively and consider the many mutual interests of management and other employees.

The *activities-oriented* manager stresses what must be done, tends to be a "one-person show," prescribes the organization structure, sets the tasks of subordinates, delegates decision-making authority, determines the best methods and exercises tight control over employee performance. The *results-oriented* manager prefers to use the full resources of his people, emphasizes goal-setting, assists in achieving goals, wants himself and his subordinates to develop self-commitment and self-direction, gives his subordinates a large role in determining the methods of work, and exercises control by results.

Your philosophy depends upon your personal values—what you consider to be *right* or *wrong, good* or *bad, desirable* or *undesirable.* You formulate your business objectives on the basis of your philosophy and value system.

The Professional Approach versus Personal Approach. There are two categories into which your philosophy may be divided:

1. An impersonal professional approach.
2. A personal, moral-ethical approach.

In counseling and consulting with prospective business owners, we have found that on occasion it is essential to approach the issues in this fashion. For example, an individual may come in to discuss the prospects of opening a bar or tavern. *Impersonally and professionally,* it is pointed out that certain licenses and permits must be obtained. The services of a local attorney familiar with these matters are necessary, because certain additional hidden payments may be needed. The approximate capital investment involved for building, fixtures, inventory, and the desirable type of location is defined. The amount of net income that may be anticipated will be stated. From a *personal, moral-ethical point of view,* it might be pointed out that there are social implications of being involved with this type of business, such as the local tendency to stigmatize people involved in it. In addition, it might be pointed out that certain local ethical sensitivities might be offended by such a business. Therefore, it might be best in the long run to avoid the business even though the economic benefits might be substantial.

20

If you want to become an entrepreneur, then you should make a penetrating analysis of your personal attributes in order to determine the types of business that best satisfy your personal objectives and needs. You might ask yourself questions about *your mental abilities,* such as these:

What Are Your Mental Abilities?

1. Can you visualize your choice of a business in its entirety?
2. Can you observe things in perspective?
3. Can you generate ideas in a freewheeling fashion?
4. Can you generate ideas relating to new methods and new products?
5. Are you technically oriented?
6. Can you translate activities into a technical framework?
7. Are you sensitive to the human factor?
8. Are you sensitive to the feelings, wants, and needs of others?

If you are thinking of entering an independent business, you should make a self-analysis of your *personal attitudes* in specific areas. Some of these areas are your:

What Are Your Attitudes?

1. Aspiration level.
2. Willingness to accept responsibility.
3. Mental and emotional stability.
4. Commitment to the idea of independent business.
5. Willingness to take risks.
6. Ability to live with irregular hours.
7. Self-discipline.
8. Self-confidence.

Each of these attitudes is discussed in detail.

Are you able to define your *aspiration level?* Aspiration is the driving force behind an individual. It is what he wants to achieve in life. You may want to express this level in such terms as education, marital and parental status, dollars, status in the community, doing physical or mental labor, or being of service to others

The degree to which you are willing to accept *responsibility* determines the relationship you will have with the public and the customer. So far in your life, have you willingly accepted responsibility? Are you willing to assume responsibility in the future? Are you willing to admit to the last error you made? Are you willing to accept responsibility even though this may mean personal sacrifice? Are you willing to accept responsibility for the actions of others even if you have given them the authority to act for you?

Are you a *stable person,* or are you impatient and unwilling to wait for success? If success is not immediately achievable, are you willing to continue to work for it? Do you seek immediate gratification of your wants, or are you willing to postpone them in order to reinvest in a firm? When given an opportunity that may not be readily achievable, many young people tend to move on to another activity. These people may generate a "good income" in their quest for "fast buck" opportunities. However, the successful entrepreneur does not work this way.

Are you *committed?* This is the trait that determines whether an individual will endure the trials, tribulations, and personal and family sacrifices necessary to achieve his or her objectives. How committed are you to your idea for the business you have dreamed of? Unless your commitment is firmly implanted, it is suggested that you forgo the idea and seek a vocation to which you can be committed.

Do you enjoy *taking risks?* Are you willing to take the chance of "losing your shirt" to gain other benefits? Or do you "play it close to the vest" and seek the "sure thing" in life? It does make a difference!

Can you live with an *irregular schedule?* Are you willing to forgo regular hours and to be worried during your time off? Are you willing to give up your weekends if something goes wrong or if it becomes necessary to prepare a proposal for that new contract? Or would you prefer regular hours, holidays, and vacations?

Are you *self-disciplined?* The old cliché "Don't take too much out the front door" still applies to early business owners. It is important that you leave sufficient working capital in the business to provide for growth and contingencies.

Are you *self-confident?* Can you make decisions alone?

If the answers to these questions are yes, or if you feel that you can make the answers yes in the near future, you may have the qualities that would make your independent business venture a satisfying and rewarding activity.

You are now at the point of deciding whether or not to go into your own business. You are in a position comparable to that of an automobile driver who is approaching a stoplight. Just as the light control mechanism is outside the influence of the driver, so there are external factors beyond your control—social, economic, cultural, and natural elements—that should influence your decision about entering a business of your own. And just as the driver approaching a traffic light must be responsive to the control mechanism, so you must be responsive to the external factors pertinent to the success or failure of your business.

See Exhibit 2 in *The Dow Jones-Irwin Business Papers* for a questionnaire that will aid you in performing a self-analysis.

WHERE TO LOOK FOR FURTHER INFORMATION

"Are You One of Them?" *MBA*, vol. 7, no. 6 (June–July 1973), p. 5.

Buchan, P. Bruce. "Corporate Risk Policies," *Journal: Management Advisor*, vol. 10, no. 5 (September–October 1973), pp. 45–51.

"Now It's Young People Making Millions," *U.S. News & World Report*, February 25, 1974, pp. 47–50.

Roscow, James P. "Can Entrepreneurship Be Taught?" *MBA*, vol. 7, no. 6 (June–July 1973), pp. 12, 16, 50, and 51.

"Some Hints on Small Business Company Success," *Iron Age*, June 1, 1967, p. 25.

PART TWO

Planning and Organizing a New Business

In Part One, you learned about some challenges of entering an independent business, some personal and business objectives of independent businessmen, and some characteristics which lead to success in owning or managing an independent business. WE ASSUME THAT YOU HAVE NOW DECIDED THAT YOU WANT TO BECOME AN INDEPENDENT BUSINESSMAN. If so, the material in Part Two should be of great use to you.

Part Two provides insights into the types of business you might enter and assistance in evaluating the business environment in which you will operate. As the prospective owner of an independent business, you have these two broad alternatives: (1) to establish a new business, or (2) to enter an ongoing business. Detailed procedures for each of these alternatives are presented.

Specifically, you will need to do the following things: Explore a business idea ⟶ Determine the economic feasibility of the idea ⟶ Develop detailed plans ⟶ Determine legal form of organization ⟶ Estimate financial needs ⟶ Arrange financing ⟶ Select business site ⟶ Obtain or build facilities ⟶ Purchase equipment ⟶ Install equipment ⟶ Acquire inventory ⟶ Select employees ⟶ Give employees preliminary training ⟶ Initiate operations ⟶ Attract potential customers ⟶ Make sales ⟶ Obtain revenue ⟶ Pay bills ⟶ Make profit.

Figure II-1 is a graphic presentation of these and other activities involved in starting up a firm. It moves you from your idea for a business through the various activities to the final objective, profit. It is intended to assist you in visualizing what is needed for your firm to become a reality.

The material in Chapter 4 will help you study the economic environment of your new business. Chapter 5 explains how to enter an existing business, and Chapter 6 explains how to start your own business.

FIGURE II-1
The Concept of Entering a Business

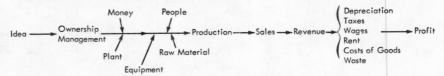

Since your new business needs to be managed effectively by someone, you must now answer a most significant question, namely, "Should I be the owner of the firm and hire someone else to manage it for me, or should I both own and manage it myself?" If you choose to be the manager yourself, you should be prepared to become a generalist manager and not try to specialize in your own area of interest and competence. The generalist manager has conceptual skills which enable him or her to analyze the total situation, detect problems, determine causes, and bring about effective solutions.

"Management is getting things done through people," said Lawrence Appley, former president of the American Management Association. We agree, but there is more to managing an independent business than that. As Figure II-2 shows, you must also make decisions and allocate scarce financial, physical, and human resources so that your business will achieve its objectives. Chapter 7 will help you with the planning function, while Chapter 8 will help you with the other functions.

FIGURE II-2
Definition and Functions of Management

Management is:
1. Doing through others,
2. Decision making, and
3. Allocating scarce resources, so that
4. Objectives are reached.

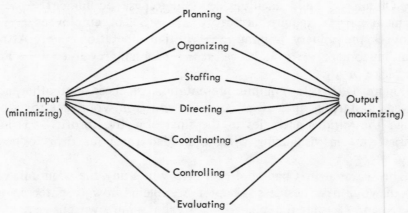

chapter 4

How to Study the Economic Environment for Your Business

It is now time for you to consider the type of business that satisfies your personal goals, to study its economic environment, and to decide whether to buy an existing firm or to start one of your own. These decisions will probably determine whether you will be successful and satisfied during your business career.

The process of picking and choosing the type of business you wish to enter will be influenced by your values, education, training, financial ability, and family situation. It is advisable to consider as broad a range of options as is feasible. However, in conducting your survey of possible business opportunities, you should not become so involved in details that you lose sight of your overall objectives. Instead, your mission should be to find the business which helps you achieve your objectives.

Since the economic environment will play a vital role in the success or failure of your firm, you should study it carefully. All too often, it becomes obvious from later events that little effort was made to determine whether the economic environment was friendly or hostile. This chapter outlines a procedure for you to use in studying the economic environment for your business. The material in this chapter should also help you determine whether your idea for a business is economically feasible and to aid you in deciding whether to buy an existing firm or to start one of your own.

SELECTING THE TYPE OF BUSINESS YOU WOULD LIKE TO ENTER

Probably your best point of departure in selecting the type of business to enter is to review the personal analysis you made in Chapter 3. The purpose of this reevaluation should be to eliminate options which are not compatible with your likes and dislikes. You would probably be miserable if you chose a business which you found to be inconsistent with your abilities and personality.

The main thrust of your personal analysis should be to identify your physical, mental, emotional, and spiritual abilities, including your:

1. Intellectual abilities.
2. Education, training, and experience which determine the expertise you have for certain types of business. As a rule of thumb, you should have at least three years' experience—some preferably managerial—in the line in which your proposed company will be engaged. This experience should have given you valuable information about the management, operations, and "statistics" of the company.
3. Philosophy and ethical value system, which will keep you from being satisfied in many kinds of business.
4. Attitudes and feelings, which will limit your success to a limited variety of activities.
5. Physical health and stamina.
6. Personal goals, which should probably include "desired income" from your business.

A significant question that you should answer is: How much profit do I expect to receive from this business for my time and investment in it? You should determine the profit potential for at least the first year of operation.

Other considerations are the likes and dislikes of your spouse, whether to be near relatives and friends, and what it would take to satisfy you.

This analysis should drastically reduce the number and variety of choices available to you.

If taking attitude, interest, and aptitude tests to assist you in making your decision would make you feel more comfortable, such tests are available through universities, colleges, junior colleges, or vocational-technical schools. You may also find a professional psychologist to assist you.

The next process is to eliminate businesses which will not provide you with the challenges, opportunities, and rewards you are seeking. Be rather ruthless in asking "What's in it for me?" as well as "What can I do to be of help to others?" Ask yourself questions like the following about each business you consider:

1. How much capital do I need to enter and compete successfully in this business?
2. How long will it take me to recoup my investment?
3. How long will it take me to reach an acceptable level of income?
4. How will I live until that time?
5. What risk is involved? Am I willing to take that risk?
6. Can I hack it on my own, or will I need help?
7. How much work is involved in getting the business going and in running it? Am I willing to put out that much effort?
8. Do I want to acquire a franchise from an established company, or do I want to "start from scratch"?
9. What is the potential of this type of business? What are my chances of achieving that potential?

10. Is enough information available for me to reach meaningful decisions? If so, what are the sources?

You might want to use a checklist in order to be more methodical and objective. Figure 4-1 shows a list used by a consultant who helps people decide what business to enter. This list may be modified to meet your unique needs.

FIGURE 4-1
Business Selection Survey Checklist

Capital Required	Degree of Risk Involved	Amount of Work Involved	Independent Ownership or Franchise	Potential of the Business	Source of Data

Where can you find the information you need? The first place to look is in the technical section of your nearest library—or in the government documents section. The librarians in either section can help you find industry data. You will probably want to study carefully the U.S. census data on population, business, housing, and possibly even agriculture. The Small Business Administration in Washington or a regional office can be of great help to you. Contact also:

1. The research division of your local chamber of commerce.
2. The trade association of the industries you are interested in.
3. Local business leaders.
4. Bankers and other financial experts.
5. Your congressman.

How You Can Classify the Types of Businesses

Although there are several ways of classifying the types of business available, we chose to group them as (1) retailing, (2) service, (3) wholesaling, (4) research and development, (5) consulting, and (6) manufacturing. A more detailed grouping is shown in Figure 4-2.

How You Can Choose the Business to Enter

At this point you need an exercise in "brainstorming." Get a group of your friends together and ask them what products or services they need. Then, ask them if their needs for products and services are being met adequately. If not, what would be required to satisfy those needs?

FIGURE 4-2
Some Business Options, Classified into Related Groups

A. *Retailing*
    1. Food
        a. Grocery
        b. Fast-prepared
        c. Convenience
        d. Restaurant
        e. Lounges
        f. Specialty shops
    2. Appliance
    3. Hardware and building material
    4. Specialty
    5. Clothing

B. *Service*
    1. Service station
    2. Auto repair
    3. Appliance repair
    4. House and commercial repair and renovation
    5. Janitorial
    6. Plumber
    7. Electrician
    8. Floor covering
    9. FBO (fixed-base operation aircraft)
    10. Travel agency

C. *Wholesaling*
    1. Jobbers
    2. Brokers
    3. Distributors
    4. Manufacturing agents

D. *Research and Development*
    1. Materials
    2. Products
    3. Software information systems
    4. Specialized machinery
    5. Manufacturing systems

E. *Consulting*
    1. Management
    2. Management information systems
    3. Financial
    4. Investment
    5. Marketing
    6. Risk management
    7. Land use and development
    8. Engineering
    9. Economic
    10. Government
    11. Various additional highly specialized areas

F. *Manufacturing*
    1. Metals
        a. Sheet metal
        b. Machine Shop
            (1) General
            (2) Special equipment
        c. Foundry
        d. Mini-steel mill
    2. Plastics
        a. Extrusion
        b. Applicators
        c. Formulators
    3. Food
        a. Processors
            (1) Meat
            (2) Vegetables
            (3) Bakery
            (4) Specialty items

Try to get them to identify not only existing types of business, but also as many new types as possible. You should then consider the kinds of products and services which are needed and could—if available—find a market.

You might also assemble a group of local independent businessmen to "brainstorm" with you on business opportunities. Another possible source of participants for this exercise might be members of the local ACE (Active Corp of Executives) or SCORE (Service Corp of Executives) chapters.

When you are obtaining advice from outsiders, always remember that your resources are at stake when the commitment is made. Thus, the final decision must be yours.

After this exercise in freewheel thinking, your next step is to actually select the business which seems best for you. In fact, you may want to make more than one choice and leave yourself some options. Your earlier checklist would now come in handy.

Remember to consider your personal attributes in order to best utilize your capabilities. The business should fit your reason for being and your life objectives. Yet, you should try to maintain an attitude of objectivity and let your mind govern—not your emotions.

Once you have made your choice, it is necessary to conduct an economic feasibility study to determine its economic possibilities.

STUDYING THE ECONOMIC ENVIRONMENT

In studying the economic environment, you may use the analytic and rational approach of a computer, or you may play the odds and rely on chance, as in playing a slot machine. However, the "game" of business requires the most objective, rational, and reasoned effort you can give it if you are to "win."

Studying the Economic Environment for the Industry

You should begin your study by analyzing the economic status of the industry in which you are interested. An overview of the economic status of the industry may be provided by obtaining answers to these questions:

1. How many firms are there in this industry?
2. Do the firms vary in size, or are they more or less uniform in size and general characteristics?
3. Are the firms in the industry concentrated in one area, or are they widely distributed? (Rising transportation costs have increased the importance of this factor.)
4. What is the relationship between independent firms in this industry and larger firms in other industries? There may be adverse features associated with this relationship. For example, carpet plants solely dependent on the auto industry for customers are subject to the whims of auto sales for their business.
5. Does the industry serve only the domestic market or, does it serve foreign markets as well?
6. What are the attitudes of federal, state, and local government agencies toward this industry?
7. What is society's attitude toward this industry?

After studying the overall economic environment of the industry, you need to study the business climate for your business in the area in which you would like to operate. One approach that is frequently used in analyzing an area is to evaluate the objective and subjective factors which influence the area's business climate. Additional data which pertain to your particular type of business may also be obtained.

Exhibit 3 of *The Dow Jones-Irwin Business Papers* can help you study the environment for the industry you are interested in.

Studying the Market for Your Business

You should next determine what is happening in the marketplace, and the possible future your business will have in the marketplace. The size, nature, and other characteristics of the market, as well as your firm's future possibilities, may be derived from answers to questions such as these:

1. What is the relationship of the population to the proposed business?
    a. Identify the age distribution of the population. Is a specific age group of greater importance to this business than are other age groups?
    b. Identify the population by sex, race, education, fertility rate, occupations, and other characteristics that affect the demand for goods and services.
    c. Define the size of the population and trends in size, age, sex, racial, educational, and occupational distributions. A declining population, or a declining population segment, in a specific geographic area may indicate an unsuccessful future for some businesses. The declining birthrate is affecting many industries oriented toward the baby, teenager, and youth markets.
2. What are the size and distribution of income within the population?
3. Is the sales volume for this kind of business growing, stable, or declining?
4. What are the number and size of competitors?
5. What is the success rate of competing businesses?
6. What are the technical aspects (state of the art)?
7. What are the sources of supply?
8. What are the capital requirements?
9. What is the rate of return on investment?

This information should help you estimate the size of your market. Additional data may be obtained from trade associations, chambers of commerce, and various federal, state, and local government agencies. Specific sources include the U.S. Department of Commerce (through its Office of Business Economics) and the Bureau of the Census. The research divisions of colleges and universities may also be of assistance to you.

Statistical information gathered and tabulated by the Bureau of the Census may be particularly useful in evaluating the following variables which determine the size and composition of your market:

1. Population characteristics.
2. Employment patterns.
3. Personal income.
4. Business sales and income.

Now, you should be able to arrive at a "ball park" figure for your total sales volume and your share of the market. In arriving at this estimate, you should select reasonable figures. For example, you—as the planner of a new business—should first define the geographic boundaries of the market area and then, from your knowledge of the potential customers in that area, make an estimate of the products that might be purchased. It is better to plan for a lower level of sales in order to budget the operation of the business more effectively.

In studying the market area, you should find out how many similar businesses have been liquidated or have merged with a competitor.

You should also find out what kind of technology is being applied by other firms in your industry. For example, are other machine shops using hand equipment, or are they using the latest equipment, including numerically controlled devices? The state of technology is significant in determining operating costs.

The adequacy of the size and cost of inventory is determined by the number and location of suppliers.

If you call on your own resources and on those of other people who are specialists in your business area, you may be able to develop a detailed plan for your business. This plan would include land, building, equipment, inventory, working capital, and personnel. You should then be able to determine the capital requirements for each of these productive factors, as well as your total capital requirements. Some additional capital should be provided for contingencies.

Information concerning your capital requirements may even be obtained from potential competitors. You may find that owners of existing businesses will cooperate with you by supplying useful information, so long as you approach them in a manner to merit confidence. Some owners cling to secrecy. However, our experience indicates that such people are in the minority. Other sources of information may include suppliers, wholesalers, and manufacturers.

> A consultant was searching for comprehensive information relating to the opening of a retail fabric shop. He called a major textile manufacturer who informed him that the information he needed was readily available from McCall Patterns and Simplicity Patterns. Both patternmakers maintain comprehensive market research programs and make such information readily available.

By determining your capital requirements and developing an estimate of your expected profits after taxes, you should be able to estimate the rate of return you can hope to receive on your investment and on each dollar of sales. You will probably want to set a "return on investment" objective which, when added to your estimated value of your own services, should compare favorably with the profit potential for your type of business. There is no generally acceptable guideline as to how much this rate of return should be.

By using the rate of return figure you decided upon and your knowledge of the market in which you plan to operate, you can compute what sales you will need.

> Suppose that you invest $25,000 in an independent business and that your objective is to receive a 12 percent return on your investment. You also think you could earn $12,000 a year working for someone else. You should then expect to receive an annual income from the business of at

least $15,000, which is the equivalent of $12,000 salary plus $3,000 return on investment.

You further estimate your market to consist of 5,000 companies spending an average of $1,000 per year for the items you will sell. This represents a total market potential of $5 million. You know that the typical profit-to-sales ratio for your industry is about 6 percent. By dividing your hoped-for earnings of $15,000 by the profit margin of 6 percent, you find that you must have sales of $250,000 in order to achieve your profit objective. This means that you would need at least a 5 percent share of the market for your products.

In addition to the data sources previously listed, the Small Business Administration has developed a variety of information resources that may be obtained from the nearest Small Business Administration office, one of the U.S. Government Printing Office retail outlets, or the Superintendent of Documents, Washington, D.C.

After completing all of these mental exercises, you should know whether the rate of return for the business you have chosen is acceptable, based on current economic information. Since you want to achieve the highest possible rate of return, you should make fresh comparisons with alternative investment opportunities. You should then decide whether you have chosen the right business. If you have, then the decision is "Go!"

You may use the questionnaire in Exhibit 4 of *The Dow Jones-Irwin Business Papers* to help you in studying the market for your business.

STARTING A NEW NEW BUSINESS VERSUS BUYING AN EXISTING ONE

You have now decided that you are the entrepreneurial type and that you want to own a business. You have also determined what type of business you want to enter and have found it to be economically feasible. Your next step is to choose a specific business. In surveying the situation, you may want to look at the alternative of entering an established business versus conceiving, planning, organizing, and operating a new business of your own. You will want to make the choice which seems to afford you the best opportunity of accomplishing your goals.

The following material should help you make this choice most effectively. It presents the reasons for and against entering an existing firm or starting a new one.

Buying an Established Business

Before you are able to make your analysis, you must first locate the businesses that are available for purchase. You will find that some firms are not available at any price, that others will become available at a high price, and that the owners of still others are actively seeking a buyer.

Sometimes a successful ongoing business may be acquired at a bargain price. For some reason, it can be bought at a fraction of its dollar cost or of its replacement value. You should be ready to grab such an opportunity.

However, you should be cautious. A retailer may be willing to sell his business for the current price of his inventory. You should not purchase his accounts receivable, and you should be certain that his payables and other liabilities are established. Be sure to have your own CPA audit the records and verify the inventory and its values.

Another element to consider in buying an ongoing firm is *your managerial ability*. There are those who have a talent for acquiring businesses that are in economic difficulty or are not achieving optimum results. These persons are able to initiate changes that turn the business around. Once the business prospers, the new owner sells out to another buyer and then seeks another similar opportunity.

Reasons for Buying an Established Business. Among the advantages of acquiring an established business are the following:

1. The facilities—building, equipment, inventory, and personnel—are in a functioning status.
2. A product or service is already being produced and distributed.
3. A market has been established.
4. Revenue and profits are being generated.
5. The location may be very desirable.
6. Financial relationships with banks and trade creditors have been established.

Reasons against Buying an Established Business. Buying an ongoing business may also have these disadvantages:

1. The physical facilities (building and equipment) may be old and obsolete.
2. The personnel may be stagnant and have a poor production record.
3. Union-management relations may be poor.
4. The inventory may contain an excessive amount of "dead stock."
5. Too high a percentage of the assets may be in poor-quality accounts receivable.
6. The location may be bad.
7. The financial condition of the firm and its relations with financial institutions may be deteriorating.
8. Some customers may be draining the assets of the firm.

Starting a New Business

In considering the possibilities of establishing a new enterprise, you should recognize that doing this gives you more freedom of choice in defining the nature of the business than if you purchase an existing firm. However, there are both pluses and minuses in choosing this alternative. You should view a particular new business in terms of whether it will enable you to achieve your personal objectives. Also, how do the advantages and disadvantages of this option compare with those of entering an ongoing business?

Some people find pleasure in establishing new ventures, getting them operating at a profit, and then finding a buyer for them. Then they start the process over again.

Other people who also enjoy the challenge and sense of accomplishment which come from creating something new. They prefer to keep the business they have founded and to run it themselves. Yet, they too may later start and operate other firms.

Reasons for Starting a New Business. The reasons for starting a new business may include the opportunities to:

1. Define the nature of your business.
2. Create the type of physical facilities you prefer.
3. Take advantage of the latest technology in selecting equipment, materials, and tools.
4. Utilize the most recent processes and procedures.
5. Obtain fresh inventory.
6. Have a free hand in selecting, training, developing, and motivating personnel.
7. Design your own management information system.
8. Select your competitive environment—within limits.

Reasons against Starting a New Business. Some of the disadvantages of starting a new business from scratch are:

1. The problems of selecting the right business.
2. Unproved performance records in sales, reliability, service, and profits.
3. The problems associated with assembling the composite resources—including location, building, equipment, material, and people.
4. The necessity of selecting and training a new work force.
5. The lack of an established product line.
6. Production problems associated with the start-up of a new business.
7. The lack of an established market and channels of distribution.
8. Problems in establishing a basic accounting system and controls.
9. Difficulties in working out the "bugs" that develop in the initial operation.

A new restaurant, catering to a high-class clientele, was established in a questionable and not very accessible neighborhood. In spite of advertising and the support of influential people, the restaurant failed. A specialist in independent businesses had counseled the potential investors against undertaking the venture because of the many negative factors.

The questionnaire in Exhibit 5 of *The Dow Jones-Irwin Business Papers* will help you in deciding whether to start a new business or to enter an existing one.

34

chapter 5

How to Enter an Existing Business

Having chosen to enter an independent business, having determined that your idea is economically feasible, and having decided to enter an existing firm, you are now ready to take that important step. This chapter presents a plan of action.

By this time you should be aware of the many hazards that await the individual who moves into small independent business ownership and management. There are times, however, when the pitfalls of an established business are well concealed. This chapter will aid you in seeing the strengths and weaknesses of the established business.

There are several significant differences between establishing a new business and entering an ongoing enterprise. These are covered in this chapter. The procedures and analyses that follow are intended to aid you: (1) in determining whether or not to purchase a given firm, and (2) if you do buy it, in beginning operations.

After you consider your options in selecting an established business, it is likely that you will narrow them down to a single choice. At that point, you should check the business out before making your final decision. The process might be compared to the steps involved in moving an aircraft from the boarding gate of the terminal to the taxiway, to the runway, and into the air. Certain items must be checked off at each step, with the pilot having the right to abort the flight—up to the point where he is committed to taking the aircraft into the air. So it is with your purchase of an established business; up to a given point, you may cancel out, but at that point you are committed to taking over the business. Figure 5-1 illustrates this comparison.

TO BUY, OR NOT TO BUY

35

FIGURE 5-1
To Go or Not to Go

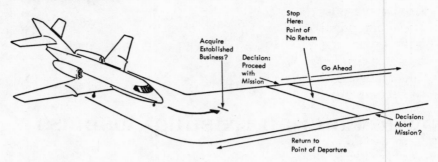

You should determine why the firm is available for purchase, as this—in itself— is a "red flag" warning that something is wrong. You need to determine what is wrong, why, and what you should do about it.

The following discussion is designed to help you determine whether a particular available business is right for you.

The question "Why is this business available for purchase?" should help you establish the validity of the owner's stated reason for selling the business. Some reasons provide a positive opportunity, while others do not. The following analysis should help you determine the potential opportunity to be found in a firm.

Does the present owner have "too many irons in the fire"? Are too many business being run by one individual who is unable to allocate sufficient time to manage all of them successfully?

> Bob Bleckley went to work for a partnership engaged in the construction of commercial buildings. He was made manager of the metal door division. The partners were so busy with their other activities that they gave him little assistance or interest. Bob was running the division. He offered to buy the division from the partners, and they accepted. He is now the owner-manager of that firm and two other small activities.

What Is the Condition of the Business? You should also seek answers to the following questions.

Are the Physical Facilities Worn Out? If the plant, equipment, tools, and furniture are worn out, it is likely that maintenance costs will be excessive. It is also likely that the firm can no longer effectively compete in the marketplace.

Does the Inventory Contain Mostly "Dead Stock"? The firm's inventory may be unsalable at any price because it is no longer in demand, or has deteriorated.

Is the Market Declining? The demand for a product may be declining for one or more of the following reasons:

1. Changing neighborhood—there may be a change in the residents' economic status, a change from one ethnic group to another, a change from one age group to another, or a change in life-style.
2. Declining population—the outward movement of the population in both urban and agrarian areas has had a devastating economic effect on some firms.
3. Technological change—the advent of new technology may cause a firm to become obsolete.

The owners of a Florida company processing large cans of grapefruit juice decided to build a new, more efficient plant. As soon as it was completed, they found themselves competing with a new plant producing "fresh frozen juice" concentrates.

Is the Business Solvent? There have been instances in which purchasers have discovered all too late that the firm they bought had more liabilities than assets.

A building contractor sold 150 homes for down payments of over $500,000. Because of *abysmally inadeaquate financing,* he was unable to complete the houses. The firm was sold, but the new owners had to either return the money or give title to their property to the purchasers.

An audit by a reputable accounting firm could uncover such information. Another protective measure is the use of escrows, whereby part of the purchase price is put in safekeeping until all aspects of the sale have been completed.

What Are the Owner's Intentions? Sometimes, for reasons of location or the age of the facility or the equipment, an owner can decide to dispose of his firm, open another one, and compete with the purchaser of his old firm. For protection, you should have an attorney draw up an agreement that the present owner will not reenter a similar business in the community or the market area for a reasonable period of time. Such agreements are sometimes difficult to enforce, but most businessmen live up to them.

If the owner claims to be in poor health, you should be sure that his problem is physical and not economic.

Bob Howard wanted to own his own business. One Sunday he spotted an item of interest in the want ads. "For reasons of health, owner willing to sacrifice successful, profitable sandwich shop. Priced for immediate sale." Bob dashed over to "Easy Sandwich Shop." The place was full, and business looked great. (All the owner's friends just needed a sandwich that day.) After some haggling, Bob wrote a check for $10,000. A month later, Bob learned that the business was "ready to fold" when he took the bait. The former owner's friends were gone, and business was "lousy." The $10,000 received by the former owner had worked a fast "cure."

The owner may wish to retire, which is a valid reason for offering a business for sale. For tax purposes, he may want to be paid for the business over a number of years. In addition, he may want to serve as a consultant or to fill some managerial role for a specified number of years.

Here a word of caution is appropriate. Sometimes the continued association of a former owner may be detrimental to the new owner. By continued association with the firm, the former owner may cause the new owner to be unsuccessful and may thereby regain ownership. At the least, the presence of the old owner restricts the freedom of action of the new man.

> Joe Jones became the controlling partner in an insurance company which also owned a savings and loan association. The previous owner, 75 years old, remained as chairman of the board of the savings and loan association and as an active partner in the insurance company. The next ten years were miserable for Joe, for he was treated as a junior clerk by the minority partner. He finally sold his interest.

The following procedure should be helpful in uncovering undesirable economic conditions in a firm you plan to buy.

Analysis of Accounting Information

The reason for analyzing a firm's accounting data is to determine its economic health. You should do a physical inventory to determine the accuracy of the recorded information, as well as a qualitative analysis of the economic value of the assets and liabilities.

In performing your analysis, there are many items you should check. The most important of these are now presented in general terms. (The specific details and examples will be discussed in Part Six.)

Cash Position. Is the firm's cash position high or low, considering the industry, location, and so forth? Due to taxes, a firm may accumulate a strong cash position. The owner may then prefer to sell the firm and take advantage of the "capital gains" benefit over ordinary income. Other reasons for having a strong cash position are to take care of poor funds management, or to enable a firm to take advantage of any profitable opportunity that presents itself.

Analysis of Ratios. Many financial ratios can be used in estimating the economic health of a firm. While these are generally used in managing a going concern (as shown in Chapter 18), they can also help you make the purchase decision.

Current ratio is defined as *current assets* divided by *current liabilities,* and is a measure of short-term solvency. Current assets normally include cash, marketable securities, accounts receivable, and inventories. Current liabilities are composed of accounts payable, short-term notes payable, income taxes payable, and accrued expenses. A general rule of thumb is that the current ratio should be two to one.

Quick ratio is obtained by dividing *current liabilities* into *current assets minus inventories*. You can use this ratio to estimate the ability of a firm to pay off its short-term obligations without having to sell its inventories. Inventories tend to lose value faster than other assets when sold in a hurry. A rule of thumb for the quick ratio is one to one.

Debt-to-equity ratio shows the firm's obligations to creditors, relative to the owner's funds. Debt includes current liabilities and bonds; owner's funds include common stock, preferred stock, capital surplus, and retained earnings.

Ratio of net income to sales is calculated by dividing *net income* by *net sales*. You may use net income before taxes or after taxes. No set guideline exists, as the ratio varies among industries, and even among companies.

Net income to investment ratio is found by dividing *net income* (before or after taxes) by *investment*. Here, again, there is no convenient rule of thumb.

Determination of Debt. You need to check both the amount of debt and the terms of debt. The *amount of debt* is important, for it shows your financial obligations. You are primarily concerned with short-term notes (less than one year), term notes (one- to five-year maturities), and long-term debt (anything in excess of five years).

Concerning *terms of debt,* you should learn the rate of interest; the firm's ability to repay the debt in its entirety, without penalty; whether a minimum deposit balance is required by the lender; and whether an acceleration clause is present in the event of default in the payment of interest and principal.

Validity of Financial Statements. Each item listed on the financial statements should be verified by a physical count. You also need to find out whether the items are of the stated value.

You should check on the *age of accounts receivable.* Some businesses continue to carry accounts receivable that should be charged off to "bad debts." A tabular summary classifying these accounts by age, such as 30, 60, 90, 120, and 180 or more days, would give some perspective on the effectiveness of the existing management's credit policies. The *age of accounts payable* should also be determined.

Cash Flow Analysis. Managers often overinvest in inventory without being aware of the cost of carrying it. Yet the annual cost may range from 25 to 35 percent. You should prepare a cash flow analysis in order to determine the effectiveness of management in allocating its resources. In preparing it, you should remember that money has a cost in the form of real or imputed interest. It is important that you consider the monthly cycle of cash revenue and cash payout. In addition, you should take into account the yearly cycle of cash inflow and outgo.

Adequacy of Cost Data. You should determine whether cost data are adequate and accurate. Accounting systems often fail to reveal the actual costs of individual activities. Thus, it is impossible to determine the price for each product or service in order to satisfy a predetermined profit criterion. Nor is it possible to explain undesirable variances..

Appraisal of Operations, Plant, and Equipment

The following discussion will help you study the total management operations of the firm you plan to buy.

Management Effectiveness. In acquiring an ongoing business, you may decide to keep key management personnel. Therefore, it is desirable to look for performance and behavioral characteristics that may serve as a basis for appraising how effectively each manager performs.

Plant Efficiency. Some questions to ask in specific production areas are:

1. *How effective are the personnel?* You can approximate the productivity of individual employees, as well as of the total group of workers. You can look for the portion of time spent productively compared to that which is wasted on nonproductive efforts. Other questions concerning labor cost are:
   a. What is the rate of labor turnover?
   b. What is the percent of absenteeism?
   c. Do employees deliberately commit acts of sabotage that reflect on the image of the product and the company?
2. *What is the amount of waste?* By being particularly observant of operations, you can determine the amount of materials and supplies being wasted. Unutilized machinery may also be an important waste.
3. *What is the quality of production?* You should grade the quality of the firm's products or services. The grading may be done by answering such questions as:
   a. What portion of production is completed without defects?
   b. What portion of the rejects may be reworked, and how much time is involved in this process?
   c. What portion of the rejects cannot be reworked?
   d. How many reshipments are needed because shipped material is not of usable quality?
4. *What is the physical condition of the plant?*
   a. Are the size and design of the plant adequate to meet current and projected requirements?
   b. How efficient is the plant layout? Where the equipment is laid out in a sequence of productive steps, only a nominal amount of *work-in-process inventory* is needed. The greater the number of operations that require doubling back and crossing over, the greater will be the requirements for such inventory. *Materials handling cost* is also important, for the more often work-in-process inventory is moved, the greater will be the cost of handling it.
   c. What is the age of the equipment? How does the present equipment compare with the latest equipment in terms of operating

costs and rate of production? What is the state of repair of the present equipment? Is it well kept, or does it appear that as little effort as possible is spent on maintenance? Occasionally, well-maintained old equipment that has been fully depreciated offers a cost advantage over newer, more modern equipment. Thus, it is possible that the continued use of older equipment will produce a greater profit. Sometimes, however, it is necessary to purchase new equipment on an installment basis.

The economic feasibility study for an ongoing business is similar to the economic feasibility study for a new enterprise, which was presented in Chapter 4. If you are to avoid either an economic disaster or stagnation, you should determine the feasibility of the business. The data for the study could be gathered and analyzed under the following classifications:

Preparing an Economic Feasibility Study

1. *Population trends of the market.* Is the area experiencing an increase or a decrease in population? Is the makeup of the population stable, or is one ethnic, economic, or age group moving out and another moving in?
2. *Age distribution of the population.* If there is a correlation between the demand for a firm's product or service and the size of a particular age group, the size of that group should be identified.
3. *Income levels and distribution of the population.* You should study the relationship between the income distribution among specific age groups and the demand for the firm's goods and services.
4. *Market size.* The *Journal of Marketing, Sales Management,* census reports, local chambers of commerce, area planning and development commissions, and local newspapers are sources of information that will help you define the size of the firm's market.
5. *Share of market.* By estimating the size of the market, and by defining the amount and the quality of the competition, you can seek out areas of weakness upon which you can capitalize.
6. *Amount of investment.* This may be determined by seeking answers to these questions: What is the owner's asking price? Is the asking price favorable? What is the opinion of an appraiser specializing in this type of business?
7. *Return on investment.* You should consider available investment opportunities to determine whether the return on investment (aftertax profit divided by investment) in this particular business is adequate.
8. *Impact of expected changes.* Changes in the legal, physical, social, cultural, economic, and religious environments can affect your chances of success. For example:
   a. Zoning changes may have some influence on a retail business.
   b. The construction of traffic arteries may cut business off from their transient traffic customers.

c. The emphasis being placed on the environment and on ecology has resulted in constraints on some businesses. Changes in the laws regulating pollution controls have increased the costs of doing business.

d. Tax law changes, as well as new government regulations, have an impact on the volume of paperwork.

e. Labor laws affect the cost of doing business. An example is the federal Occupational Health and Safety Act (OSHA), which establishes specific safety standards (see Chapter 11 for details).

f. Technological changes may affect a business adversely. Innovations in newspaper equipment, such as cheaper offset systems and computer composition, have caused many publishers to abandon their existing equipment.

IMPLEMENTING YOUR PLANS

If you have decided to buy the business, you are ready to activate "operation acquisition." Figure 5-2 indicates the sequence of steps that you will probably follow in moving from the decision to purchase the old business to the point of taking it over and running it. The rooms in the figure may be considered as the places in which the important designated

FIGURE 5-2
Points of Decisions

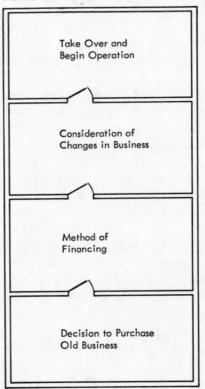

activities will take place. The sequence of rooms is intended to impress upon you the importance of following the appropriate sequence of activities.

Financing the Business.   You are now ready to develop a plan for financing the business. As indicated earlier, how you do this will depend to a significant extent on the terms asked by the seller.

Considering Changes in Methods.   As a result of the operational analysis suggested earlier in this chapter, you should have developed some ideas concerning the changes you would like to make in the existing methods of operation.

Developing a Formal Plan.   You should now prepare a formal plan of *change* to be integrated with a formal plan of *action*. You may wish to call this a "manual of operating procedures."

Taking Over the Business.   It is now time to start operations. If you have followed the procedures outlined above, your chances of succeeding in your new business will be greatly increased. However, you should be prepared for unforeseen contingencies and be ready to move promptly on any difficulties that may arise.

chapter 6

How to Establish Your New Business

By now, you should have established a basic concept of the nature of independent business and how you expect to relate to a specific type of independent business. This chapter will aid you in successfully planning a new independent business. Its intent is to enable you to move in an orderly fashion from the idea stage to making the business a reality.

The outlined procedure should aid you—the potential new entrepreneur—in avoiding costly blunders. It should conserve your time and result in a more polished final product. It should also enable you to convince potential investors that your idea has been well studied and appropriately structured.

In general, the business process involves putting financial, physical, and human resources into an organization in the form of "inputs." These are converted through some form of "operations" or "production" into "goods" or "services." These, in turn, are distributed to other processors, assemblers, wholesalers, retailers, or the final consumer as "outputs." Figure 6-1 presents a generalized chart of the business process.

The specific steps needed to start this process include at least the following:

1. Developing a timetable.
2. Establishing your business objectives.
3. Setting up your organizational structure.
4. Determining your personnel requirements.
5. Determining your physical plant needs.
6. Planning your approach to the market.
7. Preparing your budget.
8. Locating sources of funds.
9. Implementing your plans.

DEVELOPING A TIMETABLE

You should establish a timetable for developing your business in an ordered, coordinated fashion. The steps in starting the business should be

44

FIGURE 6–1
The Business Process

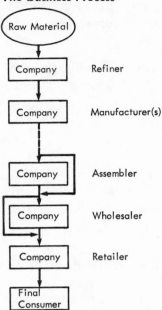

worked out. Next, a time frame for accomplishing each step should be determined. Many of the steps are often performed simultaneously.

The form in Exhibit 6 of *The Dow Jones-Irwin Business Papers* can help you develop your timetable for establishing your new business.

ESTABLISHING YOUR BUSINESS OBJECTIVES

For your enterprise to have purpose and direction, you should establish the objectives you hope to achieve for yourself and your firm. These should be compatible with the objectives discussed in Chapter 2. Some possible categories of objectives are:

		After One Year	After Five Years	After Ten Years
I.	Size			
	Physical			
	Financial			
II.	Type of products			
	Number			
	Kind of product lines			
III.	Number of employees			
IV.	Sales			
V.	Profits			

SETTING UP THE ORGANIZATIONAL STRUCTURE

You must develop a unified organizational structure, taking into consideration the legal, financial, and administrative aspects of your business. Given the basic premise that "My business is very personal," it is important that you select those forms that are in *your best interest.* You should organize for both the "long run" and the "short run." The outline which follows will aid you in considering the options available to you and in making the best choice.

1. *Legal alternatives.* You must choose the form which seems most appropriate to you, based upon your needs, objectives, qualifications, and philosophies.

    a. Proprietorship.
    b. Partnership.
    c. Corporation.
    d. Holding company.

2. *Capital structure.* The extent to which equity and debt are used will be determined by the interrelationships and the interactions among:

    a. The amount of personal funds you wish to commit to the business.
    b. The amount of personal funds other principals wish to commit.
    c. The amount of leverage desired.
    d. The availability and costs of equity and borrowed capital.
    e. The degree of risk you wish to assume.

3. *Administrative structure.* You must now develop a formal organizational plan based upon these factors:

    a. The *raison d'être* (reason for being) of the business.
    b. Your primary personal and business objectives.
    c. The plans, programs, policies, and practices that will enable you to achieve your objectives.
    d. The authority and responsibility relationships that will permit you to accomplish your mission.

An element often overlooked by the independent business manger is the importance of having access to a board of directors (or advisers, if not a corporation) to evaluate the firm's operations and to make recommendations relating to future activities. You *must* be willing to be responsive to the guidance of such a board. You should expect to pay its members a minimum of $100 per meeting, plus expenses, and as the firm prospers, an increased amount. The board should be composed of at least three people from outside the business and an equal number from within.

In selecting outside members, you should look toward a balance of expertise and experience, such as: (1) a business manager with a record of success, preferably in a related but different field; (2) another business manager with a different background, but equally successful; and (3) if available, a professorial type with a general management background that encompasses the operations of small businesses.

See Chapter 7 for further details on setting up your organizational structure.

Your next organizational step is to determine the duties and responsibilities (job descriptions and specifications) needed to perform the activities of your business. Then the process of estimating your personnel requirements can be undertaken. (See Chapter 9.)

One problem area seems to be more prevalent in smaller firms than in larger organizations. Frequently the business is closely related to the family unit, and this relationship may contribute to morale problems if outsiders are brought in. The owner-manager of an independent business should be aware of these potential problems and take deliberate steps to prevent them.

There are two important decisions you must now make, namely, (1) what location to choose, and (2) whether to buy (build) or lease your physical facilities.

You should seek that location which satisfies your requirements and provides you optimum benefits. For example, if you are going into the retail business and are considering a specific piece of vacant property, you should determine why it is vacant. Often, a particular location seems to be a "born loser." You should also evaluate the means of transportation (foot, car, or public), traffic patterns, and traffic volume.

Factors that you should consider in choosing a location are: access to your work force, the availability of utilities, the type of business, access to your market, and the availability of transportation.

Access to Work Force. The availability of people with the personal attributes and skills your business requires is essential for success. You should consider the possibility of blending part-time with full-time personnel in order to provide more flexibility and a more economic operation. Another consideration is the distance and type of the residential areas from which you will draw people. If you locate where people can walk to work and possibly even go home for lunch, you may have an advantage in pay negotiation, worker loyalty and interest, and attendance.

Availability of Utilities. Access to needed utilities, such as electric power, gas, water, sewerage, and steam, is also very important. Two other factors to consider are flexibility in operation and economics (not only the costs of initial installation, but also operating costs).

Type of Business. The type of business you are going to operate will also influence your locational decisions. This factor relates to access to customers, suppliers, work force, utilities, transportation, and compliance with zoning regulations.

Availability of Vendors. Are there enough vendors to supply the needs of your business? In selecting vendors, you should determine which of the following types of supportive service each can provide: (1) assistance in product design; (2) aid in selecting machinery and plant; (3) assistance in

DETERMINING YOUR PERSONNEL REQUIREMENTS

DETERMINING YOUR PHYSICAL PLANT NEEDS

Location

solving problems; and (4) assistance in pricing and in formulating trade credit practices.

Relationship to the Market. Is it a central location? Are there an adequate number of customers in the market area to sustain your business? What competitive advantages can you offer that will enable you to obtain your target share of the market? Evaluate any "tie-ins" that will enable you to expand your business, such as equipment sales, service, gas, and supplies.

Access to Transportation. Will the most economical form of transportation for both your inbound and outbound shipments be available? Are there railroad spurs to the location? Truck lines? Buses?

The form in Exhibit 7 of *The Dow Jones-Irwin Business Papers* should help you in determining the location of your business.

Buy or Lease?

The question of whether to buy or lease your physical plant is important. The supply of capital may be the determining factor. The return you can receive on capital invested in other ways will be another consideration. Your space requirements and the availability of a suitable structure are also significant. You should not overlook the effect of depreciation on cash flow. Also, do your building requirements indicate the need for a specialized or general-purpose structure? You should be cautious about committing yourself to a special-purpose structure because of the difficulties in disposing of it if you decide to move or go out of business.

Exhibit 8 of *The Dow Jones-Irwin Business Papers* has a form which will help you decide whether to buy or lease your physical facilities.

PLANNING YOUR APPROACH TO THE MARKET

Three marketing factors that you need to consider before opening your business to the public are: (1) building an image; (2) channels of distribution; and (3) pricing. While these factors are discussed in greater detail in Chapter 15, 16 and 17, the information you should have before starting your business is provided here.

Building an Image

A number of factors should be considered in building an image for your firm. What segment of the market offers the best potential opportunity? What advertising media will best reach this market?

Too much money may be spent on the exterior of the building, the decor, billboards, or an ineffective advertising program. Funds spent in these areas often result in a reduction in the quality of service and merchandise. It would be better to reverse the pattern by giving excellent service and high-quality merchandise, for these are remembered longer and provide the desired customer appeal and following.

The nature of your business and the economic characteristics of the industry will partially determine your channels of distribution. There are various classes of businesses, and each has a number of options for marketing its products. These options include:

I. Industrial products.
   A. Direct sales to customers.
   B. Manufacturer's agents.
   C. Distributors (wholesalers' warehouses).
II. Consumer products.
   A. Direct sales.
      1. Door-to-door.
      2. Independent retail outlets.
   B. Wholesalers.
   C. Chain retail outlets.
   D. Your own retail outlets.
      1. Direct ownership.
      2. Franchise.
III. Services. Examples include: TV, radio, appliance, and automobile repairing; day-care nurseries; catering; real estate; insurance; care of the aged; and consumer finance. The usual channel is direct to the ultimate consumer.

Whatever the business, pricing is important. However, the focus usually should be not on *price* but on *service.* In pricing your good or service, you should consider *all* the *cost factors,* and then add an additional percentage to provide you with your planned profit. (See Chapter 20.)

Certain rules of thumb are used to determine the price in most businesses. For example, in the restaurant industry food costs generally have not exceeded 33 percent of the sales price. More recently, food costs of from 33 to 44 percent have been considered more realistic. In the upper range, the owner may depend on word-of-mouth advertising rather than spend money on advertising.

A restaurant owner in financial difficulty sought the aid of the Small Business Administration. A SCORE volunteer was assigned as a consultant. His first question was, "What's the most popular item on your menu?" The restaurant owner replied, "Our $2.25 steak." The consultant asked for a scale and a raw steak. He showed the restaurant owner that the raw steak cost $1.85. Obviously, the reason for the steak's popularity was the markup of less than 22 percent. It was also the reason why the business was in financial trouble.

The questionnaire in Exhibit 9 of *The Dow Jones-Irwin Business Papers* will help you in planning your approach to the market for your good or service.

PREPARING YOUR BUDGETS

It is now time to pull together all the revenue and cost items for which you have planned. This process, called budgeting, will be discussed in Chapter 22.

The budget should be considered as an instrument of both planning and control. Its main objective is to maximize your revenue, minimize your cost, and increase your profit. Profit should be included in the total budget. Specific profit figures depend upon many factors, including the industry you enter, your location, and your efficiency.

Concerning "management information," you need to ask yourself these two questions:

1. What decisions do I need to make?
2. What information do I need in order to make those decisions?

Your answers to these questions should serve as guidelines in preparing your budgets. Some of the items you should consider are: expenses, including the cost of the money you will use, depreciation, obsolescence, utilities, maintenance, supplies, personnel, fringe benefits, insurance, materials handling, waste, transportation, and start-up revenues, including those derived from sales from your product or service, sales of property, and interest on money invested; and the resulting profit—or loss.

Types of Budgets

The most important budgets for an independent firm such as yours are:

1. An operating budget.
2. A capital budget.
3. A cash flow budget.

The Operating Budget. In preparing the operating budget, you try to anticipate the costs of obtaining and selling your products and the income received from selling them. This budget will serve as a basis for comparing budgeted activities with actual performance and as a basis for determining the causes of variances from your plans.

Capital Budget. The capital budget reflects your plans for obtaining, replacing, and expanding your physical facilities. It assists you in beginning operations and in obtaining the needed buildings, tools, equipment, and other facilities.

Cash Flow Budget. The cash flow budget states what *cash* will be needed to pay what expenses at what time and indicates where the cash to pay them will come from. The lack of *ready cash* resources is the primary cause of forced liquidations. By using the cash flow budget, such an outcome may be avoided.

Anticipating Difficulties

At the risk of being called "alarmists," we wish to point out that you should anticipate failure and begin to prepare for it. In preparing the budget for your new business, you should look at the costs involved in acquiring assets, using them, and then having to liquidate the business if it fails. Figure 6–2 should help you understand your risks.

FIGURE 6–2
The Value of Assets in a Going Concern and in Case of Liquidation

Items	Going Concern Value	Liquidation Value
Start-up costs	0	0
Cash drain until break-even level of operation is attained	0	0
Basic working capital investment for a mature level of business (includes cash position adequate to take care of _____ weeks of payroll and operating expenses)	Good value	Cash—100% Accounts receivable—depends on quality of debtors or on inventory market (less handling cost)
Equity in plant, product, and equipment	Some value	Some value
Goodwill and other intangible assets	No value	No value

LOCATING SOURCES OF FUNDS

After you have budgeted the amount of funds needed for capital expenditures and to begin operations, you must locate the sources from which you can obtain those funds.

Your ability to raise funds is one of the significant determinants of the size and type of business you can enter. You should recognize that methods of financing change and that there is no one best method. While some methods have advantages over others, the attitude and desires of the investors or lenders will determine the sources of financing available to you at a given point in time.

The following discussion should help you find the needed money to begin operations. (See Chapter 7 and the related materials in Parts Four and Six.)

Your Own Funds

Some people believe in using only their personal funds. Other people believe that they should use as little of their personal funds as possible. Assuming that you either must or wish to use the funds of others, there are several sources of outside funds.

The Funds of Other Individuals

You may find private individuals who are interested in investing in a venture opportunity among your friends or through your attorney, CPA, banker, or securities dealer. In general, such people prefer to invest in a business with which they are familiar.

Trade Credit

Trade credit should not be overlooked. This refers to the purchase of inventory, equipment, and supplies on an open account in accordance with the customary terms for your type of business.

Financial Institutions

Commercial and industrial financial institutions may provide you with funds. The proportion of funds such institutions make available may range from 25 to 60 percent of the value of the total assets. Usually, the cost of such financing is higher than is the cost of other alternatives, but such funds may be the most accessible. These institutions may help you through:

1. Loans on your fixed assets.
2. Lease-purchase arrangements.
3. Accounts receivable financing.
4. Factoring arrangements on accounts receivable.

Commercial Banks. In the past, commercial banks were a good source of credit for business managers having funds of their own and with proved successful experience. More recently, banks have shifted a greater portion of their funds into consumer financing. The large demand for funds in recent years has pushed the interest rates of bank loans to higher levels and resulted in less favorable terms.

You should also consider the following services offered by commerical banks:

1. General account (demand deposit).
2. Payroll accounting.
3. Income tax service.
4. Computerized services.
5. Lock box collections to expedite payments and cash flow.
6. More individualized services.

Investment Banks. Investment banks bring together those who need funds and various sources of funds. Many of these banks have developed a reputation for integrity and for providing their clients with good service.

Preferably, you should select a banker who specializes in regional business, for such a banker is frequently more familiar with the geographic area and the economics of the region and is more accustomed to servicing specialized needs. Such bankers also maintain relationships with insurance companies, large individual investors, and investment managers of pension trusts.

The availability of an investment banker is determined by:

1. Your present financial requirements.
2. Your market potential.
3. Your projected status for two years in advance.

Unless you can reasonably anticipate that your firm will be classified as a regional or national firm within two years, you cannot expect to have access to an investment banker.

Major Nonfinancial Corporations

Major producing corporations, through their financial subsidiaries, often play a significant role in financing certain types of activities which are closely related to some phase of their operations.

General Electric, Westinghouse, and others have been active in helping finance mobile homes and apartments. The mobile home manufacturers will install the appliances of a specific supplier, who then helps finance the producer. In addition, the appliance-financing subsidiary often finances the sale of the home to the ultimate consumer.

The "Big Three" auto firms operate through financial subsidiaries to finance dealerships, provide an arrangement for financing the dealers' new car inventories, and finance the sale of new and used cars to customers.

Insurance companies may be a source of funds for your firm. You can go directly to such a company,or you can contact its agent, an investment banker, or a mortgage banker.

Insurance Companies

A primary purpose of the SBA is to provide financial assistance. Where the terms of bank loans may be limited by regulation or law, the SBA tends to permit longer periods of repayment and to make other concessions to independent firms. Yet, as far as credit risks are concerned, the SBA has requisites very similar to those of banks. The borrower should be a good credit risk.

The Small Business Administration

The SBA has been limited in its financial activities by the constraints imposed by Congress in allocating funds for loan purposes. The loans it can give you are discussed in the following paragraphs.

Direct Loans. These loans usually fit into three categories: (1) *Ethnic loans*, (2) *Catastrophic* or *disaster loans*—these loans are made in an area where some form of disaster has struck. The terms are usually 3 percent interest and an amortization period of 20 years, (3) *Small loans*—made to business firms needing between $1,500 and $3,000.

Participating Loans. With participating loans, the SBA takes a portion of the total loan on a direct cash participation basis, and the bank or other lender provides the remainder. In this type of loan, the SBA assumes a position subordinate to that of the other lender in the event of liquidation.

Guaranteed Loans. The SBA guarantees the lender 90 percent of the loan up to a total of $350,000. The borrower may contact the SBA directly or through a bank whose policy is to make SBA-guaranteed loans. Using a bank as an intermediary seems to produce more satisfactory results.

Lease Guaranty Program. The lease guaranty program was established to enable small businesses to locate in major shopping centers requiring an AAA credit rating. Current regulations require:

1. Paying three months' rent at the outset to be placed in escrow.
2. Limiting the amount of rent that may be guaranteed to $2.5 million.
3. A 2.8 percent single insurance premium guaranteeing the total rent of the lease.

Small Business Investment Corporations

SBICs are chartered by the SBA and make qualified SBA loans. The SBA matches each dollar they put into a loan. Loans are usually made for a period of five-ten years. The SBICs may stipulate that they be given a certain portion of stock purchase warrants or stock options, or they may make a combination of a loan and a stock purchase.

Industrial Development Corporations

Industrial development corporations have greater freedom in the types of loans they are able to make. They make "501" or "502" loans.

501 Loans. 501 loans are granted by state-chartered industrial development corporations whose initial capital is provided by member commercial banks which are members of the Federal Reserve System. These corporations make term loans, working capital loans, mortgage loans, and contract performance loans, and can borrow up to one half of the loan amount from the SBA.

502 Loans. 502 financing is arranged by an individual community establishing an industrial development corporation. The amount of equity and the number of stockholders required are determined by the community's population. The SBA has a ceiling of $350,000 per individual borrower, and the repayment period may extend for 25 years.

The Economic Development Administration (EDA)

The EDA makes direct loans to industries located in communities classified as economically depressed areas or in communities that are declared to be regional economic growth centers.

The loans made by the EDA may be used for acquiring plant and equipment. The agency may lend up to 65 percent of the total coast of the assets for which the loans are made, but the agency prefers to remain in the 50 percent range. A rule of thumb in determining the amount of a loan is from an average of $5,200 to a maximum of $10,000 per employee for each new job the project will create. The interest rate is reviewed quarterly. The life of the loan may reach 25 years, but the average maturity is 18 years.

State Employment Agencies

Grants may be available through your local state employment agency for obtaining employees who are given new work assignments or for training employees for a new business where the needed skills are lacking.

Agricultural Loans

A number of sources of agricultural loans are federally funded. The Cooperative Extension Service, or one of its local agents, may be checked for information concerning availability and procedures. Some sources of agricultural loans are:

1. The Federal Land Bank Association.

2. The Production Credit Corporation.
3. The Farm Home Administration.

The questionnaire in Exhibit 10 of *The Dow Jones-Irwin Business Papers* can help you in checking sources of funds for your business.

Now you are ready to take the plunge! It is time to obtain your funds, get a charter, purchase your facilities and supplies, hire and train your people, and start operating.

Capital Procurement. Using your capital structure plan and the sources of funds you have developed, obtain the funds, put them in your checking account, and start writing checks.

Corporate Charter and Permits. You should obtain the services of an attorney if you are acquiring a corporate charter. He can also help you obtain any necessary occupational licenses and permits.

Facilities and Supplies. After you obtain the funds, charter, and permits, you should refer to your timetable and start negotiating contracts and purchasing the equipment, products, and supplies you need to run your business.

Personnel Selection and Training. As the time approaches to begin operations, you should refer to your organization chart, job titles, and job specifications in order to determine your personnel requirements. Methods of selecting and procuring personnel will be influenced by local conditions. The presence of a community college, a liberal arts college, a university, or a vocational-technical school will influence your decision to use all full-time employees or some full-time and some part-time employees. You can receive assistance in obtaining employees from institutional placement offices, state employment agencies, and private employment agencies. You may have to use local advertising media to attract prospective employees. However, this usually increases the amount of time required for screening.

The nature of your business and the background of your newly hired employees will influence the amount of time you need and the methods you use in training your new employees.

IMPLEMENTING YOUR PLANS

chapter 7

Planning for Your Business

Before you actually begin operations, a few more preliminary activities are necessary, including planning for your business. This chapter will help you do this preliminary planning and implementing.

First, it emphasizes the need for effective planning for an independent business, and makes some suggestions for making planning more effective. Second, it outlines the steps involved in planning the legal, financial, and administrative structure of your firm.

EFFECTIVE PLANNING

Independent business managers need to plan as thoroughly—if not more thoroughly—than do managers of larger companies. The reasons are that most independent firms:

1. Do not have sufficient resources to overcome their future problems.
2. Cannot afford to underwrite losses that can occur while adjusting to unexpected changes.

You should recognize that changing circumstances will probably affect your plans and you should provide means for modifying your company's objectives to meet such changes. Activities that are profitable today may not be so in the future.

Your company is especially vulnerable to bold moves by competitors. Besides managing your company well, you should keep yourself informed about your competitors and be able to predict what they will do.

How to Plan

You should start planning by getting a complete picture of your operations. The types of information that you need to do better planning are:

1. A brief description of your company's present practices in all impor-

56

tant areas, including products, purchasing, quality control, labor relations, and sales outlets.

2. A statement of your present organization, procedures, and reports.
3. A list of the external factors—such as government regulations, the state of the economy, competition, the community environment, technology, and the labor markets—which affect your company most.
4. A list of the changes you expect in these factors in the next few years.
5. A list of the main strengths and weaknesses of your present operation (based on items 1 through 4).

Writing these things down will clarify your thinking and help you convey your ideas to others who will participate in implementing the plans.

Planning consists of these steps:

1. Recognizing and making a tentative statement of the problem.
2. Collecting and classifying relevant facts.
3. Setting forth alternative courses of action.
4. Evaluating the pros and cons of these courses.
5. Selecting the course of action (the plan).

In order to ensure that your plans are complete, you should be able to answer these questions:

1. *Why* must it be done?
2. *What* action is necessary?
3. *Where* will it take place?
4. *Who* will do it?
5. *How* will it be done?
6. *How much* control should be exercised?

The sequence of these questions is important. The "why" of the action should be determined first, while the questions of control should come last.

You should be able to distinguish between "organizational," "executive-level," "operational," and "project" or "program" planning.

Levels of Planning

Organizational planning occurs before and during the organization of the business. It involves determining the firm's objectives, legal and financial structure, and administrative aspects, including organizational relationships. This type of planning is necessary before you can begin operating your firm.

Executive-level planning is broad in scope, long-range, and abstract. It entails selecting the company's objectives and policies and establishing programs and procedures for achieving them. It involves long-run trends in income levels, market size, product use, business location, and manufacturing and merchandising operations. This type of planning is neglected by many independent business managers. Too often they are engaged in fire-fighting, crisis-type management, and are so immersed in daily operations and routines that they cannot perform executive-level planning.

Operational planning is limited to separate departmental or functional activities. It tends to be narrow in scope, short-range, and concrete. It depends largely on prior planning decisions made at the executive level. Often, operational plans consist of budgets which are prepared one year in advance with a detailed breakdown by months.

Planning is also concerned with specific *projects* or *programs.* However, you should recognize that in implementing a particular project you should conform to the overall objectives of your company.

Planning is especially important during your company's first year of operations. When you approach a banker, one of his first questions will concern a proposed budget.

You should delegate some planning, particularly operational and program planning, because it is required of all managers and nonmanagers in your company. Your employees' ideas are often helpful in providing solutions to your firm's problems. In addition, you should consult periodically with an attorney, an insurance agent, and various other specialists, such as a tax accountant.

Irrespective of how well plans have been formulated, crises will arise. You should act decisively when they do.

Planning to Use Your Time Wisely

The proper use of your time can help you run your business more effectively. If you or your secretary record how you spend your time during, say, 5-, 10-, or 15-minute intervals for a week and you then total your time by categories, you may find that you spend too much time on such activities as solving production problems and talking to people and too little time on more important activities.

To help you analyze your activities and their relative usefulness in achieving your firm's objectives, you should ask these questions:

1. Can this activity be eliminated or delegated?
2. Can this activity be combined with others?
3. Can the time required to perform the activity be reduced?
4. Can the sequence of activities be changed?

Other methods of saving your valuable time are:

1. Organizing the work, including the delegation of as many duties as is feasible.
2. Selecting a competent secretary to sort out unimportant mail, screen incoming calls, and keep a schedule of appointments and activities.
3. Using dictating equipment.
4. Adhering to appointment and business conference times.
5. Preparing an agenda for meetings, and confining discussions to items on the agenda; making follow-up assignments to specific subordinates.

Exhibit 11 of *The Dow Jones-Irwin Business Papers* has a questionnaire to help you use your time more effectively.

Many owner-managers of independent businesses neglect long-range planning because they are discouraged by these barriers:

1. Fear.
2. Inexactness.
3. Changeability.
4. Lack of planning knowledge.
5. Lack of proper time and place.

Fear causes some owner-managers to believe that careful thought about the future will reveal new trouble or problems. A common reaction is, "I have enough problems now without worrying about the future." Their real fear, however, should be to face the future without an adequate plan for their businesses.

Another barrier is *inexactness.* Many independent business managers believe that no matter how carefully they plan, things often do not work out according to plan. However, you should realize that even though certainty is impossible, you are better off trying to determine the best way to play the odds. The problem is to get some idea of those odds. For example, what are the odds that more customers will need your product two years or ten years hence?

Another complaint of independent business managers is that *plans change* too rapidly to make planning worthwhile. The solution lies in the frequency and flexibility with which you plan. Perhaps you should plan for only one or two years instead of five or ten years. You should consider how you might alter your plans if a change materializes. To illustrate, in planning a new plant, you could consider what to do if the demand for your product turns out to be substantially greater or less than you had expected.

Lack of planning knowledge is another serious barrier to planning. You should consider this approach:

1. Set objectives.
2. Develop plans to achieve those objectives.
3. Assess the progress being made to carry out the plans.

Another barrier is the *lack of proper time and place.* You should make a conscious effort to find the right time and place for planning—you need some peace and quiet, some protection from continual interruptions.

Many independent business managers "kill the day" doing things they enjoy while neglecting duties they dislike. Effective time utilization includes careful planning of work prior to performance and uninterrrupted concentration during performance. You should first do the things that should be done—not the things you like to do.

Figure 7–1 shows some of the more important planning functions and types of plans that you—as an independent business owner—will probably have to make. The first of these—objectives—has been covered in previous chapters. The next four—legal, financial, and administrative structures, and strategies—will now be discussed in detail. The others will be discussed in the following chapters.

Before leaving the subject of objectives, you might be interested in the objectives of another independent firm, as shown in Figure 7-2.

FIGURE 7-1
Selected Planning Functions and Types of Plans

Objectives—Purposes, goals, results of the firm and its parts

Company objectives—Overall objective is to perform useful service for society.

Product line—Manufactures and distributes high-quality, custom-made, special living room and dining room furniture

Scope of market—Markets its furniture in the states of Georgia, Florida, Alabama, and Louisiana

Personal objectives—Statement of the type of life you wish to lead

Legal structure—Determining what legal form will best help you achieve your objectives

Proprietorship, partnership, corporation, holding company, and/or trust

Financial structure—Choosing the methods of financing your business that will enable you to achieve your objectives at the lowest feasible cost

Equities, debt, or combinations

Administrative structure—Deciding what activities are necessary to achieve your firm's objectives, combining those activities into workable groups, and assigning the necessary authority-responsibility to managers

Strategies—Major objectives or goals defining what business the company is in and the kind of company it is; plans for achieving these goals

Policies—Overall guides to action which provide some consistency in decision making, particularly in repetitive situations

Personnel policy—Promoting from within, giving preference for promotions to present employees

Standards—Values to be used as norms; these are necessary for control because they assist in measurement

Specifications—Machines and materials should be arranged in order and close together in order to produce economically and effectively

FIGURE 7-1 (continued)

Budgets—Plans of income or outgo, or both, including money, sales items, purchased items, and so on

Sales budgets, cash budgets, pro forma income statements, and balance sheets

Procedure—Series of related tasks to be performed in a given sequence, using an established method of performing the work; procedure includes how and when each task is to take place and by whom it is to be performed

Selection procedure—Used to select employees with the proper qualifications and to place them in positions where their talents can best be used

Method—Prescribed manner for performing a given task

Task—Performed by a production employee in the machining department

Program—Comprehensive plan which includes objectives, standards, budgets, policies, procedures, and methods (a given program need not include all of these components)

Production program—Designates the materials, the processes to be followed, the machines to be utilized, the production schedules to be met, and the warehouses to which shipments are made

FIGURE 7-2
Objectives of an Independent Manufacturer and Distributor of Specialized Computers

Question:	What objectives are reasonable in an industry in which IBM alone has 70 percent of the market?
Basic objectives or goals	Survival
	Then, growth and profit through technical expertise embodied in superior products
	Which of these objectives would be most important would depend upon values and objectives of stockholders and top management
Strategy (more specific objectives)	Seven-year growth objectives—Average compound growth rate of 20 percent each year
	Profit-aftertax return on investment of 10 percent for the first two years (to allow for start-up) and 18 percent annually thereafter
Hierarchy of objectives	Technical expertise—leadership in technology of miniature-sized memory units to produce the most technically superior minicomputer
	Market sought—Segment requiring minicomputers; objective: 30 percent of that market
	Product line objective—Full line of at least five sizes with variations to satisfy the market.

FIGURE 7-2 (continued)

R&D objective—Update the products substantially and have a major improvement every two years through emphasis on continual miniaturization of memory units and increases in speed of processing

Financial objectives—Initial debt-equity ratio target of 55 percent, decreasing to 35 percent over the seven-year period; target return on sales of 12 percent before taxes

Sales objectives—Sales quotas for each sales representative or region

Manufacturing objectives—Cost levels, units of production, quality standards

Source: Daniel J. McCarthy, Robert J. Minichiello, and Joseph R. Curran, *Business Policy and Strategy: Concepts and Readings* (Homewood, Ill., Richard D. Irwin, Inc., 1975), pp. 225–26.

DETERMINING THE LEGAL FORM

In many independent businesses, there seems to be an appalling lack of knowledge of the advantages and disadvantages of the various forms of legal organization. Our intent here is to provide you with a better understanding of the legal forms a business may have. The most popular of these are the: (1) proprietorship; (2) partnership; (3) corporation; (4) holding company; and (5) trust.[1]

The Proprietorship

A proprietorship is an enterprise owned by a single individual. It is the simplest form of business to organize. Many people prefer this type of organization because of its simplicity and because of their preference for individual control. It provides for relative freedom of action and control and is simple to enter and leave.

You should consider at least two negative factors, though. First, since you and your business are one and the same, the legal life of the business terminates with your death. If you die, some legal action must be taken to reactivate and reinstate it. Second, you have unlimited liability for the debts of the firm. If the firm lacks sufficient assets to pay all its obligations, you must use your personal assets to pay them. Conversely, if you have unpaid personal debts, your creditors can use the assets of your business to satisfy their demands.

The Partnership

A partnership in the joining together of two or more individuals to form an organization. Partnerships are quite popular because of these *advantages:*

---

[1] If you wish further information on this subject without seeing a lawyer, refer to Harold F. Lusk et al., *Business Law: Principles and Cases*, 3d U.C.C. ed. (Homewood, Ill.: Richard D. Irwin, Inc., 1974).

1. Pooling the resources of more than one individual.
2. Pooling the specialized skills of the individual partners.
3. Enabling division of labor and management responsibility.

Partnerships are more effective than proprietorships in raising financial resources and in obtaining better management.

Yet, there are *disadvantages* inherent in the partnership arrangement, including:

1. The death of any partner terminates the life of the partnership. This may be offset by an agreement which states that the remaining partners will purchase the interest of the deceased partner from his estate. Frequently, the partnership carries insurance to cover this contingency.
2. Members of a general partnership, or the general partners in a limited partnership, have unlimited liability for the debts of the firm.
3. The partners are responsible for the acts of each and every other partner.
4. A partner cannot obtain bonding protection against the acts of the other partners.
5. An impasse may develop when the partners become incompatible.

Because of this last disadvantage, you should include in your partnership agreement a "buy-sell" arrangement to provide for the perpetuation of the business. This clause can be activated in the event of one or more of the following:

1. An impasse develops among the partners on an important issue.
2. One or more of the partners wishes to leave the partnership.
3. A partner dies.
4. A conflict of interests develops.

Types of Partnerships. Partnerships may be general or limited. In a *general partnership,* each partner is held liable for the acts of the other partners. A *limited partnership* can be created only by compliance with a state's statutory requirements. Such a partnership is composed of one or more *general partners* and one or more *limited partners.* Management of the firm is performed by the general partners, who have unlimited personal liability for the partnership's debts. The personal liability of the limited partners is limited to the amount of capital they contribute.

The exemption from personal liability of limited partners is conditional upon their not participating in any way in the management of the firm. However, the limited partners may be employees of the firm. Unfortunately, legal decisions are not very clear as to how far the limited partners can go in giving advice or reviewing management decision making without losing their exemption from personal liability. A limited partnership is not required to so designate itself in its name or its dealings. Yet the surnames of the limited partners may not be used in the firm name.

Tests of a Partnership. It is sometimes difficult to tell whether an enterprise is a proprietorship, a partnership, or a corporation. There is no simple test for the existence of a partnership, but the major requirements are: the intent of the owners, co-ownership of the business, and carrying on the business for a profit. Also, since no formalities are required to create a partnership, you may form one and not realize it. As a general rule, the sharing of profits, together with having a voice in the management of a business, are sufficient evidence to imply the existence of a partnership.

Rights of the Partners. If there is no agreement to the contrary, each partner has an equal voice in the management of the business and a majority of the partners has the legal right to make decisions pertaining to the daily operations of the business. However, all partners must consent to fundamental changes in the structure itself. Each partner's share of the profits is presumed to be his or her only compensation, and, in the absence of any other agreement, the profits and losses are distributed equally.

The Corporation

A corporation is sometimes defined as a legal entity, or an artificial being, whose life exists at the pleasure of the courts of law. The formation of a corporation is more complex than the formation of the other legal forms. The number of persons required as stockholders varies with individual state laws. Usually, the number varies from three to five, and frequently two of these may be "dummies" who serve as incorporators in name only and are not active in the firm. The procedure for formation is usually legally defined and requires the services of an attorney. Incorporation fees frequently cost from $300 to $1,000.

Advantages and Disadvantages. The primary *advantages* the corporate form offers you as an independent investor are:

1. It is a legal entity separate and distinct from you as an individual.
2. It offers permanence. If you or another owner dies, the shares can be transferred to others without the legal life of the firm being affected.
3. Your liability for the firm's debts is limited to the amount you invest in its stock.
4. You can have representative management.
5. Large amounts of capital can be raised relatively easily. (Some authorities would question the validity of this statement.)

Some offsetting *disadvantages* which might keep you from using this form of structure are:

1. Taxes and fees are high.
2. The procedures, reports, and statements required are cumbersome and burdensome.
3. Your powers are limited to those stated in the charter.

4. You may have difficulty doing business in another state.
5. The other stockholders may not be interested in the firm.
6. It tends to be a more impersonal form of business.

Because of the limited liability feature, the corporate form is considered superior to all other forms of business organization.

Other Considerations. If other individuals are involved in your venture and you decide to incorporate, a pre-incorporation agreement should be drawn up and signed by the incorporators. This agreement should provide protection against any members of the group taking off on their own with the proprietary basis for establishing the organization. It at least provides for the restitution of damages that may be incurred.

In order to protect you and the other parties involved, a buy-sell arrangement for the major stockholders should be included in the articles of incorporation. Also, if the success of the venture is dependent on your or certain other individuals' participation in the firm, "key man insurance" should be carried on you or those persons. (See Chapter 23.)

You should also maintain adequate bond and insurance coverage against losses which result from the acts of employees and others, as well as adequate liability and workers' compensation insurance coverage.

The Holding Company

As your firm grows larger, or as you wish to expand your activities while conserving your own resources, you might consider establishing a parent corporation to serve as a holding company for your corporation. You may gain tax advantages from this arrangement. Furthermore, this may protect the assets of the parent company by limiting its liability.

The Trust

For estate and other reasons identified under the tax laws, the trust arrangement established a method of providing the owner of a business with certain tax advantages. A popular one in recent years has been the "real estate investment trust" which gives individuals in higher tax brackets certain income tax advantages.

A trust differs from a corporation in that it is established for a specific period of time—or until certain designated events have occurred. It is administered by a trustee or a board of trustees. The trust receives specific assets from the person or persons establishing it. The trust covenant defines the purpose of the trust, names the beneficiary or beneficiaries, and establishes a formula for the distribution of income and trust assets.

The questionnaire in Exhibit 12 of *The Dow Jones-Irwin Business Papers* can help you select the proper legal form for your organization.

DETERMINING YOUR FINANCIAL STRUCTURE

The legal structure you choose for your firm will have a direct relationship with its financial structure. However, it should be emphasized that the methods of financing a business are varied. Innovations that work are commonplace. In the material that follows, we discuss the more popular financial practices and structures.

The Proprietorship

Frequently, we think of the proprietorship as being financed from the personal funds of the proprietor. However, in many instances he finances only a small portion of the funds required from his own resources. He may obtain a bank loan, a loan from an individual, a loan from or guaranteed by a government agency, or a loan from a business. The amount of money which can be obtained in addition to those of the proprietor will be determined by the amount of personal funds he possesses and the amount and quality of personal assets that may be pledged for a loan. The amount of money for a loan available above the assets of the proprietor will be determined by:

1. The "track record" of the individual proprietor.
2. The nature of the business venture itself, including the amount of fixed assets, size of inventory, rate of inventory turnover, market potential, profit potential, and so forth.

The usual proportion of debt ranges from 25 to 60 percent of the owner's equity.

The Partnership

In starting a partnership, one factor to consider in selecting your partners is whether the individuals possess adequate financial resources. The capital contribution of each partner goes into the "paid-in capital" account.

Occasionally, one or more partner may make the partnership a loan after it has started operating. In such instances, the loan will be evidenced by a note. The loan may be secured by fixed assets of the partnership, or it may be unsecured, that is, issued against the general credit of the partnership.

In some instances, additional funds may be obtained from outside sources, such as banks, individuals, government agencies, and other businesses. Usually, this type of financing will be in the form of short- or intermediate-term loans.

The Corporation

In establishing a new business, the amount of equity capital required of the initial stockholders will usually range from 40 to 100 percent. The amount is dependent upon such factors as the nature of the venture, the abilities and past performance of the management group, the kind of assets involved, and the market potential.

Equities. During the period immediately following World War II, more than one class of equity (*common stock*) was frequently used. For example, Class A stock would be made voting, but would be subordinated to Class B stock as far as dividends were concerned. Class B stock would be nonvoting.

Debt. A favorite debt device has been the *convertible debenture*, which provides investors with both the security of a debt instrument, and an opportunity to shift from debt to equity when the firm's stock appreciates.

Recently, many institutional lenders, because of tight money, the demand for funds, and a changing market environment, have obtained *stock purchase warrants* of up to 50 percent of the total equity. These warrants give the investors the right to purchase a certain number of shares of the firm's common stock at a stated price.

Other Considerations. Under certain conditions, it may be advantageous for the incorporating investors to invest a portion of their funds in equity securities and the remainder in debt because of tax advantages and a more favorable priority position in case the firm liquidates.

Sometimes, *subordinated instruments,* such as *second mortgages, junior notes,* or *bonds,* are used.

Preferred stock, which pays a stated percent of dividend before the common stockholders receive any returns, may be desirable even though it tends to restrict the flexibility of the capital structure.

Warrants, as mentioned above, may be used or required by certain investors as part of the financial package. Investors who have demanded these include SBICs (Small Business Investment Companies) and insurance companies.

Industrial revenue bonds provide a cheaper means of acquiring funds when your business will be located in an industrial park, community, or region where the use of such an instrument is available.

The use of debt in financing enables you to obtain *leverage* upon your equity investment, that is by using debt you are able to expand your income relative to your equity.

You should be careful that the indenture provisions of debt instruments do not limit your actions too much. You want to have the opportunity to work through any periodic adversity without being "washed out" by covenants that fail to provide adequate "running room."

Section 1244 Stock. Your corporation may be made more attractive to investors if you comply with the statutory concept of a "small business corporation," as defined in Section 1244 of the Small Business Tax Revision Act of 1958. For this to happen, (1) the total amount of stock offered under the plan, plus other contributions to capital and paid-in surplus, may not exceed $500,000, and (2) the total amount of the stock which may be offered, plus the equity capital of the corporation, must be less than $1,000,000.

Section 1244 stock is common stock (voting or nonvoting) in a domestic corporation. *Losses* on the sale, exchange, or worthlessness of this stock *are treated as ordinary losses rather than capital losses sustained by an individual.* The total amount that may be treated as an ordinary loss must be less than $25,000 or, if a husband and wife are filing a joint return, $50,000. This provision could give you a considerable tax advantage.

The stock must be issued to the taxpayer in exchange for a transfer by him of money or other property. Stock issued in exchange for stock or securities of another corporation, or for services rendered, does not qualify. Also, only the individual to whom the stock is issued qualifies for the benefits of Section 1244.

Finally, taxpayers who are owner-operators of a closely held corporation should make certain that they qualify a maximum amount of their stock under this special provision. When planning their business, most potential owners are so optimistic that they simply cannot see the need for anticipating tax differences which become important only if their new ventures fail. However, many more independent businesses fail than succeed. If for some reason your business should fail, the opportunity to obtain a tax refund based on a $50,000 ordinary net operating loss deduction is substantially more valuable to you than the potential use of a $50,000 net capital loss carry-forward. This provision should also be of special interest to you in seeking venture capital for your new corporation. High marginal tax bracket investors are attracted by the possibility of investing in a new firm if they know that the government will share their risk of loss on a 70–30 basis, but will only share in the potential profits on a 25–75 basis.[2]

PLANNING YOUR ADMINISTRATIVE STRUCTURE

You must also set up an administrative structure that will enable you to run your business most effectively.

Organizing involves deciding what activities are necessary to attain your firm's objectives, grouping those activities into small work groups, and assigning each group to a manager possessing the necessary authority to carry out the activities and reach the objectives. A major problem with many independent business managers is that they do not organize their activities properly. The material in this section should help you organize your firm better.

Planning for Growth

With respect to organizing, you should recognize that your business may undergo four stages of growth. They are:

1. The direct supervision stage.
2. The supervised supervisor's stage.
3. The indirect control stage.
4. The divisional organization stage.

In the *direct supervision* stage, you usually have fewer than 25 employees and you directly supervise all their work.

---

[2] If you desire further information on this important subject, see your tax attorney or refer to Ray M. Sommerfeld, *Federal Taxes and Management Decisions* (Homewood, Ill.: Richard D. Irwin, Inc., 1974).

In the *supervised supervisor's* stage, you have a first-line supervisor who reports to you. You analyze results through the supervisor's reports.

If your company has 250–300 employees, you enter the *indirect control* stage and will need to supervise managers who, in turn, supervise first-line supervisors. You will also have staff people to establish policies and procedures, while you depend on reports.

If your company grows to 1,000 employees, the *divisional organization* stage is entered and you have other managers in charge of certain product lines.

An important principle of organization that you should follow is unity of command. Under this principle, employees should have only one superior to whom they are *directly responsible* for certain matters. When subordinates must report to two bosses concerning the same assignment, they may receive conflicting instructions.

In assigning work to your subordinates, you should try to arrange for *authority to be coequal with responsibility.* Try to give your subordinates sufficient authority to carry out their responsibilities. On the other hand, avoid delegating greater authority to your subordinates than they need to fulfill their responsibilities.

The meaning of delegating and placing responsibility is "let others take care of the details." Delegation is perhaps the hardest thing owner-managers have to learn. Some pay lip service to the idea, but actually run everything themselves.

When you delegate, you should be assured that your subordinates are technically competent in their areas. They should either be managers or be capable of becoming managers.

Organizational Principles and Practices

The owner of a small factory established three departments—a production department, a sales department, and an administrative department—and appointed a manager for each. He specified the following responsibilities:

1. The production manager was responsible for manufacturing, packing, and shipping.
2. The sales manager was responsible for advertising, customer solicitation, and customer service.
3. The administrative manager was responsible for personnel, purchasing, and accounting.
4. The production manager was designated as "assistant general manager" and delegated authority to make all operational decisions in the owner's absence.

The owner gave each manager a detailed statement of the function of his department and the extent of his authority. Actions which the managers could take on their own initiative and actions which required approval by the owner were enumerated.

Each department manager was instructed to designate and train an assistant who could manage the department when the need arose.

The owner coordinated the departments. The sales manager and the production manager set customer delivery dates together.

Control was exercised by holding each subordinate responsible for his actions and checking the results of those actions. The owner neither "breathed down his managers' necks" nor lost control of things. He relied upon reports and periodic staff meetings.

The owner kept his subordinates informed so that they would have the facts they needed for making their decisions. He tried to communicate effectively with them. He explained the "why" of his instructions.

His managers were given freedom to do things their way. The owner judged them by their results—not their methods.

If a manager deviated too much from policy, the owner brought him back into line. He avoided "second-guessing" his managers. If the subordinate did not run his department to the owner's satisfaction and if his shortcomings could not be overcome, the owner replaced the manager.[3]

Another principle you should follow is that *decisions are best made by the person "closest to the spot."*

You should watch carefully the *span of control* of each supervisor or manager. By this span we mean the number of subordinates reporting to one superior. First-line supervisors may have 10, 15, 25, 30, or more employees reporting to them, because of the similarity of the employees' work. On the other hand, middle managers may be responsible for only 5, 8, 10 supervisors, because of the diversity of the supervisors' work. You should be especially careful not to have too many managers report to you personally. Otherwise, the operations of your business could be severely hampered.

Division of labor, or *specialization,* should be used wherever feasible, as it leads to increased expertise.

You should provide your employees with a written statement of their *duties, responsibilities, authority,* and *relationships.* Let each of them know what he or she can and cannot—or should not—do.

Forms of Organization

You should be familiar with the forms of organization, according to the types of authority:

1. Functional.
2. Line.
3. Line and staff.
4. Informal.

Your business may start as a *functional organization,* whereby each supervisor is in charge of a specific function. For example, one supervisor may be assigned repair work; another, inspection. This form of organization is effective only in the very small business.

---

[3] Stanley Wantola, *Delegating Work and Responsibility* (Washington, D.C.: Small Business Administration, 1972), Management Aids for Small Manufacturers, No. 191.

Your business may be better organized as a *line organization*. "Command" authority is used in this type of structure. Each supervisor is in charge of a specific operational unit.

Further company growth may require *line and staff* authority. "Advisory" authority, specialty, and service characterize the staff. The staff assists line personnel in carrying out their activities.

An *informal organization* will always exist within the formal structure of your business. This organization consists of many interpersonal relations which arise as a result of friendships on and off the job. Two examples are *informal leaders* and the *grapevine* communication system. You should determine who the informal leaders are, obtain their support for your programs, and encourage them to "sell" your programs to the rest of your employees.

Ways of Organizing Your Firm

With respect to your company's formal organizational structure, you may choose to group the activities into manageable units by:

1. *Function.* Like skills are grouped together to form an organizational unit, such as *production* or *marketing*. The lowest level of the organization should probably be structured on this basis.
2. *Product.* Production or sales activities may be grouped by product, such as *men's wear, ladies' wear,* and so forth.
3. *Process.* Small companies often base their organization upon manufacturing processes, such as *welding* and *painting*.
4. *Geographic area.* If your company requires a strong, local marketing effort, organizing the sales force by areas or territories can be appropriate.
5. *Customers.* A firm's customers may be classified as *industrial, commercial,* and so on.
6. *Project.* To illustrate, a small public accounting firm may be organized on the basis of its clients' projects.
7. *Abilities.* You may assign work to people according to their talents.

Preparing an Organization Chart

You should express authority and responsibility relationships in a formal organization chart. Even if you have a one-man business, a chart can be a useful reminder of how your time might be most effectively utilized

You may select a traditional formal organization structure that may be described as a triangular pyramid. (See Figure 7-3.) This requires more centralization of authority and more detailed supervision.

On the other hand, you may select the flatter, broader span of control. (See Figure 7-4.) If so, you will provide your subordinates with less centralized authority and less detailed supervision.

A chart should be both a useful tool for the present and an aid in

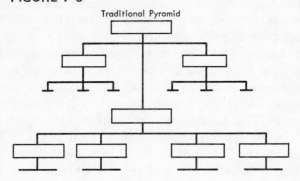
FIGURE 7-3

Traditional Pyramid

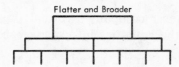
FIGURE 7-4

Flatter and Broader

planning for the future development of your organization and in projecting personnel requirements.

A list of job titles and job specifications should accompany the chart. Job specifications state the qualifications, duties, responsibilities, and working conditions of the work assignment.

If you have an independent unincorporated company, there may be no "president" or other management title. Instead, the organization structure might be similar to that shown in Figure 7-5. In fact, a tight, formal organization structure could "choke the life" out of your company.

FIGURE 7-5
Organization for an Independent Manufacturing Firm

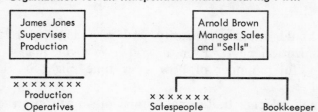

As your firm grows beyond a certain size, you will often find that specialized skills are required which you do not possess. You should first attempt to obtain outside, part-time assistance to aid, say, your sales manager, who may lack advertising expertise, or your plant manager, who may lack industrial engineering training. You may also decide that you cannot manage the detailed operations any longer because the size and complexity of your operations are increasing too rapidly. You should preferably seek people in your company to designate as managers. Figure 7-6 portrays such an organization.

FIGURE 7-6
Organization Structure of an Independent Manufacturing Firm

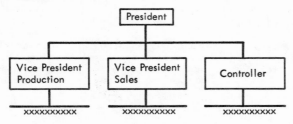

If organizational problems exist in your company, they are among the first types of problems that should be solved.

To help you detect organizational problems—and hopefully to correct them—see Figure 7-7. This figure describes the symptoms of such problems, possible causes, and some actions to remove or correct the problems.[4]

Organizational Problems

FIGURE 7-7
Organizational Problems of Independent Businesses

Symptoms	Possible Causes	Needed Action
1. Company seems to be drifting aimlessly or trying to go in all different directions	The organization lacks an effective planner	The board of directors should recognize these symptoms and formulate one-three-year plans
2. Conflicts occur among managers and key personnel; confusion arises about current objectives and operations	The manager is not working closely with his people to develop unified objectives and a team approach	Daily conferences should be held between the manager and his staff to build a working organization
3. When the manager is not available, the organization is paralyzed	The manager may believe no one else can make a decision	The manager should delegate authority; a committee of the more capable employees may suggest to the manager that they be given more responsibility in decision making

---

[4] Robert G. Murdick et al., *Business Policy: A Framework for Analysis* (Columbus, Ohio: Grid, Inc., 1972).

FIGURE 7-7 (continued)

4. Supervisors' decisions are frequently reversed by the manager	The manager has not developed a consistent set of polocies.	Some policies and procedures should be put into writing to cover the major repetitive actions and areas of decision making
5. An activity, such as sales or production, cannot keep abreast of its work	The manager is incompetent; personality problems are present	An immediate objective study is needed; if the manager cannot determine the cause of the problem, he should have a business consultant study the situation and make recommendations
6. Administrative costs have grown more rapidly than sales	Big-company organization structure is being imposed upon the independent company	The number of managers should be reduced, and the remaining managers' responsibilities broadened

The questionnaire in Exhibit 13 of *The Dow Jones-Irwin Business Papers* can help you determine the administrative organizational structure for your company.

Planning Your Strategies

Now that you've planned your legal, financial, and administrative structures, you're ready to consider the other planning functions. Most of these are covered in later chapters, and only those dealing with formulating and implementing strategies will be discussed at this point.

As stated in Figure 7–1, strategies are major objectives or goals defining what business your company is in, the kind of enterprise it is, and the plans for achieving your goals and objectives.

Your company strategy should be deliberately determined and made known to *all* employees to aid them in performing long-range planning and to inspire their organizational efforts.

As shown in Chapter 4, you begin formulating policy by studying the economy, then the industry, and then your own company. Relative to the *economy*, you try to identify opportunities and problems (risks or threats), such as technological, economic, social, and political changes. These include changes in population and government, new social mores, inflation, and war.

You analyze the *industry* you are entering to predict growth, profitability, and other key factors affecting success.

You then compare the strengths and weaknesses of your company with those of your competitors. You also match your company's strengths with key factors for success in the industry, as shown by the analysis you did earlier.

Your company strategy should:

1. Identify the particular products/services—product-market scope—which your firm will promote.
2. Select the basic ways in which those products/services will be created.
3. Determine the major steps necessary for your company to take the desired course of action.
4. Establish the standards used to measure achievement.

Your company strategy should provide central direction to the activities of your organization and your people. The public or market should also be informed about your company strategy.

The questionnaire in Exhibit 14 of *The Dow Jones-Irwin Business Papers* can assist you in evaluating your company's current strategy and in formulating a new strategy.

chapter 8

Managing Your Business

This chapter closely examines the basic managerial functions of directing and controlling. In connection with directing, the chapter discusses the exercise of leadership; communicating ideas, orders, and instructions; and motivating performance as well as the possible use of MBO.

The processes of control, self-discipline, externally imposed discipline, and indirect control are then described. The question "What kind of manager would you be?" is posed, and the importance of delegation is pointed out.

The chapter concludes with a discussion of sources of outside assistance, including private management consultants and the Small Business Administration.

Some of this material is covered elsewhere in this book in considerable detail. However, it is also treated here as part of an overview of the subject.

DIRECTING

Directing is guiding and supervising the performance of duties and responsibilities by your subordinates. It consists of:

1. Exercising leadership.
2. Communicating ideas, orders, and instructions.
3. Motivating performance.

Exercising Leadership

Effective leadership involves democratic directing rather than autocratic commanding. Leadership refers to your interpersonal influence. To exercise effective leadership, you should create a work climate which motivates better work performance. You should then be skillful in communicating your orders down the chain of command, using formal and informal channels.

You should have empathy—the ability to put yourself in the shoes of other individuals and to consider matters from their point of view.

Do you understand your personal leadership characteristics? It is probably more important for you to find subordinates who will respond to your style of management than it is for you to try to reorient your own personality, attitudes, and self-image.

Once you have chosen good subordinates, you should try to build effective supervisory relationships into your company. The following factors are significant in doing this:

1. Your attitude toward your supervisors.
2. Your choices for supervisors.
3. The training given to supervisors.
4. The opportunities for supervisor job satisfaction.
5. The rewards for work well done.

Your *attitude toward your supervisors* is at the heart of the matter. That attitude can make them believe that they are errand runners, police, or leaders. If you regard them as errand runners, they will tend to follow instructions without question or suggestion. Since they have little authority, independence, or prestige, they will be resentful and avoid responsibility. If you consider them to be police, they will see that rules are obeyed and that the work is carried out. However, if you consider them to be leaders, they will probably see that company policies are followed and that the work gets done in an efficient manner.

You should treat supervisors as members of your management team with responsibilities for human relations, training, and liaison in addition to work performance. You should listen to their ideas and respect their opinions.

You should consult all your subordinates for their ideas. They will have good ideas because they look at problems from a special point of view. Also, asking them for their ideas will give them a sense of importance.

Communication should be two-way. You should be able to communicate your ideas to subordinates, and they should be able to communicate their ideas to you. You should be an effective listener.

Communicating

To be most effective in communicating ideas, orders, and instructions, you should understand these principles of effective communication:

1. Know what message you want to communicate to subordinates and the most appropriate communication medium for "reaching" them.
2. Understand your subordinates' expectations and hopes.
3. Understand your own motives and objectives, and what you intend to gain from the communication.
4. Follow up to determine whether subordinates clearly understand the message.

Another part of communicating is counseling. In order to counsel effectively with subordinates, you should have this information:

1. What your subordinates are doing.
2. What unsolved work problems they have.
3. What suggestions they have for improvement.
4. How they feel about their jobs, their fellow employees, and their company.

Motivating

Motivation is complex and difficult to understand at best, and some writers have further complicated the subject by the use of jargon. We will present a simplified *practical* approach to help you stimulate your workers.

In essence, motivation is applying an incentive which *promises* to satisfy the predominant need of the worker. However, once that need is satisfied the incentive will no longer motivate the worker.

A practical approach to motivating your employees is shown in Figure 8-1. In general, you should know what your employees need in order to achieve self-satisfaction and then try to find an incentive that will unlock their springs to motivation.

FIGURE 8-1

Practical Approach to Motivating Your Employees

You, the Owner		Incentives You Can Use to Motivate Your Subordinates	Your Subordinates	
Your Objective	What Is Needed to Achieve Your Objectives		What Needs Must Be Satisfied for Their Objectives to Be Achieved	Their Objectives
Service and profit	Performance and productivity	Challenging work	Self-esteem	Self-satisfaction
		Merit increases and promotions		
		Praise and recognition		
		Personal publicity		
		Responsibility		
		Job enrichment	Social	
		Status systems		
		Suggestion system		
		Communications system		
		Staff meetings		
		Training and development	Security	
		Wage incentive plans		
		Savings plans		
		Profit sharing		
		Seniority systems		
		Insurance		
		Pensions		
		Other employee benefits		
		Money, or sustenance for survival	Survival	

To be most effective in managing your firm, you should consider using Management by Objectives (MBO).

Before the beginning of your company's fiscal year, you and your managers should define the company's overall objectives and the yardsticks by which performance will be measured. These objectives should be communicated to department heads and supervisors. Concurrently, your company managers should be formulating their own objectives. When your objectives are made known to your people, a reaction should occur that causes the managers to modify their goals to fit your company's objectives. Providing this integration of objectives throughout an independent company may take three to four months. Attaining a fully effective MBO program may take a year or two—or longer.

You should also establish peer goal-setting. Here individuals at a given organizational level develop their objectives together. Two benefits of this approach are:

1. Peers may give a manager unbiased viewpoints concerning major activities and suggest solutions to problems.
2. A better understanding should result between individuals because objectives will not duplicate each other.

Objectives should be specific and understandable, quantifiable, and realistic, that is, attainable—with difficulty. An objective of "increasing sales" is unclear. Instead, an objective should be set, say, "to increase sales by a minimum of 5 percent and a maximum of 15 percent over the next fiscal year at prices which will provide a gross profit of 35 percent."

Desirable objectives probably include profitability, competitive position, productivity, and employee relations. These should be stated specifically—*how much* profit, *what percent* of the market, *how much* cost of production, and *how much* labor turnover.

All of your subordinates should be asked to set objectives for themselves, their people, their material, and so forth. You should meet with each of them to reach agreement on those objectives and on how they can be accomplished.

Each subordinate should be provided a continual feedback of the results being attained, and these results should be reviewed against the objectives. You should help each person overcome obstacles to the objectives.

Near the end of the period, each subordinate should prepare a brief statement concerning how his performance compares to the objectives. Each subordinate's report should be reviewed and discussed.

An agreement should be reached with each subordinate on how good his performance has been. If the objectives were not achieved, an effort should be made to find out why.

Your company's reward structure (promotions, merit increases, training and development, and recognition) and penalty system (demotions and discharges) should be related to the performance of each individual.

An MBO program can be operated on a daily, weekly, or monthly basis. If it is working effectively, quick feedback, immediate weighing of measures of success, and good results for your company should follow.

Other applications of MBO on a *daily basis* may pertain to your production supervisor and officer manager. For example, your supervisor may receive an order for 1,000 widgets. This order sets a goal, and performance leads to its accomplishment. The office manager may be assigned to process ten contracts. This assignment also sets a goal.

In essence, we are saying that you should be concerned with the survival of your company, not only five or ten years from now, but also next week. You should act and react quickly in order to keep your firm alive—now!

The checklist in Exhibit 15 of *The Dow Jones-Irwin Business Papers*, should help you establish an MBO program for your company.

CONTROLLING

Controlling is the measurement and correction of the performance of subordinates to assure that the company's objectives and plans are accomplished.

Process of Control

The process of control consists of these steps:

1. Set up planned standards of performance.
2. Measure actual performance.
3. Compare actual performance with planned performance.
4. Determine whether deviations are excessive.
5. Determine and take appropriate corrective action.

You should appraise the employees' performance by comparing it with the objectives that were set for the time specified. Your rewards or corrections should follow the appraisal closely.

Self-Discipline

You should encourage self-discipline by your employees rather than use direct control. Here your personal example will be important. Your employees should have confidence in their abilities to perform their jobs, believe that their performance will advance their own interests, and believe that you will provide support if they run into difficulties.

Externally Imposed Discipline

You will probably find that 95 percent of your employees rarely cause any problems. However, if you do not deal effectively with the few who violate rules and regulations, employee disrespect will probably become widespread. To administer discipline effectly you should:

1. Know the rules.
2. Move promptly on violations.
3. Gather pertinent facts.
4. Allow employees to explain their positions.
5. Set up and evaluate tentative courses of action.
6. Decide what action to take.
7. Apply disciplinary action.
8. Maintain a record of actions taken.

You should distinguish between major and minor offenses and consider extenuating circumstances, such as the employee's length of service, and prior peformance record and the duration of time since the last offense. You should never be vindictive.

Indirect Control

The very small independent business usually lends itself to direct control. But indirect control is necessary at later stages of growth. Your means of indirect control are reports.

Some guidelines that you should follow with respect to reports are:

1. They should cover separate organizational units.
2. They should be designed to be updated as needed.
3. They should be factual.
4. They should be designed to indicate actions which have been taken or are planned.
5. They should be designed to highlight comparisons of the performance of organizational units and/or individuals within your company.

These reports should be given to all executive and supervisory personnel concerned. You should operate on the basis of the *exception principle,* which requires an immediate investigation of the causes of significant variations, whether favorable or unfavorable. You should arrange for immediate action to prevent a repetition of bad results or to assure the continuation of good results.

WHAT KIND OF MANAGER WOULD YOU BE?

Managerial functions described above are universal. They apply in all types of institutions, at all levels of management, and to all business functions. Thus, you should have determined by now whether or not you have the general management skills and the temperament to be in business for yourself. The material in this chapter should help you determine whether or not you have the specific know-how to be a manager in a particular industry. Often that know-how is obtained only from experience in the industry. A rule of thumb of at least three years' experience is sometimes cited.

As your business grows, you should be able to make the transition from being a "doer" to delegating authority. You will accomplish results through others so that you can concentrate on long-range planning and financing.

Too many independent business managers rely on "thinks" instead of "facts." "Thinks" consist of hunches, guesses, and intuition. You should make every effort to collect and use low-cost, readily available, published data to verify your "thinks."

The checklist in Exhibit 16 of *The Dow Jones-Irwin Business Papers* will help you decide what type of manager you will be.

SOURCES OF OUTSIDE ASSISTANCE

If you encounter problems that you cannot solve by yourself, you should seek outside assistance from a private management consultant or through the Small Business Administration (SBA).

The Private Management Consultant

A management consultant can assist you in such areas as accounting, legal matters, insurance, marketing, organizational problems, and operating problems. You should expect an objective point of view, new ideas, and a knowledge of cost-saving methods which could help you improve your decision making. Through the use of a consultant you may be able to save 10 to 20 percent of your firm's annual operating costs. The consultant can help you out of trouble or can prevent trouble by eliminating its causes. Fees will usually be more than $100 per day, plus expenses. You should insist that the consultant's fees, duties, and alloted time for the accomplishment of results be specified contractually.

You should check with past and present clients to obtain their appraisals of the consultant's competence.

The Small Business Administration

If your independent firm is in trouble, you can obtain free assistance from the Small Business Administration by contacting the nearest SBA field office.

This agency offers several kinds of assistance. First, it has developed special materials covering a variety of topics. Some are free, and the others may be purchased at a nominal cost. Forms for this printed resource material may be acquired from the SBA office that services your area.

Some years ago, the SBA organized the *Service Corps of Retired Executives* (SCORE) and the *Active Corps of Executives* (ACE). The latter group is composed of active business executives. Consultative talent may be obtained through the local chapters of these organizations or by contacting the nearest SBA office.

The SBA also operates the *406 Program* on a contract basis. It contracts with a private consulting firm to help an independent business. In this program, the consulting firm does both an analysis of activities and a follow-up by becoming involved in the day-to-day operations of the enterprise.

Free assistance may also be obtained by contacting instructors of Small Business Management courses and faculty advisers of accounting societies in colleges and universities. Furthermore, over 300 colleges and universities are members of the *Small Business Institute (SBI),* which is cosponsored by the SBA and the American Assembly of Collegiate Schools of Business (AACSB).

Through a program coordinator of the SBI, arrangements may be made to have a student team counsel and assist you in your management and operating problems.

The SBA contracts with the institution to provide consulting service on a case-referral basis, for which the agency provides a per case expense allowance. A faculty coordinator guides students from different fields in working with an individual business needing assistance. The students go into the business, make an analysis of its operation, return to the campus, and meet with the faculty coordinator and other students involved in similar activities. In a seminar-type environment, the firm's difficulties are identified and discussed and alternative courses of action are considered. The students then return to the business and try to improve its operations.

The success rate of this program seems higher than that of some other management assistance programs.

WHERE TO LOOK FOR FURTHER INFORMATION

Barker, Phyllis A. *Budgeting in a Small Service Firm.* Washington, D.C.: Small Business Administration, 1971. (Small Marketers Aids, no. 146.)

Blicksilver, Harold. "Organizatonal and Financial Planning for New Business Ventures." *The Vital Majority.* Washington, D.C.: Small Business Administration, 1973, pp. 274–75.

Broom, H. N., and **Longenecker, Justin G.** *Small Business Management.* Cincinnati, Ohio: South-Western Publishing Co., 1971, pp. 394–433.

Bunn, Verne A. *Buying and Selling a Small Business.* Washington, D.C.: Small Business Administration, 1969, pp. 3–119. (If you are serious about buying an existing business, this is *must* reading!)

Cornwell, Arthur W. *Sales Potential and Market Share.* Washington, D.C.: Small Business Administration, 1972. (Small Marketers Aids, No. 112.)

Denton, Charley M. *Franchising in the Economy, 1971-1973.* Washington, D.C.: U.S. Department of Commerce, 1973, pp. 7–16.

Golde, Roger A. *Breaking the Barriers to Small Business Planning.* Washington, D.C.: Small Business Administration, 1972, p. 2. (Management Aids for Small Manufacturers, No. 179.)

Kudrle, Albert E. *Motels.* Washington, D.C.: Small Business Administration, 1970, pp. 4–6. (Small Business Bibliography, No. 66.)

Murdick, Rogert G., et al. *Business Policy: A Framework for Analysis.* Columbus, Ohio: Grid, Inc., 1972. (For information on organizing *any* type of firm.)

Rosenblatt, Samuel M. *Franchising in the Economy, 1972-1974.* Washington, D.C.: U.S. Department of Commerce, 1974, pp. 1–15, 41–42.

Sommer, Howard E. *How to Analyze Your Own Business.* Washington, D.C.: Small Business Administration, 1973. (Management Aids for Small Manufacturers, No. 46.)

Wantola, Stanley. *Delegating Work and Responsibility.* Washington, D.C.: Small Business Administration, 1972. (Management Aids for Small Manufacturers, No. 191.)

PART THREE

Manning Your Business

According to Lawrence Appley, former president of the American Management Association, "Management is the development of people and not the direction of things. . . . Management is personnel administration."

As Mr. Appley indicates, the primary duty of every manager is the proper selection, placement, development, and utilization of the firm's personnel. How well—or how poorly—he does these things is a major factor in the success or failure of a business. Of all the resources the manager has, only people are able to vary their own productivity. While a machine can perform only the tasks for which it was designed, employees have almost limitless performance capabilities.

You, as an owner-manager, should understand that the personnel function is involved in all aspects of establishing a new business or entering an ongoing business, as well as in performing the management and business functions described throughout this book.

Every independent business manager is a "personnel manager" in the sense that work is done through people, with people, and for people. Consequently, you should be capable of handling employee relations yourself until your company becomes large enough to afford a personnel manager.

Part Three deals with the personnel function. It contains valuable insights that can help you be effective as a personnel manager in your business. It contains information about planning your personnel requirements, selecting the sources from which you can obtain new employees, recruiting, choosing the people you need, training and developing them into productive workers, evaluating their performance, compensating them, and dealing with various personnel relationships, including industrial relations. The relationships among these activities are diagramed in Figure III-1.

Some of these activities may not be necessary in the very small independent firm, but all of them will be important as your firm grows.

FIGURE III-1

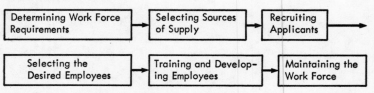

| Determining Work Force Requirements | → | Selecting Sources of Supply | → | Recruiting Applicants | → |

| Selecting the Desired Employees | → | Training and Developing Employees | → | Maintaining the Work Force |

chapter 9

Selecting Your People

This chapter focuses on the important topic of selecting employees for your firm. Selection begins with the planning of manpower requirements, which consists of determining job specifications, forecasting the number of people needed, developing manpower plans by job classification, inventorying the skills of present personnel, comparing manpower plans with your personnel inventory to identify shortages, and determining sources of supply from which to recruit the people needed. After discussing each of these subjects, the chapter covers the methods used in recruiting new employees and describes appropriate selection procedures in some depth. Finally, it presents an orientation program for new employees.

PLANNING YOUR MANPOWER REQUIREMENTS

Manpower planning is one of the most frustrating problems you will encounter in managing your firm. Perhaps the primary reason is that the independent business is not big enough to hire the exact type and number of people needed. Typically, it lacks facilities for properly recruiting, selecting, developing, and utilizing its personnel. It may also lack economies of scale in record keeping and in the administration of its personnel program. Personality conflicts may be quite troublesome. One disgruntled person represents a much larger percentage of the total work force of the independent firm than of the larger firm. Moreover, because of the usual practice of promoting from within, an incompetent worker may rise to higher levels in the independent organization.

How to Do Manpower Planning

When you do manpower planning, you are concerned with what type and quality of personnel your firm has and will need. Therefore, you should:

1. Determine the jobs to be performed and the qualities needed to perform them—namely, job specifications.
2. Forecast the total number of people needed in each category by collecting and analyzing industry growth data and by studying your firm's growth data.
3. Develop manpower plans for a given period—perhaps one year—by job classification or skill.
4. Inventory the skills of all your present personnel—their education, training, and experience; their talents, abilities, skills, and trades; and their potential for growth.
5. Compare your manpower plans with your personnel inventory to identify shortages.
6. Determine the sources of supply from which you can recruit extra people as needed.

How to Prepare Job Specifications

Because the quality and quantity of your work force are both important, your manpower plans should be complete but flexible, and updated at least semiannually. You should organize around "what is to be done" rather than "who is to do it." The use of *job specifications* will enable you to match the person to the job to be filled.

> A retailer's business was growing rapidly. While he was busy with customers, the telephone was ringing and correspondence was piling up. He thought he needed a secretary. But did he? Secretaries and stenographers are scarce and expensive. Perhaps a typist would "fill the bill." Finding a qualified typist would probably be easier, and the salary savings would be substantial. While the retailer might find it a chore to write out letters rather than dictate them, he would probably not be skilled at dictation anyway, and he could probably compose a letter more effectively by seeing how it appeared before typing.[1]

Job specifications are written statements covering the duties, authority, responsibilities, and working conditions of the job and describing the *personal qualifications* required to perform it successfully. A typical job specification includes at least the following information:

1. The physical demands of the job and the minimum physical requirements of the individual who fills it.
2. The working conditions—including psychological conditions, such as relationships with others and responsibilities for other people, money, equipment, and so on.
3. The duties and responsibilities.

---

[1] Rudolph Ralphelson, *Finding and Hiring the Right Employee* (Washington, D.C.: Small Business Administration, 1972), Small Marketers Aids, No. 106.

4. The educational background and knowledge, skills and techniques, and training and experience required to perform the job.
5. The days and hours of work.
6. The machines, tools, formulas, and other equipment used.
7. The pay classification and promotional opportunities.
8. Desirable personal characteristics.

The job specifications should state the minimum standards that must be met in order to perform the job satisfactorily. For dead-end, routine, and low-level jobs, it may also be desirable to state the maximum acceptable standards in order to prevent an overqualified person from taking the job.

Many methods are used to gather data for job specifications. The most popular ones are observation, the questionnaire, and the interview. Figure 9–1 is a questionnaire used by a bank to obtain the data it uses in preparing specifications for nonexecutive jobs.

Job specifications enable you to perform the personnel function effectively. They aid greatly in recruiting, selecting, and placing employees in your firm and in deciding what wages and salaries to pay. They are also valuable in training and developing personnel and in deciding transfers and promotions.

> A service station dealer wanted to hire an "experienced attendant." He believed it was unnecessary to specify the attendant's duties because "He'll know what the job is." But is this true? Service station attendants have different kinds of duties, including selling gasoline, lubricating cars, changing tires, and doing repair work. If the dealer needed a repair man but did not so indicate, he could have wasted considerable time interviewing men who were qualified only for driveway work.

If you do not want to prepare job specifications, you should at least establish *job descriptions* for the most important positions. These are merely statements of duties and responsibilities and do not include personal characteristics and qualifications. (See Figure 9–2 for a sample job description.)

WHERE TO FIND NEW EMPLOYEES

Once you have decided what types of employees you need, the next step is to decide where to seek them. There are two basic sources—(1) from *within the firm* through promotion, upgrading, or transfer; and (2) from *outside the company* through recruitment and selection. In general, four sources are used by independent businessmen:

1. Qualified people from within the organization.
2. Personnel from competing firms in the same industry.
3. Organizations outside the industry.
4. Educational institutions.

FIGURE 9-1

Number:_____

Name:_____ Title:_____

Division:_____ Department:_____

Supervisor's Name:_____ Title:_____

PLEASE READ THE ENTIRE QUESTIONNAIRE BEFORE MAKING ANY ENTRIES

I. RESPONSIBILITIES:

List the normal duties you personally perform in the order of their importance:

A. Daily:

B. Periodically:

C. Occasionally:

D. Describe the consequence of errors in your work for the rest of the organization:

II. AUTHORITY:

A. What are the most important decisions you can make by yourself in your job?

B. What decisions are you required to refer to your supervisor or manager?

C. What parts of your work are checked by others?

FIGURE 9-1 (continued)

III. KNOWLEDGE: MINIMUM STARTING REQUIREMENTS OF YOUR POSITION: (Note: Please do not enter your own education, experience, etc., unless it happens to agree with your opinion of the minimum requirements.)

    A. What is the minimum educational level (high school, college, other) required of a person starting in your position?

    B. What previous experience should a new employee have in order to meet the minimum starting requirements of your position?

        1. What kind of experience is required?

        2. Where can it be obtained?

        3. What is the minimum length of time required to acquire it?

    C. If a person has the above education and experience:

        1. What new factors not encountered in previous experience and training would an employee starting in this position have to learn?

        2. What would be the minimum time required to learn and practice these factors in order to perform the duties of this position?

    D. Please list any other requirements not covered above:

IV. SKILLS:

    A. What machines or other equipment do you personally operate? Do you operate them regularly or only occasionally?

    B. What contacts with other people are you required to make, other than with your subordinates and your immediate superior? (Please list contacts within the organization and outside the organization.)

FIGURE 9-1 (concluded)

C. What, in your opinion, is the most complex or difficult part of your work?

Use additional sheets of paper, if necessary, for any special features of your work not covered above, and for answers to questions for which more space is needed.

Date: _____   Signed: _____

Approved: _____

            (name)   (title)

Filling Jobs from within the Firm

There are three methods of securing employees internally: *upgrading* the employee now holding the job; *promoting* an employee from a lower level job; and *transferring* an employee from a similar job elsewhere in the organization.

Some independent companies use outside recruitment instead of training their own personnel. They permit the larger companies which can afford expensive formal training programs to develop employees. Then the smaller companies pay higher wages to attract these trained individuals.

Job interest and satisfaction may be increased for some of your employees by rotating them among jobs or by rearranging their workplaces to give them more group interaction.

The *advantages* of using internal sources to obtain your personnel include knowledge concerning your employees' capabilities, strengths, and weaknesses. Promotion from within will also probably raise the morale of all employees (except, perhaps, jealous individuals).

The *disadvantages* of internal sources may be the lack of anyone willing or able to fill the vacant job and possible inbreeding.

You should first decide what personal qualifications you are seeking and then chose the methods most likely to produce people with those qualifications. Some methods are costly in terms of your time and money; others are free.

A *balanced program* of using people from both internal and external sources is superior to using either type exclusively.

Upgrading. Increasing skill requirements have led to technological unemployment, a situation in which an employee can no longer perform a job because its demands have increased beyond his capacity. Such jobs can be filled by upgrading present employees. This involves retraining the unskilled or semiskilled worker. This method was very effective during World War II, but at present its use is limited by a lack of motivation on the part of the technologically unemployed and a lack of adequate procedures by which to select candidates for upgrading. Where these limitations can be overcome, this procedure results in improving and enhancing the individual's productive abilities.

FIGURE 9–2
Sample Job Description

Job Title: Office and credit manager
Supervisor: Store manager

Job Summary

Responsible for all office and credit functions of the store. Has control of store's assets and expenditures. Helps manager administer store's policies and methods. Exercises mature judgment and initiative in carrying out duties.

Duties

1. Inspects sales tickets for accuracy and completeness of price, stock classifications, and delivery information. (Daily)

2. Prepares bank deposits, listing checks and cash, and takes deposits to bank. (Daily)

3. Keeps sales and expenses record sheets, posting sales and expenses, and accumulating them for the month. (Daily)

4. Processes credit applications: analyzes financial status and paying record of customers, check references and credit bureau to determine credit responsibility. (Daily)

5. Sends collection notices to past-due accounts, using mail, telephone calls, and personal visits (if necessary) to collect. (Daily)

6. Sells merchandise during rush hours of the store. (Daily)

7. Checks invoices of outside purchases to verify receipt, quantity, price, etc. Gets store manager's approval. (Weekly)

8. Does all bookkeeping and prepares financial and profit-and-loss statements of store. (Monthly)

Duties	Approximate Time Spent on Each Duty (percent)
Bookkeeping	40
Credit and collection	20
Selling on retail floor	20
Inventories and stock control	10
Miscellaneous functions	10

Source: *Personnel Management,* Administrative Management Course Program, Topic 6 (Washington, D.C.: Small Business Administration, 1965), p. 56.

Promoting. Increases in salaries are sometimes misconstrued to be promotions. To be promoted, a worker must move to a higher position in which his responsibilities are increased and he has greater status or prestige. Frequently, promotions result in changes in titles or job classifications.

Promotions may be based upon *seniority* (which refers to an individual's length of service) or *merit* (which refers to the individual's ability to perform the job better than others), or a *combination* of the two. In theory, promotions based upon merit induce employees to produce more in order to demonstrate their "merit." However, for lower level jobs, particularly where unions are involved, seniority is becoming the more frequently used basis for promotion. The reason for this trend is that seniority does not involve value judgments and does not lead to as many personal conflicts.

Transferring. Filling a position by transferring an employee from the same organizational level elsewhere in the organization is usually done when this puts the person in line for greater potential advancement. Essentially, a transfer involves a change in responsibilities and duties, either with or without a change in pay.

Job Posting. If a union represents your employees, you will probably be required to post available job openings on a bulletin board to give present employees a chance to "bid" on them. This method has also been found to be a good defense against charges of violating equal employment opportunities laws. Figure 9–3 shows a form used for this purpose by a manufacturing firm.

Filling Jobs from outside the Firm

Ultimately, all jobs must be filled from outside the organization unless the company is reducing its work force. As individual positions are filled through upgrading, promoting, or transferring employees, these vacated positions must be filled externally.

Reasons for Using External Sources. A growing organization must go outside to obtain personnel for at least its lowest level jobs. But there are also reasons for going outside for high-level personnel. Inevitably, "new blood" is needed to prevent "inbreeding," conformity, and stagnation.

Another justification for external hiring is found in problems caused by mechanization and automation. Because new skills are often needed in a hurry, it is sometimes necessary to go outside the organization to find an individual who has them.

When a policy of internal promotion is followed too rigidly, there are inevitable mistakes in filling jobs. The personnel may have too much or too little education, and there may be excessive emphasis on social acceptability, experience, and so forth. It is practically impossible to anticipate the skills that will be needed in the future, to hire a man with those requirements who will enter at the bottom, and to expect him to progress all the way through the organization.

94

FIGURE 9-3

```
┌─────────────────────────────────────────────────────────┐
│                      JOB INTEREST                         │
│                                                           │
│              (Submit to Personnel in Duplicate)           │
│                                                           │
│  Do not submit for classifications in same job occupation as you │
│  are presently in.  (See charts in back of union contract.)      │
│                                                           │
│  Name _____ Classification _____ Date _____  │
│                                                           │
│  I am interested in being considered for the following classification: │
│                                                           │
│  Name of Classification _____ Chart Number _____    │
│                                                           │
│  My qualifications for the job as defined in the job description │
│  are as follows:  (Be specific—"I read complex blue prints";    │
│  "I am proficient with all hand tools listed"; "I have had six months' │
│  required product experience"; etc.  Do not use general terms such │
│  as "I am fast";"I am a good worker"; "I have watched it done and │
│  know I can do it"; etc.)                                  │
│                                                           │
│                                                           │
│                                                           │
│                                                           │
│                                                           │
│                                                           │
│                                                           │
│  Received in Personnel by_____ Date _____ │
│                                                           │
│  Keep your copy as evidence the application was received. │
└─────────────────────────────────────────────────────────┘
```

Some Sources You Can Use. Outside sources from which you can recruit new employees include:

1. Former employees.
2. Friends and relatives of employees.
3. Applications received in person or through the mail.
4. Competing firms.
5. Labor organizations.
6. Employment agencies.
7. Educational institutions, including high schools, business schools, vocational-technical schools, junior colleges, colleges, and manufacturers' training schools.
8. Leased manpower.

After you have decided the specifications for the jobs to be filled and the sources from which you are going to recruit prospective employees, the selection procedure must be set into motion. The more effective firms use some form of requisition to do this.

DETERMINING WHAT JOBS ARE TO BE FILLED

In essence, the requisition tells the personnel manager how many employees are needed, what their qualifications must be, when they will be needed, and how much they will be paid. Figure 9-4 is a form used for this purpose.

FIGURE 9-4
Employee Requisition Form

CONFIDENTIAL   CONFIDENTIAL

EMPLOYEE REQUISITION

FOR SALARIED EMPLOYEES

To: Personnel Manager   Date:_____

From: _____
          (department)

This department needs to obtain _____ employee(s) for the position of
                                              (number)
_____ with a starting salary range of _____ to
      (job title)
_____ per month.

The following qualifications will be required: _____

_____

_____

_____

_____

_____

This requisition needs to be filled by _____ if practicable.
                                                   (date)
Consideration (will) (will not) be given to the payment of any agency fees involved.

This requisition is for: ☐ Employee Replacement   ☐ Additional Requirements

                          _____

                          Department Manager

HOW TO RECRUIT NEW PEOPLE

The methods you can use in recruiting new people include:

1. School and college scouting.
2. Advertising, using newspapers, trade journals, radio, billboards, and window displays.
3. Employment agencies.
4. Employee referrals.

The following example illustrates two methods of external recruiting:

A retail store manager put a "help wanted" sign in the window. Many unqualified applicants inquired about the job, and when he turned down an applicant he stood the risk of losing the business of the applicant plus his friends and family. The manager also found that newspaper advertising brought in many unqualified people. If he included the store's telephone number in the ad, calls tied up his line and customers could not reach him.

In order to fill his vacancy, the manager should have used the services of a public or private employment agency or obtained leads from his present employees.

HOW TO SELECT PEOPLE FOR GIVEN JOBS

Mistakes in selecting and placing personnel in your firm can be greatly reduced if you use a systematic procedure for choosing the right people. The following procedure is one effective method for filling a position.

1. Review the job specifications for the position.
2. Consider your present employees, for one of them may be able to perform the job or may become qualified if his abilities are upgraded.
3. Look outside the company if none of your present employees can fill the job.
4. Use an application blank to gather information from applicants.
5. Prepare for interviews with applicants by listing the points you need to cover.
6. Conduct the interviews.
7. Bring the supervisor of the prospective employee into the act (you may even want him do do the interviewing).
8. Use psychological tests[2] to determine the applicant's knowledge, skills, and attitudes.
9. Check on qualified applicants with their previous employers.
10. Arrange to have the applicant take a physical examination.
11. Decide whether to hire the applicant on a trial basis.
12. Conduct an orientation program for the new employee.
13. After a prearranged probationary period, decide whether to retain the employee.

Figure 9–5 shows this suggested selection procedure in graphic form.

Application Blanks

Application blanks are used when a candidate applies for employment, and such blanks may be submitted in person or by mail. The candidate

---

[2] A word of caution is in order here. Discrimination against prospective employees on grounds of race, creed, color, sex, nation of origin, or age is barred by the Equal Pay Act of 1964, the Civil Rights Act of 1964, the Age Discrimination Act of 1967, and other acts; and by Executive Orders 10925, 11246, 11375, 11491, 11616, and other executive orders. You should be certain that your selection procedure conforms to national and local laws and customs.

FIGURE 9-5
Flow Chart of Selection Procedure

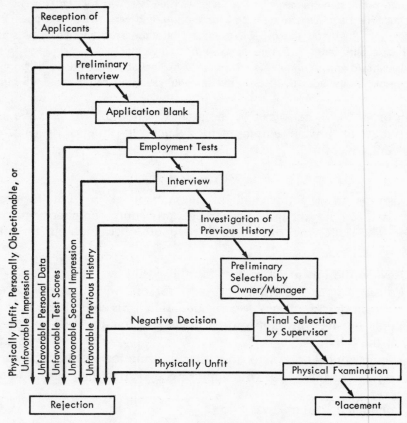

Source: Based on L. C. Megginson, *Personnel: A Behavioral Approach to Administration,* rev. ed. (Homewood, Ill.: Richard D. Irwin, Inc., 972), pp. 267 and 174.

lists employers for whom he has worked, the titles of jobs he has held, and his length of employment with each company. He furnishes information on his background, education, marital status, and military status, as well as other useful data. The blank should be car fully designed to provide information that you need about the candidates but it should not be a "hodgepodge" of irrelevant data developed from the application blanks of other firms. The completion of the blank bv the applicant will provide you with a sample of his neatness, thoroughness, and ability to answer questions. Since many states restrict the kinds of questions that may be included on an application blank, you should check any pertinent laws which your state may have.

Figure 9-6 is one of the best application blanks we have seen. Used by one of the largest firms in the country, it is a model of completeness, conciseness, clarity, and legality.

FIGURE 9-6

991-0002H

APPLICATION FOR EMPLOYMENT

EXXON

PLEASE PRINT

Exxon Corporation and affiliates

EQUAL OPPORTUNITY EMPLOYERS

PERSONAL

NAME (LAST, FIRST, MIDDLE) | CONTACT PHONE NO. (GIVE AREA CODE) | TIME TO CALL | A.M. | P.M.

PRESENT ADDRESS | ALTERNATE PHONE NO. (GIVE AREA CODE)

PERMANENT ADDRESS (IF DIFFERENT FROM ABOVE) | CONTACT PHONE NO. (GIVE AREA CODE)

SOCIAL SECURITY NO. | DO YOU HAVE RELATIVES WITH EXXON? (NAME, WHERE, RELATIONSHIP) ☐YES ☐NO | HAVE YOU APPLIED TO EXXON BEFORE? (WHICH COMPANY - WHEN)

U.S. CITIZEN ☐YES ☐NO | NON-U.S. CITIZEN — PLEASE INDICATE U.S. VISA STATUS ☐PERMANENT VISA ☐STUDENT VISA | EXCHANGE STUDENT VISA ☐ | VISITORS VISA ☐ | OTHER VISA ☐ EXPLAIN

ALIEN REGISTRATION NO. | HAVE YOU EVER BEEN DEPORTED FROM THE U.S.? ☐YES ☐NO

EDUCATION

NAME AND LOCATION OF HIGH SCHOOL | GRAD. DATE (MO./YR.) | YOUR CLASS STANDING IN YOUR MAJOR | YOUR OVERALL GRADEPOINT AVERAGE

COLLEGE NAME AND LOCATION | DATE (MO./YR.) FROM / TO | FIELDS OF STUDY MAJOR / MINOR | GRADUATION DEGREE* / DATE (MO./YR.) | MY STDG. IS 1ST IN CLASS OF 60 EXAMPLE: 1/60 | MY AVG. 3.7 ALL A'S 4.0 EXAMPLE: 3.7/4.0

*INSERT NUMBER OF COLLEGE CREDIT HOURS COMPLETED IF NO DEGREE OBTAINED.

COLLEGE FINANCING | % G.I. BILL | OWN % WORK | % SCHOLARSHIP EXPLAIN- | % OTHER EXPLAIN-

EMPLOYMENT

EMPLOYMENT DESIRED ☐PERMANENT ☐SUMMER | DATE AVAILABLE FOR WORK | LOCATION PREFERENCE (IF ANY) | SALARY EXPECTED

TYPE OF WORK DESIRED INITIALLY | TYPE OF WORK DESIRED EVENTUALLY

IS THERE SOME DIVISION OR FUNCTION IN WHICH YOU ARE ESPECIALLY INTERESTED? | IS THERE A SPECIFIC PROJECT OR STUDY THAT YOU WOULD LIKE TO DO?

EMPLOYER NAME, ADDRESS & PHONE NO. (INCLUDE GRADUATE ASSISTANTSHIP & SUMMER JOBS) | DATE (MO./YR.) FROM / TO | YOUR JOB TITLE AND DUTIES | SUPERVISOR'S NAME AND JOB TITLE

U.S. MIL.

BRANCH OF SERVICE | FROM (MO./YR.) | TO (MO./YR.) | RANK ON ENTRY | RANK ON DISCHARGE | TYPE OF DUTY (ESPECIALLY IF PROFESSIONAL)

ACTIVITIES

SUBJECTS OF SPECIAL STUDY OR RESEARCH, COLLEGE OR OTHER

HONORS, HONOR SOCIETIES, SCHOLARSHIPS, EXTRA CURRICULAR ACTIVITIES - OFFICES HELD OR RESPONSIBILITIES (EXCLUDE THOSE WHICH INDICATE RACE, COLOR, RELIGION, SEX, OR NATIONAL ORIGIN)

ADDITIONAL INFORMATION

Have you been convicted under any criminal law within the past 5 years? (Excluding minor traffic violations) ☐YES ☐NO

Have you ever been imprisoned as a result of a criminal conviction? ☐YES ☐NO
If the answer to either of the above questions is "YES", please give details on back.

Are you or have you ever knowingly been a member of the Communist Party or any organization which advocates overthrow of the United States Government by force or any illegal or unconstitutional method? ☐YES ☐NO If "YES", please give details on back.

ARE YOU UNDER TECHNICAL CONTRACT OR RESTRICTION WITH A FORMER EMPLOYER? ☐NO ☐YES — WITH WHOM?

MAY WE CALL YOUR PRESENT EMPLOYER? NOW — ☐YES ☐NO | AFTER VISIT — ☐YES ☐NO | COMMENTS

I authorize investigation of all statements contained in this application for employment. I understand that misrepresentation or omission of facts called for herein will be sufficient cause for cancellation of consideration for employment or dismissal from the Company's service if I have been employed. I understand that employment is subject to a physical examination in which my health is found to be satisfactory to the Company. I understand that if I am employed evidence of U.S. citizenship or U.S. resident status and a birth certificate or other evidence of date of birth will be required.

X SIGNATURE _____ DATE SIGNED _____

This is to inform you that as part of our procedure of processing your employment application it is understood that an investigative report may be made whereby information is obtained through personal interviews with third parties. This inquiry includes information as to your character, general reputation, personal characteristics, and mode of living, whichever may be applicable. You have the right to make a written request within a reasonable period of time for a complete and accurate disclosure of additional information concerning the nature and scope of the investigation.

(PLEASE GIVE US ANY ADDITIONAL INFORMATION ON SCHOLASTIC ACHIEVEMENT OR EXPERIENCE ON A SEPARATE SHEET OF PAPER)

Interviewing

In preparing for the interview, you should study the information in the application blank. You should know beforehand the questions you need to ask to get the other information you need. In order not to overlook anything significant, you should list the points that should be covered. You should ask the applicant specific questions, such as:

1. What did you do on your last job?
2. How did you do it?
3. Why did you do it?
4. What job did you like most? Least?

Compare your list of questions with the job specification so that you match the individual's personal qualifications with the job requirements.

If you are observant and perceptive during the interview, you can obtain some impressions about the candidate's abilities, personality, and attitudes toward work, as well as evaluate his or her appearance and speech. You can also provide information about your company and the job. Remember, the applicant needs facts to decide whether or not to accept the job, just as you need information to decide whether or not to offer it.

You may want the supervisor to conduct the interview as well as evaluate the application blank. If you are the interviewer, however, you should at least have the supervisor show the applicant the job and the work area. Failure to let the supervisor participate can lead to unfavorable attitudes later.

The interviewing may occur in one or two stages. Some firms have a *preliminary interview* during which the application is completed and general observations of the applicant are made. A *more penetrating interview* may then be held to probe his or her attitudes, values, and willingness and desire to work. Figure 9–7 is used during college recruiting by an independent manufacturer. It is completed *after* the interview.

Employment Tests

Through employment tests, you can determine the candidate's intelligence quotient (IQ), skills, aptitude, vocational interests, and personality. *IQ tests* are designed to measure a person's capacity to learn and solve problems and to comprehend complex relationships, and are particularly useful in selecting employees for managerial positions. *Proficiency and skill tests* are tests of ability to work at a particular trade, craft, or skill, and are useful in selecting operative employees *Aptitude tests* are used to predict how a person might perform on a given job, and are most applicable to operative jobs.

Vocational interest tests are designed to determine the applicant's major interests as far as work is concerned. Interest does not guarantee competence, but it can result in working and trying harder. A limitation of such tests is that the answers can be "faked."

Personality tests are designed to measure whether the applicant is an "introvert" or an "extrovert," his total personality structure, and his emotional adjustment and attitudes. These tests, along with inventories of emotional maturity, are often used to see how the applicant might fit into your organization. "Faked" answers are also possible in these tests. In addition to their use in selecting new employees, personality tests are valuable in evaluating present employees for promotion and as a basis for consulting with employees.

FIGURE 9-7

```
┌─────────────────────────────────────────────────────────────┐
│                      INTERVIEW DATA                           │
│                                                               │
│  Name _____ │
│                    (please print full name)                   │
│  School Address _____ Street     │
│                                                               │
│  City _____ State _____ Phone _____   │
│                                                               │
│  Home Address _____ Street      │
│                                                               │
│  City _____ State _____ Phone _____    │
│                                                               │
│  Married _____ No. of Dependents ____ Children:  Age ___, ___, ___ │
│                                                               │
│  Interview Date _____ 19_____ at _____  │
│                                                               │
│  Interested in Permanent _____ Summer _____ Employment │
│                                                               │
│  Interested in Elect. _____ Mech. _____ Office _____ Tech. _____ Drafting _____ │
│                                                               │
│  Shop _____ Other _____   │
│                                                               │
│  Date of Graduation _____ 19____ From _____   │
│                                                               │
│  B.S. _____ M.S. _____ in:  E.E. _____ M.E. _____ Other _____ │
│                                                               │
│  Military Service:   Army _____ Navy _____ Air Force _____ Other _____ │
│                                                               │
│      Present Classification _____   │
│                                                               │
│  Experience _____   │
│  _____    │
│  _____    │
│  _____    │
│  _____    │
│                                                               │
│  Grade-Point Average _____ out of _____   │
│                                                               │
│  Will Decide by_____ 19_____                      │
│                                                               │
│  * * * * * * * * * * * * * * * * * * * * * * * * * * * * * *  │
│                                                               │
│  Interviewer Comments _____   │
│  _____    │
│  _____    │
│  _____    │
│  _____    │
└─────────────────────────────────────────────────────────────┘
```

Aptitude tests are, by far, the most reliable indicators of an applicant's skill level. Intelligence and personality tests should be interpreted by professionals. You may be able to obtain some testing assistance from your state employment agency.

Tests used as a basis for making personnel decisions must be valid; that is, there must be a high degree of correlation between the test scores and performance on the job.

Checking References

The independent business manager is often victimized by employees whose credentials are not checked thoroughly. The importance of checking applicants' references carefully cannot be overemphasized.

Reference checks provide answers to questions concerning the candidate's performance on previous jobs. They are also helpful in verifying information on the application blank and statements made during interviews, in checking on possible omissions of information, and in clarifying specific points. Three sources of reference are:

1. Academic.
2. Personal.
3. Previous employers.

With business references, checks made by telephone or in person are preferred to written responses (Figure 9–9). The writer of a reference letter may have little or no idea of your job requirements. Also, past employers are sometimes reluctant to write poor letters of reference. Be sure to ask former employers specific questions about the candidate's performance, and whether they would consider rehiring the person. (See Figure 9–8.)

Physical Examination

The applicant's health and physical condition should be matched to the physical requirements of the job. You should have each applicant examined by a physician before hiring. The examination could reveal physical limitations which would limit job performance. It will also help you comply with your state's workers' compensation laws by providing a record of the employee's health at the time of hiring, and it could prevent compensation claims for any injury which occurred prior to his employment with you. The physical examination is usually the last step before hiring, as it is ordinarily the most expensive step.

Decision to Hire

After completing the selection procedure, you are in a position to decide whether the applicant should be hired on a trial basis or rejected. Your final decision should be made only after a probationary period. By that time, the employee should know your company well enough to decide whether or not he or she wants to stay. Some jobs may require a probationary period of six weeks, others six months—depending on how long it takes to learn to perform the job acceptably.

FIGURE 9-8

INQUIRY TO PAST EMPLOYERS

From: _____   File: _____

_____

TO: _____   Date: _____

Gentlemen:

    Mr. _____ has made application to this company for a position

as _____ and states that he was employed by you as _____

from _____ to _____ .

    Will you kindly reply to the inquiry below respecting this applicant. Your reply will be held in strict confidence and will in no way involve you in any responsibility.

    For your convenience in replying by return mail, we enclose stamped self-addressed envelope.

Very truly yours,

---

1. Is employment record with your company correct as stated above? _____

2. What kind(s) of work did he do? _____

3. Did he have custody of money or valuables? _____ Were his accounts properly kept? _____

4. Any record of salary garnishments? _____

5. If employed as a driver, specify equipment driven _____

6. Number of accidents _____ Number preventable _____

7. Was his driver's license ever suspended or revoked? _____

8. Number of on-the-job injuries while in your employ _____

9. Any back injuries? _____

10. Any award for permanent partial disability? _____

11. Reason for leaving your employ?   Discharged _____ Laid off _____ Resigned _____

12. Was his general conduct satisfactory?   Yes _____ No _____ Other _____

13. Is he competent for the position he is seeking?   Yes _____ No _____ Other _____

14. Would you re-employ?   Yes _____ No _____ Other _____

15. Any remarks with regard to questions 1-15 above? _____

_____

Date: _____ For: _____

                                                         (Name of Company)

By: _____

                              (Signature of person supplying information)

- -

(Detach here for your files)

_____ Date _____

        (Former Employer)

You are hereby authorized to give to the _____

                                      (Name of Prospective Employer)

all information regarding my services, character and conduct while in your employ, and you are released from any and all liability which may result from furnishing such information.

Witness: _____   Signed: _____

FIGURE 9-9
Reference Check—Short Form

Applicant	Position	How Contacted
Person Contacted	Position	Present Company
City and State	Phone	Are You Related? How?

Business Relationship: Where?   When?

_____

Interviewer's Comments _____

_____

_____

_____

Interviewed by _____

Date _____

Degree Verified   _____

Dates of Employment _____

Earnings Verified   _____

Strengths	Weaknesses

Performance? (Dependable, initiative, needs supervision, effective supervisor, technical ability, works well with others, sets and meets goals, attention to detail, cost-conscious, etc.) How does applicant compare with others in same classification? (Top 10%; low 25%, etc.)

(over)	(over)

Checked By	Date

FIGURE 9-10

VACANCY REPORT — AFFIRMATIVE ACTION

(This form is to be completed on each vacancy regardless of means utilized in filling vacancy. This report may be used in EEOC compliance investigations and should be filled out in detail)

Department _____   Location _____

POSITION:	NAMES OF MINORITY AND FEMALE APPLICANTS:

POSITION:

Position filled _____

Salary Grade _____

NEW EMPLOYEE:

Name_____

Sex _____ Race _____ Starting Salary _____

NAMES OF MINORITY AND FEMALE APPLICANTS:
(Place check in appropriate space if applicant was interviewed and/or offered job):

Inter-viewed	Offered position	Name	Sex	Race
[ ]	[ ]	1. _____	___	___
[ ]	[ ]	2. _____	___	___
[ ]	[ ]	3. _____	___	___
[ ]	[ ]	4. _____	___	___

NEW EMPLOYEE OBTAINED BY:

[ ]   Transfer within department
[ ]   Transfer from another department
[ ]   Promotion within department
[ ]   Promotion from another department
[ ]   New Hire (also check appropriate source in list below)

    [ ] Walk In   [ ] Newspaper Ad   [ ] Magazine Ad
    [ ] Non-Employee   [ ] Minority   [ ] College
       Referral   Newspaper Ad   Recruiting
    [ ] Employee Referral
       By Whom_____
    [ ] Employment Agency
       Agency Name_____
    [ ] Minority Agency
       Agency Name_____
    [ ] Other_____

If a minority or female is not hired, explain <u>in detail</u> why each minority or female was either not interviewed and/or not offered job. Refer to applicant's skills, ability, education, experience, etc. (Use additional pages if necessary)

(For Non-Tulsa locations only)

METHODS UTILIZED TO GENERATE MINORITY AND WOMEN CANDIDATES:
(Check all utilized) See Employee Relations Policy 102, page 4 of 6.

[ ]   Minority Ad
[ ]   State Employment Agency
[ ]   Community Organization
[ ]   Community Leaders
[ ]   Key Business People
[ ]   Other (Specify in detail)_____

_____

Return completed form within five (5) days after filling position

FIGURE 9–11

FORM 268

Social
Security No. _____

EMPLOYEE PERSONNEL HISTORY

NAME _____ Date of Birth _____ Insuring Year _____

Single _____ Married _____ Date _____ Status Change _____ __ __ Date _____

Dependents: Name _____ Relationship _____ Date _____

_____

_____

EDUCATION
(Prior to Date of Employment)

Names of Schools Attended	FROM WHAT YEAR	TO WHAT YEAR	GRADUATE	MAJOR
Grammar School				
Junior High School				
Senior High School				
Business School				
College or University				
Special Training				
Military Training				

PAST EMPLOYMENT RECORD

Firm Name and Address of Last Two Employers	POSITION HELD	FROM WHEN	TO WHEN	SALARY At Beginning	On Leaving
Name		Mo.	Mo.	Per Month	Per Month
Address		Year	Year	$	$

Reason for Leaving

	POSITION HELD	FROM WHEN	TO WHEN	SALARY At Beginning	On Leaving
Name		Mo.	Mo.	Per Month	Per Month
Address		Year	Year	$	$

Reason for Leaving

HISTORY WHILE IN BANK
DEPARTMENT TRANSFERS AND SALARY REVISIONS

DATE	DEPARTMENT	POSITION	CLASSIFICATION	SALARY Date	Per Month	Per Annum

FIGURE 9-11 (continued)

ATTENDANCE RECORD

Year	DAYS ABSENT			REMARKS	Year	DAYS ABSENT			REMARKS
	Illness	Vacation	Other			Illness	Vacation	Other	

SELF IMPROVEMENT

Special Training, Special Courses, Home Study Courses, Night School Attendance, Military Training, etc.
(Subsequent to Date of Employment)

Year	Name of School or Class	Subjects Studied	Record	AIB Point Rating

OTHER CHARACTERISTICS AND QUALIFICATIONS
(Outstanding Civic, Fraternal or Other Work Receiving Special Recognition)

SERVICES CONCLUDED

Date	Paid Thru	REASON

POSTEMPLOYMENT RECORDS

After an employee is hired, a few records must be completed for your own benefit and to comply with legal requirements.

For legal reasons, an affirmative action report should be completed and retained. It will be needed if there is an Employment Equal Opportunity Commission investigation. See Figure 9–10 on page 105 for an example of the form used by one firm. A W-4 form should also be completed.

FIGURE 9–12

NEW EMPLOYEE ORIENTATION SHEET

PURPOSE: This form is to be completed first by the Personnel Representative and then by the immediate supervisor of the department or area to which employee has been assigned. The report is placed in employee's record file upon completion.

EMPLOYEE:_____ DEPARTMENT:_____

Date Employed: _____ Position: _____

SECTION A: PERSONNEL RECORDS

      A . Complete Employment Papers   ( )

      B . Explain Benefits   ( )

      C . Review Terms of Employment   ( )

      D . Union Details (if applicable)   ( )

      E . Equal Employment Opportunity Plan   ( )

      F . Paycheck-Related Information   ( )

      G . The Red Feather Program   ( )

      H . Education Assistance Program   ( )

      I . Emergency Procedures   ( )

      J . Identification Card   ( )

      K . Parking Procedures and Permit   ( )

SECTION B: IMMEDIATE SUPERVISOR

    Introduction to Department and Associates:

    A . Accompany Employee to Department   ( )

    B . Show Person to Rest Room and Cloak Area   ( )

    C . Arrange to Take Person to Lunch   ( )

    D . Show Person Equipment in Department   ( )

FIGURE 9-12 (continued)

Page 2   NEW EMPLOYEE ORIENTATION SHEET

General Instructions

A . Detail Hours of Work (day and week)   ( )

B . Explain Start and Stop Times   ( )

C . Explain Break and Lunch Times   ( )

D . Instruct Whom to Notify when Leaving Job   ( )

E . Show Person Emergency Exits   ( )

F . Review Pay Periods and Paydays   ( )

G . Describe Overtime Compensation   ( )

H . Instruct Whom to Call when Late   ( )

I . Instruct Whom to Call when Absent   ( )

Functions of the Department

A . Summarize Department's Function   ( )

B . Describe Relationship to Others   ( )

C . Describe Relationship to Company   ( )

Job Instructions

A . Give Person Job Description   ( )

B . Explain Work Assignment   ( )

C . Demonstrate Work Assignment   ( )

D . Observe Employee until It Is Determined

Person Is Familiar with Work   ( )

Human Relations

A . Make End-of-Day Contact for Review   ( )

B . Respond to Questions from Person   ( )

General

A . Introduce to Department Personnel   ( )

B . Show where Reserve Supplies Located   ( )

C . Explain Telephone Privileges and

Show Location of Public Telephone   ( )

DATE:_____   SUPERVISOR:_____

Most progressive firms maintain an employee personnel history form. The one shown in Figure 9–11 on page 106 is used by a bank.

HOW TO INTRODUCE NEW PEOPLE TO THEIR JOBS

Frequent discussions should be held with a new employee during the orientation program. Several should be held during the first day and the first week. These talks should give the new employee the necessary facts about your firm's objectives, policies, and rules. You should also tell the new employee what performance you expect.

A formal interview with the new employee may be appropriate during the first month. Its purpose would be to correct any mistaken ideas that the employee may still have about the job, and to determine whether the employee feels that you and your people are fulfilling your commitments to him.

During the orientation and follow-up period, you should evaluate the new employee's performance compared to your expectations. You can also start to point out his or her shortcomings and strong points. Another formal meeting should be held at the end of the probationary period. You will then state whether or not you are going to keep the employee.

During the probationary period, you can make personal observations of the new employee. You can also check with the supervisor concerning progress and receive comments volunteered by co-workers.

When you make the final decision concerning retention or dismissal, again refer to the job specification. Review it item by item. The new employee's supervisor should do the same. The two evaluations should be compared. If you decide to keep the new employee, discuss both his strong and weak points with him. Encourage the employee to keep trying to improve. State when he can expect a merit increase in pay. If you decide to reject the employee, do this as gracefully as possible.

The form shown in Figure 9–12 is used by an independent manufacturing firm to introduce its employees to their new job.

The questionnaire in Exhibit 17 of *The Dow Jones-Irwin Business Papers* can be used to evaluate your selection procedure. It is divided into parts according to the usual way of determining and filling personnel needs.

chapter 10

Developing and Maintaining Your People

This chapter examines the topics of training and developing employees, setting their wages and salaries, and evaluating their performance. It points up the reasons for training both new and existing employees. It describes training methods (for example, on-the-job training, apprenticeship, and internship) and the outside assistance available in training—(such as vocational-technical education programs, the Manpower Development and Training Act, and the JOBS program). It specifies guidelines to be followed in developing supervisors and operatives.

With respect to wage and salary administration, the chapter discusses rewarding nonmanagerial employees, setting rates of pay, job evaluation, wage incentives, employee benefit plans, and rewarding management personnel.

The chapter concludes with a discussion of appraising employees' performance. It emphasizes the factors used in merit rating when an MBO program is not in effect.

The ultimate efficiency of your business will be determined by the interaction of two related factors:

TRAINING AND DEVELOPING YOUR PEOPLE

1. The caliber of the people you hire, including their inherent abilities and their development through training, education, experience, and motivation.
2. The effectiveness of their personal development by you after you hire them.

This is called *personnel development,* and it may be defined as an attempt to raise the employee's productive capacity to the highest level of the job to be performed.

111

The Need for Training

Not only must your new employees be trained, but your present employees must be retrained and upgraded in order to adjust to rapidly changing job requirements. Among the more general reasons why you should emphasize growth and development are to give you:

1. Readily available and adequate replacements for present personnel who may leave or move up.
2. Freedom to use technological advance because you have a more highly trained staff.
3. A more efficient, effective, and highly motivated work team, which improves the company's competitive position.
4. Adequate manpower resources for expansion programs.

More specific results which you will probably receive from training and developing your workers include:

1. Increased productivity.
2. Reduced turnover.
3. Increased financial rewards.
4. Decreased materials and equipment costs.
5. Decreased supervison.
6. Higher morale.

Your employees also have a stake in development, for they acquire a greater sense of worth, dignity, and well-being as they become more valuable to society. They will also receive a share of the material gains that result from their increased productivity.

Methods of Training

You, the independent business manager, can use various methods of training nonmanagerial employees. These methods include:

1. On-the-job training (OJT).
2. Apprenticeship.
3. Internship.
4. Outside training.

On-the-job training consists of giving employees training while they perform their regular jobs. Thus, they are both producers and learners. An effective OJT program consists of these steps:

1. Planning what to teach the employee.
2. Establishing a time schedule for the employee to follow.
3. Providing feedback to the employee concerning his progress.

The purpose of *apprenticeship training* is to develop well-rounded individuals who are capable of performing a variety of jobs. Such training usually involves learning the skills of a trade. The program usually lasts from two to seven years, and a union is often involved in administering it.

Internship training is a combination of school and on-the-job training. It is generally used with employees who are being prepared for marketing, clerical, or management positions.

Outside training consists of training employees at noncompany schools. Usually, the company reimburses the employees for all or part of their tuition expenses.

Other forms of development which you can probably use on a limited basis are *programmed instruction* (sometimes called "learning machines"), *educational television, extension courses,* and *correspondence courses.*

Outside Assistance You Can Use in Training

Many outside programs are available to help you train employees. You can probably use some of the following.

All states have *vocational-technical education* programs whereby vocational-technical schools conduct regular or special classes where potential employees can become qualified for skilled jobs, such as machinist, lathe operator, and power-machine operator.

The *vocational rehabilitation* programs sponsored by the U.S. Department of Health, Education, and Welfare in cooperation with state governments provide counseling, medical care, and vocational training for physically and mentally handicapped individuals.

The *Manpower Development and Training Act of 1962,* as amended, provides a program of federal assistance in training unemployed and underemployed workers. If you hire these individuals, the government reimburses you for part of their wages, instructors' fees, and materials and supplies used. It also provides advice and consultation on training problems. You do the actual training yourself.

Title V of the Economic Opportunity (Antipoverty) Act of 1964 authorizes state welfare departments to provide training programs for welfare recipients and their families. You hire and train the individual and the government pays the cost of training.

These last two programs have been incorporated into the Comprehensive Employment and Training Act, but they are still available for helping you train minorities and the disadvantaged.

The *Defense Department* has invited many companies to train servicemen who are about to be released from service. This cooperative effort, called "Project Transition," has been fairly successful in bridging the difficult period of transition from military to civilian life.

The *JOBS (Job Opportunities in the Business Sector) Program,* which was launched several years ago by NAB (the National Alliance of Businessmen), encourages you—the employer—to submit proposals for contracts to provide on-the-job training for the disadvantaged hard-core unemployed. You are paid for any additional costs you incur because of the limited qualifications of those you hire and train. The state *public employment offices* are used to recruit, select, and counsel the trainees.

The *National Apprenticeship Act of 1937,* which is administered by the Bureau of Apprenticeship and Training in the Labor Department, sets policy for apprenticeship programs. Write to this bureau for help in conducting such a program.

Some Guidelines for Developing People

Basic guidelines which can be of great help to you in developing and conducting your training and development program are:

1. The objectives of the program should be established.
2. The trainees should be carefully selected.
3. Qualified instructors and proper instructional techniques should be used.
4. A method of evaluating the results of the program should be established.
5. The trainees should not be brought along faster than they can absorb the training and demonstrate their skills. On the other hand, they should not be permitted to stagnate.
6. Feedback on performance should flow from both trainers and trainees. The former should periodically report results to the trainees and to you, and the latter should submit periodic written reports on their progress to you.
7. When trainees finish the program, they should be given new and challenging assignments with appropriate rewards.

Developing employees for your competitors should be avoided! Yet your firm will probably experience some degree of personnel turnover. People die, become disabled, retire, or quit. Quitting is a key indicator. If such separations occur often, you should find out why. The reasons may include poor supervision, dead-end jobs, and poor training or motivation.

See Exhibit 18 of *The Dow Jones-Irwin Business Papers* for a form to assist you in evaluating your personnel development program.

SETTING WAGES AND SALARIES

Another important duty you have is setting wages and salaries for your people. Their earnings must be high enough to motivate them to be good producers, yet low enough for you to maintain a satisfactory earnings level.

Rewarding Non-managerial Employees

Two aspects of wage and salary administration are particularly relevant to small business. People work for monetary and nonmonetary rewards. *Nonmonetary* rewards often motivate us even when monetary rewards fail to do so. (See Chapter 10.)

As for monetary rewards, you should understand that both *absolute* and *relative* income are important to employees. They want their *absolute* level of pay to meet their needs. However, they are also concerned about their income *relative* to that of their fellow workers. In fact, an employee could be quite satisfied with his absolute pay but highly disgruntled because an associate is receiving more.

Rates of Pay. Important factors to consider when setting pay rates are:

1. Effort: Employees want to be paid in proportion to their physical and mental outlays.
2. Time: The time spent in performing a job should be directly related to the amount of pay.
3. Your ability to pay.
4. The standard and cost of living.
5. Legislation, including laws establishing minimum wages and overtime pay.
6. Union wage patterns—whether or not your firm is unionized.
7. The supply of and demand for workers, as reflected in the wages received by employees with similar skills in the area.

One of the first things you must be concerned with is the Fair Standards Act, which currently requires that you pay your employees a *minimum wage* of $2.30 per hour plus 1½ times their hourly rate for all hours over 40 per week. Certain managerial and professional personnel are exempt from the provisions of this act, but you should check with the Wage and Hour Division of the U.S. Labor Department for further details.

One way you can provide more equitable wages and salaries is to use formal or informal *job evaluation* to determine the relative worth of each job to your firm. The *ranking system* and the *point system* are the two most commonly used job evaluation methods. The independent business manager who performs his own job evaluation generally ranks jobs on the basis of their relative value to the company. Consultants performing job evaluation programs for independent businesses generally use the point system.

In the *ranking system,* you assign a monetary figure to the worth of each job. The system is simple, relatively inexpensive, and requires little paperwork. Its disadvantages are the lack of definite standards on which to determine the ranking and the difficulty in finding raters with sufficient knowledge of the jobs.

In actual practice, *prevailing rates and classifications* are used extensively by independent business managers. In other words, these managers rely heavily on the so-called going rates in establishing their companies' wage and salary structure.

Other Aspects of Your Wage and Salary Program. In compensating your employees, you should also consider:

1. How the employees will be paid—by wage or by salary.
2. The wage and salary structure in your firm.
3. Whether to adopt a wage incentive system.
4. The employee benefits you will provide, such as life insurance; hospitalization, sickness, and accident insurance; and pension plans.

A *wage incentive plan* may be an effective motivational tool, particularly in an independent manufacturing plant. Purposes of the plan can include increased production, reduced waste, and better use of machinery.

The oldest and most frequently used plan is a straight piece-work system, whereby a given rate is paid for each unit produced. Another plan is a *cash bonus based on profit.* Whatever the plan, it should be simple, easy to administer, and accepted by the employees.

Other motivational possibilities are:

1. Using bonuses as morale boosters, particularly during "slow" periods.
2. Controlling absenteeism through incentive compensation.
3. Using profit-sharing plans to stimulate productivity.

You could also consider using one or more of the following employee benefit programs: money-purchase pension plan, pension plan, and bonus awards. Most independent businesses can afford these deferred-compensation programs whose purpose is to help attract and hold quality employees. The Internal Revenue Service has approved model plans which contain all the forms and agreements needed. You can choose from a wide variety of plans—from mutual funds, banks, insurance companies, and others.

If you wish to base your employees' retirement income on a fixed dollar contribution by the company, the *money-purchase pension plan* is appropriate. The same percentage of pay must be deposited for all employees in the plan. You should consider this plan only if your company has relatively stable earnings.

Under a *pension plan,* you provide your employees with retirement benefits that can be computed at any time. The plan is not dependent on profits or on pension fund investments. It requires an actuarial study.

For an employee benefit plan to be successful: [1]

1. Your company's plan should be the right type for your purpose.
2. Your company's contribution should generally be at least 8 percent of the employee's salary or wages.
3. You need an average annual return of at least 6 to 8 percent from investment of the plan's funds.
4. You should inform your employees about the benefits and value of their plan at least annually.
5. You should review your plan periodically and keep its benefits up-to-date.

Since the Pension Reform Act has had a great impact on independent firms, its main provisions are shown in Figure 10–1.

If you use *bonus awards* for outstanding performance, a certain sum of money or gifts are given to outstanding employees.

The owner-manager of an independent company decided to eliminate paid vacations and sick leave. Instead, he gave all employees 30 days of annual leave to use as they saw fit. At the end of the year, the employees

---

[1] Harold A. Hobson, Jr., *Selecting Employee Benefit Plans* (Washington, D.C.: Small Business Administration, 1972), Management Aids for Small Manufacturers, No. 213.

FIGURE 10-1
The Pension Reform Law

Major Provisions		Effective Dates*	
		Existing Plans	New Plans
Eligibility	Prohibits plans from establishing eligibility requirements of more than one year of service, or an age greater than 25, whichever is later.	January 1, 1976	Date of enactment (September 2, 1974)
Vesting	Establishes new minimum standards; employer has three choices: (1) 100 percent vesting after 10 years of service; (2) 25 percent vesting after 5 years of service, grading up to 100 percent after 15 years; (3) 50 percent vesting when age and service (if the employee has at least 5 years of service) equal 45, grading up to 100 percent vesting 5 years later	January 1, 1976	Date of enactment
Funding	Requires the employer to fund annually the full cost for current benefit accruals and amortize past service benefit liabilities over 30 years for new plans and 40 years for existing plans	January 1, 1976	Date of enactment
Plan termination insurance	Establishes a government insurance fund to insure vested pension benefits up to the lesser of $750 a month or 100 percent of the employee's average wages during his highest paid five years of employment; the employer pays an annual premium of $1 per participant and is liable for any insurance benefits paid up to 30 percent of the company's net worth	Benefits: July 1, 1974; other provisions: date of enactment	Phased in over 5 years
Fiduciary responsibility	Establishes the "prudent man" rule as the basic standard of fiduciary responsibility; prohibits various transactions between fiduciaries and parties-in-interest; prohibits investment of more than 10 percent of pension plan assets in the employer's securities	January 1, 1975	January 1, 1975
Portability	Permits an employee leaving a company to make a tax-free transfer of the assets behind his vested penion benefits (if the employer agrees) or of his vested profit-sharing or savings plan funds to an individual retirement account	Date of enactment	Date of enactment
Individual retirement accounts (IRAs)	Provides a vehicle for transfers as noted above and permits employees of private or public employers that do not have qualified retirement plans to deduct 15 percent of compensation, up to $1,500, each year for contributions to a personal retirement fund; earnings on the fund are not taxable until distributed.	January 1, 1975	January 1, 1975
Reporting and disclosures	Requires the employer to provide employees with a comprehensive booklet describing plan provisions and to report annually to the secretary of labor on various operating and financial details of the plan	January 1, 1975	January 1, 1975
Lump-sum distributions	Changes the tax rules to provide capital gains treatment on pre-1974 amounts and to tax post-1973 amounts as ordinary income, but as the employee's only income and spread over ten years.	January 1, 1974	January 1, 1974
Limits on contributions and benefits	(1) increases the maximum deductible annual contributions that can be made by self-employed people to HR 10 or Keogh plans to the lesser of $7,500 or 15 percent of earned income;	January 1, 1974	January 1, 1974
	(2) limits benefits payable from defined benefit pension plans to the lesser of $75,000 a year or 100 percent of average annual cash compensation during the employee's three highest paid years of service;	January 1, 1976	January 1, 1976
	(3) limits annual additions to employee profit sharing accounts to the lesser of $26,825 or 25 percent of the employee's compensation that year	January 1, 1976	January 1, 1976

*Applicable to single-employer plans; multiemployer plans are given more time to comply with some of the new standards.

Source: Donald G. Carlson, "Responding to the Pension Reform Law," *Harvard Business Review*, vol. 52, no. 6 (November–December 1974), p. 134.

were paid for the leave not used. Previously, employees had to prove they were actually ill when they took sick leave and apply for personal leave in advance. The new program reduced unscheduled absences and overtime pay, and resulted in happier, more productive employees.[2]

Employee benefits constitute one of your major costs of production. According to the U.S. Chamber of Commerce, for the average firm (large, medium, *and* small) these benefits amounted to 33 percent of payroll in 1973.[3]

There are two other financial programs which you should know about. If you use them, by all means call in experts to aid you!

The *Keogh Plan* (HR 10) permits you as a self-employed person or a partner to have a tax-deferred retirement program. You may withhold and invest up to $7,500, or 15 percent of earned income, whichever is the lower of the two amounts.

Under the *key man deferred compensation plan,* a contract is drawn between you and your employee. Your firm agrees to invest annually a specified dollar amount or percent of wages. Your firm holds title to these assets until the retirement, disability, or death of the employee, when the benefit becomes payable to him or his beneficiary.

Rewarding Management Personnel

A well-conceived and effectively operated management compensation plan can help you motivate your top assistants. It can also help you know your employment costs for these assistants.

Determining the Level of Pay. The level of pay for these managers depends on many factors. Among the more important are:

1. The kind of industry your firm is in.
2. The size of your firm.
3. The firm's geographic location.
4. The responsibilities of each position.
5. The pay method used (bonus or nonbonus).
6. The growth of your firm.

You should establish a salary range, adjust present salaries to that range, and periodically review your compensation plan. The salary range for each position should have a minimum for beginners, intermediate figures for advancement, and a maximum. Responsibility should determine the spread in a range. For example, a 60 percent spread may be needed at the vice presidential level, whereas for lower management positions a 40 percent spread might be enough. Examples of percentage spread are shown below:

---

[2]Jack H. Feller, Jr., *Keep Pointed toward Profit* (Washington, D.C.: Small Business Administration, 1972), Management Aids for Small Manufacturers, No. 206.

[3]*Employee Benefits, 1973* (Washington, D.C.: Economic Analysis and Study Group, Chamber of Commerce of the United States, 1974), p. 26.

| | | Range of Salaries | |
Percentage Spread	Minimum	Midpoint	Maximum
40	$10,000	$12,000	$14,000
50	15,000	18,750	22,500
60	20,000	26,000	32,000

After you have established salary ranges, you should compare your managers' current salaries with the ranges. If adjustments are merited and your company is able to make them, you should adjust current salaries to the appropriate place in the ranges.

What should you do if a substantial difference exists between a manager's current salary and what his salary should be? Here are some guidelines:

1. Consider carefully the possible effects of your actions.
2. If the current salary is greater than it should be, try to upgrade the manager's performance, perhaps by a promotion.
3. If the current salary is less than it should be, develop a plan for raising it to the desired level.

Since pay levels and practices are constantly changing, you should compare your compensation plan with competitive practices at least annually. Information on competitive salaries may be obtained from local surveys (including those done by chambers of commerce), informal contacts at service clubs or industry conventions, and national surveys conducted by trade associations.

Using Financial Rewards to Motivate. If your business is growing rapidly, your compensation program should normally be designed for the type of manager who is willing to take risks. Even if his salary is less than he could receive elsewhere, he will be motivated to produce for you if he is paid a substantial bonus for results and he has good opportunities for promotion. On the other hand, if your firm's sales and profits are growing slowly, your compensation plan should probably emphasize salary and perhaps an attractive retirement plan.

One effective bonus plan is *profit sharing*. Such plans usually have four features:

1. Bonuses are directly related to company profits, and a predetermined formula is used to compute the amount of profits that will be provided for bonuses.
2. Participation in the plan is reserved for managers whose performance significantly affects profits.
3. Bonuses are based on each manager's performance.
4. Bonuses are paid promptly.

FIGURE 10-2

PERFORMANCE REVIEW
NONEXEMPT SALARIED EMPLOYEES

Date

Employee Name		Classification	Department
Clock Number	Date Hired	Date Classified	Reviewer

PERFORMANCE REVIEW	RATING (See Explanation of Numbers Below)				
	1	2	3	4	5
INITIATIVE-ENTERPRISE: Drive. Capacity for independent action. Degree to which he assumes responsibility when orders are lacking. Degree to which he follows through on a job despite obstacles.					
COOPERATIVENESS: The trait of working wholeheartedly both with and for others in an open-minded objective fashion. Possession of the qualities of tact, courtesy, friendliness and tolerance.					
QUANTITY OF WORK: Amount of useful output in light of the opportunities afforded by the job. The output may be written or otherwise.					
QUALITY OF WORK: The general excellence of output, including written material, with consideration given to the difficulty of the job. Accuracy, thoroughness and dependability of output should be considered but not quantity.					
ORIGINALITY: Creativeness, including imagination and inventiveness.					
EXPRESSION: Facility in expressing ideas both orally and in writing. This implies the ability to communicate ideas in a logical coherent fashion and the ability to summarize.					
JUDGMENT: Skill in accumulating and analyzing information necessary to arrive at sound conclusions.					
OVERALL APPRAISAL: Judge the total person in terms of a perfect person in his classification.					

RATING NUMBER DEFINITIONS:

1. **OUTSTANDING:**
One whose performance is unquestionably outstanding. Must regularly make exceptional personal contributions to company progress. When compared with others in classification, will consistently rank in top performance on appraisal form.

2. **SUPERIOR:**
Clearly superior performance. Exceeds position requirements on all points; obviously a potential candidate for advancement.

3. **SATISFACTORY:**
Meets all position requirements. Accomplishes assignments in a completely satisfactory manner. Can logically expect to advance at the same rate as the majority in his classification.

4. **ACCEPTABLE:**
Performance is generally satisfactory, but may be below what is normally expected in some significant areas of the total job. Improvement can logically be expected.

5. **QUESTIONABLE:**
Generally meets absolute minimum requirements of classification, but often does not. Depending on factors contributing to low rating, he might later be declared completely unsatisfactory.

Employee's Signature	Date	Approval Signature	Date

The bonus formula usually provides that after owners receive a normal return a specified percentage of the company's profits before taxes will be paid out as bonuses. For top assistants, bonuses for superior performance are commonly 50 to 60 percent of their salaries.

The questionnaire in Exhibit 19 of *The Dow Jones-Irwin Business Papers* should help you evaluate the effectiveness of your compensation program.

Your firm should have an effective personnel appraisal or employee evaluation system to enable you to answer the question: How well are my people performing? Under such a system, each employee's performance and progress are evaluated and rewards are given for above-average performance. Often, this method is used in determining merit salary increases.

If a Management by Objectives program or its equivalent is not being used, *merit rating* is commonly based upon the following factors:

1. Quantity and quality of work performed.
2. Cooperativeness.
3. Initiative.
4. Dependability.
5. Attendance.
6. Job knowledge.
7. Ability to work with others.
8. Safety.
9. Personal habits.

Each of these factors can be evaluated, for example, as *superior, above average, average, below average,* or *poor.* The person's wage or salary is then determined from this evaluation.

Relationships should exist between merit ratings and promotions. Your personal appraisal system can also help you identify marginal employees, as well as point up areas of improvement and possible training and development needs for all your people. It can help determine your success in achieving the objectives of a Management by Objectives program. Under a personnel appraisal plan, each manager should be held responsible for establishing the written performance criteria used by him for promotion.

Figure 10–2 shows the form used by an independent firm to evaluate its nonmanagerial personnel.

chapter 11

Improving Your Relationships with Your Employees

This chapter focuses on employees' grievances, on labor legislation that affects an independent business, and on dealing with labor unions.

HANDLING YOUR EMPLOYEES' GRIEVANCES

You should encourage your employees to inform you when they think something is wrong and needs correcting. You should also tell your supervisors how to handle these grievances. An effective grievance procedure should have these characteristics:

1. Assurance to employees that expressing their complaints will not prejudice their relationships with their immediate supervisors.
2. A clear method by which employees can present their grievances, and a description of how those grievances will be processed.
3. A minimum of red tape and time in processing grievances.
4. An effective method of presenting grievances for employees who cannot express themselves well.

Unresolved grievances can lead to strikes. You should listen patiently and deal with an employee's grievance promptly even though you believe it is without foundation. You should thank the employee for bringing the grievance to your attention. Before you render judgment on the grievance, you should think about it carefully and gather pertinent facts. You should inform the employee of your decision and follow up to determine whether the grievance has been corrected.

You should maintain written records of all grievances (and disciplinary actions) in employees' files. These records can be helpful in your defense against any charges of unfair labor practices which may be brought against you.

The questionnaire in Exhibit 20 of *The Dow Jones–Irwin Business Papers* will help you evaluate how well you are handling the grievances of your employees.

122

The whole area of personnel relations in your business is affected by labor legislation. The effects of some of this legislation on your business are now explained.

You are required by the *National Labor Relations Act of 1935*, as amended by the *Labor Management Relations Act of 1947*, to bargain collectively if a majority of your employees desire unionization. You are forbidden to discriminate against your employees for union activity. Under the National Labor Relations Act, both you and the union are required to bargain in "good faith" in order to resolve difficulties and reach agreement.

The National Labor Relations Board serves as a labor court, and its general counsel investigates charges of unfair labor practices, issues complaints, and prosecutes cases. The Board can issue direct orders, but cannot levy fines or penalties. Only the courts can levy fines or penalties. You can appeal a ruling of the Board through a circuit court.

Under "right-to-work" laws in some states, the union shop is outlawed. A union shop clause provides that all employees must join the recognized union within 30 days after being hired.

The checklist in Exhibit 21 of *The Dow Jones-Irwin Business Papers* will help you evaluate whether or not you act legally when a union tries to organize your firm.

UNDERSTANDING LABOR LEGISLATION THAT AFFECTS YOUR BUSINESS
Unions and Collective Bargaining

As an independent business manager, you are both a taxpayer and a tax collector. To finance old-age and survivors insurance, you must pay a tax on each employee's earnings and deduct a comparable amount from the employee's salary. Since tax laws are subject to change, you should check the applicable rate and base amount. As the proportion of the aged in the total population rises, both taxes and benefits can be expected to increase. An unemployment insurance tax is also provided under the *Social Security Act of 1936*. The state government receives most of this tax. It may be as high as 3 percent on your payroll. If you stabilize employment in your firm, you can have lower rates under merit rating provisions. It is important that you maintain the validity of your tax trust funds because of the legal liability associated with them.

Payroll Taxes

Accidents and occupational diseases are covered under state workers' compensation statutes. You are required to pay insurance premiums to either a state fund or a private insurance carrier. These premiums are used to compensate victims of industrial accidents or occupational illness. Your premiums will be affected by the hazards in your company and the effectiveness of your safety program.

Workers' Compensation

Wages and Hours

Minimum wages and overtime compensation are prescribed by the *Fair Labor Standards Act of 1938,* as amended. The act specifies a standard workweek of 40 hours and overtime compensation at the rate of time and a half for hours in excess of standard. Many states also have wage and hour statutes which specify maximum hours for women and children.

Laws Pertaining to Age

The Fair Labor Standards Act and many state statutes prescribe the minimum age for employees. Typically, these laws specify a minimum of 14 to 16 years with a higher minimum often set for hazardous occupations. On the other hand, the *Age Discrimination in Employment Act of 1967* says that you cannot discriminate against potential employees aged 40–64.

Equal Employment Opportunities

In 1964, Congress passed the *Civil Rights Act. Title VII* of this act, as amended by the *Equal Employment Opportunities Act of 1972,* prohibits discrimination because of race, color, religion, sex, or national origin in hiring, upgrading, and all other conditions of employment. It applies to employers of 15 or more persons.

The *Equal Employment Opportunity Commission,* established by Title VII, investigates charges of employment discrimination. In order to stop violations, the Commission may take action itself or go to a U.S. district court. The Commission promotes *affirmative action* programs to carry out the principle of equal employment opportunity.

In recruiting applicants for employment, companies may no longer rely completely on "walk-in" or "word-of-mouth" advertising of job openings, especially if their own work force is predominantly of one race. Friends or relatives of present employees cannot be recruited if a company has a disproportionate amount of a certain class of employees. A company cannot set hiring standards with respect to test results, high school diplomas, height, arrest records, manner of speech, or appearance if such standards result in discrimination on the basis of race, color, sex, religion, or national origin.

Seniority systems should not "lock" minorities into unskilled and semiskilled jobs. Equal opportunity for promotions should be provided. Training and performance appraisals should be conducted on a nondiscriminatory basis. Discrimination should not exist in hourly rates and deferred wages, including pensions or other deferred payments. Recreational activities—bowling teams, softball teams, Christmas parties, and so on—should be open to all employees on a nondiscriminatory basis. So far as facilities of a "personal nature" are concerned, an employer should make every "reasonable accommodation" for male and female employees.

Generally, all jobs must be open to both men and women unless the employer can prove that sex is a bona fide occupational qualification necessary to the normal operations of that particular business.

Advertisments cannot be run by a company for "male only" or "female only" employees unless sex can be shown as a bona fide occupational qualification. Disqualifying female employees from jobs requiring heavy lifting, night shifts, and dirty work is often illegal. Automatic discharge of pregnant women and refusal to reinstate them after childbirth constitute discrimination.

All employees are entitled to equality in all conditions of employment, including:

1. Hiring.
2. Layoff.
3. Recall.
4. Discharge.
5. Recruitment.
6. Compensation.
7. Overtime.
8. Promotional opportunities.
9. Paid sick leave time.
10. Paid vacation time.
11. Insurance coverage.
12. Training and development activities.
13. Retirement privileges and pension benefits.
14. Rest periods, lunch periods, and so on.

According to the *Equal Pay Act of 1963*, an amendment to the *Fair Labor Standards Act of 1938*, you must also pay males and females the same rate of pay for performing the same general type of work.

Exhibit 22 of *The Dow Jones-Irwin Business Papers*, is a checklist to help you evaluate whether or not you are adhering to the equal employment opportunity laws.

Occupational Safety and Health

The *Occupational Safety and Health Act* (OSHA) was passed in 1970. Its purpose is to assure so far as possible safe and healthful working conditions for every employee. Under OSHA, an employee—or his representative—has these five important rights:

1. If he believes that a violation of job safety or health standards exists which threatens physical harm, he may request an inspection by sending a signed notice to the U.S. Department of Labor. He may not be discharged or discriminated against for filing the complaint.
2. When the Department of Labor inspector arrives, usually unannounced, the employees's representative may accompany the inspector on the visit.
3. If the employer is cited under OSHA and protests either the fine or the abatement period, the employee can participate at the hearing and object to the length of the abatement period.
4. The employee may observe the company's processes for monitoring exposure to toxic materials or other physically harmful agents. If an OSHA standard covers the substance, the worker is entitled to information about his exposure record.
5. The employee's authorized representative may request that the secretary of health, education, and welfare (HEW) determine whether any

substance found in the place of employment has potentially toxic effects. If HEW makes this finding, the secretary of labor may institute a procedure to set a safe exposure level for that substance.

Supporters of OSHA claim reductions in lost time and in workers' compensation, decreases in lost wages, lowered medical costs, and higher productivity. Critics believe that the act has been implemented too rapidly and restrictively, and that compliance costs are so high that a company's competitive position is threatened.[1]

Even though many accidents are caused by the employees' own carelessness, they usually do not receive citations. Instead, employers are responsible for having their employees wear safety equipment. Furthermore, employers are subject to fines for unsafe practices, whether or not any accidents actually occur. You should provide safety training for your supervisors and employees and discipline employees for noncompliance with safety work rules. OSHA has resulted in increased examination and questioning of management's manning decisions and equipment selection. To illustrate, a union could claim that a crew size is unsafe or that a machine fails to provide a safe workplace. The act makes it compulsory to train employees in driving forklifts and in wearing respirators.

Five industries in which independent businesses predominate—roofing and sheet metal; meat and meat products; lumber and wood products; manufacturers of mobile homes, campers, and snowmobiles; and stevedoring—have relatively high injury and illness rates.

"Dry-run" inspections by OSHA inspectors are not permitted because if inspectors do come to your premises they are obligated by law to inspect fully, to cite, and to fine. You can request a free health hazard evaluation by HEW's National Institute of Occupational Safety and Health. Training may be obtained from OSHA and from National Safety Council chapters. Your workers' compensation insurance carrier may be helpful. However, its approval does not guarantee OSHA approval. You may also obtain useful information from equipment manufacturers, other employers who have had an inspection, trade associations, and your local fire department. You should provide effective coordination among manufacturing, safety, medical, industrial relations, and so forth.

Occasionally, there is some frustration in attempting to comply with OSHA regulations and standards due to a lack of clarity. In addition, although an OSHA inspector may present you with a citation for noncompliance or may reject the procedures or protective measures being used, definitive corrective information may not be forthcoming. OSHA inspectors are not allowed to offer such assistance. You should recognize that the OSHA program will be in a state of transition for some time. Therefore, you are advised to utilize the resources suggested above, as well

---

[1]Businesses with fewer than eight employees are not required to maintain injury and illness records. However, these firms must report fatalities and accidents that hospitalize five or more persons.

as your local chamber of commerce, your area planning and development commission, and the office of the Small Business Administration serving your area. Small Business Administration loans could help you meet safety and health standards.[2]

Exhibit 23 of *The Dow Jones-Irwin Business Papers* contains a checklist to help you evaluate how well you are complying with the provisions of the Occupational Safety and Health Act.

DEALING WITH LABOR UNIONS

Many independent business managers have rather strong antiunion feelings because they believe: (1) they have "made it on their own," and employees want to take it away from them; and (2) an individual's drive and initiative are more productive than group-set norms. You should recognize, however, that employees join unions because they believe that they need them.

If your company is unionized, you have more constraints on what you can and cannot do in your relations with your people. Your employees may view you more as an economic opponent than as a person with whom cooperation to obtain mutual benefits can be expected. Improving personnel performance is more difficult in a unionized company than in a nonunionized company.

If a union does try to organize your firm, there are certain things you can and cannot do. See Exhibit 21 of *The Dow Jones-Irwin Business Papers*, for the things you *can* and *cannot* do.

Labor unions bargain with the employer on behalf of their members. Your unionized employees, through their elected representatives, negotiate with your company for wages, fringe benefits, working conditions, and so forth.

If your company is unionized, you should be prepared for certain difficulties. Many of your actions and statements may be reported to union officials. The union may harass you by filing unfair labor practice notices with the National Labor Relations Board. Your best defense is to know your management rights under the Labor Management Relations Act.

Bargaining with a labor union involves preparation, negotiation, and agreement. The bargaining is followed by another phase, living with the contract. *Preparation* may well be the most important step. You should obtain facts about wages, hours, and working conditions before you sit down at the bargaining table. You should have information on other contracts in the industry and in the local area. You should know about the disciplinary actions, grievances, and other key matters that arose during the day-to-day administration of the current contract. Current business literature concerning the status of union-management relations in

---

[2]Fred W. Foulkes, "Learning to Live with OSHA," *Harvard Business Review*, vol. 51, no. 6 (November–December 1973), pp. 57–67.

the nation and in your industry can be useful. A carefully researched proposal should be developed well in advance of negotiation.

You should be in a much more favorable negotiating position if you do this than if you use a negative strategy of permitting the union to develop its own ideas for a new contract and then offer defensive counter-proposals. The "I don't want to give away any more than I have to" attitude generally fails to contribute to a viable union-management relationship.

You should recognize that the *negotiation* step is critical. You should consider not only the impact of wages on your company but also the impact of seniority, discharge rules, and sick leave. You should understand that anything given up now can probably never be regained.

The *agreement* usually consists of these ten clauses:

1. Union recognition.
2. Wages.
3. Vacations and holidays.
4. Working conditions.
5. Layoffs and rehiring.

6. Management prerogatives.
7. Hours of work.
8. Seniority.
9. Arbitration.
10. Renewal clause.

The agreement establishes rules which should be obeyed by you. The management prerogatives clause defines the areas in which you have the right to act, free from questioning or joint action by the union.

Once the agreement is signed, you should *live with the contract* until it is time to negotiate a new one. All of your management personnel should be thoroughly briefed on the contents. Your supervisors' questions on the contract should be answered so that they will be better prepared to deal with labor matters.

Your company's labor relations and personnel practices should be consistent, uniform in application and interpretation, and based on a sense of "fair play." We have observed numerous instances in which owners have pursued policies that could be labeled selfish and greedy; the end product has been unionization, bankruptcy, or both.

To enable you do do the proper thing in a specific labor relations situation, you can obtain advice and information from numerous private groups and some government agencies. The *private sources* consist of employers' associations, trade associations, labor relations attorneys, labor relations consultants, leader companies, and professors. *Government sources* are federal and state mediators, wage-hour investigators, National Labor Relations Board regional offices, and state industrial relations departments. Leader companies set labor contract patterns in key bargaining sessions, and independent companies tend to follow their lead. Often, their labor relations staffs are willing to help you. The wage-hour investigator is not only a law enforcement officer, but is also interested *in helping an owner-manager* avoid violations.

Feller, Jack H., Jr. *Keep Pointed toward Profit.* Washington, D.C.: Small Business Administration, 1972. (Management Aids for Small Manufacturers, No. 206.)

Hobson, Harold A., Jr. *Selecting Employee Benefit Plans.* Washington, D.C.: Small Business Administration, 1972. (Management Aids for Small Manufacturers, No. 213.)

Murdick, Robert G., et al. *Business Policy: A Framework for Analysis.* Columbus, Ohio: Grid, Inc., 1972. Credit is given to the authors of this text for many of the ideas in this chapter.

Smith, Leonard J. *Checklist for Developing a Training Program.* Washington, D.C.: Small Business Administration, 1967. (Management Aids for Small Manufacturers, No. 186.)

Summer, Howard E. *How to Analyze Your Own Business.* Washington, D.C.: Small Business Administration, 1973. (Management Aids for Small Manufacturers, No. 46.)

WHERE TO LOOK FOR FURTHER INFORMATION

PART FOUR

Producing Your Product or Service

Previous parts of this text have been concerned with planning for and managing your business. Part Three dealt extensively with selecting, developing, and maintaining your work force.

Now it is time to look at the internal process of "producing" your good or service. This is no simple task, for many and diverse activities are required to carry on the "production" function.

You must determine what products to sell; decide whether to buy those products from someone else or make them yourself; plan, acquire, lay out, and maintain the physical facilities you require; procure or produce the "right" quantity of the "right products" at the "right" time and the "right" cost; control the quality and quantity of your inventory; maintain a work force; and do all of this as economically as possible!

All of these activities make the production function interesting, challenging, and rewarding, but also awfully frustrating.

Part Four will tell you how to:

1. Change your inputs to outputs (Chapter 12).
2. Set up your process plan and control system (Chapter 13).
3. Purchase and control your materials (Chapter 14).

Changing Inputs to Outputs

All business organizations produce either goods or services. Thus, they are all engaged in some form of "production." Yet, the term *production* may be misleading, as will be seen.

In this chapter, we will talk about "operations," or converting inputs into outputs. The inputs include manpower, money, machines, materials, and methods. The outputs are products or services for your customers.

At first, you may think that the material in this chapter applies only to a manufacturing-type business. However, the principles and procedures detailed here can also be utilized in many other kinds of businesses.

SYSTEMS FOR CONVERTING INPUTS INTO FINISHED PRODUCTS

The term *production* is often used in reference to manufacturing, because production methodology was first developed and applied in manufacturing industries. However, *production* can be defined as *the creation of value or wealth by producing goods and services*. This definition includes nonmanufacturing activities. As indicated above, all business organizations convert inputs into outputs. Managers must have a system for doing this. Figure 12-1 shows the transformation or movement of goods for a number of types of companies. Note that the conversion of inputs into outputs represents the major activity of each business—the reason for its existence—and may be a transforming of form, place, or time. Other examples of inputs and outputs are shown in Figure 12-2.

Exhibit 24 of *The Dow Jones-Irwin Business Papers* is a checklist to help you evaluate your system for converting inputs into finished products.

Productive Elements

How can the production methodology used by industrial firms be applied to all types of small businesses? The processes of changing inputs to outputs have the following common elements:

133

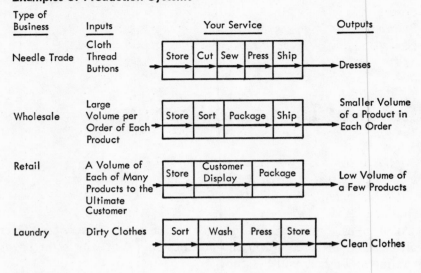

FIGURE 12-1

Examples of Production Systems

Type of Business	Inputs	Your Service	Outputs
Needle Trade	Cloth Thread Buttons	Store | Cut | Sew | Press | Ship	Dresses
Wholesale	Large Volume per Order of Each Product	Store | Sort | Package | Ship	Smaller Volume of a Product in Each Order
Retail	A Volume of Each of Many Products to the Ultimate Customer	Store | Customer Display | Package	Low Volume of a Few Products
Laundry	Dirty Clothes	Sort | Wash | Press | Store	Clean Clothes

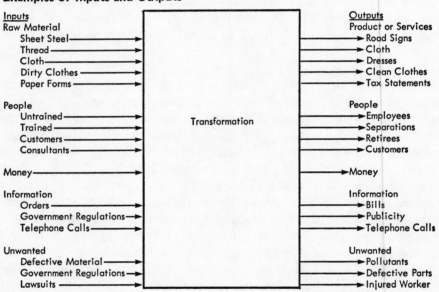

FIGURE 12-2

Examples of Inputs and Outputs

1. Systems to transform the input as to form, place, or time.
2. A sequence of steps or operations to convert the inputs into outputs.
3. Special skills and often tools, machinery, or equipment to make the transformation or conversion.

134

4. A time frame in which the work is to be done.
5. Instructions to identify the work to be performed and the units being produced.
6. Standards and maximum rates of input and output.
7. Exceptions and errors which must be handled.

The inputs and outputs within a company and among different classifications of businesses have common characteristics. Let us look at some of the different applications of these common characteristics to firms in different industries.

Manufacturing Companies To manufacture means to make or process a raw material into a finished product. "Raw material" may be the outputs from other companies, such as synthetic rubber, resistors, or plastic powder, which are changed in form and/or assembled. Usually a series of operations is performed by machines in the conversion process. Formerly, blue-collar workers using tools and machines generally performed these operations. Now, manual labor has been largely replaced by machines, some of which are controlled either automatically or by other machines. These devices require less skill and turn out more uniform products, with greater precision, and in greater volume than does manual production.

Some manufacturing companies produce only one standard product, while others produce each product to special order, never making the same product twice. The former type of process, called *continuous production,* operates automatically. Its inputs and outputs can be stored with less chance of obsolescence or loss of value because of style or use changes.

Companies producing goods for customers requesting nonstandard products are called *job shops*—they produce to the customer's order, or by the job. Seasonal and other variations in demand cause production to vary considerably, and tend to result in idle time and varying employment levels.

In both processes planning and controls must be exercised. The product is usually designed by an engineer, who usually also converts it into production specifications. The operations to be performed and the machines, skills, and inputs needed are determined for each product or order. Production schedules are set, and instructions are prepared. The instructions are used in performing and checking the work ot assure the conformity of output with specifications.

Service Companies with Manufacturing Characteristics. Many independent businesses fall into this category. Cleaning and laundering, cabinetmaking, short-order food processing, patient processing, printing, and machining organizations are examples. The inputs are converted into finished products through one or a series of operations. The required operations are repeated with variations for special orders. However, different emphases are placed on the design of the system to transformation than in manufacturing.

The service company usually receives smaller orders, with some variation in the input and the desired output. For example, a customer may bring such different items as sheets, clothing, rags, and linens to a laundry. These, in turn, are made from different combinations of white, colored, natural, and synthetic cloth. The laundry must put greater emphasis on individual handling and contact and requires complex systems to identify the product and to plan and control the processes. This results in higher unit costs than are incurred in single-product, high-volume processes.

These companies fit the job shop classification. However, when they are designed properly, they may take on the characteristics of continuous production. In the laundry, for example, all clothing is sorted into different types of cloth. Then, a set process is used for each type of cloth.

However, some units, such as short-order food processors, can reduce the supporting systems needed by building controls into the physical facilities. The amount of communication may be reduced by limiting the variety of the product. A hamburger stand with high volume works on an inventory replenishment basis, and the hamburgers follow set variations.

Wholesalers. This group of companies receives large volumes of many items and distributes smaller volumes of selected items. The transformation process involves converting large packages of like items into large and small packages of a variety of items. Wholesalers can plan and control the sequence of operations in the same manner as manufacturing companies. The emphasis, however, moves from transforming the product by machinery to storing, materials handling, and packaging.

Retailers. The process within a store also has subprocesses, but the organization includes movements of customers, as well as the materials. The primary emphasis is directed toward covenience to the customers, and material flow is a secondary consideration. The place of goods in the store and the movement of customers in relation to the goods are important contributors to or detractions from the sale of goods.

Other Types of Companies. Many independent businesses not included in the above classifications can benefit from the same type of internal analyses as those presented. Automobile repairing, home building, and accounting firms have similar flows of material, people, or forms.

The set of processes in each organization tends to reflect its reason for existence. For example, materials and parts are converted to finished goods in a manufacturing company; patients are processed through operations in a hospital; and the customer is guided to the goods in a self-service store. All supportive processes, including paperwork, are needed to achieve the objectives of the firm.

DECIDING WHETHER TO MAKE OR BUY

Changing raw materials to finished products is a long process, usually involving many companies. One company may refine the raw materials; several may perform manufacturing processes; another may assemble the parts into the finished product, and so on. A given company may perform a large or small part of this process. The place and size of the segment is an important decision.

Part Two discussed how you would decide what segment you wanted for yourself. The size of each segment depends on what you decide to buy and process, and to whom you decide to sell. The following examples will illustrate this point. For birdhouses made of wood, you can:

1. Buy wood and cut the parts, or buy precut pieces.
2. Assemble the birdhouse, or sell the packaged pieces to be assembled by the customer.
3. Sell to a wholesaler, a retailer, or the final user.

A food processor can:

1 Grow or buy vegetables.
2 Sell its output to a wholesaler, a retailer, or the consumer.

For best results, you should try to specialize in the segment of the total process in which you have the greatest expertise. The *advantages of specializing* and concentrating in a small area that the company performs best are as follows:

1. Less capital investment is needed for machinery and for people with differing capabilities.
2. Management can concentrate better on a small segment.
3. Planning, directing, and controlling are less complex.

The *advantages of a larger segment* are:

1. More control of the process.
2. Less idle machine and man time.
3. Greater potential for growth.

The decision as to what segment you will seek is usually based on the economics of the situation. It might be advantageous for you to make some of the parts you normally buy in order to use the idle time of machines and people. You might drop some early or late operations instead of buying more machinery when you do not have enough capacity. Remember that any additions or reductions must be evaluated from a cost viewpoint and that some costs may vary with changes in volume.

Exhibit 25 of *The Dow Jones-Irwin Business Papers* is a form which will aid you in deciding at what point in the process you should start and stop your company's operations and purchase a component rather than produce it yourself. Having decided on the segment of the total transformation process you wish to perform, you can begin to plan, obtain, and install your producing unit.

The physical facilities of your company—including the building itself, machines and equipment, and furniture and fixtures—must be designed to aid the employees in producing the desired product or service at a low cost. The design function includes the layout and selection of machines and equipment and the determination of the desired building features. Our discussion of the design function is divided into two parts: (1) planning and (2) implementation.

PLANNING YOUR PHYSICAL FACILITIES

Good selection and arrangement of your physical facilities can pay dividends. Planning your physical facilities requires these steps:

1. Determine what services you plan to perform (discussed in earlier chapters).
2. Break down your production into *parts, operations,* and *activities.*
3. Determine the time you require to perform each operation.
4. Using these time figures as a guide, estimate the number of machines and workers you need.
5. Decide what type of arrangement is best for the sequence of operations.
6. Determine the general layout, using blocks for sections of the plant.
7. Plan the detailed layout which will provide the most effective use of your personnel, machines, and materials.

Exhibit 26 of *The Dow Jones-Irwin Business Papers* provides a form to aid you to maintain the proper steps in planning physical facilities.

Step 1: Determining Your Services

This step was discussed in earlier chapters, but in general the business you are in will determine what goods you will produce or what services you will perform.

Step 2: Break Down Your Product or Service into Parts, Operations, and Activities

Assuming that you are going to make a product you need to break the product down into:

1. The parts going into it.
2. The operations needed to produce it.
3. The activities surrounding its production.

Parts are the divisions of the product which, when assembled, form the output. Some outputs have only one part; others, such as radios, have many. The part or parts must be identified. (See Figure 12–3.)

Operations are the steps or segments of work performed to accomplish the conversion of inputs into outputs. The segments are often identified by the specialized work of a machine, for example, drilling, typing, or wrapping. The conversion process usually requires a series of operations. Figure 12–4 and 12–5 show the operations for making metal signs and collecting groceries. The circles indicate operations. The work order form in Figure 12–6 shows how the list of required operations and materials can be combined in one order. An example of a form used to establish the sequence of operations is shown in Figure 12–7.

FIGURE 12-3
Product Specifications Sheet

KEY	PRODUCT	CODE	PART NO & CODE		QTY	DESCRIPTION	PRICE	MATERIAL COST
71990	50MWT-GBD							
			1	C-9	1.0000	50LCL CTN.	1.07325	1.07
			7	T-39	2.0000	28 X 54 T	3.26000	6.52
			8	G-68-1	1.0000	APR-68G TGCC 61 1/2''	1.19000	1.19
			9	G-73-1	1.0000	APR-73BG BGCC 60''	.95000	.95
			10	G-72-2	4.0000	APR-72G SGCC 56''	.67000	2.68
			11	G-71-3	1.0000	APR-71G HDRC 61''	2.43000	2.43
			12	G-70-2	1.0000	APR-70G SILLC 60''	1.01000	1.01
			13	G-98-1	2.0000	APR-98G JSC 56 3/8''	.84000	1.68
			14	S-5	6.0000	#8 X 1 GLZG.	.01025	.08
			15	L-1	28.4000	C166 7/32'' GLZG.	.02345	.67
			16	Z-7	6.0000	S-1 ANCHOR	.00550	.03
			17	Z-10	2.0000	#7714 BUMPER	.00850	.02
			18	Z-11	4.0000	#C GUIDE	.00865	.03
			19	Z-3	4.0000	#193 ROLLERS	.05750	.23
			20	S-11	8.0000	#8-32 X 3/8 TRUSS HD	.00595	.05
			21	S-8	6.0000	#8 X 1 G	.00650	.04
			22	Z-2	1.0000	6 X 8 PL. BAG	.01665	.02
			23	Z-12	7.0000	F PAPER 20''	.00910	.06
			24	G-96-2	.5000	APR-96G TB 115''	1.03000	.52
			25	B-10	4.0000	APR97G BKT. 55/64''	.30000	1.20
			26	Z-8	4.0000	AL POST	.01450	.06

TOTAL MATERIAL COST   20.54

FIGURE 12-4
Operating Process Chart and Calculations for Making a Typical Metal Sign

Operations	Symbols for Sequence	Machine	Hours Required per Machine	Forecast Volume per Hour	Number of Machines Needed
Cut Sides	①	Shear	.12/100 Cuts	500 Cuts	1
Cut Corners	②	Press	.17/100 Corners	600 Corners	2
Punch Holes	③	Press	.10/100 Holes	500 Holes	1
Wash	④	Tank	.005/Sign	300 Signs	10 Ft.*
Dry	⑤	Oven	.01/Sign	300 Signs	15 Ft.*
Phosphate Coat	⑥	Tank	.008/Sign	300 Signs	12 Ft.*
Dry	⑦	Oven	.02/Sign	300 Signs	30 Ft.*
Paint Metal	⑧	Spray Gun	.28/100 Signs	300 Signs	1
Bake	⑨	Oven	.10/Sign	300 Signs	150 Ft.*
Print Sign	⑩	Silk Screen	Varies (see table)	300 Signs	2
Bake	⑪	Oven	.10/100 Signs	300 Signs	1
Box Signs	⑫	Bench	1.00/100 Signs	300 Signs	3 Workers

*Conveyers are used to move sings into, through, and out of tanks and ovens at 10 feet per minute. Tanks and ovens are measured in feet.

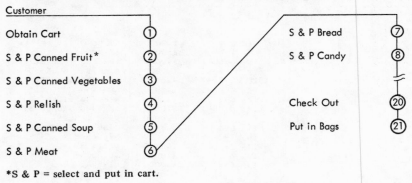

FIGURE 12–5
Operation Process Chart for a Customer in a Supermarket

Customer

Obtain Cart	①	S & P Bread	⑦
S & P Canned Fruit*	②	S & P Candy	⑧
S & P Canned Vegetables	③		
S & P Relish	④	Check Out	⑳
S & P Canned Soup	⑤	Put in Bags	㉑
S & P Meat	⑥		

*S & P = select and put in cart.

Activities, such as moving materials, are necessary for the performance of operations. Nonactivities, including delays, are caused by imbalances in the timing of operations. Activities and nonactivities may not be identified fully until the final layout planning is done. Nonactivities should be minimized.

To determine the parts and operations, you start with the output and work backward to the inputs. In an assembled product, the disassembly processing is called *exploding.* The process identifies the parts. Then, the operations on each part and their sequence can be identified and the machines selected. Exhibit 27 of *The Dow Jones-Irwin Business Papers* provides a form which can assist you in determining what equipment is needed.

The sequence may be fixed, or rigid. For example, the cutting of boards must precede their assembly as a bookshelf. Or the sequence may be unimportant, as in the order of cutting the boards. In still other cases, the proper sequence of operations is needed to obtain a high volume of sales, as in a cafeteria or a supermarket. Flexible sequences of operations are desirable to allow for high utilization of machines and personnel.

Step 3: Determine When to Perform the Operations

Each operation required to produce a good or perform a service consumes the time of machines and personnel. The times can be obtained by making an estimate, or by using one of the several time measurement methods discussed in the next chapter. The total time includes the time to perform the operation plus time for unavoidable delays and personal needs. Some operations are routine and easily measured; others are more variable and not so easily measured. The times obtained are used to determine how many machines and people are needed to perform the work, and the speed of conveyors.

FIGURE 12-6
Work Order

WORK ORDER												

WORK ORDER

Description | | Drawing No. | Date Issued | W.O. Number

Department Routing — From / To | Catalog No. | Sales Class | Quantity

Dept. No.	Oper. No.	Operation Description	Std. Hr. Prod.	Premium Rate	Mach. No.	Tool No.	Bin No.	No. Oper.	Cost Rate

DATE SCHEDULED | DATE COMPLETED

MATERIAL LIST

Catalog Numbers Used on	Material Description	Size—Part—Drawing No.	Material Code No.	Unit Weight	No. Pcs. Req.

FIGURE 12-7
Operation Sheet

OPERATION SHEET						
Part Name: Mainshaft			Part No.: 114			
Material: Steel			Used on: Automobile Transmission			
Opr. No.	Operation Description	Mach. No.	Machine Name		Std. Time	Hourly Prod.
1	Rough Turn & Cutoff	31	Gridley		Hrs/scs .0179	56
2	Grind Burrs	61	Chevy Grinder		.0018	550
3	Center Pilot End	14	Cinn. Bickford Drill		.0031	320
4	Tap & Blow Out Chips	2	Allen Drill		.0031	320
5	Rough-Hob 6 Teeth & Hob 10 Spline	56	Cleveland Hobber		.0133	75
6	Undercut	30				59
7	Finish Hob 6 Teeth		King Grinder			
	Teeth	64	Fitchburg Grinder		.0073	
21		69	Norton Grinder		.0073	137
22	Grind Second Speed Bearing Face	63	Cinn. Tool Grinder		.0068	146
23	Grind 1.0598 – 1.0606 Dia. (Second-Speed Bearing)	69	Norton Grinder		.0073	137
24	Grind Pilot	69	Norton Grinder		.0063	160
25	Burr Diameter	34	Porter Cable Lathe		.0050	200

Step 4: Estimate How Many Machines and Workers are Needed

Knowing how much time a machine takes to perform an operation on a product, and knowing your planned production, you can determine the number of machines needed. Figure 12-4 shows the number of machines required to make 300 signs per hour. Operation 3, punching holes, requires half the time of a press [(0.10÷100) × 500 holes]. Either one machine can be purchased for this operation, or it can be combined with operation 2, cutting corners, which requires less than half the time of a second machine.

Step 5: Decide the Best Arrangement for the Sequence of Operations

You should try to obtain the least movement of product and people. However, people and machines should not be idle and space should not be wasted. The plant can be planned according to one or a combination of two types of layout:

1. Product, or service.
2. Process, or function.

142

The *product layout* places the machines or serving units in such a way that the product moves along a line as it moves through its sequence of operations. Assembly lines in the automobile industry are the best-known examples of this type of layout. As the automobile frame moves on a conveyer, the engine, axles, steering mechanism, and other components are added until a finished car comes off the conveyer.

This type of layout has been spreading from the large manufacturing operations to nonmanufacturing and independent businesses as more standardized routines have been developed and as demand volume and the capacities of machines and people have been better matched. The use of this layout by independent businesses includes the cafeteria short-order line, packing materials for a warehouse order, and the one-product company. In fact, all layouts should generally conform to this concept, as shown in Figure 12-8.

FIGURE 12-8
Product Layout

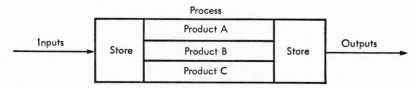

With this type of layout, materials or people move forward from operation to operation with little backtracking. A supermarket could set up this type of layout if it knew that a large enough number of customers wanted the same items. The customers could move down the line picking up the items as they went, and be through in a short time. If the customer selects purchases according to the order in which the goods are displayed, there is no need to backtrack. The advantages of this type of layout include:

1. Specialization of workers and machines.
2. Less inventory.
3. Fewer instructions and controls.
4. Faster movement.
5. Less space for aisles and storage.

The *process* type of layout is based on keeping the machines and workers busy, thus keeping the idle time to a minimum. Machines performing the same type of work are grouped together, and the same is true of workers with like skills. Examples of this type of layout include grouping presses together so that each press can keep busy and putting typists in a "pool" to service many offices. This type of layout increases the movement of materials or people, and necessitates higher inventory. *Advantages* of the process layout include:

1. Flexibility to take care of change and variety.
2. The use of general-purpose machines and equipment.
3. More efficient use of machines and personnel.

Few layout plans are confined to either the product or process type. Most consist of combinations of the two to take advantage of the given situation. Idle time created by differing production rates is more than compensated for by decreased inventory.

Layouts can be planned to move materials, people, tools, or machines. Thus, in some stores the customers move through self-service lines; in others, the salesperson brings the goods to the customer. Products move through some production processes; in others, people and tools move to the product. For part of the physical examination in a clinic, doctors and nurses move to the patient; for others, the patient moves from room to room.

Some of the factors to be considered in planning for movement are:

1. The size of goods and machines.
2. The safety requirements.
3. The volume of input and output.
4. The type of service.

Step 6: Determine the General Layout

The next step is to determine the general layout, using blocks for sections of the layout. A block can be a machine, a group of machines, a group of products on shelves, or a department. This step is intended to establish the general arrangement of the plant, store, or office before spending much time on details. Estimates are made of the space needed in each block by using past layouts; summing the space for machines, men, aisles, and other factors; or employing the best judgment available. The intent is to plan the general arrangement before planning the detailed layout.

Figure 12–9 illustrates a block layout. The dashed and solid lines show the general block areas for presses, painting, shipping, and so forth.

In addition to the space required for activities directly concerned with the main services of the company, space is provided for maintenance, planning, food, personal needs, and other services. These services should be convenient to the units being serviced. Estimates of the space required can be obtained from books, pamphlets, trade associations, and past experience.

If you are replanning the layout of an existing building, the location of outside walls is predetermined. The size and shape of the land may be confining.

On the other hand, if you are planning a new building, you can design it so that changes may be made easily in the future. Buildings are usually designed to provide space for several years, while the number of machines is planned for only the near future—as machines can be added at a later date. In most operations, single-story, square, and columnless build-

FIGURE 12-9
Plant Layout for Metal Sign Company

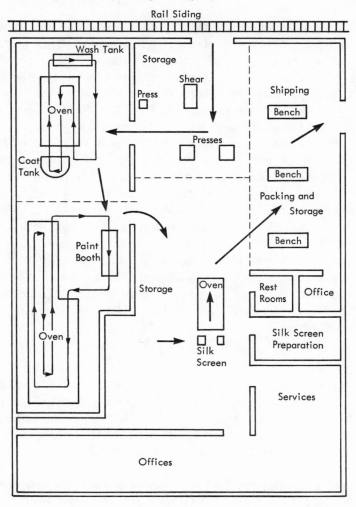

ings with movable utility outlets are preferred. The building is designed from the inside out.

Entrance locations are important in the layout, particularly for service establishments. Customers enter downtown stores from the street, and goods usually enter from the back. These entrances may be fixed, setting the flow of goods from back to front. Some producing plants use the same transportation units for delivering supplies and materials as for shipping the finished goods. The flow is thus U-shaped. Other—usually less important—external factors are:

1. Entrances for employees.
2. Connections to utilities.
3. Governmental restrictions.
4. Weather factors.

The layout should include plans for expansion and other future conditions.

Step 7: Plan the Detailed Layout

You must plan in detail the layout of your people, machines, and materials if you are to have efficient performance. Each piece of equipment is located, and space allocated for its use. As with blocks, templates—or models—of the machines, equipment, and workers help you perform this step. These templates can be moved about to obtain your best plan. Figure 12-9 shows machine locations for the Metal Sign Company plant after templates were used for placing machines.

In manufacturing, many methods are used to move materials. Conveyors, carts, trucks, and cranes are examples. For example, the materials shown in Figure 12-4 could be moved by forklift, carts, and overhead and belt conveyers. Notice that, as shown, the conveyor carries the metal plates through washing, drying, coating, and drying without stopping. The objective is to minimize materials handling and its cost without increasing other costs.

Each operation should be examined to assure easy performance of work. If the worker spends too much time standing, walking, turning, and twisting, the work will take longer and be more tiring. Large-volume items or tools should be located close at hand. An understanding of methods study is helpful here.

Specific matters which you should include in your final layout planning are:

1. *Space for movement.* Are aisles wide enough for one- or two-way traffic? Is there enough room if a queue forms? Can materials be obtained easily, and is space available when they are waiting?
2. *Utilities.* Have adequate provisions been made for incoming wiring and gas or for the disposal of water at each machine? Will future moves be necessary?
3. *The supply of equipment.* Can shelves be restocked conveniently?
4. *Safety.* Has equipment using flammable material been properly isolated and proper fire protection been provided? Are moving parts and machines guarded and the operators protected from accidents?
5. *Working conditions.* Does the worker have enough working space and light? Have you provided for low noise levels, proper temperature, and the elimination of objectionable odors? Is the worker safe? Can he socialize and take care of his personal needs?
6. *Cleanliness and maintenance.* Is the layout designed for good housekeeping at low cost? Can machinery, equipment, and the building be maintained easily?
7. *Product quality.* Have provisions been made to protect the product as it moves through the plant or sits in storage?

Although we have been talking about manufacturing facilities, many of the same generalizations hold true for retail and wholesale establishments. For assistance in planning the physical facilities for a retail establishment, see Exhibit 28 of *The Dow Jones-Irwin Business Papers*. See Exhibit 29 if you are interested in planning wholesale facilities.

The first step in implementing your plans is to test them to see whether they are sound. There are many ways to do this. One method is to have employees—or other persons who can give experienced opinions—review the plans and give you their suggestions. Another method is to simulate the process by using templates or models of the goods or people so that you can foresee their movements. You might deliberately include some mishaps to see what happens. It might be well to use the processing plans which will be discussed in Chapter 13 to see how the production plan works with your layout.

IMPLEMENTING YOUR PLANS

The actual implementation of your plans will depend on whether this is a brand-new venture, a layout for an existing building, or a rearrangement of the present layout. Construction of a new building requires further steps in the design of the building and its surroundings. These steps include consideration of at least the following factors:

1. The type and method of construction.
2. Arrangements for parking.
3. Roads and the transportation of goods.
4. Landscaping.

Changes may be required by a new layout or the rearrangement of the layout in an existing building, but the latter may be mainly a matter of scheduling the changeover to keep production downtime to a minimum. Periodically, decisions on the replacement of machines are needed in order to maintain or improve productivity, reduce costs, expand production, or improve service. Exhibit 30 of *The Dow Jones-Irwin Business Papers* will help you decide what equipment to replace.

Exhibit 31 of *The Dow Jones-Irwin Business Papers* will help you determine whether your physical distribution function is being performed economically and effectively.

Exhibit 32 of *The Dow Jones-Irwin Business Papers* will help you do a conservation audit of your people, equipment, materials, utilities, and inventory.

A continually recurring problem of business organizations is maintaining adequate housekeeping. Many firms now use contract personnel or outside organizations to perform this function. Whether you do it yourself or have someone else do it, the form in Exhibit 33 will help you see that the housekeeping function is being performed properly.

Another problem of business organizations is maintaining the "image" of being neat, clean, and appealing. The form in Exhibit 34 of *The Dow Jones-Irwin Business Papers,* which deals with the maintenance and appearance of your structures, machines, lighting, signs, grounds, parking lots, loading ramps, and other equipment and facilities, should help you audit your "image" as it is projected to the public.

chapter 13

Designing and Controlling Work

You have determined what goods and services you plan to produce or perform, what physical facilities you need, and how those facilities should be laid out. Now you are ready to start producing the goods and services This includes designing work methods, measuring work, providing instructions, and directing and controlling the work activities. (Some of these activities have been designed into the systems already described.)

The planning and control process is a communications system designed to convey to employees the who, what, when, where, how, and why of the work to be done. It is also a check on what has been done to assure that the customer receives good service—in terms of both time and quality.

As in Chapter 12, procedures described as applying to manufacturing activities may also be utilized in a service, retail, and other types of business activity. The objective is to develop a plan for operational activity and control that will achieve the most effective utilization of the organization's resources.

WORK DESIGN

In Chapter 12, we showed how to plan the overall layout of a plant. In this chapter, we will take up the detailed movement of materials and the layout of the workplace. For example, in the metal sign plant discussed in Chapter 12, are the metal plates placed so that the operator cutting the corners has short and easy moves? How many machines can one man operate? Are there new methods of moving materials? The following steps are used in work design and improvment:

1. State the problem.
2. State the function of the work.
3. Collect information.
4. List alternatives.
5. Analyze the alternatives.
6. Select and test the changes.
7. Install and follow up the changes.

As usual, you should begin by stating the problem. Is the cost of the work too high? Is the work delaying other work? Is quality low? Is service slow? The reasons for studying the work should be clearly stated in order to provide direction.

State the Problem

Often, the need for a given production function appears obvious. However, you should begin by asking whether the function is necessary and whether it is the only alternative. A clear statement of the reason for the function starts you toward finding the best method.

State the Purpose of the Work

Collecting data breaks the work into parts and establishes appropriate relationships. The purposes are twofold—to train and to inform.

Collect Information

Training develops your ability to observe work as a series of activities. For example, a machine operation might include such statements as "prepare material," "do the work," and "remove finished product." The term *prepare material* might include reaching for material, selecting material, grasping material, moving material to the machine, and positioning material. This type of training, combined with the use of some common-sense principles, develops your ability to identify inefficiencies.

Informing aids you in recording for later analysis the details of the work being done. Several types of charting procedures are shown in Figures 13-1, 13-2, and 13-3.

Figure 13-1 shows a flow process chart for the first and second operations in making a metal sign, as shown in Figure 13-3. This chart shows not only the cutting of sides and corners but also includes transportations, delays, and storage. Observe the number of delays and trans-

FIGURE 13-1
Flow Process Chart for Making Metal Signs

Item Description	Operation / Transportation / Inspection / Delay / Storage	Distance in Feet	Pick-Ups / Lay-Downs	Time in MIN.	Quantity	Analysis		Notes
						Why? What?	Where? When? Who? How?	
IN STORAGE AREA	O ⇨ □ D ▽							
TO SHEARS BY CART	O ⇨ □ D ▽	15'	1	2	1	√	√	FORK TRUCK CONVEY
IN STACK	O ⇨ □ D ▽			10	1	√		
CUT SIDES, SHEAR	O ⇨ □ D ▽		1	2				
IN STACK	O ⇨ □ D ▽			10	3	√		CONVEYOR- ROLL TO PRESS
TO PRESS, CART	O ⇨ □ D ▽	10	1		6	√	√	"
IN STACK	O ⇨ □ D ▽			3	3			
CUT CORNERS, PRESS	O ⇨ □ D ▽		1	1	1			

ports which occur for each operation. You will want to reduce these. Symbols are used to simplify your understanding of the process. Data are also collected on methods of movement, distances, time, and quantity.

Figure 13–2 presents a motion study of the simple operation of assembling a bolt, washer, and nut. Note that the assembler is holding the bolt well over half the time. His hand is a very expensive vise.

Figure 13–3 shows the relationship between an operator and a machine. The operator loads and unloads the machine, and the machine performs its operations automatically. Note that the operator is idle well over half the time. Figure 13–4 can be used to analyze the decisions involved when you get up in the morning.

FIGURE 13–2
Motion Study of Assembling Bolt, Washer, and Nut

Left-Hand Description	Activity	Activity	Right-Hand Description
To bolt	→	→	To washer
Grasp bolt	0	0	Grasp washer
To washer	→	→	To bolt
Hold	D	0	Assemble
Hold	D	→	To nut
Hold	D	0	Grasp nut
Hold	D	→	To assembly
Hold	D	0	Assemble
Dispose	→	D	For disposal

Legend: 0 = Operation; → = Movement; D = Delay.
Note the large percentage of delay.

FIGURE 13–3
Operator Running an Automatic Machine

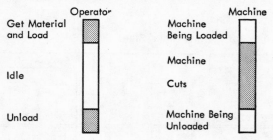

List Alternatives

Listing alternatives is a critical step in decision making. All work and services can be performed in many ways, and products can be made from many different materials. Your pencil can be made of wood, metal, or plastic; a hole can be punched, drilled, burned, or cut. You should question the whole process, parts of the process, and each individual activity by recording all alternatives. The following questions are helpful.

1. Why is the activity being performed?
2. Can it be eliminated?
3. What is the activity, where is it being performed, and who is performing it?
4. Can the activity be combined with other operations?
5. When is the activity performed?
6. Would changing the work sequence reduce the volume of work?
7. How is the activity performed?
8. Can it be simplified?

How many alternatives can you list for the bolt and washer assembly in Figure 13–2? Why assemble? Can you devise a holder to eliminate the *hold* and *dispose* activities? Can the operator in Figure 13–3 run another machine also? Or inspect? Or perform the next operation? The objective is

FIGURE 13–4
Computer Diagram on How to Get Up in the Morning

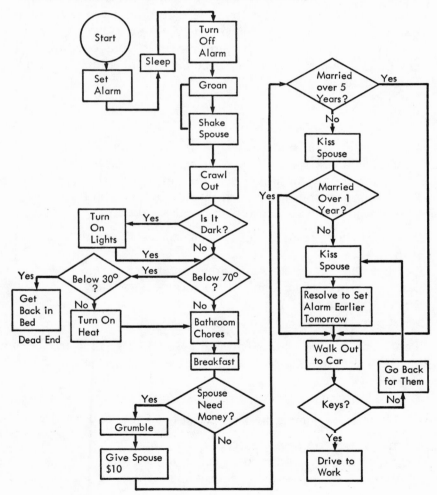

to remove or simplify as many activities as possible without reducing the quality and quantity of output.

Analyze the Alternatives

In this step, alternatives are evaluated on the basis of practicality, cost, acceptance by workers, and effect on output. In a good list of alternatives, only a small percentage will be acceptable. However, the extra time invested in exploring alternatives improves your chances of finding the best design.

Select and Test the Changes

This step converts ideas into reality, checks for any errors or missed possibilities, and makes sure that the proposals will perform as expected.

Install and Follow Up the Changes

Installation includes placing the physical equipment (for example, a foot pedal), gaining acceptance by the people involved with the operation, and training workers. The objective is to optimize performance.

Exhibit 35 of *The Dow Jones-Irwin Business Papers* is a form which will help you identify possible improvements in your operations. The use of this form should help you determine areas to eliminate, simplify, or make more effective.

WORK MEASUREMENT

We have few precise tools for work measurements, but rely heavily on the fallible judgment of people to make such measurements. Physical work can be measured more precisely than mental work.

This section is concerned with measuring the time for doing physical work. Once time standards are set, they can be used to:

1. Determine how many people or machines are needed for a desired output.
2. Estimate the cost of sales and other orders.
3. Determine the standard output for incentive systems.
4. Schedule production.
5. Measure performance.

Performance time can be divided into (1) the time to perform the work and (2) the time for personal needs and irregular activities.

The Time for Work Performance

Methods for obtaining the time to perform the work are:

1. Estimates by people experienced in the work.
2. Time study, using a watch or other timing device.
3. Synthesis of the elemental times obtained from tables.

152

Time Standards Set by Experienced People. This is the simplest and least costly method of obtaining a time for work, but it is also the least precise. No breakdown of the work is made, and the standards often include past inefficiencies. Such standards are often adequate if the person setting them is careful.

Time Study., This is probably the best method. Yet it has the poorest reputation, because time studies have often not been done or used properly. A time study is made by a person—usually an industrial engineer—actually observing the work being done. The observer uses a stopwatch; makes many recordings of the time for each segment of the work; evaluates the worker's performance against the observer's standard of normal speed and effort; adjusts the time values; selects the *normal* time, using some averaging method; and adds a certain amount of time for personal needs and irregular activities. See Figure 13-5 for a copy of a time study sheet.

Synthesis of Elemental Times. This is a pencil-and-paper method based on the accumulation of data from research studies. Tables of manual times have been developed for a wide range of activities, including reaching, moving, grasping, positioning, turning, walking, and bending. A synthetic time can be set for assembling the bolt, washer, and nut shown in Figure 13-2. Tables are also available to compute times for machining operations. By analyzing the work into the proper elements, times from the tables can be applied to obtain a *normal* time for an operation. Figure 13-6 shows sample pages of Methods-Time-Measurement (MTM) data.

Personal and irregular time allowances are added to normal time to obtain the total time in which an operation should be performed under "normal" conditions. Time study and synthesis methods include time allowances for use of the rest room, poor working conditions, and fatigue. Tables are available for such allowances. The time for irregular activities— for example, getting material, receiving instructions, repairing minor breakdowns, and cleanup—can be determined by work sampling or by estimating the frequency and length of time for each type of activity.

Adding Time for Personal Needs

Work Sampling is based on making a large number of observations at random times. For each observation, you record whether a worker is producing, idle, or doing irregular work. The percentage of observations in each category is the estimate of the percentage of his total time spent in that activity. Figure 13-7 shows the tallies and summary of a work sampling study. Your secretary might use this technique to help you measure how you or others use time.

Work Sampling

Standard time is usually expressed in *standard allowed hours* (SAH) per unit of output. Workers who are paid on the basis of their SAH will usually earn 5 percent-30 percent more SAH than their actual hours.

FIGURE 13-5
Time Study Sheet

Side 1

TIME STUDY OBSERVATION AND COMPUTATION SHEET

Wristwatch Time		1	2	3	4	5	6	7	8	9	10	11	12	13
1. Start														
2. Finish														
3. Elapsed														
4. Total on Stopwatch														
4 + 3														

Foreign El. Time

Sta. Fin. Net

A | R | T
Reason
B | R | T
Reason
C | R | T
Reason
D | R | T
Reason
E | R | T
Reason
F | R | T
Reason

Calculations

Total time in —
No. of readings
Average
Median
Mode
Selected time
Rating factor
Normal time

(Carry figures to back of page)

Side 2

Study No. ___ Date ___ Sheet ___ of ___

Part Description

Operation Name ___ No. ___ Department ___

No.	Element Description	Tools, etc.	Feed	Speed	No. Per Cycle	Normal Time

1. Total Normal Time
2. Allowances – Fatigue ___%, Personal ___%, Delays ___%, Total ___%
3. Setup time allowed ___ per ___ Separate allow. ___
   Standard time per ___ (What is your unit?)
4. Standard time per ___ (What is your unit?)
5. Rate per hour ___ Rate per ___ (What is your unit?)

Layout

Material
Operator Name ___ No. ___
Experience on job ___ No. ___
Equipment
Tools
Conditions
Observer
Approved

Sketch of part:—

Remarks

FIGURE 13-6
Methods-Time-Measurement

TABLE IV—GRASP—G

Case	Time TMU	DESCRIPTION
1A	2.0	Pick Up Grasp—Small, medium or large object by itself, easily grasped.
1B	3.5	Very small object or object lying close against a flat surface.
1C1	7.3	Interference with grasp on bottom and one side of nearly cylindrical object. Diameter larger than ½".
1C2	8.7	Interference with grasp on bottom and one side of nearly cylindrical object. Diameter ¼" to ½".
1C3	10.8	Interference with grasp on bottom and one side of nearly cylindrical object. Diameter less than ¼".
2	5.6	Regrasp.
3	5.6	Transfer Grasp.
4A	7.3	Object jumbled with other objects so search and select occur. Larger than 1" x 1" x 1".
4B	9.1	Object jumbled with other objects so search and select occur. ¼" x ¼" x ⅛" to 1" x 1" x 1".
4C	12.9	Object jumbled with other objects so search and select occur. Smaller than ¼" x ¼" x ⅛".
5	0	Contact, sliding or hook grasp.

TABLE V—POSITION*—P

CLASS OF FIT		Symmetry	Easy To Handle	Difficult To Handle
1—Loose	No pressure required	S	5.6	11.2
		SS	9.1	14.7
		NS	10.4	16.0
2—Close	Light pressure required	S	16.2	21.8
		SS	19.7	25.3
		NS	21.0	26.6
3—Exact	Heavy pressure required.	S	43.0	48.6
		SS	46.5	52.1
		NS	47.8	53.4

*Distance moved to engage—1" or less.

TABLE VI—RELEASE—RL

Case	Time TMU	DESCRIPTION
1	2.0	Normal release performed by opening fingers as independent motion.
2	0	Contact Release.

TABLE VII—DISENGAGE—D

CLASS OF FIT	Easy to Handle	Difficult to Handle
1—Loose—Very slight effort, blends with subsequent move.	4.0	5.7
2—Close — Normal effort, slight recoil.	7.5	11.8
3—Tight — Considerable effort, hand recoils markedly.	22.9	34.7

TABLE VIII—EYE TRAVEL TIME AND EYE FOCUS—ET AND EF

Eye Travel Time = 15.2 x $\frac{T}{D}$ TMU, with a maximum value of 20 TMU.

where T = the distance between points from and to which the eye travels.
D = the perpendicular distance from the eye to the line of travel T.

Eye Focus Time = 7.3 TMU.

TABLE I—REACH—R

Distance Moved Inches	Time TMU				Hand In Motion		CASE AND DESCRIPTION
	A	B	C or D	E	A	B	
¾ or less	2.0	2.0	2.0	2.0	1.6	1.6	**A** Reach to object in fixed location, or to object in other hand or on which other hand rests.
1	2.5	2.5	3.6	2.4	2.3	2.3	
2	4.0	4.0	5.9	3.8	3.5	2.7	
3	5.3	5.3	7.3	5.3	4.5	3.6	
4	6.1	6.4	8.4	6.8	4.9	4.3	**B** Reach to single object in location which may vary slightly from cycle to cycle.
5	6.5	7.8	9.4	7.4	5.3	5.0	
6	7.0	8.6	10.1	8.0	5.7	5.7	
7	7.4	9.3	10.8	8.7	6.1	6.5	
8	7.9	10.1	11.5	9.3	6.5	7.2	**C** Reach to object jumbled with other objects in a group so that search and select occur.
9	8.3	10.8	12.2	9.9	6.9	7.9	
10	8.7	11.5	12.9	10.5	7.3	8.6	
12	9.6	12.9	14.2	11.8	8.1	10.1	
14	10.5	14.4	15.6	13.0	8.9	11.5	**D** Reach to a very small object or where accurate grasp is required.
16	11.4	15.8	17.0	14.2	9.7	12.9	
18	12.3	17.2	18.4	15.5	10.5	14.4	
20	13.1	18.6	19.8	16.7	11.3	15.8	
22	14.0	20.1	21.2	18.0	12.1	17.3	**E** Reach to indefinite location to get hand in position for body balance or next motion or out of way.
24	14.9	21.5	22.5	19.2	12.9	18.8	
26	15.8	22.9	23.9	20.4	13.7	20.2	
28	16.7	24.4	25.3	21.7	14.5	21.7	
30	17.5	25.8	26.7	22.9	15.3	23.2	

TABLE II—MOVE—M

Distance Moved Inches	Time TMU			Hand In Motion B	Wt. Allowance			CASE AND DESCRIPTION
	A	B	C		Wt. (lb.) Up to	Factor	Constant TMU	
¾ or less	2.0	2.0	2.0	1.7	2.5	0	0	
1	2.5	2.9	3.4	2.3				
2	3.6	4.6	5.2	2.9	7.5	1.06	2.2	**A** Move object to other hand or against stop.
3	4.9	5.7	6.7	3.6				
4	6.1	6.9	8.0	4.3				
5	7.3	8.0	9.2	5.0	12.5	1.11	3.9	
6	8.1	8.9	10.3	5.7				
7	8.9	9.7	11.1	6.5	17.5	1.17	5.6	
8	9.7	10.6	11.8	7.2				
9	10.5	11.5	12.7	7.9	22.5	1.22	7.4	**B** Move object to approximate or indefinite location.
10	11.3	12.2	13.5	8.6				
12	12.9	13.4	15.2	10.0	27.5	1.28	9.1	
14	14.4	14.6	16.9	11.4				
16	16.0	15.8	18.7	12.8	32.5	1.33	10.8	
18	17.6	17.0	20.4	14.2				
20	19.2	18.2	22.1	15.6	37.5	1.39	12.5	**C** Move object to exact location.
22	20.8	19.4	23.8	17.0				
24	22.4	20.6	25.5	18.4	42.5	1.44	14.3	
26	24.0	21.8	27.3	19.8				
28	25.5	23.1	29.0	21.2				
30	27.1	24.3	30.7	22.7	47.5	1.50	16.0	

TABLE III—TURN AND APPLY PRESSURE—T AND AP

Weight	Time TMU for Degrees Turned											
	30°	45°	60°	75°	90°	105°	120°	135°	150°	165°	180°	
Small— 0 to 2 Pounds	2.8	3.5	4.1	4.8	5.4	6.1	6.8	7.4	8.1	8.7	9.4	
Medium—2.1 to 10 Pounds	4.4	5.5	6.5	7.5	8.5	9.6	10.6	11.6	12.7	13.7	14.8	
Large— 10.1 to 35 Pounds	8.4	10.5	12.3	14.4	16.2	18.3	20.4	22.2	24.3	26.1	28.2	

APPLY PRESSURE CASE 1—16.2 TMU.   APPLY PRESSURE CASE 2—10.6 TMU.

Source: From MTM Association for Standards and Research, Ann Arbor, Michigan. (Do not attempt to use this chart or apply Methods-Time-Measurement in any way unless you understand the proper application of the data. This statement is intended as a word of caution to prevent difficulties resulting from misapplication of the data.)

Research indicates that introducing a good incentive system will increase production by about 30 percent.

Exhibit 36 of *The Dow Jones-Irwin Business Papers* is a form to help you carry out your work measurement activities most effectively.

THE SALES PLAN

Sales forecasting and marketing research will be discussed in Chapter 16. Converting sales forecasts into a sales plan is the starting point for your production plan. Before the sales plan can be fixed, your production

FIGURE 13-7

WORK SAMPLING OBSERVATION SHEET

Sheet <u>1</u> of <u>1</u>
Starting Date <u>7/12</u>
Ending Date <u>7/23</u>

Area or Person Being Observed <u>Jerry Lant</u>

Supervisor <u>Nelson Sower</u>

Observer <u>J. M. Doar</u>

Activities	Observations	Total	%
Machine Operation	﹖﹖﹖﹖﹖﹖﹖﹖﹖﹖﹖﹖﹖﹖﹖﹖﹖﹖﹖	105	38
Collating Papers	﹖﹖﹖﹖ /	21	8
Wrapping	﹖﹖﹖﹖﹖﹖ //	32	12
Talking to Customer	﹖﹖﹖﹖﹖﹖﹖﹖﹖﹖ //	52	19
Talking to Others	﹖﹖﹖	15	5
Telephoning	﹖﹖﹖﹖﹖ ////	29	10
Walking	﹖ //	7	3
Other	﹖﹖ //	12	4
Absent from Room	///	3	1
Total		276	100

capacity must be checked. The best sales plan from a marketing viewpoint may not be the best plan for the company as a whole. It may require too much overtime or too much idle time.

The optimum plan from a production standpoint is to maintain a constant level of production—near capacity for both machine and worker—of one product, with inputs arriving as needed and outputs taken by customers as they are completed. This is an ideal to shoot for.

If the sales plan does not keep production busy, what can be done? Should the company advertise more heavily, reduce prices, or redesign its product to increase the volume? Should another product, or a variation of your product, be added? Or would this increase the changeover costs and cause such confusion in production that it would cost more than is gained from the added sales?

Maybe the sales plan is for more output than your production capacity. If so, the plan can be satisfied by expanding capacity, by overtime, or by subcontracting. Each of these can be very expensive and is capable of causing you more problems than benefits.

You will be told that it is impossible to predict the sales of an independent business with any reasonable degree of accuracy. This may be true, but even crude estimates are usually better than none at all. Time is required to purchase, produce, and deliver an item if it is not in stock when the customer orders it. On the other hand, the company incurs extra costs when mateial is held in inventory. As is mentioned in Chapter 12, inventory gives flexibility to a production process. This results in savings, but it also increases costs. These costs and savings should be balanced.

The largest inventories are planned for the beginning and end of the production process, where the company has least control over its environment. The sales plan is affected primarily by the customer. Sales volume fluctuates from one time period to another. How can the production and sales plans be aligned for optimal results?

Planning starts with longer periods and proceeds backward to day-to-day operations. Chapter 12 discussed the long-range planning needed for physical facilities. The next step is to plan for the next shorter time period, which may be the annual plan. The sales plan, which is usually done for the year ahead, is broken down into months (or perhaps by quarters for the last six months). The production plan should be prepared for these same periods.

Alternative *production plans* (PP) which you might consider are:

PP-1. Produce what your customers demand at the time they need the goods.

PP-2. Produce at a constant level equal to the average monthly demand for the year. Inventories will increase when the volume of demand is lower than the production volume, and will decrease when it is higher.

PP-3. Produce complementary products which balance out increases and decreases in the volume of demand for individual products. This should result in a constant production level.

PP-4. Subcontract production in excess of a certain level.

PP-5. Decide not to expand production to meet demand.

PP-6. Have special sales inducements, perhaps extra advertising and lower prices, when your sales volume is expected to be low.

A major cause of variations in demand is seasonal change. Examples include variations in the demand for sports equipment, heating and cooling facilities, and landscaping. Alternative production plans will be discussed, using seasonal variations in the examples.

Figure 13-8 shows a possible monthly plot of the sales plan for your company for the year ahead. The measure of sales volume can be dollars, standard allowed hours (SAH), tons, or other units, whichever best measures production capacity, inventory level, and sales demand. Under Production Plan One (PP-1), production and sales volume lines are the same, and the inventory of finished goods can be held at a constant minimum level. As plant capacity is large—80 units—overtime work can be avoided. Production is at plant capacity during only a small part of the year, and the plant is idle up to 30 units per month during another part of the year. With the trend toward greater fringe benefits, annual wage systems, and severance pay, this type of production plan is becoming outdated.

FIGURE 13–8
Sales and Production Plans with Seasonal Changes in Demand

Production Plan Two (PP-2) shows a constant level of production with a heavy buildup of inventory. The advantages of this plan are:

1. Less capacity needed.
2. Constant manpower level, with a minimum of hiring and layoff costs.
3. Reduction in the paperwork needed in running the production system.

PP-2 is ideal from the production viewpoint. The major disadvantage of PP-2 is the large inventory cost, which can bankrupt your company if it is not evaluated carefully. (See Chapter 14.) Companies ordinarily try to find some compromise between PP-1 and PP-2. A minimum cost plan can be developed by using the following formula:

Annual added costs = Inventory costs + overtime costs
+ change in level costs.

Production Plan Three (PP-3)—producing complementary products— might be likened to producing both furnaces and air conditioners. The furnaces are produced for winter, air conditioners for summer. If the same machines and skills can be used in producing both, and if the volumes produced and sold can be balanced, the sales and production forces will be kept working at a constant year-round rate. This is one reason why many companies make a variety of products.

Production Plan Four (PP-4)—subcontracting excess production—has several variations. You might make more of the parts yourself during slack periods, and subcontract to others during peak periods.

Production Plan Five (PP-5)—not expanding production to meet sales—is often rejected without much thought. However, extra sales may result in losses because they require extra capacity or overtime.

Production Plan Six (PP-6)—offer special sales inducements—is a marketing activity which will be covered in Part Five.

After you have established your production plan for the year, you can develop other plans or budgets and determine the required amount of materials, parts, and goods; and financing.

The previous section discussed the development of the general annual production plan. This section covers day-to-day scheduling. As orders are received, they are filled from inventory or ordered into production.

Most companies keep an inventory of standard items in order to give quick service. They stock the items for which they have forecast sufficient demand and for which the advantages of fast service outweigh the added cost of carrying the inventory. Such items are produced when the plant would otherwise be idle.

Orders are scheduled into production:

1. On a preplanned schedule.
2. When inventory is reduced to a certain level.
3. When orders are received and inventory is not available.

The preplanned schedule works best for standard items, the demand for which can be forecast. Customer order scheduling is used for specialty items and for items too expensive to keep in inventory. Here the size of the customer order usually sets the size of the production order, except when future orders of the same item are expected. In each case, the number of units in a production order is determined by balancing the costs involved. A large order increases the inventory costs per unit; a small order increases the planning, machine setup, handling, and paperwork per unit. (A further consideration of these costs is included with the discussion of purchase order sizes in Chapter 14.)

Schedules set the times to produce specified goods. A company producing the same units continuously can automatically set how many units to produce by setting the total number of man- and machine-hours per week. Job shops, on the other hand, must schedule each order. This scheduling can be done by one of the following methods:

1. Sending orders into the shop in sequence. The shop processes the jobs on a first-come, first-served basis.
2. Setting priorities, and processing orders accordingly. "Rush" orders have top priority.
3. Using either 1 or 2 for each operation.
4. Setting a specific time for each operation for each job.

Note the following relationships:

Method	Scheduling Cost	Idle Time	Processing Time	Inventory Level
1	Low	High	High	High
4	High	Low	Low	Low

In doing all your scheduling, you should try to keep inventory as low as practical. A long-time sequence of operations on a part which is to be assembled to a short-time sequenced part should be started early. This can be illustrated by the often used bar, or Gantt chart, shown in Figure 13–9. Part A is scheduled to start on May 10 and Part B is scheduled to

FIGURE 13–9

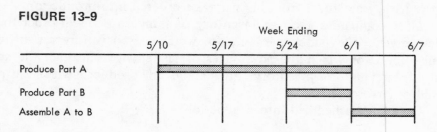

start on May 24 so that the two parts can be completed when they are needed for assembly. If the delivery date for the order is June 7, the delivery may be made soon after the parts are completed. Figure 13–10 shows a Broadmaster panel used to picture the progress of production orders in comparison with planned schedules for easy checks on shop loads and delayed orders.

FIGURE 13–10
Control Panel for Easy Check on Schedule of Jobs

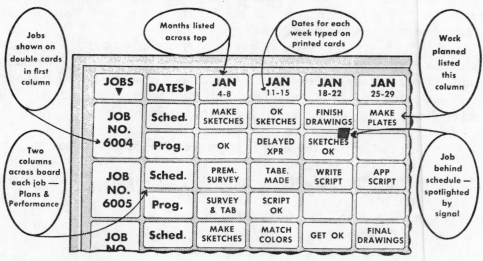

Source: Graphic Systems.

160

A recently developed chart is used for scheduling "networks"—sequences of operations, each of which may be dependent upon the completion of several other activities. This chart, called the *critical path method* (CPM) or the *program evaluation and review technique* (PERT), is used by many companies in the construction industry. Figure 13–11 shows a chart for the installation of an underground pipe.

The circles represent the start and finish of activities, and the lines show activities (the line length has no meaning). The times at the circles give the earliest and latest times for the end of the prior operation and the beginning of the next one; the difference is called "slack." The circles with zero slack time are on the "critical path," and the sum of the times for all the activities between those circles determines how long the whole process will take. The times are usually the best estimates of knowledgeable people.

Exhibit 37 of *The Dow Jones-Irwin Business Papers* has a form for helping you see that your work is properly scheduled to keep costs down and machines busy and to assure punctual delivery.

Orders received and plans made must be communicated to those doing the work. The information is provided by written or oral instructions, by training workers, and by having a fixed flow of materials. Each worker must know what and how many he is to produce, when and where

INSTALLING AN INFORMATION SYSTEM TO DIRECT WORK ACTIVITIES

FIGURE 13–11
PERT Chart for Putting in a Pipeline

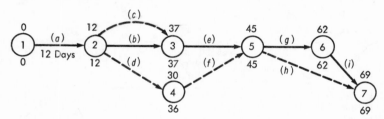

Legend:	Days	Completion Earliest	Date Latest
(a) Survey Ditch	12	12	12
(b) Dig Ditch	25	37	37
(c) Order and Receive Rock	3	15	37
(d) Order and Receive Pipe and Fittings	18	30	36
(e) Rock Ditch	8	45	45
(f) Assemble Valves and Fittings	9	39	45
(g) Lay Pipe	17	62	62
(h) Install Fittings	13	58	69
(i) Cover Ditch	7	69	69
Earliest Day Estimated to be Completed	12		
Latest Day Can Be Completed	12		
Critical Path	—		

he is to produce them, and what he needs in order to perform the job satisfactorily. You should design a simple, yet adequate, system to provide this information in your firm.

The route sheet shown in Figure 13-12 is used in a garment plant and travels with a bundle of cut cloth. It tells the workers what to sew, the type of operation, the time for the operation, and what the next operation is. The size of the bundle sets the quantity. As each operator completes an operation, the proper tab is clipped to be returned to the office. More complex systems are needed for other processes. A simple route card is shown in Figure 13-13. The outside envelope cover in Figure 13-14 provides customer instructions for production. It also identifies material in process.

Figure 13-15 shows a work order for an automobile repair garage, and Figure 13-16 shows one for a shower door manufacturer. A sample of a set of production specifications is shown in Figure 13-17.

CONTROLLING THE QUANTITY AND QUALITY OF PRODUCTION

Even if the best of plans are made and communicated, and the best of work is performed, controls are still needed. Without controls, the process will fail. Thus, the principle of exception should be followed.

Controlling by exceptions involves comparing your plans with the plant's performance. In simple systems, this can be done informally by personally observing the performance. Usually, though, a system of formal checks is needed.

FIGURE 13-12
Route Sheet Used in Garment Plant

	SKIRT	SCH.NO. LOT NO. AMT.	7732 24	SKIRT	
	.NR-24-7732 Thread bkle.on tab.tack to fnt. ****			.060-24-7732 Reverse	
					1:00
11:00	.448-24-7732 Hem Waist & Btm. BS			.132-24-7732 Serge Btm.	
					3:00
3:00	.128-24-7732 SS 2nd Side Seam ***			.196-24-7732 Serge Elastic to Waist	5:00
4:00	.164-24-7732 SS One Side Seam T&L			1.134-24-7732 Topst.fnt.pleats bste.across top **	27:00

FIGURE 13-13
Route Card or Job Order Instruction Card

```
┌─────────────────────────────────────────────────────┐
│                    ROUTE CARD                          │
│                                                        │
│  Production Order No._____         │
│                                                        │
│  Product _____         │
│                                                        │
│  No. of Units_____         │
│                                                        │
│  Special Instructions:                                 │
│                                                        │
├──────────────────┬───────┬───────────┬────────────────┤
│    Required      │       │   Date    │  Initials of   │
│   Operations     │ Dept. │ Completed │  Foreman or    │
│                  │       │           │   Operator     │
├──────────────────┼───────┼───────────┼────────────────┤
│                  │       │           │                │
├──────────────────┼───────┼───────────┼────────────────┤
│                  │       │           │                │
├──────────────────┼───────┼───────────┼────────────────┤
│                  │       │           │                │
├──────────────────┼───────┼───────────┼────────────────┤
│                  │       │           │                │
├──────────────────┼───────┼───────────┼────────────────┤
│                  │       │           │                │
├──────────────────┼───────┼───────────┼────────────────┤
│                  │       │           │                │
├──────────────────┼───────┼───────────┼────────────────┤
│                  │       │           │                │
├──────────────────┼───────┼───────────┼────────────────┤
│                  │       │           │                │
└──────────────────┴───────┴───────────┴────────────────┘
```

Source: From R. Lee Brummet and Jack C. Robertson, *Cost Accounting for Small Manufacturers,* 2d ed. (Washington, D.C.: Small Business Administration, 1972), Small Business Management Series, No. 9.

Orders may be filed by due dates, the work to be completed in each department may be recorded each day; or bar charts or graphs may be used. The record of performance is obtained through feedback, or by having forms returned with information on the work performed. For example, press operators clock their time in and out on the edge of a job envelope carrying instructions; workers in a garment plant clip off pieces of the route sheet and return it pasted on their time ticket; a garage repairman enters his time on the order form. A sample job time card is shown in Figure 13-18, a daily production report in Figure 13-19, records of material and labor usage for a job in Figure 13-20, and an inspection ticket in Figure 13-21.

You need not make changes when performance equals or exceeds your plans. An exception exists when performance does not reach the level desired. Then you need to decide what to do to improve future performance.

FIGURE 13–14
Customer Order

MAY 21 1974

GALLEY PROOF ____ ; REVISED GALLEY ____ ; PAGE PROOF ____ ; REVISED PAGE ____ ; VELOX ____

PROOF Yes ( ) No ( ) | Proof OK with Corrections _____ | Letterpress *set change*

TO _____ | Proof OK _____ | № 25188

DATE _____ | Give Revised _____ | OFFSET (X) _____

JOB BY _____ *Brewer State Junior College* DATE *May 14, 1974*
NAME _____
ADDRESS _____
JOB PROMISED *Friday Morning* PURCHASE ORDER NO. _____
JOBS IN SHOP _____ MAKE-UP MAN _____
Deliver (X) *UPS* Will Call ( ) Paid ( ) Collect ( )

QUANTITY	DESCRIPTION		PRICE
1500	*Fight Inflation Flyers*	Last Price	380/M - $74
		Art	40.40
		Cuts	
		Printing	2.46
		TOTAL	43 —

T.E.

Printed on Back ( ) Head to Head ( ) Tumble Head ( ) 42.86

SPECIAL INSTRUCTIONS — *2 Folds for Mailing - Prints on*

FOLDER _____ PAGES _____
SADDLE STITCHED _____
SIDE STITCHED _____

ORIGINAL DUP. TRIP. QUAD. **INVOICED**

COLOR OF INK (BLACK) (RED) (BLUE) OTHER: _____ MAY 29 1974
PADDED _____ TAGBOARD _____ MARBLEBOARD _____ BOX _____ Invoice No. 19530
PUNCHING: NO. OF HOLES _____ SLOT _____
PERFORATIONS: ____ Across ____ Up and Down ____ On Press ____ Round Hole ____ Slit
BEGIN NUMBER _____ END NUMBER ____ (Hand) ROUND CORNER ____
CARBONS: Pencil ( ) Typewriter ( ) SNAPOUT: Black ( ) Blue ( )

FINISHED SIZE *8½ X 11* SHEET SIZE _____
NO. OUT _____ CUT FROM _____ QUAN. _____
GRADE & WT. *50 lb Offset White* _____

№ 25188

RETURN: ART WORK ☐ PICTURES ☐ ENGRAVINGS ☐
TO _____ DATE RETURNED _____

FIGURE 13-15
Three-Part Work Order

(Front)

REPAIR ORDER

MATERIAL USED				
QUAN	PART No	DESCRIPTION	PRICE	
		SUBLET REPAIRS		
		BROUGHT FORWARD		
		TOTAL PARTS		
QUAN	ACCESS No	ACCESSORIES	PRICE	
		TOTAL ACCESSORIES		

MAZDA with the rotary engine. **MARK II**

KIRKLAND GARAGE
2319 University Blvd. East   Phone 553-6121
TUSCALOOSA, ALABAMA 35401

BEAR

6457

FORM RO-554

NAME			RECEIVED	DATE
			A P M	
ADDRESS			PROMISED	CUSTOMERS ORDER No
			A P M	
CITY		PHONE	TERMS	ORDER WRITTEN BY
MAKE	TYPE or MODEL	YEAR	SER No	LICENSE No	SPEEDOMETER
			MTR No		

OPER No	INSTRUCTIONS:	LABOR CHARGE

I hereby authorize the above repair work to be done along with the necessary material, and hereby grant you and/or your employees permission to operate the car or truck herein described on streets, highways or elsewhere for the purpose of testing and/or inspection. An express mechanic's lien is hereby acknowledged on above car or truck to secure the amount of repairs thereto.

X_____

NOT RESPONSIBLE FOR LOSS OR DAMAGE TO CARS OR ARTICLES LEFT IN CARS IN CASE OF FIRE, THEFT OR ANY OTHER CAUSE BEYOND OUR CONTROL.

	F S		PHONE WHEN READY	YES ☐ NO ☐
			TOTAL LABOR	
			TOTAL PARTS	
			ACCESSORIES	
GAS, OIL & GREASE	PRICE		GAS OIL & GREASE	
GAL GAS @			SUBLET REPAIRS	
QTS. OIL @				
LBS GREASE @			TAX	
TOTAL GAS, OIL & GREASE			TOTAL AMOUNT	

(Back)

ADDITIONAL MATERIAL USED				
QUAN.	ITEM NO.	DESCRIPTION	PRICE	

ADDITIONAL MATERIAL USED					LABOR RECORD				
QUAN	ITEM NO.	DESCRIPTION	PRICE		EMP. NO.	OPER. NO.	COST	ELAPSED TIME	TIME CLOCK
									OFF
									ON
									OFF
									ON
									OFF
									ON
									OFF
									ON
									OFF
									ON
									OFF
									ON
									OFF
									ON

FIGURE 13–16
Work Order

Coral Industries, Inc.

ORDER
07/222/6

920 19TH AVE. E., TUSCALOOSA, ALABAMA 35401

PHONE (205) 556–2880

SOLD TO _____

SHIP TO _____

CUSTOMER'S ORDER NUMBER	DATE	WHEN SHIP	SALESMAN	SHIP VIA		
QUANTITY	MODEL NO.	DESIGNS	DESCRIPTION and/or DIAGRAM		UNIT PRICE	AMOUNT
					TOTAL	

REMARKS:

Office Copy

Customer Confirmation

Salesman's Copy

Shop Copy

Packing Slip

Frank

FIGURE 13–17
A Drawing for Production

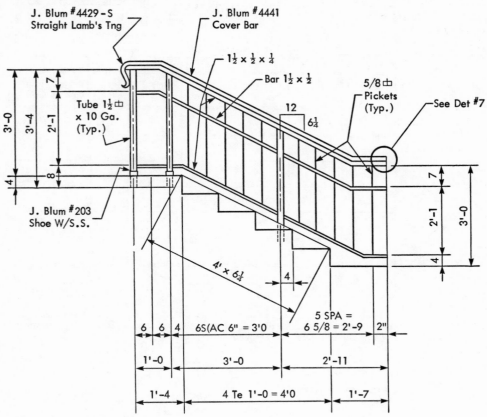

ONE – RAIL – M∠1R6^R (AS SHOWN)
ONE – RAIL – M∠1R6^L (OPP HAND)

FIGURE 13-18
Job Time Card

JOB TIME CARD							
Name _____					Card No. _____		
Department _____					Clock No. _____		
Date	Prod'n Order No.	Machine No.	Time Started	Time Stopped	Total Hours	Wage Rate	Total Cost
No. of Pieces Finished _____			Approved by _____				

Source: From R. Lee Brummet and Jack C. Robertson, *Cost Accounting for Small Manufacturers*, 2d ed. (Washington, D.C.: Small Business Administration, 1972), Small Business Management Series, No. 9.

FIGURE 13-19
Daily Production Report

DAILY PRODUCTION REPORT FOR _____					
				Date	
Order No.	Product Description	Dept.	No. of Items Finished	No. of Items Spoiled, Lost, or Wasted	Remarks

Source: From R. Lee Brummett and Jack C. Robertson, *Cost Accounting for Small Manufacturers*, 2d ed. (Washington, D.C.: Small Business Administration 1972), Small Business Management Series, No. 9.

FIGURE 13–20
Material and Labor Usage Card (front and back)

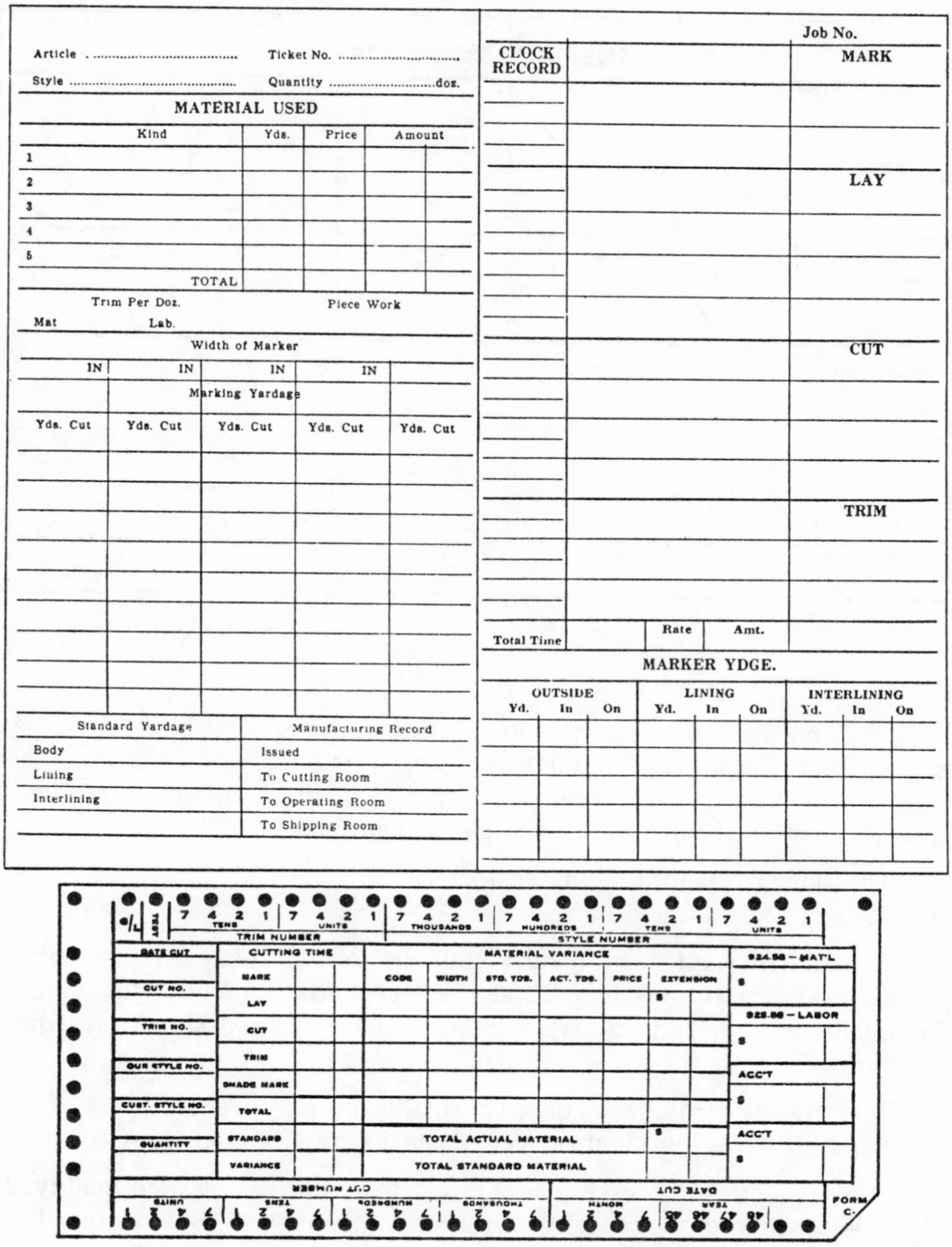

Article .... Ticket No.	CLOCK RECORD	Job No.
Style .... Quantity .... doz.		MARK

MATERIAL USED

	Kind	Yds.	Price	Amount
1				
2				
3				
4				
5				
	TOTAL			

Trim Per Doz.   Piece Work

Mat   Lab.

Width of Marker

IN	IN	IN	IN	

Marking Yardage

Yds. Cut	Yds. Cut	Yds. Cut	Yds. Cut	Yds. Cut

LAY

CUT

TRIM

Total Time	Rate	Amt.

MARKER YDGE.

OUTSIDE			LINING			INTERLINING		
Yd.	In	On	Yd.	In	On	Yd.	In	On

Standard Yardage   Manufacturing Record

Body	Issued
Lining	To Cutting Room
Interlining	To Operating Room
	To Shipping Room

13 / Designing and Controlling Work   169

FIGURE 13–21
Inspection Report

INSPECTION REPORT

RECEIVED FROM:			DATE
ADDRESS:			P. O. No. REC. No. STORE No. PARTIAL or COMPLETE

DWG. NO.	DESCRIPTION	QUANTITY RECEIVED	QUANTITY PASSED	QUANTITY REJECTED

REASON FOR REJECTION

REMARKS

INSPECTED BY

The methods used in quality control systems have been developed further than those of other control systems, and are used in many other systems, including cost control. The quality control system begins with setting the level of quality desired. This is based on:

1. The value of quality to the customer.
2. The cost of the quality.

Customers want high quality, but are often willing to pay only a limited price for the product. Production costs rise rapidly as the demand for quality rises beyond a certain point. Therefore, you should ask these questions:

1. Who are my customers, and what quality do they want?
2. What quality of product or service can I obtain, and at what costs?

Then you need to establish controls to obtain the desired quality. If you try to exceed that level, your costs will increase. But if you allow quality to go below that level, you will lose customers. Design your process to produce products or services within the desired quality range. Then, design your quality control system to check performance.

The steps needed in any control system are:

1. Set standards for your quality range.
2. Measure your actual performance.
3. Compare 1 and 2.
4. Make corrections when needed

Standards of quality may be set for dimension, color, strength, content, weight, service, and other characteristics. Some standards may be measured by instruments (for example, rulers or gauges can be used to measure length), but color, taste, and other standards must be evaluated by skilled individuals. Measurement may be made by selected people at certain points in the process—usually upon the receipt of material, and always before it goes to the customer. You can spot-check (sample), or check each item.

Inspection reduces the chances that poor-quality products will be passed through your process and to your customers. But not all defective work is eliminated by inspection. By recording the number of defective units per 100 units, you can observe the quality performance of the process and make needed corrections. A final check might be to keep a record of the number of complaints received per 100 sales made.

Exhibit 38 of *The Dow Jones—Irwin Business Papers* has a form to help you see that your quality control is being performed so that your product or service is at the proper level of quality.

Exhibit 39 has a form to help you see that your strategic planning of production and your control of production are being carried out properly.

chapter 14

Purchasing and Controlling Materials

The profitability of an independent business is often dependent upon the purchasing and materials control expertise of its owner-manager. The absence of know-how in these areas is often revealed only during the postmortem of a failed business.

This chapter emphasizes the importance of purchasing and controlling materials and provides information on sound procedural practices.

PLANNING AND CONTROLLING MATERIALS OR GOODS

In the previous chapters, we discussed the flow of materials in a business and the use of inventory to take care of seasonal variations in demand. Now, we need to consider the decisions regarding materials planning and control, including:

1. Amount of material needed for the output desired.
2. Amount of inventory and its storage and recording.
3. Quantity and time of order.
4. Vendor relations.
5. Quality of materials and price per unit.
6. Methods of receiving and shipping.
7. Handling of defective materials and stock-outs.

Policies and procedures should be established so that most of these decisions become routine. When exceptions occur, they should be handled by you or someone whom you delegate. Your policies and procedures should minimize the total cost of materials to your company. But remember that total cost includes more than just the price of the materials. It includes costs which are charged to the goods and costs which are hidden in other expenses—usually in overhead.

Trade-offs must be made to obtain the best cost. Materials are a form of investment, and until they produce revenue, the money expended on them cannot be used for other income-producing purposes. Consequently,

172

you want to buy materials in small quantities and sell them rapidly in order to obtain income. But if the quantities you have on hand are too small, you may miss income-producing opportunities and lose customers. Also, purchasing in small quantities usually results in higher prices.

Another problem concerns the controls established to minimize losses from theft. While increasing controls may reduce the cost from losses, it also increases the control cost. The problem is to find the optimum balance between the two costs.

In materials planning and control, you should recognize that most of your income will come from a small percentage of your products or services. About 80 percent of the average firm's income comes from 20 percent of its products. Materials planning and control should be directed mainly toward the 20 percent. You may want to classify the goods in categories and set a procedure for each category. Thus, for the most valuable 20 percent, you may set standards and procedures for each time; for the next, say, 30 percent, you may handle items in groups; and for the last 50 percent, you may consider all items as a single group.

Another important area is the study of the products and services to determine whether all the inputs are needed. This is called *value analysis,* and it is based on relating the purpose of each part to its cost or value. It determines the best material or design for each part or input.

The form in Exhibit 40 of *The Dow Jones-Irwin Business Papers* will help you evaluate your planning and controlling of materials.

INVENTORY

The inventory of materials, parts, goods, and supplies represents a high investment in all businesses. Many companies have failed because their inventories tied up too much money, or because the items in inventory were obsolete, impaired, or lost. You should have appropriate policies concerning the items to carry in inventory and the level and control of inventory.

The purpose of an inventory is to disconnect one segment of a process from another, so that each segment can operate at its optimum level of performance. A process composed of several operations, with inventory between them, might be diagramed as in Figure 14-1.

Note that the inventories are shown at different levels at different stages of the process. The level depends on the prior activities of the supplier to, and the user of, the inventory. For example, operation 1 may have been running recently and operation 2 may have been shut down.

FIGURE 14-1

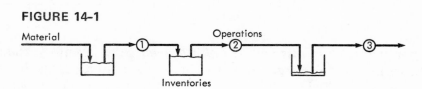

Also notice that operation 3 may not have enough material if operation 2 does not start up soon.

Inventories exist in various places in a business, and in different stages of production, as:

1. Raw materials and parts.
2. Goods in process or between operations.
3. Finished goods at the factory, storehouse, or store.
4. Purchased goods and materials.
5. Repair parts for machines.
6. Supplies for the office, shop, or factory.
7. Patterns and tools.

Each of these types of inventory performs basically the same function and can be studied in the same way. However, some inventories may represent a much greater investment, cause more serious trouble if they are depleted and be more costly to restock. More attention and time should be given to such inventories.

Even a small company may have thousands of items in stock. The total investment in inventory should be kept in a proper relation to the finances of the company. (This relationship will be discussed in Chapter 20 when the financial analysis of the company is considered.) It should not be so great that it deprives you of enough cash to pay your current bills.

Figure 14–2 shows how the number of units of a *purchased item* varies over a period of time. When a purchased item is received, the inventory increases instantly. Units are removed from inventory as they are demanded. At a certain point in time, or when the inventory reaches a given level, a purchase order is sent to the vendor for a certain quantity. The order will be received some time later. In the meantime, more units may be drawn from inventory. This cycle is repeated for each item purchased.

FIGURE 14–2
Graph of the Changing Level of Inventory of an Item

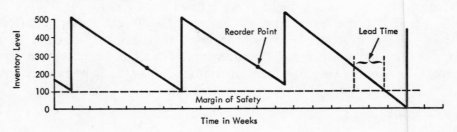

For items *in process* and *in finished goods,* the inventory builds up over a period of time as goods are produced, so the vertical line in Figure 14–2 would be sloping upward to the right. The inventory builds up because production is greater than demand. The following discussion pertains to purchased items, but with minor adjustments it would apply to in-process and finished goods also.

The level of inventory at which an order should be issued is based on:

1. The quantity to be used between the time an order is issued and the time the items are received.
2. The quantity needed to provide a margin of safety.

The time to be allowed in (1) is determined by the sum of the times for:

1. The order to be processed in your company.
2. The order to be transported to the vendor.
3. The vendor to make and package the items.
4. The items to be transported to your company.

The total delay varies from time to time, so a margin of safety is added to obtain the quantity at the reorder point. The margin of safety, in turn, depends upon:

1. Variability of the time to obtain the items from the vendor. A higher variability requires a higher margin of safety.
2. Variability of usage.
3. Cost of not having inventory—losses from stock-outs.
4. Costs of carrying inventory, estimated for each item or group of items. These inventory costs include:
   a. Space charges.
   b. Insurance and taxes.
   c. Profits lost because money is tied up in inventory.
   d. Obsolescence of items.
   e. Deterioration.
   f. Theft.

Estimates of the costs of carrying inventory range from 15 percent to over 100 percent of the average inventory for a year. Values of 20–25 percent are often used.

You can compute or estimate the reorder-point quantity by trying various levels and reordering points and adding the cost of carrying the inventory and the cost of running out of goods multiplied by the probability of running out. The lowest total cost is the best reorder point. Note that you should focus more attention on some items than on others.

Exhibit 41 of *The Dow Jones-Irwin Business Papers* has a form which will help you do an audit of your inventory to see whether it is being handled efficiently and effectively.

The quantity you include on each order affects the level of inventory and the time between orders. You may place your orders:

QUANTITIES PER ORDER

1. At certain intervals, such as once a week, month, or quarter, when you order an amount which brings the level of the inventory up to a predetermined standard amount.
2. When the inventory reaches a certain quantity, such as 250 units in Figure 14–2. The quantity ordered is a fixed amount called the *economic order quantity* (EOQ).

The quantity to order in (1) and (2) can be computed or estimated in the same manner, but in (1) it is used only as an expected average. The economic order quantity is determined by balancing:

1. The cost of the order, which includes:
    a. The cost of processing and handling the order.
    b. The costs of the item, realizing that larger orders usually warrant price discounts.
    c. Transportation costs.
2. The inventory carrying costs.

Figure 14–3 shows the way costs per unit vary as the quantity ordered is changed. The point of lowest cost is the EOQ. This can be found by using a formula or by comparing the unit costs for different order quantities. Note how a discount affects the curve and that a range in quantities has approximately the same low cost.

FIGURE 14–3
Changes in Purchase Unit Costs

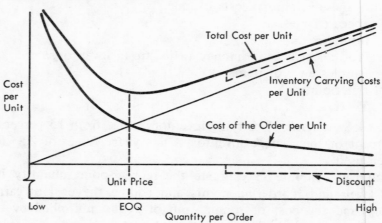

ORDERING PROCEDURE

Many items can be ordered on a routine basis. The procedure starts with the need as reflected by the reorder point and requires:

1. Keeping a perpetual inventory, which records when the inventory has reached the reorder point. Figure 14–4 shows a perpetual inventory card.

FIGURE 14-4
Inventory Record Form

| Date | Received | | Issued | | Balance |
	Order No.	Units	Req. No.	Units	on Hand
7/13	3401	400			450
7/17			1075	10	440
7/22			1090	10	430

Reorder Point: 70 Bags   Reorder Quantity: 400 Bags

Item No.	Description	Unit
315	Zinc Oxide (3Z33)	50# Bags

2. Having a quantity set aside which will not be used unless a purchase order is made out.

3. Having a method for calling attention to the need for the order, such as a gauge for a tank of oil.

The amount to reorder is shown on the inventory card or on some other form. The vendor and the method of packaging and transporting are on a record.

The major items of purchase require more analysis, as their cost and quality can have a greater effect on your company. You, or someone in authority in your firm, should be involved in these purchases. A number of the considerations which require higher level decisions are:

1. Expected changes in price. Short delays in buying for expected decreases in price or buying increased quantities for expected increases in price can result in savings. However, stock-outs or too heavy inventory costs should be guarded against.

2. Expected changes in demand. Seasonal products fall into this category.

3. Orders to meet a demand for specialty goods. The quantity ordered should match the amount demanded so that no material is left over. When the quantity of the demand is known, estimates of losses in process are added to the order. When the quantity of the demand is not known, you must depend on forecasts and estimates of losses.

4. A short supply of materials.

You should avoid speculative buying unless you are in that business. While all business decisions have a certain element of speculation, an independent businessman cannot afford to gamble with money required in his business. The procedure for processing a purchase order and receiving the goods is flow-charted in Figure 14-5.

One person should have the responsibility for ordering all materials, but he should obtain the help of people knowledgeable in the areas in which the goods are needed. Having a single person responsible, avoids

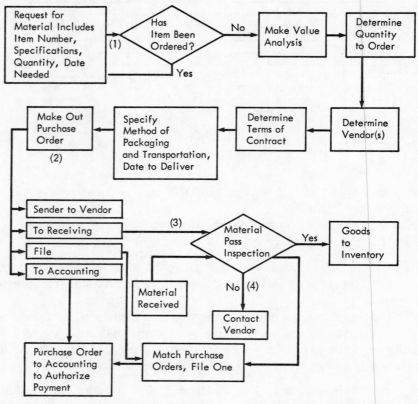

FIGURE 14-5
Purchase Order Procedure

Key: (1) See Figure 14-6, purchase requisition. The reorder point is obtained from Figure 14-4.
(2) See Figure 14-7, purchase order.
(3) See Figure 14-8, receiving report.
(4) See Figure 13-1, inspection report.

duplicate orders, utilizes the specialized skills needed for purchasing, and localizes responsibility for improvements in the buying process.

The number of forms needed for obtaining and controlling products, and the number of copies of these forms, depend on the amount of formality desired. A simple requisition form can be forwarded to the purchasing agent. He, in turn, reviews requisitions, issues purchase orders to vendors, follows up on orders when necessary, checks the receipt of materials, takes corrective action when needed, and sees that materials are delivered to the proper place.

SOURCES OF SUPPLY

Sources from which you obtain your inputs are important because:

1. Price of purchased goods is a major cost in your outputs.
2. Reliability in delivery and quality affects your operations.

178

FIGURE 14-6
Purchase Requisition

```
┌─────────────────────────────────────────────────────────────┐
│        PURCHASE REQUISITION        No._____               │
│                                                              │
│  Please Purchase the Following        Date_____           │
│  for Delivery Not Later Than _____          │
├──────────┬──────────────┬───────────────────────────────────┤
│          │ Material or  │                                    │
│ Quantity │ Part Number  │           Description              │
│          │              │                                    │
├──────────┼──────────────┼───────────────────────────────────┤
│          │              │                                    │
│          │              │                                    │
│          │              │                                    │
│          │              │                                    │
│          │              │                                    │
│          │              │                                    │
│          │              │                                    │
│          │              │                                    │
│          │              │         Signed _____     │
├──────────┴──────────────┴───────────────────────────────────┤
│  Quantity on Hand _____   Order No._____          │
│  Average Monthly Usage_____                               │
│                                Date of Order_____          │
│  Desired Maximum_____.                                 │
│  Desired Minimum_____    Vendor _____            │
└─────────────────────────────────────────────────────────────┘
```

Source: From R. Lee Brummet and Jack C. Robertson, *Cost Accounting for Small Manufacturers*, 2d ed. (Washington, D.C.: Small Business Administration, 1972), Small Business Management Series, No. 9.

3. Vendors can be valuable sources of information.
4. Vendors can provide valuable services.

The prices of different vendors vary. Higher prices may be charged for:

1. Higher quality.
2. More reliable and faster delivery.
3. Better terms for returning goods.
4. More services, such as in advertising. type of packaging, and information.
5. Better, or delayed, payment plan.

You may be able to purchase an item at a lower price, but your total cost of processing the item may be higher. For example, the price plus transportation cost from a distant source may be less than from a local source, but the faster service from the local source may allow you to carry less inventory. The reduction in inventory may more than compensate for the higher local price. One source may be able to supply a wide assortment of the goods you need, reducing the expense of ordering from many sources.

FIGURE 14–7
Purchase Order

PURCHASE ORDER		19___

M_____

Address_____

Please Ship to_____

Address_____

Ship via_____When_____Terms:_____

QUANTITY	ITEM NO.	DESCRIPTION	PRICE
		SPECIMEN	

ORDER № 3657

KINDLY SHOW OUR ORDER
NUMBER ON YOUR INVOICE.

Yours truly,

RICKS & SONS HARDWARE

2116 University Boulevard, East

PHONE 553-6620

By_____

Your sources of supply may be brokers, jobbers, wholesalers, manufacturers, or others. Each of these sources provides a type of service which may be valuable to you. For example, the wholesaler stocks many items so that he can give fast delivery of a wide variety of items. The manufacturer ships directly, but he is restricted in the products he can supply. However, he may have sales representatives or agents who can help the small business. Regional and national trade shows and private trade associations provide valuable information and services for keeping up-to-date on sources and their products and services.

Should you buy from one or many sources? The argument for a single source is the closer and more individual relationship which can be established. When shortages occur, you can probably obtain better service if you have a single source. Discounts may be obtained with larger volume buying. On the other hand, using multiple sources allows you to find the sources with a greater variety of goods and, often, better terms. Some companies put out requests for bids, and negotiations can result in better arrangements.

Care should be exercised on the ethics of the supplier and your relationship to him. You should guard against unethical practices, including gifts, entertainment, misrepresentation, and reciprocity. An independent

FIGURE 14–8
Receiving Report

Materials or Parts Received from _____ Vendor			
Purchase Order No._____ Date Received_____			

No. of Packages	No. of Items	Specs.	Description

Comments:

Prepared by _____

Source: From R. Lee Brummet and Jack C. Robertson, *Cost Accounting for Small Manufacturers*, 2d ed. (Washington, D.C.: Small Business Administration, 1972), Small Business Management Series, No. 9.

company should try to maintain a good image in its dealings with vendors in order to obtain good service.

RECEIVING MATERIALS

The receipt and forwarding of materials to inventory is the last step in acquiring inputs. This step is performed to check that the material is what has been ordered, is in the proper condition, and is of the proper quality. Purchasing is informed that the goods have been received and are ready for processing.

A copy of the purchase order and other desired specifications are sent to those receiving the material. The material is checked for damage in transportation; for specified characteristics, such as color and size; and for quantity and price. Those processing the materials are delayed if they do not find the right kind and quantity of material in inventory. Proper receiving procedures can eliminate these discrepancies.

Materials can be stored in the containers in which they are received, in separate containers, or individually. Receiving prepares materials for storing.

Issuance of material can be accounted for through a material requisition, a sample of which is shown in Figure 14–9.

FIGURE 14–9
Material Requisition

```
┌──────────────────────────────────────────────────────────────────┐
│                      MATERIAL REQUISITION                          │
│                                                                    │
│   Date _____    Requisition No. _____   │
│                                                                    │
│   For _____     Production Order No. _____   │
│        Department or Operator                                      │
│                                                                    │
│   Requested by _____        │
│                                                                    │
```

Stores No.	Quantity Requested	Description	Quantity Issued	Unit Cost	Total Cost

Received by _____   Date _____

Source: From R. Lee Brummet and Jack C. Robertson, *Cost Accounting for Small Manufacturers,* (Washington, D.C.: Small Business Administration, 1972), Small Business Management Series, No. 9.

The form in Exhibit 42 of *The Dow Jones-Irwin Business Papers* will help you evaluate your purchasing procedure to see that it assures the proper amounts and types of material, reduces costs, and maintains proper product quality.

WHERE TO LOOK FOR FURTHER INFORMATION

Buffa, E. S. *Modern Production Management,* 4th ed. New York: John Wiley and Sons, 1973.

Hedrick, F. D. *Purchasing Management in the Small Company.* New York: American Management Association, Inc., 1971.

Hopeman, R. J. *Production: Concepts-Analysis-Control,* 2d ed. Columbus, Ohio: Charles E. Merrill, 1971.

Improving Materials Handling in Small Business, 3d ed. Washington, D.C.: Small Business Administration, 1969. (Small Business Management, No. 4.)

Kline, J. B. *Pointers on Scheduling Production.* Washington, D.C.: Small Business Administration, 1970. (Management Aids for Small Manufacturers, No. 207.)

Mayer, R. R. *The Equipment Replacement Decision.* Washington, D.C.: Small Business Administration, 1970. (Management Aids for Small Manufacturers, No. 212.)

Miles, L. *Techniques of Value Analysis and Engineering,* 2d ed. New York: McGraw-Hill Book Company, 1972.

Moore, F. G., *Production Management,* 6th ed. Homewood, Ill.: Richard D. Irwin, Inc., 1973.

PART FIVE

Marketing Your Product or Service

Manning, production, marketing, and financing are all essential business functions. Each of them should be performed economically and effectively for your firm to be successful. The following chapters should help you perform the marketing function better.

Marketing refers to the distribution of your firm's product or service to your customers in order to satisfy their needs and to accomplish your firm's objectives. Marketing includes developing the product or service, pricing, distributing the product, advertising, doing personal selling, promoting, and directing the sales and service people. Unless your firm has or can develop a market for its product or service, the other functions of manning, producing, and financing are unnecessary.

The marketing function and the philosophy that underlies its performance are presented in Figure V-1.

FIGURE V-1
Schematic of Marketing Function

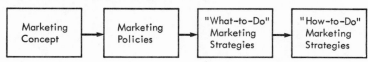

This logical approach to the performance of the marketing is covered in this part. Chapter 15 will cover the subject of developing marketing strategies. Specifically, it will deal with the marketing concept, strategic marketing policies, and developing your "what-to-do" marketing strategies. Chapter 15 is followed by three chapters that deal with "how-to-do-it" marketing operations.

Chapter 16 covers sales forecasting and promoting. It includes the subjects of marketing research and sales forecasting and advertising and sales promotion.

Chapter 17 discusses personal selling through agent middlemen or your own sales force.

Chapter 18 covers such other marketing problems as setting up sales territories, planning and controlling the activities of your salespeople, and determining your marketing mix, as well as some contemporary marketing problems and their solutions.

chapter 15

Developing Market Strategies

The marketing activity is an area that frequently seems to be neglected by the owner of an independent business. In the final analysis, what occurs in the marketplace determines the success or failure of the firm. Therefore, in this chapter we have attempted to "lay out" in a step-by-step fashion what you must do to succeed in the marketplace.

The chapter focuses attention on the marketing concept, strategic marketing policies, and "what-to-do" strategies. It covers these aspects of the marketing concept, determining what customers' needs are and how those needs can be satisfied; specifying the market to be served—called market segmentation; and deciding what advantages the company has—called its competitive edge.

The strategic marketing policies described are: morality and public service, products, markets, profits, personal selling, customer relations, promotion, and credit.

The chapter concludes with a discussion of the following "what-to-do" marketing strategies: expanding sales into new classes of customers; increasing penetration into market segments corresponding to existing classes of customers; and making no marketing innovations, but rather emphasizing product design and manufacturing innovations.

THE MARKETING CONCEPT

The marketing concept is based upon the importance of the customers to a firm. If you decide to use this approach in your firm, you will need to: (1) determine what your customers' needs are, and how those needs can be satisfied; (2) select the market you will try to serve; and (3) decide what advantage you have which will give you a competitive edge over other firms.

Meeting Customers' Needs

The underlying principle of the marketing concept, as it applies to your business, is that your firm should seek to meet the needs of

187

customers—at a profit to you. The marketing concept should guide all your employees. They should be devoted to stimulating and satisfying the wants and needs of customers. Too often, only the salespeople in a company follow the concept, while other employees (say, delivery people, cashiers, or clerks) are rude and create customer ill will.

You should learn your customers' likes and make them feel that you are interested in them. You should give them extra service, because your customers will remember it and inform others. You should be an expert on your products and tell the truth about them even if sales are lost. You should build your trade around existing customers.

You should sell your customers only as much as they can afford. An "oversold" customer will not be a "repeat." You should encourage your salespeople to build personal followings among customers.

You should have a customer policy whereby salesmen give the benefit of doubt to customers who return merchandise.

Be Conscious of Your Image. You should rate your business once each quarter and determine what kind of image your firm has by letting yourself think about it as a customer would. Looked at from his standpoint, ask yourself:

1. Is my firm doing all that it can to be customer-oriented?
2. Can the customer find what he wants, when he wants it, and where he wants it at a cost-effective price?
3. Do my employees and I make sure that the customer leaves with his needs satisfied and with a feeling toward our company that will bring him back again?

Customers want a business to be helpful! The American Institute of Banking makes this observation: "The easiest way to make money is to learn what people want and sell it to them. The fastest way to lose money is to offer something, regardless of what people want, and try to make them buy it."[1]

You should do little favors for your customers; they like your thoughtfulness more than any gift. However, people dislike receiving big favors which they cannot repay.

Look for Danger Signals. If you are interested in the marketing concept, you will look for these *danger signals:*

1. Many customers walk out of your store without buying.
2. Many of them no longer visit the store.
3. Customers are not urged to buy additional or more expensive items.
4. Traffic (pedestrian and vehicle) in front of your store has fallen off.
5. Customers are returning more merchandise than they should.
6. Your company's sales are down this month over the same month last

---

[1] Robert G. Murdick et al., *Business Policy: A Framework for Analysis* (Columbus, Ohio: Grid, Inc., 1972), p. 71.

188

year, and sales for the year-to-date are down over the same period last year.

7. Your employees are slow in greeting customers.
8. Your employees appear indifferent and make customers wait unnecessarily.
9. Your employees' personal appearance is not neat.
10. Your salespeople lack knowledge of the store's merchandise.
11. The number of mistakes made by your employees is increasing.
12. The "mantle of greed" is evidenced through raising prices.
13. Your better qualified employees leave for jobs with competitors.

All of these signals are evidence that your store is not following the marketing concept.

Market Segmentation

Your firm should specify what market it is attempting to serve. A product or service which fulfills the needs and wants of a specifically defined group of people is preferable to a product or service that is a compromise to suit widely divergent tastes. A marketing segment should be defined in terms of various characteristics, such as economic status, age, education, occupation, and location. Your best opportunity is to identify a market segment which is not well served by other firms. One authority has said:

> If we are to market successfully, we must in one way or another continually search for "holes" in the market. These holes are nothing but consumer needs and wants that exist because of inadequate or nonexistent products or services.[2]

In determining your segment of the market, you should ask yourself these fundamental questions.

1. What is my place in industry, and how can I find my competitive niche?
2. Am I known for my quality or my price?
3. If I sell industrial products, do I sell to more than one customer?
4. What image do the customers and the public have of my firm?
5. I serve only a limited number of customers. Why?

A common error of many independent retailing firms is "straddling the market," or attempting to sell both high-quality and low-quality goods. As a result, the retailer carries limited inventory of everything but does not have a good selection of anything.

Competitive Edge

To be successful, your firm should seek a "competitive edge." Your firm, like all other firms, needs some reason for being, something that is

---

[2] Allan Wickman, Jr., "Marketing Ideas Make or Break a Company," *Marketing Insights,* January 19, 1970, p. 3.

desirable from the customers' viewpoint that gives it an edge over its competition. You should stress quality, reliability, integrity, and service rather than lower prices.

The competitive edge should be realistic. To determine whether it is realistic in your firm, you should answer these questions:

1. Is the competitive edge based on facts?
2. Do you know what your customers are looking for?
3. Do you have an edge that can entice customers away from their present source of supply?
4. Have you used market research to make this determination?
5. Is the competitive edge compatible with your firm's capabilities and constraints?
6. Does your firm have the necessary resources—for example, manpower—to accomplish it?
7. Is the competitive edge based on conditions that are likely to change rapidly?[3]

Your firm should focus on earning profits instead of increasing the volume of sales. You should not increase sales without considering production costs, adequacy of capital, the position of competition, and so forth. Expenses incurred in achieving the increased volume may exceed the revenues achieved and result in losses. You can literally "Sell yourself into bankruptcy." Sales increases should not far exceed your company's well-rounded growth in vital areas, such as working capital and productive capacity.

The form in Exhibit 43 of *The Dow Jones-Irwin Business Papers* should help you determine whether you are using the marketing concept properly.

STRATEGIC MARKETING POLICIES

You and the top managers in your firm should formulate strategic marketing policies for certain areas, including:

1. Morality and public service.
2. Products.
3. Markets.
4. Profits.
5. Personal selling.
6. Customer relations.
7. Promotion.
8. Credit.
9. Credit cards.

Morality and Public Service

Policies on morality and public service consisting of general statements expressing your firm's desire to be honest in its dealing with the public and its customers.

---

[3]Murdick et al., *Business Policy.*

Policies on products will determine the direction in which your firm may grow in the future and may keep your company from "running off in all directions." If you are a manufacturer, you should generally restrict your products to custom, special-purpose, low-volume products and not attempt to make high-volume, assembly line products where big companies are competitors and have advantages over you. If you have a department store, you may deal in either low-quality, low-priced goods or high-quality, high-priced goods. If you are a retailer, you may specialize in either soft goods or durable goods. **Products**

The independent firm often finds its most effective competitive weapon in product strategy. It may concentrate upon a narrow product line, develop a highly specialized product or service, or provide a product-service "package" containing an unusual amount of service. Competitors' products, prices, and services should be obtained and examined to determine whether your company can outmatch them.

Market policies are designed to clarify what geographic areas you wish to serve and other market characteristics appropriate for your firm. Perhaps you desire to remain only a local business. You may decide to market only consumer, industrial, or defense goods. You may decide to sell only at retail, wholesale, or to manufacturers. **Markets**

Profit policies may require that sales goals be specified which will provide your firm a sufficiently large sales volume and a certain dollar profit. Or profit as a percentage of sales may be specified, calling for low marketing costs. **Profits**

Personal selling policies may range from those guiding the structure of your sales organization to those covering your sales representatives' behavior. For example, you may have a policy stating that only one representative of your company may call upon an account. You may not permit "hard selling." Other sales policies may relate to your representatives' qualifications and compensation and to constraints on your sales managers. **Personal Selling**

Your company's relationship with your customers may be illustrated by this question: Should you have a policy that the customer is always right? **Customer Relations**

Your firm's advertisements may reveal its promotion policies. You should follow a policy of tasteful advertising at all times. You may restrict **Promotion** your promotion to trade shows, to industrial publications, or to some other advertising medium.

Credit

In order to stimulate sales, you should provide credit for your customers. However, an appropriate credit policy is essential if you wish to be successful in granting credit.

Some retail and service firms have been bankrupted by the over-extension or unwise extension of credit. However, retailers lose far more from slow accounts than from bad debts. Costs related to slow accounts are the most important item in the total cost of doing credit business. Some adverse effects of slow-paying charge accounts are:

1. Increased bad-debt losses.
2. Increased bookkeeping and collection expenses.
3. Increased interest expense due to greater capital requirements.
4. Reduction of capital turnover and profit.
5. Loss of business because "slow payers" tend to transfer their patronage elsewhere.

The longer a charge account goes unpaid, the more difficult it is to collect. (See Chapter 22 for further details.)

You should establish a definite credit policy covering the following factors:

1. To grant or not to grant credit.
2. To require or not to require a down payment.
3. How much the typical down payment should be.
4. How much time should be allowed on installment sales.

In selecting your credit customers, you can use the three C's of credit as your guideline:

Character: What is the customer's reputation in business and in the community?
Capacity: What is the customer's ability to repay?
Capital: What is the customer's financial condition, or how much equity does he have invested in his company?

You should explain your credit terms to your customers clearly and unmistakably.

The credit applicant's position should be investigated to obtain the following credit information:

1. Address and length of residence in your locality.
2. Occupation and earnings.
3. Marital status and number of dependents.
4. Ownership of property.
5. Amount of debts or payment and other credit accounts.
6. References, including bank references.

Additional questions include the following: Does the credit applicant change residence frequently? Change jobs often? Pay accounts slowly?

In many retail stores, the initial step in credit investigation is the completion of an application form, an example of which appears in Figure 15-1. The information obtained is used to determine the credit applicant's financial responsibility. Your retail credit bureau can also be asked to provide reports on prospective credit customers.

Other credit pointers are:

1. Set definite limits to the amount a customer can charge.
2. Keep accurate, complete records.
3. Send statements at regular intervals.
4. Watch past-due accounts.
5. Take legal steps when necessary.

A well-planned collection policy is very beneficial to your firm.[4] The policy should include specific rules on such matters as:

1. When accounts are to be payable.
2. How soon after the due date the first reminder shall be mailed.
3. How soon after the due date the credit privileges shall be suspended on a past-due account.
4. How many steps shall be in the standard follow-up procedure, and what duration of time shall elapse between the steps.
5. What tools and methods shall be used in the follow-up.
6. When past-due accounts shall be given to a collection agency or an attorney.

Credit Cards

In order to stimulate sales, you, as a retailer, should seriously consider the use of credit cards. Their objectives are to attain more rapid completion of credit sales, to reduce customer waiting time and inconvenience, and to eliminate certain record-keeping costs.

Bank credit cards, such as BankAmericard and Master Charge, have become important in generating sales. In 1977, Americans were holding 280 million credit cards.[5] Merchants report sales, sales returns and allowances, and other credits; and banks charge and credit their deposit accounts. Retailers pay a joining fee, a fee on sales made, and other fees.

You should recognize the advantages of not having bad debt losses or collection problems and of not requiring personnel, equipment, or space for servicing accounts receivable.

Your credit policy should be examined in relation to your company's strategic marketing plans. Is it consistent with your marketing strategies?

---

[4] *Records and Credit in Profitable Management* (Washington, D.C.: Small Business Administration), Administrative Management Course, pp. 32-33.

[5] *Business Week*, April 18, 1977, p. 90.

FIGURE 15-1
Credit Application Blank

CREDIT APPLICATION BLANK

Date _____

Credit Limit Requested _____ Set_____

IDENTIFICATION

Name of Applicant_____ Age_____

Present Address _____

Last Prior Address _____

EMPLOYMENT

Employer _____

Employer's Address _____

Position Held _____

Length of Employment _____

FINANCIAL STATUS

Monthly Salary _____

Value of Securities Owned _____

Amount of Life Insurance _____

Home Owned ( )   Rented ( )

    Value _____ Mortgage_____

    Monthly Payment _____   Monthly Rent _____

Other Income _____

_____

Bank Account with_____ Average Balance_____

FAMILY DATA

Ages of Children _____

Ages of Other Dependents _____

    Credit Bureau Report Findings _____

_____

FIGURE 15-1 (continued)

```
3 Trade References _____

               _____

               _____

Sales Terms _____


NOTICE:  Interest will be charged at 1½ percent per month on amounts past due 30 days.



                              _____
                                    Signature of Applicant
```

Source: Adapted from H. N. Broom and Justin G. Longenecker, *Small Business Management,* 4th ed. (Cincinnati, Ohio: South-Western Publishing Co., 1975), p. 178.

The form in Exhibit 44 of *The Dow Jones-Irwin Business Papers* should help you evaluate whether you have proper strategic marketing policies.

MARKETING STRATEGIES

In order to obtain a competitive edge, your company must innovate in product design, marketing, or manufacturing. You may find it necessary to adopt developments made by others in two of these areas while you innovate in the third. You should determine which of these three "what-to-do" marketing strategies to follow:

1. Expand sales into new classes of customers.
2. Increase penetration in market segments corresponding to existing classes of customers.
3. Make no market innovations, but copy new marketing techniques and try to hold your present market share by product design and manufacturing innovations.

Expand Sales into New Markets

To reach new markets, you might consider these possibilities:

1. Develop additional products or models within your product line.
2. Develop completely new products unrelated to your present line.
3. Find new applications in new markets for your product.
4. Develop customized products.

In introducing new and improved products, you should consider their relationship to your existing product line and channels of distribution; the costs of development and introduction; the availability of personnel and facilities; and competition and market acceptance.

The new and improved products should be consistent with your existing product line. Otherwise, costly changes in manufacturing methods, channels of distribution, advertising, and personal selling may be necessary.

Significant capital outlays for design and development, personnel and facilities, market research, advertising and sales promotion, patents, and equipment and tooling may be involved. It may take up to three years to realize profits on the sale of the new product, and financing should be adequate to cover this "breaking-in" period.

Competition should not be too severe. A rule of thumb is that new products can be introduced successfully only if a 5 percent share of the total market can be obtained. Your independent firm may compete effectively by means of: (1) a nonstandard product (either a higher priced or an economy product); (2) fast deliveries or short production runs of special items; or (3) high quality.

The following example pertains to the acquisition of a product or product line to preset specifications.

> The management of a defense-aerospace-oriented, precision metal-stamping and machine shop desired to acquire a product or product line that met these specifications:
>
> *Market*—The product sought is used by industrial or commercial firms of a specific industry, but not by the government or the general public, except incidentally.
>
> *Product*—The product sought is one on which 60 percent of the total direct manufacturing cost consists of metal stamping and/or machining processes.
>
> *Price Range*—The price range is open, but preferably should be $300 to $400.
>
> *Volume*—The volume is open, but preferably should produce $200,000 in sales in the first year with potential annual sales of $1 to $2 million.
>
> *Finance*—Capital of $50,000 in addition to present plant capacity is available for manufacturing the product.
>
> *Type of Acquisition*—Royalties are preferred, although purchase of a patent, a joint venture, merger, or outright purchase of a company will be considered.[6]

You should carefully consider diversificaton, or product line expansion. The advantages may be:

1. Increased profits.
2. Contribution to long-range growth.
3. Stabilization of product, employment, and payrolls.

---

[6]John B. Lang, *Finding a New Product for Your Company,* (Washington, D.C.: Small Business Administration, 1972), Management Aids for Small Manufacturers, No. 216.

4. Filling out a product line.
5. Lowering of administrative overhead cost per unit.

The availability of the necessary facilities and skill is relevant. Your diversification costs may exceed your income from increased sales.

If you have been selling replacement parts primarily, you might attempt to expand by selling to original equipment manufacturers. Or you might reduce the variety of products and models—this can bring about substantial operating economies.

Increase Your Penetration of Your Present Market

The strategy of adopting current marketing practices without trying to innovate is particularly suitable for your firm if its strength lies in its technical competence. In retailing, it is often advisable for store managers to follow this strategy.

Make No Marketing Innovations

Over the long range, your firm may follow one strategy for a number of years with the intention of changing it after certain marketing goals have been achieved.

The form in Exhibit 45 of *The Dow Jones-Irwin Business Papers* should help you evaluate whether your firm is following the appropriate marketing strategies.

chapter 16

Sales Forecasting,
Pricing and Promoting

Many people think that market research and sales forecasting have little or no value for independent businesses. These people think that market research and sales forecasting apply to larger firms and are too time-consuming and complex to be used by smaller firms.

Yet our experience seems to refute the idea. Determining the nature, location, and potential volume of the market and the most effective procedure for penetrating it is essential to independent businesses as well as larger organizations. The quality of market research and sales forecasting plays a significant role in product design, packaging, display, advertising, and the degree of success achieved as measured in sales and profit.

This chapter presents some of the marketing "means," or "how-to-do-it" strategies. It covers strategies in these areas: market research and sales forecasting, pricing, channels of distribution, and advertising and sales promotion.

The chapter describes the areas of market research, the sources of marketing information, the steps involved in performing market research, and some of the difficulties encountered. Illustrations of sales forecasts are also presented.

In the area of pricing, the chapter examines markups, price-lining, odd-pricing, as well as other factors affecting pricing.

It then discusses some of the problems in designing your own channels of distribution and presents suggestions for modifying the channels as necessary.

Product and institutional advertising are discussed. Attention is also going to advertising programs, expenditures, policies, and results.

The chapter concludes with a description of sales promotion activities, with particular emphasis on effective media.

Market research consists of fact-finding and forecasting. It should provide a basis for more effective decisions by you and your marketing managers.

MARKET RESEARCH AND SALES FORECASTING

Areas of Market Research

Areas of market research that you should consider are: identification of customers for your firm's products or services; determination of your customers' needs; evaluation of the sales potential for your industry, and your firm; selection of the most appropriate channels of distribution; and evaluation of advertising efficiency.

Market research studies may measure population, income level, purchasing power, and other indexes of sales potential in your trading area. The establishment of accurate sales quotas and measurements of effectiveness in selling depend upon the determination of sales potential.

The following example shows the importance of researching the customers for a company's product.

> The manager of a customer durables manufacturing firm set a goal of industry leadership and a target share of the market to be obtained within a certain period of time.
>
> *Problem:* The company did not attain the desired share of the market. The product line was styled above mass tastes. The designer was designing the product line for department store buyers (prestige stores at that). But three fourths of the company's sales were through furniture stores. The manager realized that he had failed to research the customer adequately.
>
> *Solution:* He arranged for market research. The results indicated that many furniture store buyers were seeking products styled quite differently.[1]

Market research consists of the following steps:

1. Recognizing a problem.
2. Preliminary investigation and planning.
3. Gathering information.
4. Classifying and interpreting the information.
5. Reaching a conclusion.

The difficulties facing your firm should be determined by a careful analysis. Your next step is to review the facts already known, perhaps by discussing them with people inside or outside your firm and by reading trade publications. Once the facts are gathered, their siginficance, interrelationships, and implications for your firm should be determined.

---

[1] T. Stanley Gallagher, *Sound Objectives Help Build Profits* (Washington, D.C.: Small Business Administration, 1965), Management Aids for Small Manufacturers, No. 11.

Sources of Marketing Information

The sources of marketing information consist of: (1) secondary sources of published data, (2) primary sources of published data, and (3) primary sources of unpublished data.

Secondary Sources of Published Data. Secondary sources pertain to data originally compiled and published elsewhere. Examples include:

1. Government publications, such as *Survey of Current Business* and *Statistical Abstract of the United States.*
2. Trade associations reports.
3. Chambers of commerce studies.
4. University research publications.
5. Trade journals.
6. Newspapers.

The U.S. Bureau of the Census regularly collects data on the number of industrial establishments and their sales volume, as well as the number of employees for many industry groups, broken down by county and Standard Metropolitan Statistical Areas (SMSAs). An SMSA contains one city of 50,000 or more inhabitants or "twin cities" with a combined population of that size.

The data are reported by Standard Industrial Classification (SIC) codes. This facilitates research by firms whose sales can be related to their customers' type of activity. The code starts with broad industrial categories, for example, such apparel classification as men's, youth's, and boys' furnishings, work clothing, and allied garments; these are broken down into subclassifications, such as shirts, collars, nightwear, underwear, and neckwear.

Many trade associations and other organizations which gather industrial data also use SIC codes.

Metropolitan newspapers often develop important market data, such as purchasing power information, for their advertising clients. Examples are the Scripps-Howard publications and the Memphis *Commercial Appeal.*

Primary Sources of Published Data. Primary sources of published data are the initial publications containing the data. The U.S. census reports are examples.

Primary Sources of Unpublished Data. Examples of primary sources of unpublished data are your firm's records and data you obtain from your dealers, customers, and competitors.

Sales Forecasting

You should measure your company's potential market in terms of both units and dollars. A sales forecast, both long- and short-range, should be prepared. It is the foundation of your firm's budgeting. Typically, it indicates sales during the last planning period, current sales, and future sales. (See Figure 16–1.)

Using Sales Quotas in Forecasting. Your firm's sales quotas can be used in sales forecasting. They can be used to set targets for your firm, individual salespersons, departments, or sales territories. The quotas should be realistic. Market sampling studies and a study of census data may be used in deriving the quotas.

FIGURE 16-1
Jones Soap Company: Sales Forecast for Brands A, B, and C

Sales	Geographic Market Atlanta, Ga.
Last Year	
Brand A	$10,000
Brand B	56,000
Brand C	37,000
This Year	
Brand A	$12,000
Brand B	69,000
Brand C	42,000
Next Year	
Brand A	$15,000
Brand B	62,000
Brand C	45,000

The Jones Company obtained actual data from its records.
Source: Harry Lipson and John R. Darling, *Introduction to Marketing* (New York: John Wiley and Sons, 1971), pp. 184–85, 347.

An independent manufacturer of automobile dashboard accessories had a problem.

Problem: What new sales territories should be added?

Solution: The manufacturer used *Census of Population* data as an aid in making his decision. His first question was: Where are the high concentrations of automobiles? Then he determined which of the geographic areas being considered had concentrations of automobile supply stores and variety stores, the most appropriate kinds of retail outlets. He found this information in the *Census of Business.*

A manufacturer of paneling and room accessories had franchise arrangements with local contractors who used his products to convert basements into finished rooms.

Problem: What new areas would be best for franchises?

Solution: From census statistics on housing, the manufacturer determined: (1) the types of houses that predominated in a particular area; and (2) whether the houses were built on concrete slabs or with a full basement. He eliminated areas without basements.

Another question: Could people in a given area afford to finish off their basements?

Answer: To answer this question, the manufacturer examined census data on family income, number of children, and car ownership—particularly ownership of more than one car, which indicated discretionary income that might be spent for home improvement. He granted franchises in areas with a good market potential.[2]

Using Sales Representatives' Knowledge. The knowledge obtained

---

[2]Solomon Dutka, *Using Census Data in Small Plant Marketing* (Washington, D.C.: Small Business Administration, 1972), Management Aids for Small Manufacturers, No. 187.

by sales representatives through their customer contacts should also be used in establishing sales quotas.

> An independent company used its salesmen in developing its market plans for a new product, an item used by the steel industry.
>
> *Problem:* The manager needed to estimate the new product's market potential.
>
> *Solution:* A steel plant's use of the new product would be proportionate to the amount of water used by it for cooling purposes. On their regular calls, the company's salesmen asked about the amount of water used at each plant.
>
> The water usage data were compared with each plant's known production. A ratio between production capacity and water usage was calculated. Statistics from the American Iron and Steel Institute were used to calculate the total amount of cooling water used by the steel industry. A list of water usage data was compiled for every steel plant in the country. With this list, the company's salesman determined which plants had the best potential.[3]

Using Questionnaires. When information is needed from a large number of companies, you should consider using mail questionnaires. Sometimes confidential information can be obtained in this way that customers prefer not to give to salesmen. For example, information on the commission percentages that your competitors pay their agents, the market shares obtained by your competitors, and the market potential for your products in various geographic areas may be obtained from mail surveys.

> An independent company made a product used by meat-packing plants.
>
> *Problem:* The manager wanted to determine the sales potential of a 300-county area.
>
> *Solution:* From *County Business Patterns* (a series of booklets published by the U.S. Department of Commerce), he determined the total number and employment of meat-packing plants. He mailed questionnaires to those plants. By analyzing the replies, he learned that an average plant bought $200 worth of his product per employee per year. By multiplying the total employment by $200, he derived the potential sales.[4]

Using Personal Contacts. Certain kinds of questions can best be answered by interviews with your customers and distributors. Some of these questions are:

1. Why are you losing business? Because of price?
2. Is something wrong with your product? Your sales staff?
3. Why don't your distributors push your line harder? Is it your discount schedule? What is the future for your product?

---

[3] Warren R. Dix, *Getting Facts for Better Sales Decisions* (Washington, D.C.: Small Business Administration, 1966), Management Aids for Small Manufacturers, No. 12.

[4] Ibid.

4. Are your customers experimenting with processes that may replace your product? Are they likely to shift to in-house manufacturing of your product?

Sometimes, respondents tell you what they think you want to hear. Some people don't want to hurt your feelings, and they won't tell you that they think your company is behind the times or that your competitor's new models give better service.

You should consider the extent and intensity of your competition. One way to determine how much merchandise you and your competitors sell is to use direct data.

> The manager of a furniture store obtained information on total furniture sales for counties A and B, and determined that his store accounted for 25 percent of county A's furniture sales and 10 percent of county B's. For county A, total furniture sales totaled $3 million, and his store's sales were $750,000.

If sales data are not available for your type of goods in your market area, you should *estimate the volume of business* by relating the sales of your type of merchandise to the sales of other merchandise which is sold in conjunction with yours, or by relating known national data to known local data.

> A tire dealer found the national sales of replacement tires in any one year consistently equaled 10 percent of auto sales three years earlier. He could have used 10 percent of the 1971 automobile sales in his area as his market potential for 1974.

Using Statistical Analyses and Projections. You may also use statistical analyses and projections based on your firm's past sales in developing sales quotas. You may make an accounting analysis of the profitability of selling to particular customers or of selling particular products and in this way you may identify certain low-quality, high-cost customers to whom sales are unprofitable. Furthermore, analysis of your sales records on profitable credit customers may provide good information for merchandising decisions and sales promotion programs. An analysis of your company's accounts receivable aging data—current, 30-day, 60-day, 90-day, and over 90 days—may prove beneficial.

If your store sells many varieties of products, its market share should be measured in total dollar volume rather than in units sold. You should determine your company's total sales and the growth rate of its sales.

Overcoming Market Research Difficulties

A major disadvantage associated with market research in independent businesses is lack of know-how in research techniques. However, the services of outside experts may be secured. Other possibilities include help from trade associations, local chambers of commerce, banks, and field offices of the U.S. Department of Commerce and the Small Business Administration. You should also consider cooperative research with other independent businesses—say, evaluations of traffic flow and parking facilities.

Your firm should closely follow market changes due to shifts in the composition values and preferences, and locations of your customers. "Fad" items and services tend to have a short life cycle. You should plan to "get in and get out" at the right time in order to maximize profits.[5]

You cannot afford all the market research you would like, so you should select projects with the greatest payoff. The objectives of each research project should be carefully specified. You should make market tests before introducing new products.

The form in Exhibit 46 of *The Dow Jones-Irwin Business Papers* should help you determine whether your company's market research and sales forecasting functions are being performed economically and effectively.

PRICING

All items should be priced at a level that provides an adequate profit margin. The policy of pricing "to cover costs" has dangerous long-run implications. Particularly in periods of rapid inflation, costs should be monitored constantly and price changes made to provide for continued profitability.

In order to make use of idle facilities, you may price some items at less than total cost. However, your price should cover the variable costs and make some contribution toward the fixed costs.

You should constantly check your package price structure and your profits based on units sold.

> A new lessee of a club food-beverage concession decided to sell food at cost and make his profits from the sale of beverages. He overlooked the fact that many of his customers were nondrinkers or light drinkers. Therefore, his profits were lower than anticipated.

Your goal should be to find the price-volume combination that will maximize profits. When setting a price strategy, you should consider these factors:

1. Customers and channels of distribution.
2. Competitive and legal forces.
3. Annual volume and life-cycle volume.

---

[5]Successful products go through a life cycle. The stages of the cycle are: (1) the introductory period, in which there is low customer acceptance; (2) a growth period, in which gains are rapid; (3) maturity, in which sales level off; and (4) decline, in which sales fall. In general, the average life of products is decreasing due to rapid technological development and business change.

4. Opportunities for special market promotions.
5. Product group prices.

The product, price, delivery, service, and fulfillment of psychological needs form the total package which the customer buys. A price should be consistent with the product image. Since customers often equate the quality of unknown products with price, raising prices may increase sales.

Price-cutting should be considered as a form of sales promotion. You should reduce a price whenever the added volume resulting from the reduction produces sufficient sales revenue to offset the added costs. However, if an inelastic demand exists for your product, a lower price will not result in greater sales. Your competitors' probable reactions should be considered in determining whether to reduce prices. Independent firms generally should not regard themselves as price leaders.

Markups, price-lining, and odd-pricing are other aspects of pricing you should consider. In calculating the selling price for a particular product, retailers, wholesalers, and manufacturers should add a *markup* to the purchase or manufacturing costs. An initial markup should cover operating—particularly selling—expenses, operating profit, and subsequent price reductions (for example, markdowns and employee discounts). An initial markup may be expressed as a percentage of either the sales price or the product cost. A markup of $8 on a product costing, say, $12 would produce a selling price of $20. The markup would be 40 percent of the sales price and 66 2/3 percent of cost. Consistency should be followed in the use of either base. You need effective cost analysis by products in order to price products effectively. You should recognize that modifications of markup percentages may be needed because of such factors as competitors' prices and the use of loss-leader, or promotional, pricing.

Price-lining refers to the offering of merchandise at distinct price levels. To illustrate, women's dresses might be sold at $40, $60, and $80. Income level and the buying desires of a store's customers are important considerations. Price-lining simplifies customer choice and reduces inventory.

Some independent business managers believe that customers react more favorably to prices ending in odd numbers (*odd-pricing*). Prices ending with "95," such as $29.95, are common for merchandise selling under $50.

By adding extra service or warranties, or paying transportation costs, your firm may sometimes effectively lower price without incurring the retaliation of competitors.

The form in Exhibit 47 of *The Dow Jones-Irwin Business Papers* should help you determine whether your pricing policies and practices are appropriate.

CHANNELS OF DISTRIBUTION AND LOGISTICS

A marketing channel is the pipeline through which a product flows on its way to the ultimate consumer. The choice of channels of distribution is difficult but important.

A small firm manufactured perishable salads which were sold direct to retail food stores. The salads required frequent delivery and close control to ensure freshness. The company diversified into pickles and jelly and selected the same marketing channel for these lines as for the salads. Since pickles and jelly had a longer shelf life, a separate, less expensive channel—wholesalers and chain warehouses—could have been used.

An independent manufacturer added an infant cereal to its product line, and distributed it through its existing marketing channel of drugstores.
Problem: Consumers bought cereal at food stores.
Solution: The manufacturer started using food brokers as a channel.[6]

Designing Your Own Channels of Distribution

Channels should be tailored to the needs of your firm. For example, in order to obtain regional or national coverage of its products, your company may find it productive to use distributors or manufacturers' agents in conjunction with its own sales force.

Your distribution plan should consider these factors:

1. Geographic markets and consumer types arrayed in order of importance.
2. The coverage plan (whether distribution will be through many outlets, selected outlets, or exclusive distributors).
3. The marketing effort expected of each outlet.
4. The marketing effort you, the manufacturer, will contribute.
5. Policy statements concerning areas of conflict.
6. Provision for feedback.
7. Adequate incentives to motivate resellers.

New products commonly require different distribution channels from those needed for well-established and widely accepted products.

A company started selling its new high-priced germicidal toilet soap through drugstores and prestige department stores. When consumer acceptance made the soap a staple, the company selected food stores.[7]

A company may have new markets for its products, and new marketing channels may be required.

A pneumatic drill manufacturer originally sold directly to the mining industry.
Problem: Sales and profits were inadequate.
Solution: The manufacturer selected distributors who were able to cater to the construction market.

[6] Richard M. Clewett, *Checking Your Marketing Channels* (Washington, D.C.: Small Business Administration, 1963), Management Aids for Small Manufacturers, No. 9, p. 38.
[7] Ibid.

A paint manufacturer distributed a new household floor wax through hardware and paint stores, its existing channel.

Problem: The new product was reaching only a small part of the potential market.

Solution: The manufacturer switched to food stores.[8]

If you are a manufacturer, your ultimate outlets should be willing to work with you on product promotion. You may arrange cooperative advertising with your dealers to share promotion costs. You should specify in advance your criteria for the selection of outlets.

Another problem a manufacturer may face is whether to ship directly from the factory or to establish regional warehouses. The latter will provide more rapid service, but probably at higher inventory-carrying costs. However, transshipments among warehouses may permit lower inventories.

Avoid Multiple Channels. Multiple distribution channels sometimes create conflicts. Distribution can be adversely affected unless these conflicts are resolved.

A manufacturer introduced a ladder attachment and selected a large mail-order house as its channel.

Problem: Shipping small quantities to many points greatly increased costs.

Solution: The manufacturer sold the attachments through hardware stores.

Results: Hardware stores refused to sell the attachments because of the greater discounts given to the mail-order house.

Changes in buyers' locations may dictate a change in marketing channels. Changes in buyer concentration may also require a change in marketing channels. Due to the rapid growth of markets in the Far West and the Southwest, many manufacturers have stopped using agents and started selling directly to wholesalers and distributors. **When to Change Your Channels**

Changes in your marketing channels may be revealed through the following indicators:

1. Shifting trends in the types of sources from which users buy.
2. The development of new needs for service or parts.
3. Changes in the amount of the distributors' profits.
4. Changes in the policies and activities of each type of outlet according to customer types and areas, inventory, and promotion.
5. Changes in the financial strength, the sales volume, and the marketing personnel of your own firm.
6. New objectives concerning customer groups and marketing areas.

_____
[8]Ibid.

7. New products.
8. Changes in competitors' distribution plans.

The form in Exhibit 48 of *The Dow Jones-Irwin Business Papers* will assist you in evaluating your channels of distribution and your logistics function.

ADVERTISING

Advertising is used to inform your customers of the availability and uses of your products or services and to convince customers that your products are superior to those of your competitors. In order to be successful, advertising should be based upon quality workmanship and efficient service. It should be closely related to changes in your customers' needs and desires. Rather than advertise on a random, unplanned basis, you should establish an advertising program.

Institutional or product advertising may be used. The purpose of institutional advertising is to keep the public conscious of your company and its good reputation. However, most independent business advertising is of the product type. Determinants of the type of advertising used are:

1. The nature of the business.
2. Company objectives.
3. Industry practice.
4. The media used.

Developing Your Advertising Program

Your advertising programs should be continuous. One-shot advertisements which are not part of a well-planned program are usually ineffective. The proportion of your advertising budget allocated to each medium should be determined by the nature of your market.

> The owner of three well-maintained Laundromats had only a few loyal customers in one of them.
>
> He had advertised in newspapers on a "one-shot" basis every four months at high expense. The money was wasted because most of the newspaper readers lived outside the marketing area of the problem unit.
>
> He decided to make three successive mailings of handbills to potential customers in the immediate vicinity of the problem Laundromat. The desired volume was soon reached.

On the other hand, noncontinuous advertising can be used to prepare your customers for a new product, to suggest new uses for established products, or to announce special sales.

The question of *when to advertise* is very important for your business. Advertising media should reach your present or desired market. You should choose the media that will provide the greatest return for your advertising dollar. You should determine whether your advertising and sales promotion will be used to back up your sales representatives or in place of them. To back up sales representatives, advertising should pave the way by making your company and product well known.

You should develop an *advertising budget*. Standard advertising ratios for your line of business or type of industry are effective guides. *Advertising expenditures* vary with:

1. The type of product.
2. The location, age, and prestige of your firm.
3. The extent of your market.
4. The media used.
5. The business cycle.
6. The amount of advertising by your competitors.

If advertising is a percentage of sales, then your advertising will be at a minimum when it is needed most to increase sales. On the other hand, diminishing returns may be realized from increases in your advertising.

Your *advertising policy* may also govern the amount you spend for advertising given products.

Advertising should be truthful and in good taste. An advertising agency may be invaluable in designing your firm's advertising program, evaluating and recommending advertising media, evaluating the effectiveness of advertising appeals, performing artwork, advising on sales promotion problems, furnishing mailing lists, and making marketing studies to evaluate product acceptance and sales potentials. Suppliers and trade associations may also perform these activities.

When and How to Use an Advertising Agency

Most independent business owner-managers plan and execute their own advertising programs.[9] However, this is often false economy since significant differences exist between materials prepared by professionals and those prepared by amateurs.

Before considering the use of an advertising agency, you should recognize that most advertising expenditures are in the newspaper medium, and that most newspaper advertising is developed within the newspaper organization.

These aspects of using an advertising agency are covered below: the functions of advertising agencies, evaluating agencies, the selection of your agency, the agency-client contract, and achieving an effective agency-client relationship.

The Functions of Advertising Agencies. An advertising agency is an organization of skilled advertising specialists with experience in serving successful business firms in many different industries. Such an agency can help you by:

1. Doing a preliminary study and analysis.
   a. Making a study of your product or service to determine its advantages and disadvantages relative to that of competitors.
   b. Analyzing the location, season, trade and economic conditions, and competition of your present and potential markets.

---

[9] See Frederic R. Gamble, *How Advertising Agencies Help Small Businesses* (Washington, D.C.: Small Business Administration, 1958), Management Aids for Small Business Annual, No. 2, for more information on this subject.

c. Studying your distribution channels.
d. Determining what advertising media can be used most profitably to distribute your product.
2. Developing, implementing, and evaluating your advertising plan.
   a. Developing and presenting an advertising plan for your approval.
   b. Designing, writing, and illustrating your advertisements.
   c. Contracting for your advertising space in its own name.
   d. Forwarding your advertisements to the media with proper instructions.
3. Servicing your radio or television advertising.
   a. Writing or obtaining the program and the commercial copy.
   b. Arranging to have performers present your message on the air.
   c. Contracting for advertising time.
   d. Supervising the production of the program or commercial.
4. Following the appearance of your advertising.
   a. Checking and verifying insertions, displays, or broadcasts.
   b. Auditing, billing, and paying for services and for space or time.

An advertising agency will also coordinate its work with your other sales activities to ensure maximum effect from the advertising. It can help you (usually for a special fee) in such areas as package design, sales research, sales training, the preparations of sales and service literature, merchandising displays, the preparation of house organs, and public relations and publicity.

Evaluating Agencies. Advertising agencies are listed in the National Standard Advertising Register and in classified telephone directories. Interviews with business acquaintances, agency representatives, media representatives, and trade publications and associations will be helpful in evaluating agencies. You might also consider retaining a management or advertising consultant to make the initial contacts.

You should also interview typical clients of several agencies. A key question is: What proportion of its advertising success does the client attribute to its agency's performance? Also, former clients can be asked why they changed agencies.

Agencies which survive the interview process are ready for a formal presentation to you and your management. This presentation should consist of:

1. Agency materials designed to show the agency's ability to solve your needs.
2. Agency reaction to the performance standards suggested by you.
3. Agency reaction to the method of compensation suggested by you.

You may ask advertising agencies to conduct preliminary research, submit a speculative advertising plan, or create a speculative advertising campaign for your products. These activities may be performed at shared cost, covering the direct expenses incurred, or possibly subsidized by you.

In these ways, you should locate bona fide advertising agencies which are qualified to give you the advertising counsel you need.

The Selection of Your Agency. After you narrow down your list to one agency, you should investigate whether it meets these basic qualifications:

1. It should be a bona fide, independent operation, free from undue control by any one advertiser.
2. It should be free from control by a medium owner.
3. It should keep all commissions allowed by media (that is, not rebate any part of the commissions) and devote those commissions to the service and development of the advertising specified in its media contracts.
4. It should possess adequate personnel to serve your needs.
5. It should be able to meet its financial obligations to media owners.

Agency size is less important. You may find that a smaller agency gives you more attention and has smaller overhead costs. You may find it covenient to use a local agency with whose reputation you are familiar. Or you may need the greater staff and specialization of a larger agency.

The Agency-Client Contract. The terms of the contract, or letter of agreement, should be clear, understood, and in writing. The contract should include at least these four points:

1. The term of the contract.
2. The services which the agency will perform.
3. The agency's billing terms—for materials, special services, and all forms of advertising.
4. The rights and duties of the agency and your company if the contract should be terminated.

Achieving an Effective Agency-Client Relationship. A productive relationship between the client and the agency requires mutual confidence and a free exchange of information. The agency's understanding of your needs and wants is critical to the success of the relationship. You should take the initiative in specifying your requirements and in obtaining acceptance of them.

The client should pay the agency promptly so that the agency may meet the media's due dates. The 2 percent cash discount allowed by most media to stimulate prompt payment is given to the client when he pays the agency promptly. The agency is not responsible for the failure of media or suppliers to fulfill their commitments.

An effective agency-client relationship is based upon the following principles:

1. The agency will not handle a product directly competitive with yours.
2. You will not engage the services of a second agency without the first agency's consent.

3. The agency will secure your approval on all advertising expenditures.
4. You will pay the agency at the media's published rates, and the agency will retain the commissions allowed by the media.

You also need to reach agreement with the agency on compensation. The basic methods of compensation may include:

1. Media commissions.
2. Media commissions subject to a minimum fee.
3. Media commissions plus percentage charges, a retainer fee, an incentive fee, and fees for new product development, testing, and commercialization.

The agency needs to know how its performance will be evaluated—that is, by sales results and/or reaching advertising objectives. It also expects information on company products, objectives, and marketing strategies, and on the role expected from advertising.

Your employees should fully understand the collaborative relationship with the agency. They should regard the agency as having a peer relationship with your company.

Copy strategies should be the result of team effort and mutual agreement. These strategies refer to what is stated in the advertising and to whom it is addressed. You know more about your products and their uses, strengths, and limitations than anyone else. You should help the agency to match product benefits with consumer needs.

You should meet regularly with agency representatives to systematically review the agency's work and tell the agency where it stands. Evaluation sessions should be held with agency management to identify strengths, outstanding performance, and troubles—if any. These evaluations should lead to mutually agreed-upon courses of action designed to improve the agency-client relationship and agency performance.

Measuring the Results of Advertising

Assume that you are the owner of an independent retail firm and that you wish to determine whether your advertising is doing the job that you intend it to do. Before the advertisement is composed, you should answer this question: What do you expect the advertising to do for your store? You should divide your advertising into two kinds: *immediate response* and *attitude* advertising. The purpose of immediate response advertising is to entice the potential customer to buy a particular product from your store within a short period of time—today, tomorrow, this weekend, or next week. The results of this type of advertising should be checked daily and at the end of one week, two weeks, and three weeks. The carry-over effects are checked after the first week.

Attitude or "image-building" advertising is the type you use to keep your store's name and merchandise before the public. You continually remind people about your regular products or services or inform them about new or special policies or services. The results of this type of Advertising are more difficult to measure, because you cannot always attribute a specific sale to it. You can measure the results of some attitude advertising, such as a series of ads about your store's brands, one month after their appearance or at the end of a campaign.

Your success in measuring the results of your advertising will depend upon how well the ads have been planned. These pointers are pertinent in planning your ads:

1. Identify your store completely and clearly.
2. Select similar illustrations.
3. Select a typeface and stick to it.
4. Develop easily read copy.
5. Use coupons for direct mail advertising.
6. Get the audience's attention in the first five seconds of a television or radio commercial.

In using radio spots, saturation or blitz may prove to be successful techniques. Radio stations usually have a special package of spot rates, for example, 70 spots in seven days. Alternating between saturated coverage and prime-time spots is economical and effective.

You should consider using these tests for immediate response ads:

1. Coupons to be brought to your store.
2. Letter or phone requests referring to the ads.
3. Split runs by newspapers.
4. Sales of the particular item.
5. Check on store traffic.

Record keeping is essential in testing attitude advertising, because you want to compare ads and sales for an extended time. You may make your comparisons on a weekly basis.

When ads appear concurrently in different media—newspaper, radio and television, direct mail, handbills—you should try to evaluate the relative effectiveness of each medium.

The results of advertising cannot be measured precisely because there are many complicating factors, including the time element, other forces affecting the customers' behavior, changing business conditions, and changes in competitors' advertising.

SALES PROMOTION

Sales promotion consists of activities which have the purpose of making your other sales efforts more effective. Some of the more popular sales promotion techniques are:

1. Creating special displays.
2. Offering premiums.
3. Running contests.
4. Distributing free samples.
5. Offering free introductory services.
6. Demonstrating products.

Sales promotion may be directed toward the ultimate consumers, the trade, and sales representatives.

If you are a retailer, you may consider using promotions, stamps, "two for the price of one," and premiums to obtain new customers. However, you should determine whether these techniques are really effective or are merely reducing your profits. Your window and counter displays should be changed frequently to help bring the merchandise to your customers' attention. Some manufacturers and wholesalers advise on store layouts and personnel training programs, provide free advertising mats, provide short training courses for sales personnel, and maintain a staff of sales engineers to assist in solving customers' problems.

If you are a manufacturer, you may consider the use of trade shows as an advertising and sales promotion medium. These shows are particularly beneficial when your buyers are widely scattered and when you are making significant innovations in equipment each year.

Your sales representatives should be furnished good sales kits, up-to-date promotional materials, and catalogs. If you are selling two or more products, you should decide whether to promote them jointly or separately.

The form in Exhibit 49 of *The Dow Jones-Irwin Business Papers* should help you determine whether your advertising and sales promotion functions are being handled effectively and whether to use an advertising agency.

chapter 17

Selling Your Product or Service

This chapter on personal selling continues the discussion of "how-to-do-it" marketing strategies begun in the previous chapter. It deals with the use of agent middlemen and your own sales force to sell your products or services.

In spite of all your market research, sales forecasting, and advertising and sales promotion, ultimately someone must do some personal selling of your products or services. If you are a manufacturer selling to wholesalers or jobbers, retailers, or industrial users, you should decide whether to use your own sales force or to sell through agent middlemen. Without these middlemen, independent manufacturers would find it difficult to compete.

SELLING THROUGH AGENT MIDDLEMEN

Typically, a new manufacturing firm starts as a local or regional operation seeking sales in a limited market. Since it has a small amount of capital, it generally utilizes existing agency middlemen. If the manufacturer succeeds, he or she may expand to new markets, again probably working through middlemen.

Sometimes, a sequential plan for distribution is adopted by a new manufacturing firm. Having a limited product line, limited finances, and geographically dispersed markets, the firm may use the full-service wholesaler. With growth in financial stability, capabilities, and product line, it may move to a limited use of wholesaler services or to a selling agent, or broker, in selected areas. Still later, it may establish contractual arrangements with manufacturer's agents. Ultimately, the firm may develop its sales force and set up branches. The firm's control over sales increases as this sequence progresses.

Brokers

A broker represents either the buyer or the seller in negotiating purchases or sales. However, the broker is usually the agent of the seller.

Each broker usually specializes in a limited number of items and sells by description or sample. The broker possesses only limited authority over prices and the terms of sale. After a sale is arranged, the seller ships the goods directly to the buyer. The broker receives his commission—usually 1-5 percent of sales—from the principal who sought his services.

Each transaction between a manufacturer and a broker is separate; no obligation exists to maintain a continuing relationship. Firms using brokers are usually buyers or sellers of highly specialized goods and seasonal products not requiring constant distribution. Independent canners, for example, often use brokers.

Selling Agents

On the basis of an extended contract, the selling agent negotiates all sales of a specialized line of merchandise or the manufacturer's entire output. Usually the selling agent has full authority concerning prices and terms, is the sole seller for the line represented, and is not confined to a given market area. Some agents even provide working capital to the manufacturer.

Under this arrangement, the independent manufacturer shifts most of the marketing responsibility to an outside organization and can concentrate on production and other nonmarketing problems. The agent advises the manufacturer on styling and design, and often does sales promotion and advertising—usually on a straight commission.

The manufacturer should recognize the risks involved, since the bargaining power rests predominantly with the agent. First, the agent may engage in price-cutting instead of devoting sufficient effort to selling the manufacturer's output. The manufacturer may also become over-obligated financially to the agent.

Selling agents are engaged primarily in the marketing of textiles, but they also sell coal, lumber, metal products, and canned food. New high-technology companies sometimes use sales agents. However, the highly speculative nature of their unproved products often dictates contractual requirements highly favorable to the agents, particularly if market success is achieved.

Manufacturer's Agents

The manufacturer's agent (or representative) is an independent businessman who sells a part of the output of two or more manufacturers of related but noncompeting products on a continuous, contractual basis in a limited or exclusive territory. Manufacturer's agents are used more often than any other type of agent middlemen.

The manufacturer's agent does not take title to goods, is paid a commission, and has little or no control over prices, credit, or other terms of sale.

Characteristics of Firms Using the Manufacturer's Agent. The manufacturing firm which uses the manufacturer's agent usually:[1]

1. Has sufficient resources for production but not for maintaining its own sales force.
2. Produces a single product—or a narrow line of products—the revenue from which is insufficient to support its own sales force.
3. Has an item going to a market different from that of its major line, where the cost of maintaining separate sales personnel may be too great.
4. Has its own sales force but wishes to expand to areas where the expected sales volume does not warrant the use of its own sales representatives.
5. Finds the administrative problems of maintaining a sales force to be troublesome and undesirable.
6. Wants to retain primary control of distribution policy while shifting some selling to others.
7. Desires to maintain rigid control of selling costs.
8. Desires rapid regional or nationwide distribution.

Characteristics of the Products Handled by the Manufacturer's Agent. The product handled by the manufacturer's agent usually:

1. Is being introduced by a new manufacturer, and the manufacturer's agent can lend his or her prestige to the product.
2. Cannot be handled satisfactorily by wholesale merchants because their salespeople must be conversant with many products.
3. Requires sales personnel with considerable technical knowledge.
4. Involves long periods of negotiation before a sale is completed, necessitating large presale costs and expenses which the manufacturer desires to avoid.

Characteristics of Markets Served by the Manufacturer's Agent. The markets most effectively served by manufacturer's agents are usually:

1. Too small to support a manufacturer's own sales force.
2. Distant, making sales cultivation expensive.
3. Thin, with a few geographically dispersed customers and prospects.
4. Characterized by relatively infrequent sales to individual customers with whom close contact is desirable to avoid possible loss of orders.
5. Somewhat seasonal, but requiring continuous representation to ensure sales.

Selecting the Manufacturer's Agent. The independent firm should try to select a manufacturer's agent who meets the following criteria:

---

[1] Thomas A. Staudt, *A Managerial Introduction to Marketing*, 2d ed. (Englewood Cliffs, N.J.: Prentice-Hall, Inc., 1970), pp. 364–70.

1. His product lines are sufficiently limited to enable him to achieve aggressive representation for the firm.
2. Each product within his line is closely related to the others.
3. The price and quality of the lines he handles are compatible.
4. The territories for all his products are similar or identical so that he is able to obtain maximum trade cultivation and continuous representations of all his client manufacturers.

The independent manufacturer should learn a great deal about the operations of each available agent. No basic conflict should exist between the manufacturer's distribution policies and those of the agent.

Sources of Information about Manufacturer's Agents. The independent manufacturer can obtain information regarding manufacturer's agents from a number of sources, including classified ads in trade papers whose readership is geared toward the type of agent sought; editors or sales representatives of trade magazines; and trade associations of manufacturer's agents. Examples of these associations are the Materials Marketing Associates, Inc., which represents principals who market materials and equipment to the chemical industry; and the Manufacturers' Agents National Association (MANA), which includes agents for all types of goods and services, from costume jewelry to foundry facilities, that are sold throughout the United States.

Many independent manufacturers learn about potential outlets through direct inquiries from manufacturer's agents who express an interest in handling their product lines. A sales inquiry report, such as that shown in Figure 17-1, can be used to indicate prospects, what they asked about, what material they have been sent, the source of their inquiry, and the results of the inquiry follow-up.

Criteria for Selecting a Manufacturer's Agent. Questions that the independent manufacturer should pose in selecting a manufacturer's agent are: What sort of selling skills are needed to sell our products? Does the agent need technical knowledge and experience? Must the agent service our product as well as sell it? Is a one-person agency or a larger organization needed? If the latter, how large? What is the agent's record of success in products and territories similar to those of our company? How long has the agent been in business? What is its reputation, and how well can your company trade on it? Will the other lines carried by the agent be compatible with ours? Will the agent's contracts for its existing lines help gain entry for our line? Is the trade the agent specializes in the one our company wants to reach? Does the agent cover the geographic area needed, and in what depth? Are our two organizations compatible? Do we need an agent that merely follows instructions or one that offers constructive suggestions? Will we enjoy working together?

Contracts and Advance Preparation. The manufacturer should have a comprehensive written contract with its agent. The contract usually includes these items: a definition of the relationship; the territory and

FIGURE 17-1
Sales Inquiry Report

SALES INQUIRY REPORT

Date _____

PROSPECT:

_____
Individual

_____
Position

_____
Company

_____
Address

INQUIRY CONCERNING:

_____

HAS BEEN SENT:

_____ Catalog

_____ Price Schedule

_____ Letter

SOURCE OF INQUIRY:

_____ Ad

_____ Trade Show Exhibit

_____ Direct Mail

_____ Undetermined

_____ Other

RESULTS OF INQUIRY FOLLOW-UP:

Prospect Contacted on _____
                              Date

Inquirer Plans to Sell $ _____

of _____
          Products

_____ Good Future Prospect

Follow-Up on _____
                      Date

_____ Wanted Information Only

_____ No Interest

Comments: _____

_____

_____

_____

Signed _____

Date _____

Source: Adapted from Roger M. Pegram, *Selecting and Evaluating Distributors* (New York: National Industrial Conference Board, Inc., 1965), Studies in Business Policy, No. 116, p. 14.

coverage; the products to be sold; the sales policy; prices, terms, and customer credit responsibility; product warranties; invoices; collections; cancellations; order changes; returns; commissions and methods of computing and allocating them; servicing obligations of the factory and representatives; sales aids; and the rights of the principal and the representative under consummation and termination.

Policies to Consider in Managing a Manufacturer's Agent. The independent manufacturer should consider these policies: training, merchandising aids and support, commissions, and relationships with the agent.

Training. Following the appointment of a manufacturer's agent, arrangements should be made by the manufacturer to have the agent spend enough time at the plant to obtain an intimate knowledge of the product, the manufacturing processes, company policies, and the marketing program. The training period should be brief (because the agent cannot afford to be away from his or her own business very long), and it should be carefully planned and conducted.

Merchandising Aids and Support. The agent should be supplied with adequate tools to operate effectively. Display stocks, swatch or sample books, and other promotional aids, as well as market data, should be integrated with the agent's operations. Engineering and sales assistance should be made available when necessary. Manufacturers should solicit suggestions from agents about the most effective methods of merchandising and should make a sincere effort to honor any reasonable requests from agents for information, records, and other data.

Commissions. Adequate commissions should be established, both to attract high-caliber agents and to promote aggressive representation. Agents usually receive straight commissions of about 6 percent, with a range of 2-20 percent, depending on the type of the goods.

Relationships with the Manufacturer's Agent. Once a manufacturer's agent is operating in the field, the manufacturer should try to build up mutual confidence and cooperation. The manufacturer should state sincerely that permanent representation is anticipated. The manufacturer should develop a friendly personal relationship with its agent. However, the agent should not be overburdened with detail.

Evaluation of the Performance of the Manufacturer's Agent. The performance of your agent should be evaluated periodically. Standards of performance should be developed and measurement techniques devised. Sales quotas may be established for each territory, product line, and customer group. Actual performance can be evaluated by continuous examination of orders, invoices, and reseller inventories. Other indices are: reseller and consumer satisfaction, the quantity and quality of advertising, promptness in paying bills, and the amount of new business.

USING YOUR OWN SALES REPRESENTATIVES

Having your own sales representatives will require the greatest investment. Yet, in the case of a highly specialized technical product, it will probably be most effective.

Effective selling should be built upon a foundation of product knowledge. The sales representative who understands the product's advantages, uses, and limitations can educate the potential customer and may be able to suggest new uses of the product.

The critical part of personal selling is the sales presentation to the prospect. A sales representative should adapt the sales approach to the customer's needs and meet every objection. Enthusiasm, friendliness, and persistence are valued traits in a sales representative. A "hard-sell" approach is sometimes advocated for intangible products and services, for example, selling life insurance.

You should decide whether to assign your sales representatives to industry, government, and institutional customers or to assign them by product classification.

Your firm should have a basic sales strategy which includes these features:

1. The number of accounts per representative and the average account size.
2. The compensation plan—salary, commission, salary plus commission, salary plus commission with bonus—and the method of paying expenses.
3. The cost of obtaining new accounts versus the cost of holding old accounts. This comparison determines how much time a representative should spend servicing accounts of a certain size.
4. The use of overlapping or exclusive territories.
5. The use of sales representatives who are specialists in one of your products or lines or of generalists who will handle your entire line.

Specialists are easier to train and provide greater impact. One generalist representative per customer may be less confusing. Fewer high-quality, highly paid representatives may be preferable to a larger number of less competent representatives. Owner-managers of independent businesses often find that only a few customers account for a major proportion of total sales.

> The owner of a company distributing supplies to an industrial market analyzed the firm's accounts, and found that 2 percent of the customers accounted for one half of the total sales and more than one half of the gross profits. More than 90 percent of the customers accounted for less than 10 percent of the sales. An analysis of representatives' call reports showed that they were spending most of their time on the small accounts and that many big accounts with good sales and profit potential were being neglected.[2]

Through analysis of your sales records, you may find out which products should be promoted, which products should be carried even though their profit margin is small, which products should be dropped,

---

[2]Warren R. Dix, *Getting Facts for Better Sales Decisions* (Washington, D.C.: Small Business Administration, 1966), Management Aids for Small Manufacturers, No. 12.

which territories are overstaffed or undermanned, and which customers are profitable.

You should provide for continuous or special training programs for your representatives and hold regularly scheduled meetings with them. *Contests* tied into promotions are often desirable. The effectiveness of contests may be improved when the rewards include benefits for the representatives' spouses. A guide for improving a sales representative's performance is presented in the appendix at the end of Chapter 18.

Your sales organization should be working closely with the manufacturing department. The representatives' delivery promises and production's output should be matched. Good working relationships should also exist between your sales organization and market research.

You should determine whether to place your best sales representatives in the most lucrative markets to compete with your top competitors or to have these representatives seek untapped markets. Efficient routing of your traveling representatives and the making of appointments prior to their arrival are cost-saving practices that should be adopted.

Your representatives can maximize profits by emphasizing high-margin items. But they should look beyond the immediate sale to build customer goodwill and to help create satisfied future customers. *High ethical standards are vital.*

In determining whether to enter a territory, you should compare incremental costs and incremental income. You should drop a territory when its cost contribution exceeds its income contribution.

Either you or one of your top executives should support a representative when he is experiencing difficulties in obtaining a big account. Preferably, he should initially seek and request your assistance. Your representatives should be given an opportunity to be trained and promoted into management positions.

You should utilize sales reports, and stress major facts and trends rather than details. The reports should show all variances between budgeted and actual sales. You should immediately investigate all excessive deviations upward or downward in order to find their causes. Long-term sales contracts with customers should have protective escalation clauses incorporated in them, particularly under inflationary conditions.

To assist your sales manager in managing your sales force effectively, you should consider using the following techniques: job descriptions for salespersons, market evaluation reports, lost sales reports, product service reports, and sales performance evaluations.

Using Job Descriptions for Salespersons

The general use of job descriptions was covered in Chapter 9. However, since they are of great importance in achieving personal selling effectiveness, they merit additional coverage at this point.

The components of the job description of salesperson, as shown in Figure 17-2, are: (1) the job title; (2) a statement of the basic objective

FIGURE 17–2
Job Description of Salesperson

1. POSITION TITLE:

    Salesperson

2. BASIC OBJECTIVE:

    Will represent the _____ in the territory described in the agreement
    Company

    by maintaining excellent relations with current customers and by seeking to
    increase the number of such customers. Will be sensitive to special customer
    situations that may call for special treatment. Will be alert to all events and
    situations that affect the success of the _____ in maintaining and
    Company

    improving its position as a supplier of its product to corporations in the
    territory.

3. LINE RELATIONSHIP:

    Reports to the sales manager.

4. FUNCTIONAL RELATIONSHIPS:

    Reports market and credit information to appropriate staff managers.

5. SPECIFIC RESPONSIBILITIES:

    The salesperson should:

    1. Average at least five sales calls per day.
    2. Whenever possible, encourage customers to place their orders
        directly by telephone.
    3. Keep transportation and other expenses to a minimum and seek
        prior approval for entertainment expenses in excess of $____ per
        week.
    4. Inform the sales office of whereabouts by filing weekly itineraries.
    5. Submit orders in the form prescribed by the company and keep
        the sales manual up to date.

    Source: Adapted from Victor P. Buell and Carl Heyel, *Handbook of Modern Marketing*
    (New York: McGraw-Hill Book Company, 1970), p. 12–27.

of the job; (3) a description of the line organizational relationship; (4) a
description of the functional relationships; and (5) a listing of the salesperson's specific responsibilities.

A market evaluation report, such as the one shown in Figure 17–3, **Market Evaluation**
may be used by each salesperson to report to your sales manager, field **Report**
observations pertaining to promotions, competition, direct accounts, retailers, and personal activities.

Unfortunately, lost sales do occur, even in the best of businesses. **Lost Sales Report**
However, important information can be gleaned from salespersons' experi-

FIGURE 17–3
Market Evaluation Report

MARKET EVALUATION REPORT

Field Observations to Sales Manager (promotions, new products, displays, account advertising, etc.):

_____
_____
_____
_____

Competitive (new products, new promotions, new prices, new policies, etc.):

_____
_____
_____

Direct Accounts (promotions established, sales meetings, sales drives, new distribution, etc.):

_____
_____
_____

Retailers (new stores, creative aids used, promotions established, etc.):

_____
_____
_____

Personal Activities (trade relations, creative selling, etc.):

_____
_____

Invoicing Current Month: Objective $_____   Plans for Making Objectives: _____

                                      To Date   _____   _____

                                      To Go   _____   _____

Explanation of Absence from Territory: _____

_____

Source: Adapted from E. Patrick McGuire, *Salesmen's Call Reports* (New York: The Conference Board, Inc., 1972), p. 85.

FIGURE 17-4
Lost Sales Report

```
┌─────────────────────────────────────────────────────────────────────┐
│                          LOST SALES REPORT                            │
│                                                                       │
│   Quantity:  Product and Model    Intended End Use—Location    Reason for Loss of Sale │
│                                                                       │
│   ─────────────────────────────────────────────────────────────────  │
│                                                                       │
│   ─────────────────────────────────────────────────────────────────  │
│                                                                       │
│   ─────────────────────────────────────────────────────────────────  │
│                                                                       │
│   ─────────────────────────────────────────────────────────────────  │
│                                                                       │
│   ─────────────────────────────────────────────────────────────────  │
│                                                                       │
│                                                                       │
│   Report for Month of _____   Submitted by _____  │
│                                                                       │
└─────────────────────────────────────────────────────────────────────┘
```

Source: Adapted from E. Patrick McGuire, *Salesmen's Call Reports* (New York: The Conference Board, Inc., 1972), p. 91.

ences in connection with such sales. A form for obtaining this information is presented in Figure 17-4.

Product Service Report

Customers often complain about products or services. You may consider using the product service report, presented in Figure 17-5, to obtain information pertaining to such complaints and to assess how to handle them most economically and effectively.

Sales Performance Evaluation

Employee evaluation was described in Chapter 10, and a form for that purpose was shown in Figure 10-2. However, since the effectiveness of salespersons is so vital to the success of your business, the use of a sales performance rating form may be justified. Figure 17-6 illustrates a trait-rating approach that should enable your sales manager to evaluate the performance of each of your salespersons.

The form in Exhibit 50 of *The Dow Jones-Irwin Business Papers* should help you evaluate whether your selling function is being performed economically and effectively.

FIGURE 17–5
Product Service Report

```
┌─────────────────────────────────────────────────────────────┐
│                   PRODUCT SERVICE REPORT                      │
│                                                               │
│  To: _____ Date _____  │
│            Department                                         │
│                                                               │
│  Account: _____ │
│                                                               │
│  Dealer: _____ │
│                                                               │
│  Address: _____ │
│                                                               │
│  Invoice No.: _____ Invoice Date: _____ │
│                                                               │
│  1. The complaint is the result of:                          │
│                                                               │
│        _____ Truck Damage                                 │
│                                                               │
│        _____ Factory Defect                               │
│                                                               │
│        _____ Salesperson or Administrative Error          │
│                                                               │
│        _____ Other                                        │
│                                                               │
│  2. Description of Complaint: _____ │
│                                                               │
│     _____ │
│                                                               │
│     _____ │
│                                                               │
│     _____ │
│                                                               │
│  3. Date Inspected: _____                 │
│                                                               │
│  4. Will Customer Repair Material? _____ │
│                                                               │
│  5. What Allowance Will the Customer Accept?   $ _____   │
│                                                               │
│  6. Remarks: _____ │
│                                                               │
│     _____ │
│                                                               │
│     _____ │
│                                                               │
│                                         Territory_____  │
└─────────────────────────────────────────────────────────────┘
```

Source: Adapted from E. Patrick McGuire, *Salesmen's Call Reports* (New York: The Conference Board, Inc., 1972), p. 86.

FIGURE 17-6
Sales Performance Rating Form

	Exceptional	Good	Fair	Poor
New business development	Develops new business to the fullest extent of the territory. Has intimate familiarity with customers' business. Develops the best possible contacts. Develops new applications. sells our service, and knows where products are used on various types of equipment. Initiates many new projects. Knows competition and handles competitive bidding exceptionally well. Always follows through to close the sale.	Develops new business with major accounts. Maintains contacts with appropriate people. Obtains new applications; initiates projects well. Knows of various applications for our products. Knows competition and handles competitive bidding well. Rarely fails to follow through to close sales.	Has sold standard products to major accounts but avoids new product development. Contacts the same people in a company. Rarely initiates a new project or new application. Knows only a few customers. Follows major bids only and has pet products and projects. Avoids contacting government agencies and has only spotty information about competition and product applications. Often fails to close sales.	Does not develop new business in territory. Does not make or maintain appropriate contacts at various major companies. Pays little attention to competition or to product applications. Fails to follow competitive bids. Sells only pet products and spends most of his time on advertising leads. Rarely closes a sale.
Directed effort	Enthusiastically follows company sales programs, often expanding objectives. Has exceptional planning ability. Prepares special sample selections and data prior to calls. Faithfully reports specific applications. Searches leads furnished by the company and finds other sources. Follows instructions in an outstanding fashion. Often offers suggestions and ideas. Reads trade magazines. Devotes appropriate time to all products. Uses all sales tools. Has thorough knowledge of all company policies.	Enthusiastically follows company sales programs without letting normal promotions decline. Has good planning ability. Uses all sales tools, directories, sales kits and so on. Reports product applications. Follows product applications. Follows instructions well. Sells all products. Knows major policies of company.	Accomplishes only the minimum of company sales programs. Gives excuses for declines in business. Trips haphazard and without specific purpose. Often misses calls that should be included. Often not equipped with basic sales tools, personnel to see, and so on. Follows instructions reluctantly at times. Has limited understanding of company policies.	Accomplishes only a small part of company sales programs and appears to ignore company objectives. Usually poorly equipped. with sales tools. Ignores management requests and fails to perform or report. Leaves important regions of territory uncovered. Ignores company policies.
Service	Knows customer operating problems. Can solve them. Works well with customer's organization. Allots sufficient time to customer complaints, handles them tactfully, and explains the company point of view.	Looks for customer's problems. Usually works well with customer's organization. Keeps customers' complaints to a minimum and maintains their confidence. Handles complaints tactfully with a proper balance of customer and company interests.	Fair knowledge of customers' problems. Weak in defining problems. Has some difficulty in working with customer's organization and some irate customers. Customers have little confidence in his handling of their complaints. Generally takes the customer's side completely.	Pays little attention to customers' problems. Lets the company worry about complaints. Allots little or no time to servicing customers Customers demonstrate no confidence in him. Frequently expresses sullen attitude toward company due to customers' complaints.

FIGURE 17-6 (continued)

| Overall performance | Maintains and protects present business. Is a good closer on all types of accounts. Engages in self-improvement. Impresses customers with neatness, voice, self-confidence, and courtesy. Is enthusiastic and persevering. Has high character. Is very valuable. | Maintains present business. Sells additional items to most accounts. Puts new knowledge to practical use. Is well-groomed, neat, and pleasant. Makes good overall impression. Has enthusiasm and is a good worker. Has good character. Is valuable. | Calls on most accounts regularly. Gets fair amount of new business. Occasionally applies new knowledge. Has fair appearance. Lacks self-confidence. Is not always persuasive | Makes spotty regular calls. Cannot sell new accounts. Is poor closer. Is not well-groomed and might show poor taste. Is unenthusiastic. Is of questionable value. |

Source: Adapted from David A. Weeks, *Incentive Plans for Salesmen*, (New York: National Industrial Conference Board, Inc., 1970), Studies in Personnel Policy, No. 217, p. 61.

chapter 18

Managing Your Sales

This chapter is about setting up sales territories and planning and controlling the activities of your salespeople.

SETTING UP SALES TERRITORIES

Independent firms can improve their marketing performance by carefully controlling their selling activities, especially through giving specific salespeople responsibility for definite territories. Consequently, you and your managers should consider setting up sales territories and establishing routine schedules for your sales representatives.[1]

Why Have Territorial Assignments?

In addition to your broad objective of controlling sales operations, your more specific objectives would include:

1. Attaining thorough coverage of the market.
2. Assigning each sales representative a reasonable overall task.
3. Placing definite responsibility on each sales representative.
4. Providing management with valid criteria for judging the performance of sales representatives.
5. Reducing sales expenses by eliminating duplication of effort and obtaining more effective coverage.
6. Facilitating the budgeting of sales expenses and the performance of distribution cost accounting.
7. Improving your relations with customers.

Assigning Market Responsibilities

One method for assigning market responsibilities to your sales representatives is to permit each sales representative to handle a specified list of

---

[1] Edwin H. Lewis, *How to Set Up Sales Territories* (Washington, D.C.: Small Business Administration, 1958), Management Areas for Small Business, Annual No. 3, pp. 16–23.

customers. This method is frequently used by companies having a small sales organization. Every salesperson retains the accounts which he or she has obtained and contacts them regardless of their location. When a new salesperson is hired, he or she obtains new accounts wherever they can be found. Over time, however, your salespeople would follow routes that tend to resemble a poorly designed spider web. Once this method takes root, it becomes more difficult to shift to another approach. Adopting another system disrupts working relationships between sales representatives and customers, endangers the morale of the sales organization, and frequently results in the loss of both customers and salespeople.

A preferable way of handling field assignments is to make each sales representative responsible for a geographic area. Each salesperson is then responsible for obtaining his or her full share of the potential business in that area. Appropriate sales quotas and cost controls can be set up by territory. Each salesperson understands the selling problems peculiar to his or her territory.

Guideposts You Should Use

Five guideposts for setting up territories are:

1. Keep the size of the territory practical.
2. Plan efficient sales-call routes.
3. Use established geographic boundaries—political or census areas—wherever possible.
4. Group territories by trading areas.
5. Design territories for equal potential.

Steps in Setting Up Sales Territories

You should follow seven principal steps in establishing sales territories for your firm.

1. Secure information on the distribution of sales by states, counties, metropolitan centers, or trade areas for each product or product class. For example, estimates of total retail sales by metropolitan county areas and by ten store groups (food, lumber, hardware, drugs, and so on) are made by *Sales Management* annually and published in its June issue, "Survey of Buying Power."

Sales data for products and product classes may be secured from the decennial census, trade associations, and other sources. Using actual past sales by territories, you can prepare an index showing the proportion of total sales made in each territory.

An alternative is to develop an index of potential demand. *Sales Management* prepares an annual "Buying Power Index" which provides breakdowns by counties, metropolitan areas, and principal cities. Even though this index does not pertain to particular products, it can be used to determine that a particular county might be expected to take, say, 2 percent of the total sales of a product. Such data can be applied to estimate either your industry sales or your company's sales. To illustrate, if from past industry sales and an analysis of business conditions you estimate that total sales for the next year will be 200,000 units, or $100 million, the county could be expected to take 2 percent, or 4,000 units, or $2 million.

2. Determine, on the basis of past experience and the strength of competition, the percentage of potential sales which your company can expect to obtain in each territory. Applied to potential industry sales, these percentages should provide you with estimates of your firm's potential sales. For example, if you estimate that you should receive 10 percent of total industry sales in the county, you would sell 400 units in the county.

You may also secure unit and dollar sales estimates from your sales representatives or branch managers. These estimates are then combined to make an industry sales forecast or a company sales forecast, or both.

3. Pinpoint on a map the location of customers or potential customers. The latter should be classified in terms of their relative importance. It is often unnecessary or undesirable to call on all customers on every trip.

4. Determine the average number of calls that can be made in one day. Make a detailed study of the sales representative's job and of the time he spends on his various activities. The travel time required for each call should be included.

5. Group the customers into logical territories. Start at some geographic point, preferably a major trading center. The full-time services of one or more people may be needed in a large city.

6. Beginning with the city, bring together contiguous counties which constitute either a complete trading area or an appropriate portion of a trading area. Large sales territories may consist of sections of several cities. Small territories usually comprise a number of counties around the trading center. There are now about 230 Standard Metropolitan Statistical Areas in the United States.

One of the published trading area studies could be used. These are maps of the United States which show trading centers, together with the boundaries of their trading areas. The maps show either wholesale or retail trading areas. Several kinds of trading-area maps are available. For example, the U.S. Department of Commerce has analyzed wholesale trading areas for groceries and dry goods. The National Wholesale Druggists Association has outlined wholesale areas for drugs. Consumer trading area maps include "Market Areas in the United States," published by Curtis Publishing Company; "Consumer Trading Areas," published by Dartnell Corporation; and "The New Marketing Map of the United States," published by Hearst Magazines, Inc.

7. Each territory should be rechecked in terms of the total business expected and problems of physical coverage. In determining the total potential business available in a given territory, the following publications should be consulted: *County Business Patterns;* the *Sales Management*

"Survey of Buying Power"; the U.S. censuses of business, population, and housing; and the *Survey of Current Business.*

In addition to past sales and sales potentials, other factors that should be considered include:

1. Variations in the product.
2. The extent of market development.
3. The channel of distribution.
4. The nature of the work assigned.
5. Competition.
6. The caliber of the salespersons.
7. Changes in business conditions.
8. The possibilities of specialization.

Routing Sales Personnel

Should definite routes be set for sales personnel, or should they be free to route themselves? Usually no clear-cut answer exists to this question. Salespeople should be consulted about routing patterns, and they should be satisfied that the schedule is workable. An important source of data is field experience with the selling job to be done, the frequency of calls, the possibility of following a regular route, and the caliber of the salespeople. If calls are made irregularly, and if the sales representatives are primarily troubleshooters or service people, a fixed routing schedule would probably have little value. Routing schedules are most useful when calls are regular and frequent and when relatively little time needs to be spent with each customer.

Firms which sell to retailers often make good use of a routing pattern. Firms selling to manufacturers and wholesalers find such patterns less valuable.

The first step in routing is to make a list of customers, together with the frequency of calls on them. The average length of a call is determined either for each customer group or for each individual customer. Routes are then constructed to cover an area efficiently.

Routes should be tested and revised until both you and your salespeople believe they are the best that can be developed. The routes should be followed, and reports should be filed by the sales representatives and checked by the sales supervisor.

The owner-managers of many independent companies ask their salespeople to plan a route for each trip in advance, make the necessary arrangements for it, and adhere to it instead of following the above procedure.

The Territory Agreement

To assist your sales manager and your salespeople in increasing the effectiveness of their sales planning, you may consider using a "territory agreement." The agreement usually includes: (1) a preamble; (2) specification of markets and customers; (3) specification of products and services; and (4) specification of current targets and objectives.

Since the agreement is a contract between the employer and the sales representative for an extended period typically one year, it is usually

FIGURE 18-1 Territory Agreement

Preamble

This agreement is to be between _____ and the _____ for a period
                                Salesperson   Company

of 12 months from January 1 to December 31, 19___. During the period,
_____ agrees to represent the Company, and the Company agrees that he
Salesperson

shall represent it, in the territory described below. _____ will use his best
                                                        Salesperson

efforts to maintain excellent relations with current customers in his territory and
to increase the number of such customers. For its part, the Company will keep
_____ fully informed at all times of changes in its policies, product lines, or
Salesperson

services and will provide him with all the technical support that, in the opinion
of his manager, will best enable him to pursue these goals.

Markets and Customers

The territory assigned to _____ includes all establishments engaged in
                            Salesperson

the business of _____. Specifically, _____ will cultivate
                                                        Salesperson

the following firms, which are now regular customers of the company.

List of Regular Customers

However, _____ is not to limit his efforts to satisfying these customers
            Salesperson

and should seek every opportunity to secure new customers.

Products and Services

This territory is designed to include the right and responsibility to sell the
Company's equipment; _____ has no right or responsibility to sell any
                        Salesperson

other products manufactured by the Company.

It is _____ responsibility to develop expert knowledge of his assigned
        Salesperson's

products and to maintain his sales manual in up-to-date status by filing additional
and replacement pages within one day after their receipt. It is further
_____ responsibility to understand fully the technical services offered by
Salesperson's

the Company's sales support department and to work closely with the support
representative assigned to his branch office.

Targets and Objectives

In the 12 months from January to December 19 _____, the following are the
objectives for this territory:

1. A sales dollar volume of $_____.
2. An expense-to-sales ratio of _____ percent.
3. Gaining seven new major accounts.

Source: Adapted from Victor P. Buell and Carl Heyel, *Handbook of Modern Marketing*
(New York: McGraw-Hill Book Company, 1970), pp. 12–28.

written in semilegal terms. The salesperson should be asked to read the document carefully and sign it. An example of this type of agreement is shown in Figure 18-1.

The form in Exhibit 51 of *The Dow Jones-Irwin Business Papers* can help you determine whether your sales territories have been established correctly.

PLANNING AND CONTROLLING THE ACTIVITIES OF YOUR SALESPEOPLE

There are many techniques, forms, and activities that you can use to help your salespeople. In essence, they involve you and your salespeople in planning their activities and you and your managers in controlling how those activities are carried out.

Among the forms which can be used are the account objectives form, the salesperson's annual planning work sheet, the call and route planning report, the call planning form, the weekly itinerary form, and the salesperson's daily call report.

The Account Objectives Form

An annual sales objective can be established for each account your salespeople call on. The objectives can be established and entered on an account objectives form, as shown in Figure 18-2. This figure is then allocated among the 12 months, considering seasonal patterns.

FIGURE 18-2
Account Objectives Form

ACCOUNT OBJECTIVES FORM

Account Objectives for Year 19-- - 19-- Salesperson____________________

Location	CF	Account Name	Jan.	Feb.	Mar.	Apr.	May	Jun.	Jul.	Aug.	Sept.	Oct.	Nov.	Dec.	Total for Yr.

Source: Adapted from *Sales Analysis* (New York: National Industrial Conference Board, Inc., 1965), Studies in Business Policy, No. 113, p. 8.
Note: CF = Call frequency per month.

The salesperson's annual planning work sheet (Figure 18-3) shows the sales volume goals of each sales representative, based on individual accounts, and the support needed by the salesperson.

The Salesperson's Annual Planning Work Sheet

FIGURE 18-3
Salesperson's Annual Planning Work Sheet

SALESPERSON'S ANNUAL PLANNING WORK SHEET

Salesperson__________ Route______ Date Completed________

Sales Manager: ________________

Name and Address of Account:____________________

Sales in Dollars
2 Years Ago______ Last Year______ Goal this Year________

Salesperson's Plan:

Support Needed:

Source: Adapted from William J. McBurney, Jr., *Goal Setting and Planning at the District Sales Level* (New York: American Management Association, Inc., 1963), AMA Research Study 61, p. 33.

The Call and Route Planning Report

Another form that can be beneficial is the call and route planning report in (Figure 18-4). It enables the salesperson to set objectives, determine the most important activities, and establish a monthly work plan.

Call Planning Form

Planning for each phase of the sales call—including the approach, presentation, objectives, and closing—is vital. A form which may be used to train your sales representatives in call planning is presented in Figure 18-5.

FIGURE 18-4
Call and Route Planning Report

```
CALL AND ROUTE PLANNING REPORT

Sales Plans Guide—Month of: _____

For: _____

Objective: _____
_____
_____

          The Most Important Things to Do—in Order of Importance
1._____    4. _____
2._____    5. _____
3._____    6. _____

                    Work Plan for the Month

          Monday   Tuesday   Wednesday   Thursday   Friday
1st
Week
_____
2d
Week
_____
3d
Week
_____
4th
Week
_____
5th
Week
_____
```

Source: Adapted from E. Patrick McGuire, *Salesmen's Call Reports* (New York: The Conference Board, Inc., 1972), p. 29.

The Weekly Itinerary Form

The weekly itinerary form is designed to stimulate careful scheduling of sales calls each week. A copy of the form may be given to each salesperson and the sales manager every Friday. An example is shown in Figure 18-6.

FIGURE 18-5
Call Planning

```
┌─────────────────────────────────────────────────────────────┐
│                      CALL PLANNING                           │
│                                                              │
│  Company:                                                    │
│                                                              │
│  Address:                          Phone:                    │
│                                                              │
│  Name of Customer or Prospect:                               │
│                                                              │
│  A.  Objective of Call:                                      │
│                                                              │
│  B .  Essential Information                                   │
│          Company:                                            │
│                                                              │
│        Individual:                                           │
│                                                              │
│  C.  Techniques                                              │
│                                                              │
│      Approach:                                               │
│                                                              │
│                                                              │
│      Presentation:                                           │
│                                                              │
│                                                              │
│      Objections                                              │
│                                                              │
│                                                              │
│      Closing:                                                │
│                                                              │
│                                                              │
└─────────────────────────────────────────────────────────────┘
```

Source: Adapted from Victor P. Buell and Carl Heyel *Handbook of Modern Marketing* (New York: McGraw-Hill Book Company, 1970), pp. 12-26.

On the salesperson's daily call report (Figure 18-7), information for customer calls and prospect calls are shown separately. The salesperson's success in winning new customers and holding old ones may be determined by tracing the reports from quarter to quarter.

The Salesperson's Daily Call Report

The following calculations may be made for each salesperson: number of days worked, total calls made, total orders taken, average number of calls per day, and average number of calls needed to secure an order. All of this information is helpful in reviewing the individual salesperson's performance over time and in comparing the salespersons with one another.

You should develop a marketing mix. Basic variables in this mix are the "four P's:

THE MARKETING MIX

1. Product.   3. Promotion.
2. Place.   4. Price.

FIGURE 18-6
Weekly Itinerary

```
┌─────────────────────────────────────────────────────────────┐
│                    WEEKLY ITINERARY                          │
│                                                              │
│  To: _____  Week Ending: _____    │
│                                                              │
│  Location: _____                                   │
│                                                              │
│  From: _____                                       │
│                                                              │
│         Account Name              Reason(s) for Call         │
│      _____        │
│  Mon.                                                        │
│      _____        │
│                                                              │
│      _____        │
│                                                              │
│      _____        │
│                                                              │
│      _____        │
│                                                              │
│      _____        │
│                                                              │
│      _____        │
│                                                              │
│  Hotel/Motel _____        │
│                                                              │
│  Tues.                   ...                                 │
│                                                              │
│  Wed.                    ...                                 │
│                                                              │
│  Thurs.                  ...                                 │
│                                                              │
│  Fri.                    ...                                 │
│                                                              │
└─────────────────────────────────────────────────────────────┘
```

Source: Adapted from *Sales Analysis* (New York: National Industrial Conference Board, Inc., 1965), Studies in Business Policy, No. 113, p. 30.

The right *product* for the target market should be developed. *Place* refers to the channels of distribution. *Promotion* refers to any method that communicates with the target market. The right *price* should be determined to move the right product to the right place with the right promotion for the target market.

The manufacturer of a line of good-quality costume jewelry sold to retail jewelry stores. The owner wanted his company to grow faster. The company used no sales representatives, but advertised in monthly trade magazines, employed order-takers, attended trade shows, and had good service, pricing, and packaging.

FIGURE 18-7
Salesperson's Daily Call Report

```
┌─────────────────────────────────────────────────────────────────┐
│                 SALESPERSON'S DAILY CALL REPORT                   │
│                                                                   │
│  Name:_____ Date:_____No.:_____   │
│                                                                   │
│  Hotel/Motel:_____ Town and State:_____    │
│                                                                   │
│  No. Customer Calls—Name and City    Direct   Phone   Out  Remarks│
│                                      Order                        │
│  ───────────────────────────────────────────────────────────────│
│  1                                                                │
│  ───────────────────────────────────────────────────────────────│
│  2                                                                │
│  ───────────────────────────────────────────────────────────────│
│  3                                                                │
│  ───────────────────────────────────────────────────────────────│
│                              · · ·                                │
│                                                                   │
│  7                                                                │
│  ───────────────────────────────────────────────────────────────│
│                          Prospect Calls                           │
│  ───────────────────────────────────────────────────────────────│
│  1                                                                │
│  ───────────────────────────────────────────────────────────────│
│                              · · ·                                │
│  5                                                                │
│  ───────────────────────────────────────────────────────────────│
│  Salesperson Complete:   Total Calls Made  _____        │
│                                                                   │
│                          Total Orders Taken _____       │
│                                                                   │
│                              Approved by_____  │
│                                              Sales Manager        │
└─────────────────────────────────────────────────────────────────┘
```

Source: Adapted from *Sales Analysis* (New York: National Industrial Conference Board, Inc., 1965), Studies in Business Policy, No. 113, p. 13.

Owner's Study: The sales volume of each area of the country was examined over a three-year period. Sales were lagging in the southeastern area.

New Marketing Mix: Advertising outlays were reduced in the southeastern area, and a sales representative was hired for the area.

Results: Sales grew more rapidly in the southeastern area than in any other area of the country. The sales representative concentrated her efforts on retail jewelry stores with the largest growth potentials.

Next Phase: Point-of-purchase displays and advertising mats for retailers were developed. More sales representatives were hired.

Results: Sales doubled in two years and continued to increase substantially thereafter.[2]

After developing an integrated marketing strategy, you should check it by getting affirmative answers to these questions:

1. Are all marketing activities—market research, personal selling, advertising and promotion, distribution, and pricing—directed toward selling the same product and product image?
2. Are trade-offs made so that each activity contributes the same net marginal benefit? For example, if money is taken away from the sales organization to be used in market research, are profits likely to fall? Have priorities been established in the use of personal selling, advertising, sales promotions, packaging, and pricing within limits dictated by the volume of sales needed and the funds available for the marketing program?
3. Are programs, budgets, and schedules prepared at regular intervals (yearly, quarterly, and so forth)?

The form in Exhibit 52 of *The Dow Jones-Irwin Business Papers* can be used by you and your managers to determine whether your company has the appropriate marketing mix.

SOME MARKETING PROBLEMS AND THEIR SOLUTIONS

You should be familiar with the viewpoint that independent businesses (in fact, all businesses) are operating in an age of disruptions[3] and that marketing is the department that most needs reorienting or reorganizing.

Marketing faces problems and challenges in many areas, including the following:

1. Forecasting sales.
2. Retraining personnel.
3. Upgrading the system of responding to customers' inquiries.
4. Increasing the effectiveness of promotion.
5. Preparing contingency plans for gasoline rationing or the curtailment of car travel because of high fuel and car costs.
6. Participating in the creation of new products and services appropriate for the times.

An error factor should be included in forecasts, say, "5,000 units

---

[2] Harvey C. Krentzman, *Managing for Profits* (Washington, D.C.: Small Business Administration, 1968).

[3] Mel Mandell, *1001 Ways to Operate Your Business More Profitably* (Homewood, Ill.: Dow Jones-Irwin, Inc., 1975), pp. 77–96.

plus or minus 7 percent"; or forecasts should give a range with high and low figures and perhaps a mean. Forecasting should be a group effort, with current projections subject to review at least quarterly.

Using the telephone properly in sales should be stressed in retraining. Salespeople should be trained to offer alternatives in a shortage economy. Accommodations for sales meetings and entertainment can be more modest.

Smaller cars are recommended for sales personnel. Visits to customers should be scheduled to minimize mileage. Public transportation should be considered. Flying can be cheaper, especially to a city several hundred miles away. A new way to pay travel expenses is through the Travelorder, which involves paying small sums and is issued weekly. The Travelorder provides employees with immediate funds and avoids delays in receiving checks. Over 2,000 motels, hotels, and commercial banks cash them.

The Traveletter Corporation has developed Rapidrafts, a low-cost way to make small cash disbursements in the field, such as to merchants for promotions. Lower cost auto insurance for all your employees, not just your salesman, may be arranged. The IRS requires that if an employee is permitted to make personal use of a car provided by your company, he must reimburse you for this usage. Otherwise, such personal use is considered as extra income.

Quick responses to inquiries maintain the "presence" of your company effectively. A system of color-coding all incoming inquiries by the weekday in which they arrive may be implemented. Form letters should be used to handle most responses.

"Hard-sell" advertising should be emphasized, and advertising that supposedly contributes to image should be de-emphasized or eliminated. More fractional-page ads should be bought. The amount of copy in ads should be reduced in industrial advertising, but maintaining it may be essential in consumer advertising. Ways to obtain quantity discounts should be considered. If company salespersons are developed into consultants, they should become more reliable sources for viable products, product modifications, and new services. Still, the overriding responsibility of all salespeople is sales and customer service.

Salespersons should be encouraged to help provide sound credit information. They should ask for customer cooperation in coping with supplier problems and in eliminating anything that increases product cost unnecessarily. They should be provided with documented evidence of price increases in raw materials. Price may be quoted as of delivery, but this policy should be explained in person to important customers. Price lists should not be issued during shortages.

Businesses may need to adapt to overdemand; marketing in sellers' markets is "demarketing." Demand containment—by reducing advertising and sales promotion, selling time and effort, increasing prices, reducing outlets, and so on—may be necessary. Products may have to be allocated to customers. However, such practices are carried too far if they endanger future relations with customers.

The form shown in Exhibit 53 of *The Dow Jones-Irwin Business Papers* will help you do a short, quick evaluation of your sales activities. It is called a sales analysis.

APPENDIX: GUIDE FOR IMPROVING A SALES REPRESENTATIVE'S PERFORMANCE[4]

The three steps in improving a sales representative's performance are *planning, measuring,* and *correcting.*

Planning

Get the representative's agreement about goals to be attained or exceeded in the next year:

1. Total profit contribution in dollars.
2. Profit contribution in dollars for each major product line, each major market (by industry or geographic area), and each of 10–20 target accounts (for significant new and additional business).

Get the representative's agreement about expenses for the next year:

1. Total sales expense budget in dollars.
2. Budget for travel, customer entertainment, telephone, and other expenses.

Have the representative plan the number of calls to accounts and prospects during the next year.

Measuring

Review at least monthly the representative's record for: (1) year-to-date progress toward the 12-month profit contribution goals, and (2) year-to-date budget compliance.

Correcting

Meet with the representative if the record shows a variance of 10 percent or more from target. Review the number of calls, plus major accomplishments and problems. In addition, you may need to take these steps:

1. Give more day-to-day help and direction.
2. Accompany the representative on calls to provide coaching.
3. Conduct regular sales meetings on subjects the representatives want covered.
4. Increase sales promotion.

---

[4]From Raymond O. Loen, *Measuring the Performance of Salesmen* (Washington, D.C.: Small Business Administration, 1972), Management Aids for Small Manufacturer, No. 190.

5. Transfer accounts to other representatives if there is insufficient effort or progress.
6. Establish tighter control over the price variances allowed.
7. Increase or reduce selling prices.
8. Add new products or services.
9. Increase the financial incentive.
10. Transfer, replace, or discharge representatives.

WHERE TO LOOK FOR FURTHER INFORMATION

Cornwell, Arthur W. *Sales Potential and Market Shares*. Washington, D.C.: Small Business Administration, 1972. (Small Marketers Aids, No. 112.)

Dutka, Solomon. *Using Census Data in Small Plant Marketing*. Washington, D.C.: Small Business Administration, 1972. (Management Aids for Small Manufacturers, No. 187.)

Feller, Jack H. *Keep Pointed toward Profit*. Washington, D.C.: Small Business Administration, 1972. (Management Aids for Small Manufacturers, No. 206).

Goodpasture, Bruce. *Danger Signals in a Small Store*. Washington, D.C.: Small Business Administration, 1970. (Small Marketers Aids, No. 141.)

Grubb, Kenneth. *Are Your Salespeople Missing Opportunities?* Washington, D.C.: Small Business Administration, 1970. (Small Marketers Aids, No. 95.)

Lang, John B. *Finding a New Product for Your Company*. Washington, D.C.: Small Business Administration, 1972. (Management Aids for Small Manufacturers, No. 216.)

Lipson, Harry and Darling, John R. *Introduction to Marketing*. New York: John Wiley and Sons, 1971, pp. 184-85, 347.

Loen, Raymond O. *Measuring the Performance of Salesmen*. Washington, D.C.: Small Business Administration, 1972. (Management Aids for Small Manufacturers, No. 190.)

McCarthy, E. Jerome. *Basic Marketing,* 5th ed. Homewood, Ill.: Richard D. Irwin, Inc., 1975.

Murdick, Robert G., et al. *Business Policy: A Framework for Analysis*. Columbus, Ohio: Grid, Inc., 1972, pp. 61, 99-121. Credit is given to these authors for the approach used in developing this chapter and for many of the ideas included in it.

Schabacker, Joseph C. *Strengthening Small Business Management*. Washington, D.C.: Small Business Administration, 1970.

Schwartz, Irving. *Personal Qualities Needed to Manage a Store*. Washington, D.C.: Small Business Administration, 1970. (Small Marketers Aids, No. 145.)

Small Business Administration. *Why Customers Buy (and Why They Don't)*. Washington, D.C.: Small Business Administration, 1972. (Administrative Management Course.)

Sorbet, Elizabeth. *Measuring the Results of Advertising*. Washington, D.C.: Small Business Administration, 1972. (Small Marketers Aids, No. 121.)

Wikman, Allan, Jr. "Marketing Ideas Make or Break a Company," *Marketing Insights,* January 19, 1970, p. 4.

PART SIX

Profit Planning
and Control

No business is stronger than its financial strength and vitality. Among the greatest requirements for success in an independent business are the devotion of time, energy, and initiative to financial management. The rewards are worth the effort, though, for this is how your firm will be profitable, grow, and develop.

In Part Six, you will study how to analyze and evaluate your financial operations and position (Chapter 19); "how to" maintain adequate and accurate records (Chapter 20); the methods to use in planning your profit (Chapter 21); how to budget and maintain financial control (Chapter 22); and how to safeguard your assets (Chapter 23).

How to Keep Score

The main purpose of this chapter is to help you learn how to set up an accounting system for your firm and how to read, evaluate, and interpret the accounts and the resulting profit (or loss) figure. The chapter will also guide you in estimating your firm's financial position and in determining its value. Finally, the chapter provides some ratios which can guide you in forecasting whether your operations will be successful or unsuccessful.

The operations of your firm result from your decisions and the resulting activities of your staff. These decisions and operations change your firm's financial position. Cash received for sales increases your bank balance. Cash spent for materials increases your inventory. Machines decrease in value; goods are processed by employees; utilities are used. The value of your firm is constantly changing.

HOW YOU CAN EVALUATE YOUR FINANCIAL OPERATIONS AND POSITION

However, the important question is whether your company is improving its chances of attaining its objectives. One objective is to make a profit, but some companies have made a profit and still have failed. Profits are not necessarily cash; they may be reflected in uncollectible accounts receivable. Too much of your money may be tied up in assets which are unavailable to pay your bills.

Your accounting records must accurately reflect the changes in your *assets, liabilities,* income, expenses, and *equity.* You must make certain that the interrelationships among these accounts remain "satisfactory." The continued operation of your company depends upon maintaining the proper balance between its investments, expenses, and income. These subjects are discussed in the balance of this chapter, and are divided into two parts:

1. How each of the accounts affects your company's operations.
2. Methods of evaluating your company's financial condition, and important ratios and their meanings.

247

The financial structure of your firm is reflected in its assets, liabilities, and equity. These accounts interact with one another. See Figure 19–1 for location of the accounts on the balance sheet.

FIGURE 19–1

THE SAMPLE CO.
Balance Sheet
December 31, 19 ___

Assets

Current assets:

Cash	$ 3,527	
Accounts receivable	30,242	
Inventory	40,021	
Prepaid expenses	523	
Total Current Assets		$74,313

Fixed assets:

Equipment		$30,250
Building	20,475	
	$50,725	
Less reserve for depreciation	8,450	
Net fixed assets		42,275
Total Assets		$116,588

Liabilities

Current liabilities:

Accounts payable	$25,674	
Accrued payables	1,530	
Total Current Liabilities		$27,204

Long-term liabilities

Mortgage payable		10,354
Total Liabilities		$ 37,558

Net worth (equity)

Capital stock	$60,000	
Retained earnings	19,030	
Total Net Worth		79,030
Total Liabilities plus Net Worth		$116,588

Assets

Assets are the physical, financial, or other values of your company. They are divided into *current* and *fixed* assets. Current assets turn over—change from one form to another—within one year. For example, it is expected that accounts receivable will be converted into cash and that inventory will be converted into sales within one year.

Current Assets. The first item of current assets is cash. It includes the bills and coins in your cash register and the deposits in your checking account. When cash is available, it means that you can pay today's bills. It is the most liquid of the accounts.

A certain level of cash is necessary to pay your bills. However, cash does not produce income. Too much cash means that the company has reduced its income-producing capacity.

Accounts receivable is a current asset which results from giving credit to customers when they buy your goods. Your company may sell entirely on credit. Your customers will usually want credit. However, since some customers—fortunately, only a few—do not pay their accounts, you must be careful to extend credit only to customers who will pay within a reasonable period of time. You should also set policies on the terms of payment and on the amount of credit that will be extended.

Credit is a cost to your company. The money owed you cannot be used to pay your own expenses or to buy goods. Among the means that are used to decrease the impact of credit are the following:

1. Your company may factor its accounts receivable—that is, sell its accounts receivable and receive cash less a fee.
2. Your company may honor credit cards.

Both types of transactions make it easier for your company to pay its obligations, but they also result in an expense to the company. This expense may be offset by increased sales and a reduction in needed assets.

Too large an investment in accounts receivable will place your company in considerable financial strain. Your investments of financial resources in the company will have to be increased, and your chances of incurring a high expense because of bad debts will be greater.

Inventory is an asset which provides a buffer between the production and sale of a product, as discussed in Chapter 14. Some sales are made on the basis of availability, and a company must therefore maintain some level of inventory to serve customers when they demand a product. On the other hand, a customer may want a special item and be willing to wait until it is ordered and delivered.

However, costs result from carrying inventory. Your money is tied up, space is used, products must be maintained and can become obsolete, and so forth. Also, inventory is not an income-producing asset. Thus, determining the amount of inventory to carry requires a judicious balancing of costs.

Other current asset accounts might include *short-term investment, prepaid items,* and *accrued income.* Usually, these are only a small percentage of the current assets and need little attention.

Fixed Assets. *Buildings, machinery, store fixtures, trucks,* and *land* are fixed assets. The company expects to own them for a considerable time and writes off part of their cost each period as a depreciation expense.

Different types of fixed assets have different lengths of useful life. Land is not depreciated; buildings are usually depreciated over a period of 20 years; machinery, over 5–10 years; and store equipment, 2–10 years. The amount of fixed assets should be related to the needs of your company. Idle fixed assets are a financial drain and are usually avoided when possible.

Some companies find it advantageous to rent fixed assets instead of owning them. A retailer rents a store to reduce his need to make a large investment. Whether you decide to rent or own your fixed assets will depend on the rental cost, the ownership cost, the availability of capital, and your freedom to operate.

Liabilities

A company obtains its funds by borrowing and by owner investment. The first results in a liability to pay someone; the second results in owners' equity. *The total of the liabilities and the owners' equity always equals the total of the assets.* A company should maintain a proper balance between the higher risk of investment by creditors and the investment by owners. The investment by creditors is divided into current liabilities and long-term liabilities.

Current liabilities are obligations which are to be paid within one year. They include *accounts payable, notes payable,* and *accrued items*—such as payroll—services performed for the company but not yet paid.

Accounts payable are usually due within 30 to 60 days, depending on the credit terms. The delay is the service a vendor provides to the buyer. A company maintains current assets to pay these accounts. It should determine whether early payment is beneficial. Some companies offer a cash discount for early payment, such as 2 percent if paid in ten days. A high level of accounts payable requires a high level of current assets.

Notes payable—written obligations to pay—usually give the company a somewhat longer period before payment is required and usually require the payment of interest. An example is a 90-day note.

Bonds and *mortgages* are the usual types of *long-term liabilities.* A company contracts such liabilities when it purchases fixed assets and the owners do not have sufficient equity to pay for the assets. *Long-term loans* may also be used to supply a permanent amount of *working capital,* which is current assets less current liabilities. Independent businesses use long-term borrowing as a source of funds much less frequently than do large businesses. This type of borrowing requires current payment of a fixed amount on the principal and a smaller amount for interest. Such payments increase the risk that a company will be unable to meet its obligations during slack times.

Owners' Equity

Equity is the owners' share of a company after the liabilities are subtracted from the assets. The owners receive income from the profits of the company in the form of dividends or an increase in their share of the company through an increase in the retained earnings. They also absorb losses, which decrease the equity.

Capital stock is the value the owners invest in the company. A share of stock is issued in the form of a certificate and has a stated value on the books of the company. Additional shares can be sold or issued in place of cash dividends.

Retained earnings are the profits which are not distributed to the owners. *Cash dividends* reduce current assets. A company usually does not pay out all its profits in dividends, but retains some earnings as protection for the firm or to provide for its growth. Many independent firms have failed because the owners paid out the profits as dividends too quickly. You should establish a long-range plan for paying dividends.

The assets, liabilities, and equity accounts tend to change over time. At regular intervals, a *balance sheet* is prepared to show the value of a company and how its funds are distributed.

The financial structure of a company is changed by its profit-making activities. These activities are reflected in the revenue and expense accounts. (Net income = Revenue − expenses.) During a given period, the company performs services for which it receives values. The financial values exchanged are shown by the profit-and-loss statement below.

FIGURE 19-2

THE SAMPLE CO.
Profit-and-Loss Statement
January 1 through December 31, 19 ___

Net sales		$231,574
Less cost of goods sold		145,631
Gross profit		$ 85,943
Operating expenses:		
Salaries	$41,569	
Utilities	3,475	
Depreciation	5,025	
Rent	1,000	
Building services	2,460	
Insurance	2,000	
Interest	1,323	
Office and supplies	2,775	
Sales promotion	5,500	
Taxes and licenses	3,240	
Maintenance	805	
Delivery	2,924	
Miscellaneous	875	
Total Expenses		72,971
Net income before taxes		$ 12,972
Less income taxes		3,242
Net income after taxes		$ 9,730

Revenue and Expenses

Revenue is the return from services performed. Revenue—usually called sales income—is received by the company in the form of cash or credit—an obligation of the customer to pay. Many companies also have other income, such as interest from investments.

Expenses are the costs of performing services. They include materials, wages, insurance, utilities, transportation, depreciation, taxes, supplies, and sales promotion. These items are deductions from revenue.

Profit

Profit is the difference between revenue and expenses. Profit is often classified as gross, operating, net before taxes, and net after taxes—depending on the type of expenses deducted.

The values of these items are related to one another and to the structure of the company. Earlier, it was stated that a company has fixed assets which are income-producing. Are those assets being used efficiently? To find out, the relationship between the volume of sales income and the value of the fixed assets is determined and evaluated.

**METHODS OF
EVALUATING THE
FIRM'S FINANCIAL
CONDITION**

Now that we have considered the financial structure and operations of a company, we will examine the methods of evaluating its financial condition. Look at Figures 19-1 and 19-2, which present the financial statements of The Sample Company. Is the company in a good financial position?

The evaluation of the financial condition of a company is based upon establishing relationships between two or more variables. For example, the amount of current assets needed depends on other conditions of a company, such as the size of its current liabilities. So, a *current ratio*—current assets divided by current liabilities—shows how easily a company can pay its current obligations. Another comparison can be made by subtracting current liabilities from current assets, with the resulting value called *working capital.* Unfortunately, no standard figures have been determined to be best, nor have any figures been found which can assure your success. Yet a reasonable evaluation is necessary. Two sets of values which can be used for evaluation purposes are:

1. A comparison of the current value of ratios with those of the past.
2. A comparison of the ratios of your firm with the ratios of similar firms.

**Values of Each Ratio
in the Past**

A change in the value of selected ratios for a firm indicates a change in its financial position. For example, suppose that the current ratio for The Sample Company has moved gradually from a value of 1.0 to 3.0. The firm has moved to a more liquid position and therefore looks good. However, this change may be due to keeping old uncollectible accounts on the books. In that case, the company would not be more liquid. Although the trend does indicate a change, only in-depth analysis can determine the causes.

**The Ratios of
Like Companies**

Average values and the range of values for the ratios are published for a large variety of companies. Some of these firms will fail, but the averages and ranges provide a guide to what other companies are doing.

Suppose that the current ratio of companies with assets of $250,000 or less is found to be 2.3 to 1, while The Sample Company has a ratio of 3.0 to 1. Again, the company's ratio looks good. However, it may be losing income by maintaining too many unproductive assets.

In the past, a ratio of 2 to 1 has been used as a rule of thumb for the current ratio. However, no one ratio is optimum for all companies.

IMPORTANT RATIOS AND THEIR MEANINGS

You can use the ratios and percentages to correct deficiencies in the operations and structure of your company. When a ratio is mentioned, look at Figure 19-3 for the method of computing it. Spaces are provided for you to compute the ratios for The Sample Company, using the data provided in Figures 19-1 and 19-2. Comparable figures for the industry are provided for comparative purposes.

Are you making reasonable return on your investment? The *ratio of net profit to net worth* (often called return on investment, or ROI) is used to evaluate this, but several other ratios should be considered to aid in profit planning.

What is your company's return on its sales dollar? The *ratio of net profit to net sales* provides this information. Suppose that The Sample Company makes four cents per dollar of sales. How does it compare with like companies? Is the trend up or down? If down, why? Your costs may be increasing without an increase in price. Perhaps your competitors are keeping their prices low, and as a result you need to keep yours low. Perhaps you are trying to obtain a large sales volume at the expense of profit. An increase in sales volume with the same net profit per dollar of sales will increase your ROI, but if increasing sales volume forces you to reduce the return on a dollar of sales, your ROI may decrease.

Does your company obtain enough sales from its producing assets? This is reflected in the *ratio of net sales to fixed assets*—your fixed assets representing the producing units of the company. This ratio is only a general guide, for so many variables exist—such as leasing instead of owning fixed assets—that the ratio can change with changes in policies. Still, trends and good use of industry data make this a valuable ratio.

Does your company have enough sales for the amount of investment? The *ratio of net sales to net worth* provides a guide to this evaluation. Note that this ratio can be combined with the profit to sales ratio to obtain the ROI.

Can you pay your current obligations? A number of ratios can help you answer this question. The best known is the *current ratio,* that is, the ratio of current assets to current liabilities. You may be making a good profit, yet not be able to pay your debts, for cash does not necessarily increase when you make a profit.

The *acid test ratio,* that is, the ratio of current assets minus inventory to current liabilities, can be used to make a further check.

Still another check can be made by using *working capital,* or current

FIGURE 19-3
Financial Ratios

Ratio	Formula	The Sample Company	Industry Average
1. Net profit to net worth	$\dfrac{\text{Net profit before taxes}}{\text{Net worth}}$ = _____		18.4%
2. Net profit to net sales	$\dfrac{\text{Net profit before taxes}}{\text{Net sales}}$ = _____		3.1
3. Net sales to fixed assets	$\dfrac{\text{Net sales}}{\text{Fixed assets}}$ = _____		5.8
4. Net sales to net worth	$\dfrac{\text{Net sales}}{\text{Owners' equity}}$ = _____		7.5
5. Current ratio	$\dfrac{\text{Current assets}}{\text{Current liabilities}}$ = _____		1.3
6. Acid test	$\dfrac{\text{Current assets} - \text{inventory}}{\text{Current liabilities}}$ = _____		1.0
7. Receivables to working capital	$\dfrac{\text{Accounts receivable}}{\text{Working capital}}$ = _____		1.2
8. Inventory ot working capital	$\dfrac{\text{Inventory}}{\text{Working capital}}$ = _____		0.4
9. Collection period	$\dfrac{\text{Accounts Receivable}}{\text{Average daily credit sales}}$ = _____ *		43.0 days
10. Net sales to inventory	$\dfrac{\text{Net sales}}{\text{Inventory}}$ = _____		22.0
11. Net sales to working capital	$\dfrac{\text{Net sales}}{\text{Working capital}}$ = _____		10.0
12. Long-term liabilities to working capital	$\dfrac{\text{Long-term liabilities}}{\text{Working capital}}$ = _____		0.7
13. Debt to net worth	$\dfrac{\text{Total liabilities}}{\text{Net worth}}$ = _____		1.6
14. Current liabilities to net worth	$\dfrac{\text{Current liabilities}}{\text{Owners' equity}}$ = _____		1.1
15. Fixed assets to net worth ..	$\dfrac{\text{Fixed assets}}{\text{Owners' equity}}$ = _____		1.2

*If 80% of sales are on credit: Average daily credit sales = $\dfrac{\text{Annual sales}}{365}$ × 0.80 = _____ × 0.80 = _____ = $\dfrac{\text{_____}}{365}$ ×

assets less current liabilities, as a basis. Working capital is the margin of safety your company has in paying its current liabilities.

The *ratios of accounts receivable* and *inventory to working capital* provide an insight into the company's ability to make current payments.

How good are your current assets? Cash in hand is the best current asset. Accounts receivable represent cash that the company will receive from customers sometime in the future. However, the older an account is, the greater the expectation of loss. The *collection period ratio,* that is, the ratio of accounts receivable to average daily credit sales, provides a guide to the "goodness" of your accounts receivable. Suppose that The Sample Company has set a 30-day payment period for its customers and that its collection period ratio is 50 days. Since many accounts are less than 30 days old, many other accounts must be over two months old. Apparently, Mr. Sample is not checking adequately on those to whom he extends credit, is carrying bad accounts, or is not exerting enough effort to reduce the slow payments of accounts. Periodically, each account in accounts receivable should be reviewed for its collectibility. (A system for controlling accounts receivable is discussed in Chapter 20.)

Inventories can be evaluated in about the same way as accounts receivable. Goods in inventory become obsolete if they are not sold within a reasonable time. Therefore, inventory should be "turned over" during the year. The turnover rate is expressed by the *ratio of net sales to inventory*. A turnover of inventory of six times each year for a company is good if turnover for the industry is five. If your company is turning over its inventory too slowly, you may be keeping obsolete goods. Too high a ratio may result from an inventory so low that it is hurting production or not providing necessary customer services.

To obtain an idea of the support a company is receiving from its current assets, the *ratio of net sales to working capital* may be computed. Accounts receivable and inventory should increase with an increase in sales, but not out of proportion. Payroll and other expense increases require a higher level of cash outflow. On the other hand, too low a ratio indicates that surplus working capital is available to service sales.

How much equity should your company have? Assets are financed by either equity investments or the creation of liabilities. Retained profits are part of equity and can be used to increase your assets or decrease your liabilities. You can maintain a high level of equity with a relatively low level of risk, or a relatively high level of liabilities with a higher expected return on equity.

Most small companies do not like to maintain a large amount of long-term debt. The risk is too great. The common ratios used for checking a company's source of funds relationships are:

1. Debt to net worth.
2. Current liabilities to net worth.
3. Long-term liabilities to working capital.
4. Fixed assets to net worth.

If any of these is extremely high, the company is in a risky situation. A bad year decreases company income, but the obligation to pay continues.

More questions can be asked, and you can develop more relationships to guide you in analyzing your company's financial strengths and weaknesses. Each ratio is an indicator of only part of the company's position. The ratios overlap because a company is a complex system so that a change in the size of one account, such as cash, will change other values.

The financial ratios for the items on the profit-and-loss statement are usually expressed in percentages of sales. When this information is obtainable from competing firms, it can point to out-of-line costs. A high cost of goods sold as a percentage of sales income may indicate a poor choice of vendors, inefficient use of materials, or labor, or too low a price. A high percentage of salaries may indicate overstaffing.

chapter 20

Maintaining Adequate—
and Accurate—Records

Have you ever considered how many records you generate as an individual? You probably have a driver's license, credit cards, a social security card, and a checkbook.

Without these, you would be unable to transact much of your business. When you use one of these, records are generated. For example, suppose that you use a credit card. This generates a sales slip, an account for you, a bill, and a record of payment. You use the bill to write a check and to deduct the amount from your bank balance. At the same time, you keep some information in your head to save time in filling out forms. While this informal method may be all right for you as an individual, it is not sufficient for you as an independent business manager. Instead, you need a system of records to aid your memory. A business has a much more extensive set of records than an individual does, because it has many more transactions and because more people are involved.

You have already read about the information needed to make personnel, production, marketing, and financial decisions. Much of this information can be carried around in the heads of the owner, managers, and employees. However, certain types of information are more valuable if they are brought together from a variety of sources, related systematically, maintained accurately, recorded permanently, and made available to the people who need them. A procedure is needed to provide the needed information in a proper manner. Exhibit 54 in *The Dow Jones-Irwin Business Papers* will help you analyze your information system.

Accounting information—we prefer to think of these data as "management information"—seems to become more important as the economy and business operations become more complex. Although the increasing complexity of business has expanded the amount of paperwork, records still need to be kept as simply and inexpensively as possible—while providing the required information. This can be achieved by knowing what information is needed and by obtaining and storing that information for easy retrieval with little copying and recording.

Historically, accounting data have been developed to satisfy tax-reporting needs and to report the condition of the firms to their owners. The emphasis has been placed on gathering historic data rather than on gathering projective data for use in the future. However, both categories have their role. In addition to the traditional accounting information, your accounting system should provide information that will help you in making decisions. In setting up an accounting system, you should consider these questions: What are the decisions I need to make? What information do I need to make those decisions? How can I best record and retrieve that information?

WHAT MANAGEMENT INFORMATION IS NEEDED?

In determining what information you need, you should ask: Why do I want the information? The usual answers are:

1. To plan ahead. Past information can be used in planning. Examples include past sales trends, sales per salesperson, the output of a machine, the delivery time for a purchase, the quality of an employee's output, payment experience with a given customer, and the demand for a particular product at a given time.
2. To meet obligations. For example, money is borrowed, material is purchased on credit, delivery is promised for a certain day at a certain price, and taxes are due.
3. To control activities. Many vital activities are routine and can be checked by a clerk. For example, material ordered has not arrived, inventory has reached zero, losses in supplies are occurring, and too much time is being spent on routine work. By means of guidelines and "warning flags," a clerk can perform the control function.
4. To satisfy the government. For example, the government collects taxes; requires conformity with safety, fair employment, and price control standards; and demands ethical standards of business practice.
5. To evaluate performance. Review selected records and reports.

In addition to determining what information is needed, you must know how to use it. This involves classifying it into a usable form. The information for accounting purposes has been classified as follows:

1. Assets.
2. Liabilities.
3. Owners' equity or net worth.
4. Revenue or sales income.
5. Expenses.

Much other information is needed, including information on economic and market conditions, personnel history and capabilities, sources of materials, and specifications for products. Systems and procedures need to be established to assure the availability of critical information. This area is beyond the scope of this book.

Services to Customers

These transactions provide both the income and the expenses of doing business. When you perform a service—such as the sale of a product, the repair of an auto, or the rental of an apartment—cash, check, or an IOU is received in exchange for goods or labor. Recordings on slips and tapes are used to accumulate the changes in the affected records. For example, the cash sale of a pair of socks increases your cash. Yet, it creates the obligation to pay sales taxes and reduces your inventory of socks. See Figure 20-1 for a flowchart of the transfer of data, cash, and goods. A credit slip is used to reverse this transaction if the socks are returned.

FIGURE 20-1
Accounting for Sales

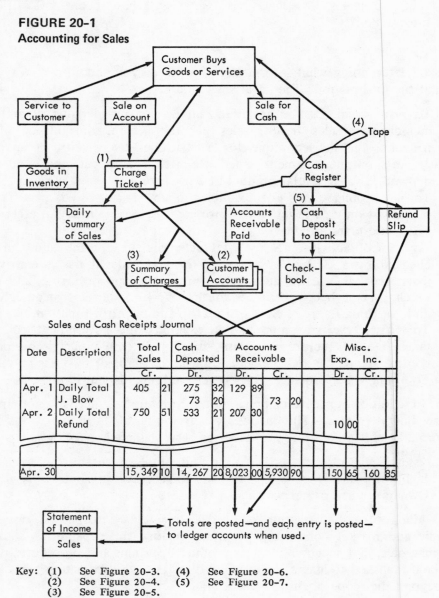

| Date | Description | Total Sales | | Cash Deposited | | Accounts Receivable | | | | | | Misc. | | | |
		Cr.		Dr.		Dr.		Cr.				Exp. Dr.		Inc. Cr.	
Apr. 1	Daily Total	405	21	275	32	129	89								
	J. Blow			73	20			73	20						
Apr. 2	Daily Total	750	51	533	21	207	30								
	Refund											10	00		
Apr. 30		15,349	10	14,267	20	8,023	00	5,930	90			150	65	160	85

Sales and Cash Receipts Journal

Totals are posted—and each entry is posted—to ledger accounts when used.

Statement of Income

Sales

Key: (1)   See Figure 20-3.   (4)   See Figure 20-6.
     (2)   See Figure 20-4.   (5)   See Figure 20-7.
     (3)   See Figure 20-5.

258

These transactions originate your expenses of doing business. Materials, parts, and finished products are purchased to be transformed or sold. Employees are paid for work performed. Electricity is consumed, taxes are paid, advertising promotes products, and supplies are used. Also, the service may increase the assets of your company—such as equipment and machine purchases, building construction, and stock investments. A somewhat different type of service that fits into this category is the floating of bonds to obtain cash or credit. All of these transactions generate obligations and initiate transfers of data within an accounting system, as is shown in Figures 20-1 and 20-2.

FIGURE 20-2
Accounting for Purchases

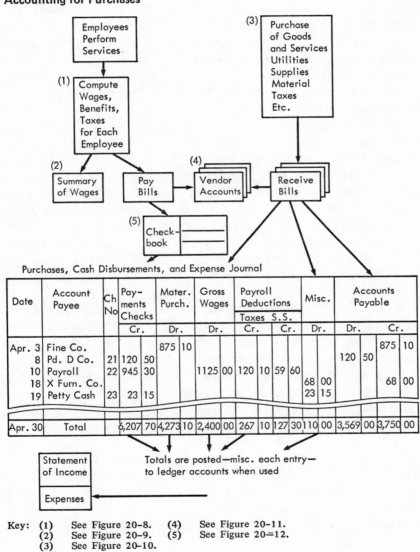

Purchases, Cash Disbursements, and Expense Journal

Date	Account Payee	Ch No	Pay-ments Checks Cr.	Mater. Purch. Dr.	Gross Wages Dr.	Payroll Deductions Taxes Cr.	Payroll Deductions S.S. Cr.	Misc. Dr.	Accounts Payable Dr.	Accounts Payable Cr.
Apr. 3	Fine Co.			875 10						875 10
8	Pd. D Co.	21	120 50						120 50	
10	Payroll	22	945 30		1125 00	120 10	59 60			
18	X Furn. Co.							68 00		68 00
19	Petty Cash	23	23 15					23 15		
Apr. 30	Total		6,207 70	4,273 10	2,400 00	267 10	127 30	110 00	3,569 00	3,750 00

Statement of Income

Expenses

Totals are posted—misc. each entry— to ledger accounts when used

Key:
(1) See Figure 20-8.
(2) See Figure 20-9.
(3) See Figure 20-10.
(4) See Figure 20-11.
(5) See Figure 20=12.

Other records are initiated by many matters of a nonaccounting nature, such as letters of inquiry, agreements on sales, complaints, and implementation of controls over physical units.

RECORDING THE INFORMATION

All transactions involving accounting information must be recorded. Some very small firms use a single-entry system for its simplicity. This type of system records a transaction in only one place—a sale for cash is recorded as cash income. This type of system does not provide much needed information or control. With a double-entry system of accounting, your accounts are kept in "balance" by entering a transaction in two places. When a sale is made for cash, income is increased and cash—an asset—is increased by the same amount; conversely, inventory is decreased. When material is purchased on credit, inventory—an asset—is increased and accounts payable—a liability is increased by a like amount. A machine wears out. So depreciation is periodically deducted from assets, and expenses are increased by the same amount. Notice in all of these transactions that the changes are made so that the *sum* of assets + expenses = the *sum* of liabilities + equity + income. The totals may change, but they change by the same amount.

The accounting system starts with the tapes and other items discussed under *sources*, and includes journals and ledger accounts. The journal is the original book of entry, and records the daily transactions in chronological order. To group like items together, the chronological entries are entered individually or as totals in ledger accounts. A ledger account might be set up for each of the accounts listed in Figure 19-1. The amount of detail depends on the needs of your company and its other records. For example, journals and statements might be used to show the income and expenses, whereas only the profit—the difference between income and expenses—is shown in a ledger account. Under all circumstances, the ledger accounts must balance.

Figures 20-1 and 20-2 diagram the flow of data for some of the more common entries in the accounting records of an independent business. The following sections discuss some transactions and entries to help you understand the system of recording information. (The month is used as the time period for adjustments to emphasize the need for frequent review of the results of your operations. Some of the formal accounting illustrated may be performed only once a year, often by an accountant. But we hope that the examples explain the concepts.)

Sales

The sale of your products or services is your source of profit. In every company, a record must be kept of each sale. The auto repair shop makes a record of the charges to the customer for labor hours and parts. A *sales slip* is completed when a radio is sold. The number, type, unit price, and total price of the radio should be entered on the slip. The sales tax on all items sold must be recorded. When cash registers are available, a tape can be used as the sales slip.

Information on the sales forms is used to accumulate the sales income, to reduce inventory, to make analyses for future plans, and—in the case of a credit sale—to enter in the *accounts receivable record* for the customer. To eliminate the totaling of sales slips, cash registers which total the daily sales can be used. When many different items and people are involved, the registers can total by variables, including type of product, salesperson, or department. The classification should be aligned with the types of analysis you will make and with the controls to be exercised.

Sales are entered in a *sales journal.* This shows the daily summary or the individual item, depending on the detail desired. The sales journal can be multicolumnar paper to provide additional information, such as how much was sold for cash (or credit card and account) in each department, of each type of product, and by each salesperson. If you analyze this sheet, it can provide information on sales trends, where the major volume is, and who is selling the most. Figure 20-1 provides an illustration of a sales and cash receipts journal.

The totals of the columns of the sales journal are transferred to the income statement and/or the sales income ledger account.

Cash Income and Outgo

When services are sold, the total of the recordings for cash, credits, and other values must equal the sales income recorded in order to balance the accounts. The accounting for cash is most important, as cash is negotiable anywhere. The person handling cash can mishandle it so that losses will occur. The recording system for cash should be designed and established with care so as to minimize losses.

When sales are made for cash, the goods sold and the cash received should be recorded independently of each other—if possible. Also, in order to maintain control, only certain people should be allowed to handle company cash, and only on an individual basis. Each person should start with a standard amount for change, and the cash balance should be reconciled each day or more often to see that the cash on hand equals the beginning cash on hand plus cash sales less cash returns.

Checks are not as negotiable as cash, but are handled with cash. One extra step is required. To guard against losses from bad checks, a method of identification of the person presenting the check should be established. Past experience with payment by check often determines the policy followed. Some companies accept only cash; some require identification, such as driver's license and social security card, the numbers of which are recorded on the check; and some accept the check without formal identification. (Stamp the back side of a check as in Figure 20-13, and enter the required information.) You should maintain a proper balance between safeguarding against losses and making the customer feel that a personal service is being performed.

At the end of each day, standard amounts of money are retained to make change the next day and the rest is deposited in the bank. *Deposit slips* are forwarded to the bank with the money and the amount deposited is added to the checkbook stub balance.

Payments are made by check or from petty cash. The *checkbook* can be used as a ledger account by adding bank deposits and deducting each check on the checkbook stubs. Each check is entered in the *cash journal* to show the account to which it is charged.

It often becomes too expensive to pay small bills—say, $5 and under—by check. A *petty cash fund*—say, $25 or $50—can be used to pay these bills. Each payment should be recorded on a form to keep track of the account and amount paid. (See Figure 20–14.) The sum of the amounts on this record, plus the cash in the account, should always total the figure set for the size of the petty cash fund. Periodically, the fund is replenished by check to the set figure, and the expenditures recorded transferred to the appropriate accounts in the *cash journal.*

The form in Exhibit 55 of *The Dow Jones-Irwin Business Papers* will help you determine whether you are maintaining adequate control of your cash.

Accounts Receivable

When your customer uses *credit cards* or *open accounts* to buy goods, each sales slip is either entered on a customer account record or filed under the customer's name. These records are details of the *accounts receivable account* and are totaled periodically to compare with the account. Any differences should be investigated. At the end of each period —usually a month—all customers' accounts are totaled and bills sent to them. As payments are received, the amounts of the checks are recorded in each customer's account and totaled for entry in the *sales and cash receipts journal.* A discussion of the decisions regarding credit is included in Chapter 22.

Periodically, a review of the individual *accounts receivable records* provides information about the status of the accounts, who is slow in paying, and which accounts need follow-up. The follow-up methods include delinquent notices, personal contact, and use of a collection agency. Some should be written off by charging them to *bad debts* when they cannot be collected. Other information can also be obtained, including identification of your large customers, what kinds of items they buy, and who has stopped buying your services.

Credit card sales are totaled by each credit card company and, after service charges are deducted, are processed through the bank. Gross sales are entered as sales income, as are accounts receivable and cash sales; the service charge is charged to that account; and the accounts receivable or cash account posted.

Some transactions—such as installment sales, damaged or lost goods, and income from insurance of damaged equipment—require more complex accounting procedures than are being presented. For these, we recommend consulting with an accountant or studying an accounting text.

An operating business incurs many obligations for material and equipment purchases, wages, utilities, taxes, and notes payable. These are reported in a *purchase and cash disbursements journal.* Practically all purchases are paid by check, and the number of individual payments is relatively small. A weekly report of cash receipts and disbursements is shown in Figure 20-15. This report plus the cash and sales audit in Figure 20-16 can be used for analysis of the operations of a retail store.

Bills and *invoices* can be filed by date to be paid, and when paid, filed as a history of *accounts payable.* As each initiating record is received, it is entered in the purchases and cash disbursements journal, as shown in Figure 20-2. Notice the columns used to classify the expenses and the "Miscellaneous" column used for expenses or assets for which there are few bills each month. Columns are used for accounts in which many entries occur duing a month. For example, each month many purchases are made of a variety of materials, products, parts, and supplies for which one or more columns are provided. Few purchases of office equipment are made in a year, so they are handled in the miscellaneous column. Utilities might warrant a separate column. As a payment is made, the bill is marked and filed and the amount is entered on the check stub and in the purchases and cash disbursements journal. As with accounts receivable, there are complex transactions about which you should consult an accountant or an accounting book.

Accounts Payable

Inventory records are troublesome to keep. The problem of inventory was discussed in Chapter 14. A number of methods are used to assist the manager in maintaining records of his stock. All are based on a systematic means of spotting a low-inventory item—that is, they help "wave a warning flag" when the inventory is below a predetermined standard. These methods include setting aside the standard amount, setting aside an amount of space, making a regular physical count, and for bulky material, flashing a light. A business selling a high volume of many items, such as a grocery store, depends on visual inspection of the number of items on the shelf by several people, each assigned to certain items. For slower-moving and fewer items, the paperwork is not increased very much by keeping a *perpetual inventory record.* (See Figure 14-4.) All the methods require

Inventory

determining the minimum or standard amount left in inventory before ordering.

A record is made of a sale and of the physical movement of the item sold. The recording of the removal to expense is handled in two ways. First, for high volume and a multiplicity of items, the purchased items are charged to expense directly and adjusted at the end of the period for the inventory obtained by a physical count of the items. This reduces the volume of transfer recordings out of inventory into expense required of the second method. The second method uses the perpetual inventory record described above, with added columns in the form for dollar values of units. The total cost of the units used is the material expense. This method is generally used by manufacturing companies.

Expenses

Your business will purchase services from other people, and these will become expenses as they are used. Materials are transformed and sold, electricity is used, machines decrease in value, and insurance protection is based on time. The bases of payments for these costs of doing business vary from daily to over five years, and the use of an item may be delayed for years. In order to determine your true profit, income and expenses must be determined for the same period, say, for January, 19___.

Many independent businesses compute their profit on a cash basis rather than on an accrual basis. The *accrual basis* makes adjustments to align income and expenses. The *cash basis* charges the items as they are actually paid. The cash basis is used for simplicity and, as will be seen, is not a pure cash procedure. The cash basis assumes that payments and use are in the same period or that payments do not vary from one period to another.

The procedure for obtaining the expenses by the accrual method is:

1. Obtain the values for all assets, payments, and obligations.
2. Determine how much of each has been used during the period.
3. Transfer the used portion to expense, reduce the asset, or increase the obligation.

A number of examples of this procedure are shown below. (See Figure 20–17 for sample recordings of each.)

1. *Material for sale in a retail store.* The expense of material = Beginning inventory + purchases – ending inventory.

2. *Insurance.* Insurance may be paid monthly, quarterly, or annually for the period ahead. Annual payments usually reduce the cost, and payment can be distributed to different months by spreading the payment of different policies over the year. Insurance is usually charged to expenses when paid and, for monthly statements 1/12 is charged to expenses and the remainder of payments placed in an asset account for prepaid insur-

ance. This adjustment is not necessary when the monthly payment is close to 1/12 the annual cost (the latter is a cash-basis type of accounting).

3. *Wages and salaries.* These expenses are paid regularly after employees have performed a service for the business. If salaries are paid for a month at the end of the month, salaries are the expense of the month and need no adjustment. When wages are paid, say, every two weeks, the payment is for the past two weeks, which often covers work in the previous month. At the end of the month, wages have not been paid for part of the month, so a liability exists for accrued wages. Adjustments between labor and accrued wages are made. Subsidiary records are usually kept to compute wages, salaries, employee benefits, company payments for social security, and so forth.

4. *Machinery, equipment, and buildings.* These are used up over a period of years. On a monthly basis, the expense of a machine

$$= \frac{\text{Cost of machine} - \text{sale value at end of expected life}}{\text{Expected life}}$$

This figure remains constant until the assets are sold, added to, or used.

Maintaining a record of the original cost of machinery and equipment is valuable. The cost of using the machine, which is called *depreciation*, is an estimate, and the reduction in value for depreciation is kept in a separate account, called *reserve for depreciation*.

Many other items of expense and income need the same types of adjustment as those just discussed. The main points to determine are: How much of the cost is used up during the period? How much is an asset? How much is a liability? Find the easiest way to assign the proper values to expenses, income, assets, and liabilities. These records can then be used for analysis and for making reports.

Financial Statements

During each period—say, daily or weekly—a check should be made of a few critical accounts, such as sales, for trends and other changes. This enables you to anticipate action that may be needed. For example, you may detect shortages or overages of stock.

Financial statements are prepared from accounting records to aid management in its analyses. They are the *balance sheet* and the *profit-and-loss statement* (see Figures 19–1 and 19–2). The accounts are grouped so that a financial analysis can be performed, as discussed in Chapter 19. Profit-and-loss statements should be prepared monthly, and balance sheets less often—perhaps semiannually.

Tax reports are completed for the various government divisions many times during the year. These include reports for income, sales, social security, and excise taxes. As reporting requires an understanding of regulations which change periodically, you are advised to consult the Internal Revenue Service, accountants, or an appropriate tax pamphlet.

THE STORING OF INFORMATION

The records of your company are very important to you and should be treated accordingly. Care should be exercised to see that records are not lost, stolen, burned, or otherwise destroyed. Critical records should be kept in a safe; others may be placed where they are readily available. Systematic arrangements for keeping records can save time and money in processing information and protecting the records.

JOB COSTS

You should know not only the costs for a period but the costs of units or jobs so that you can determine how profitable each is. Estimates and standards of materials, labor, and overhead are used to establish planned costs for bidding on and pricing a product. Figure 20–18 shows the calculations for a bid. Actual data are collected from material requisitions (Figure 14–9) and time tickets (Figure 20–19), and the costs for a job or product are calculated on a job cost record (Figure 20–20). Comparison of the planned and actual costs provides a basis for analyses of operations and prices. A summary report of production and costs for a month is shown in Figure 20–21. Note that many records of operations are used for both noncosting and costing purposes. Figure 20–22 shows a hospital form which contains many different types of information.

The questionnaire in Exhibit 56 of *The Dow Jones-Irwin Business Papers* can help you determine whether your accounting records are accurate. Exhibit 57 will help you see whether your production accounting records are accurate.

FIGURE 20-3
Charge Ticket

RICKS HARDWARE

LUMBER
&
BUILDING MATERIALS

DRAWER K EAST SIDE STATION
2116 UNIVERSITY BLVD. EAST
TUSCALOOSA, AL. 35401

ELECTRICAL
&
PLUMBING SUPPLIES

SOLD TO

PHONE
553-6620

DATE
DELIVERED
TO

CUSTOMER ORDER NO.			SOLD BY		DELIVERED BY			

DELIVERED	ORDERED	SIZE	LENGTH	DESCRIPTION	UNIT	PRICE	AMOUNT

This transaction, as evidenced by purchases listed hereon, constitutes the entire agreement between buyer and seller and signature of buyer is acknowledgment of same. Failure to make payment within thirty days is basis for legal action to be taken, and buyer agrees to pay all court costs and reasonable attorney fees and hereby waives all rights of exemption under the laws of the State of Alabama or any other State of the Union.   A SERVICE CHARGE OF 1½% PER MONTH WILL BE ADDED TO ANY ACCOUNT 30 DAYS PAST DUE, WHICH IS AN **ANNUAL PERCENTAGE RATE OF 18%.**

TAX	
TOTAL	

INVOICE
NO. **13266**

Rec'd By

All claims and goods returned MUST be accompanied by this bill.

Thank You

ORIGINAL INVOICE

FIGURE 20-5
Summary of Charges

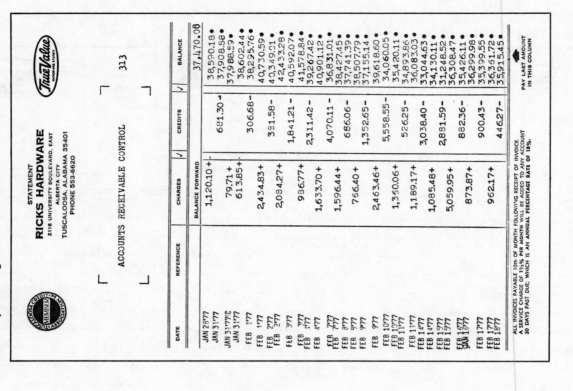

STATEMENT
RICKS HARDWARE
2116 UNIVERSITY BOULEVARD, EAST
ALBERTA CITY
TUSCALOOSA, ALABAMA 35401
PHONE 553-6620

ACCOUNTS RECEIVABLE CONTROL   313

DATE	REFERENCE	CHARGES	√	CREDITS	√	BALANCE
		BALANCE FORWARD				37,470.08 ●
JAN 28??		1,120.10 +-				38,590.18 ●
JAN 31??				681.30 -'		37,908.58 ●
JAN 31??SC		79.71 +				37,988.59 ●
JAN 31??		613.85+				38,602.44 ●
FEB 1??				306.68-		38,295.76 ●
FEB 1??		2,434.83 +				40,730.59 ●
FEB 2??				391.58-		40,349.01 ●
FEB 2??		2,084.27+				42,433.28 ●
FEB 3??				1,841.21-		40,592.07 ●
FEB 3??		936.77+				41,578.84 ●
FEB 4??				2,311.42-		39,267.42 ●
FEB 4??		1,633.70 +				40,901.12 ●
FEB 7??				4,070.11 -		36,831.01 ●
FEB 8??		1,596.44 +				38,427.45 ●
FEB 8??				686.06-		37,741.39 ●
FEB 9??		766.40 +				38,507.79 ●
FEB 9??				1,352.65-		37,155.14 ●
FEB 9??		2,463.46+				39,618.60 ●
FEB 10??				5,558.55 -		34,060.05 ●
FEB 10??		1,350.06 +				35,420.11 ●
FEB 11??				526.25 -		34,893.86 ●
FEB 11??		1,189.17+				36,083.03 ●
FEB 14??				3,038.40 -		33,044.63 ●
FEB 14??		1,085.48+				34,130.11 ●
FEB 15??				2,881.59-		31,248.52 ●
FEB 15??		5,059.95 +				36,308.47 ●
FEB 16??				882.36-		35,426.11 ●
JAN 16??		873.87+				36,299.98 ●
FEB 17??				900.43-		35,399.55 ●
FEB 17??		962.17+				36,361.72 ●
FEB 18??				446.27-		35,915.45 ●

ALL INVOICES PAYABLE 10th OF MONTH FOLLOWING RECEIPT OF INVOICE.
A SERVICE CHARGE OF 1½% PER MONTH WILL BE ADDED TO ANY ACCOUNT
30 DAYS PAST DUE, WHICH IS AN ANNUAL PERCENTAGE RATE OF 18%.

→ PAY LAST AMOUNT IN THIS COLUMN

FIGURE 20-4
Customer Account

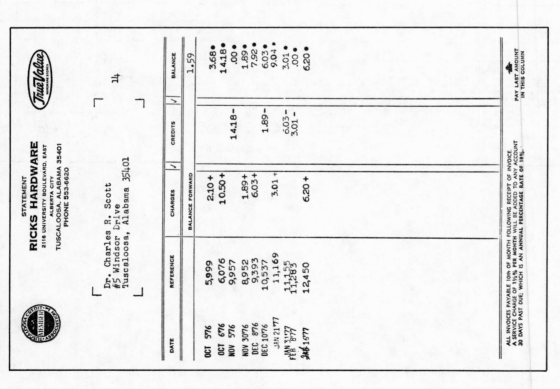

STATEMENT
RICKS HARDWARE
2116 UNIVERSITY BOULEVARD, EAST
ALBERTA CITY
TUSCALOOSA, ALABAMA 35401
PHONE 553-6620

Dr. Charles R. Scott
#5 Windsor Drive
Tuscaloosa, Alabama 35401   14

DATE	REFERENCE	CHARGES	√	CREDITS	√	BALANCE
		BALANCE FORWARD				1.59
OCT 5?6	5,999	2.10 +				3.68 ●
OCT 6?6	6,076	10.50+				14.18 ●
NOV 5?6	9,957			14.18-		.00 ●
NOV 30?6	8,952	1.89+				1.89 ●
DEC 8?6	9,393	6.03+				7.92 ●
DEC 10?6	10,537			1.89-		6.03 ●
JAN 21?7	11,169	3.01 +				9.04 ●
JAN 31?7	11,155			6.03-		3.01 ●
FEB 8?7	11,283			3.01 -		.00 ●
JAN 16?7	12,450	6.20 +				6.20 ●

ALL INVOICES PAYABLE 10th OF MONTH FOLLOWING RECEIPT OF INVOICE.
A SERVICE CHARGE OF 1½% PER MONTH WILL BE ADDED TO ANY ACCOUNT
30 DAYS PAST DUE; WHICH IS AN ANNUAL PERCENTAGE RATE OF 18%.

→ PAY LAST AMOUNT IN THIS COLUMN

FIGURE 20-6
Bank Deposit Ticket

(Front)

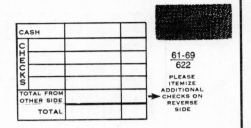

DEPOSIT TICKET

CHARLES R. SCOTT, JR.
OR ADDIE M. SCOTT

5 WINDSOR DRIVE
TUSCALOOSA, AL.   35401

DATE_____19____

ALL ITEMS ARE RECEIVED BY THIS BANK FOR THE PURPOSES OF COLLEC-
TION AND ARE SUBJECT TO PROVISIONS OF THE UNIFORM COMMERCIAL
CODE WHERE APPLICABLE AND THE RULES AND REGULATIONS OF THIS
BANK. ALL CREDITS FOR ITEMS ARE PROVISIONAL UNTIL COLLECTED.

First Alabama Bank
of Tuscaloosa, N.A.
Tuscaloosa, Alabama 35401

HARLAND 101 (5/75)

CASH		
C H E C K S		
TOTAL FROM OTHER SIDE		
TOTAL		

61-69
622

PLEASE
ITEMIZE
ADDITIONAL
→ CHECKS ON
REVERSE
SIDE

(Back)

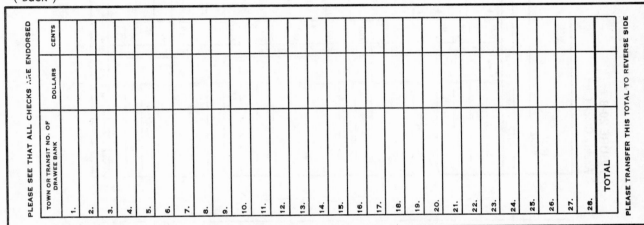

FIGURE 20-8
Weekly Clock Card

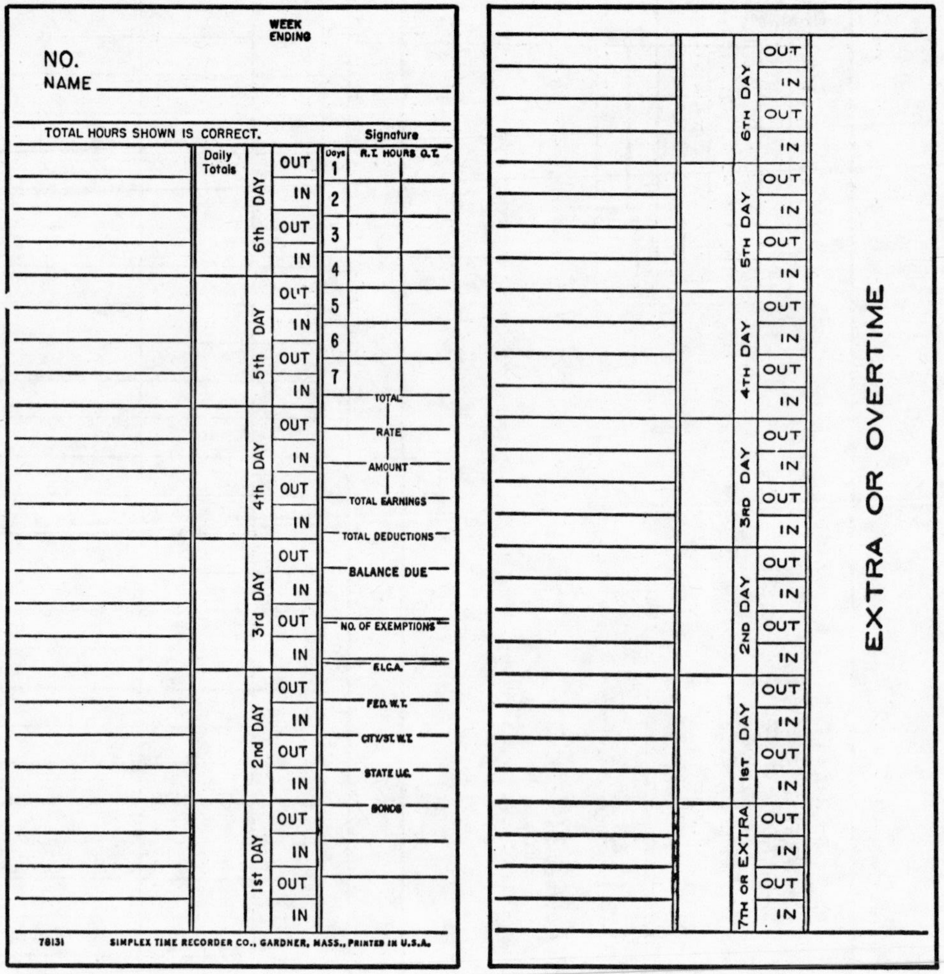

FIGURE 20-7
Cash Register Tape

G   .87 GR
G   1.74 DY
G   1.19 MT
G   .53 FF
G   .53 FF
G   .39 FF
G   .79 GP
G   .75 FF
G   .69 DY
G   2.36 MT
G   3.99 MT
C   .35 NF
G   .39 PR
G   .81 DY
G   .69 BK
         1LB/ .19   D 7
G   1.83LB .35 PR
         1LB/ .49   D26
G   1.13LB .55 PR
                1.02 TX
               17.99 TL

             20.00CATO
              2.01CACG

169

6319   2 A 8/23/76
             40002

FIGURE 20-9
Weekly Payroll Form

Department _____

Payroll for week ended _____   Page _____

Line no.	Name of employee	Empl. no.	Card no.	Hrs. worked	Reg. rate	Totals			Deductions						Net pay	Check no.
						Reg.	OT	Gross wages	Income taxes	FICA	Group ins.	Union dues	Other	Total		
1																
2																
3																
4																
5																
6																
7																
8																
9																
10																
TOTALS																

FIGURE 20-10
Invoice from Vendor

INVOICE

KRISHNAN ELECTRICAL PVT. LTD.
Hardinge Road, Bombay

No._____

Date:_____

Order No._____

Terms:_____

Sold To:_____

Address:_____

Salesman:_____

Quan.	Size	Description		Price	Amount

Customers P.O. No._____

Written By:_____   Ship Via:_____   Rec'd. By:_____

Copy 1: Shipment

272

FIGURE 20–11
Vendor's Account

STATEMENT
RICKS HARDWARE
2116 UNIVERSITY BOULEVARD, EAST
ALBERTA CITY
TUSCALOOSA, ALABAMA 35401
PHONE 553-6620

```
Wimberly & Thomas Hardware
P. O. Box 518                            82
1809 1st Avenue, South
Birmingham, Alabama 35201
```

DATE	REFERENCE	CHARGES	√	CREDITS	√	BALANCE
		BALANCE FORWARD				.00
NOV 5'76	2,466			773.39 –		773.39 CR
NOV 11'76	10,038			1,317.99 –		2,091.38 CR
OCT 14'76 CM	112,151	18.12 +				2,073.26 CR
NOV 18'76	111,262			67.64 –		2,140.90 CR
NOV 16'76	116,322			8.00 –		2,148.90 CR
NOV 18'76	116,562			408.44 –		2,557.34 CR
NOV 26'76	23,404			238.26 –		2,795.60 CR
NOV 26'76	24,296			166.35 –		2,961.95 CR
DEC 10'76	6,612	2,902.50 +				
DEC 10'76 DS	6,612	59.45 +				.00 CR
DEC 2'76	110,606			627.65 –		627.65 CR
DEC 6'76	206,071			35.64 –		663.29 CR
DEC 9'76	207,459			521.83 –		1,185.12 CR
DEC 14'76	214,417			8.00 –		1,193.12 CR
DEC 16'76	213,170			34.02 –		1,227.14 CR
DEC 16'76	214,592			506.22 –		1,733.36 CR
DEC 23'76	122,142			275.24 –		2,008.60 CR
OCT 28'76 CM	122,804	7.10 +				
DEC 6'76 CM	122,916	35.64 +				1,965.86 CR
JAN 10'77	6,749	1,927.65 +				
JAN 10'77 DS	6,749	38.21 +				.00 CR
JAN 7'77	105,005			558.55 –		558.55 CR
JAN 7'77	105,060			33.60 –		592.15 CR
JAN 13'77	112,032			754.01 –		1,346.16 CR
JAN 11'77	114,159			8.00 –		1,354.16 CR
JAN 17'77	117,136			34.28 –		1,388.44 CR
JAN 21'77	119,176			506.69 –		1,895.13 CR
JAN 27'77	125,391			451.60 –		2,346.73 CR
JAN 31'77	131,179			113.28 –		2,460.01 CR
JAN 7'77 CM	131,281	19.75 +				2,440.26 CR
FEB 10'77	6,887	2,391.22 +				
FEB 10'77 DS	6,887	49.04 +				.00 CR

ALL INVOICES PAYABLE 10th OF MONTH FOLLOWING RECEIPT OF INVOICE.
A SERVICE CHARGE OF 1½% PER MONTH WILL BE ADDED TO ANY ACCOUNT
30 DAYS PAST DUE; WHICH IS AN ANNUAL PERCENTAGE RATE OF 18%.

PAY LAST AMOUNT
IN THIS COLUMN

FIGURE 20–12
Check and Stub

CHARLES R. SCOTT, JR.
OR ADDIE M. SCOTT
5 WINDSOR DRIVE
TUSCALOOSA, AL.   35401

499

_____ 19___ $\frac{61\text{-}69}{622}$

PAY TO THE
ORDER OF _____ $_____

_____ DOLLARS

First Alabama Bank
of Tuscaloosa, N.A.
Tuscaloosa, Alabama 35401

FOR_____   _____

No.   499

_____ 19___

PAY TO _____

FOR _____

DEPOSIT _____

DEPOSIT _____

BALANCE

AMOUNT THIS CHECK

HARLAND 80   BALANCE

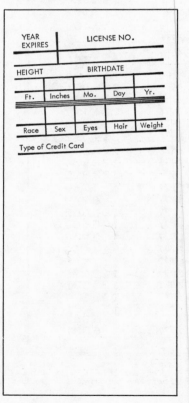

FIGURE 20–13
Identification Stamp

YEAR EXPIRES		LICENSE NO.		
HEIGHT		BIRTHDATE		
Ft.	Inches	Mo.	Day	Yr.
Race	Sex	Eyes	Hair	Weight
Type of Credit Card				

FIGURE 20-14
Slip for Petty Cash

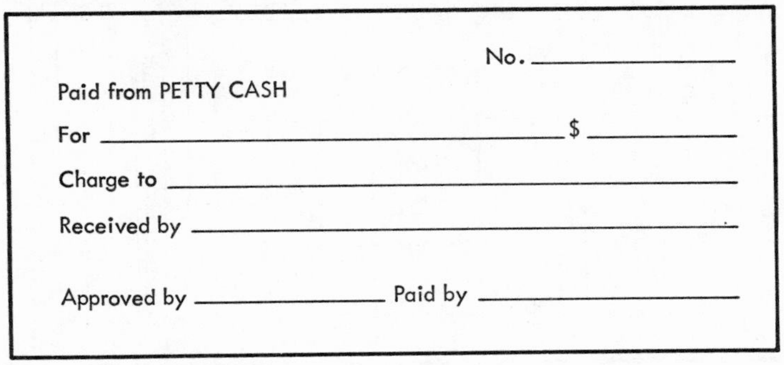

No. __________

Paid from PETTY CASH

For __________ $ __________

Charge to __________

Received by __________

Approved by __________ Paid by __________

FIGURE 20-15
Weekly Cash Report

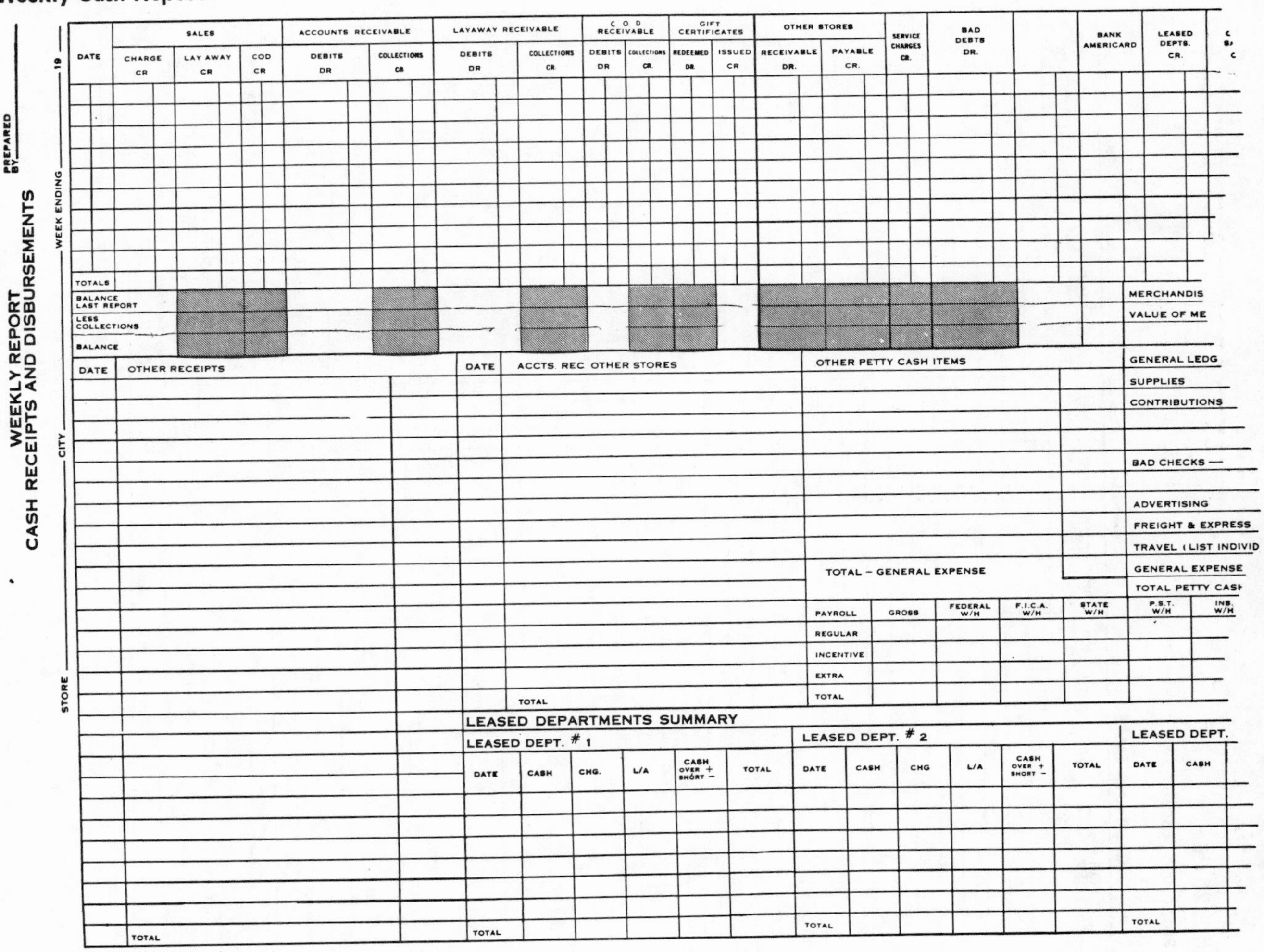

WEEKLY REPORT
CASH RECEIPTS AND DISBURSEMENTS

PREPARED BY __________

WEEK ENDING __________ 19 ____

STORE __________ CITY __________

DATE | SALES: CHARGE CR, LAY AWAY CR, COD CR | ACCOUNTS RECEIVABLE: DEBITS DR, COLLECTIONS CR | LAYAWAY RECEIVABLE: DEBITS DR, COLLECTIONS CR | C O D RECEIVABLE: DEBITS DR, COLLECTIONS CR | GIFT CERTIFICATES: REDEEMED DR, ISSUED CR | OTHER STORES: RECEIVABLE DR., PAYABLE CR. | SERVICE CHARGES CR. | BAD DEBTS DR. | BANK AMERICARD | LEASED DEPTS. CR.

TOTALS

BALANCE LAST REPORT

LESS COLLECTIONS

BALANCE

MERCHANDIS

VALUE OF ME

DATE | OTHER RECEIPTS

TOTAL

DATE | ACCTS. REC. OTHER STORES

TOTAL

OTHER PETTY CASH ITEMS

GENERAL LEDG

SUPPLIES

CONTRIBUTIONS

BAD CHECKS —

ADVERTISING

FREIGHT & EXPRESS

TRAVEL (LIST INDIVID

TOTAL – GENERAL EXPENSE

GENERAL EXPENSE

TOTAL PETTY CASH

PAYROLL | GROSS | FEDERAL W/H | F.I.C.A. W/H | STATE W/H | P.S.T. W/H | INS. W/H

REGULAR

INCENTIVE

EXTRA

TOTAL

LEASED DEPARTMENTS SUMMARY

LEASED DEPT. # 1: DATE | CASH | CHG. | L/A | CASH OVER + SHORT – | TOTAL

TOTAL

LEASED DEPT. # 2: DATE | CASH | CHG | L/A | CASH OVER + SHORT – | TOTAL

TOTAL

LEASED DEPT.: DATE | CASH

TOTAL

FIGURE 20-16
Cash and Sales Audit

CASH AND SALES AUDIT

Prepared by _____ Date _____

REGISTER TRANSACTION NUMBER		REGISTER NUMBER	SALES PERSON NUMBER	REGISTER READING	CHARGE RETURN	LAY-AWAY RETURN	VOIDS & ADJUSTMENTS	REFUNDS & EXCHANGES	LAY-AWAY SERVICE CHARGE	NET SALES BY SALES PERSON	CHARGE SALES LESS RETURNS	LAY-AWAY SALES LESS RETURNS & SER. CHG.	LAY-AWAY DOWN PAYMENTS	C.O.D. SALES		CASH SALES	GIFT CERTS. REDEEMED	DEPOSIT	CASH OVER + SHORT -
BEGIN	END																		
1	2	3	4	5	6	7	8	9	10	11	12	13	14	15	16	17	18	19	20

Trans. L/A—Chg.
Subtotal
Leased Dept. 1
Leased Dept. 2
Leased Dept. 3

Totals

Serial Nos. of Gift Certificates Redeemed

Balancing Formula
5 — 6 — 7 — 8 — 9 — 10 = 11
11 — 12 — 13 — 15 = 17
14 + 17 — 18 — 19 + or — 20
22 — 23 + or — 24 — 26 = 27
Column 11 = Column 27

DEPARTMENTAL AUDIT

DEPT. NUMBER	DEPT. REGISTER READING	CREDITS & ADJUSTMENTS	DEPT. TRANSFERS + (—)		LAY-AWAY SER. CHG.	NET DEPT. SALES
21	22	23	24	25	26	27

SCHEDULE OF MISCELLANEOUS COLLECTIONS

	TAPE OF RECEIPTS	
C.O.D. Collections		
Miscellaneous Collections	XXXX	
Gift Certificates Issued	XXXX	
Charge Collections	XXXX	
Lay-Away Collections		
Total	XXXXX	

Gift Certificates Charged
Charge Sales to Other Stores' Customers
Tickets Charged to Our Customers in Other Stores
Total Debit to Accounts Receivable — Customers

FIGURE 20-17
Examples of Recordings and Adjustments of Transactions

1. Receive order for material X, $100, entered when received.
   Used $80 of material X, entered at end of period.

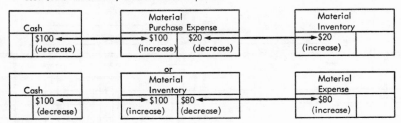

or

2. Paid insurance policy, $75, entered when paid.
   Monthly expense of insurance, $50 (1/12 of annual $600), entered
   at end of period.

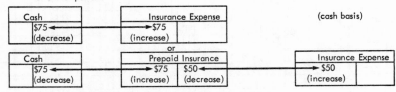

3. Paid wages, $2,400 (160 hours x $3.00 per hour x 5 workers) (from
   payroll book). Wages paid for last month's work, $480 (32 hours
   x $3.00 per hour x 5 workers). Work not paid this month, $600 (40
   hours x $3.00 x 5 workers).

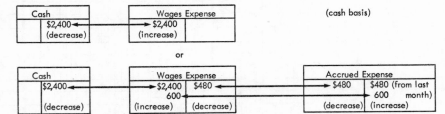

4. Have machine which cost $1,300. From machine records, machine
   expense, $20—machine cost, $1,300 less estimated scrap value,
   $100—divided by estimated life, 5 years (60 months).

Reserve for Depreciation		Depreciation Expense	
$20 ◄──		──► $20	
(increase)		(increase)	

FIGURE 20-18
Calculation Sheet for Bid on a Job

RECAPITULATION

LOCATION _HOUSTON BUILDING_   JOB___

ARCHITECT _JAY PARK_   _60X180_   ITEM___

DATE___   PR.___ CK.___   SHEET No.___ EST. No.___

ITEM	DESCRIPTION OF WORK	QUANTITY	UNIT	LABOR Unit Cost	LABOR	MATERIAL Unit Cost	MATERIAL	SUB-BID	TOTAL
	LAYOUT				100—				
	MISC. EXPENSES				125—				
	FOUNDATION								
	MACHINE EXCAVATION	26	CY						
	HAND EXCAVATION	6	CY	9	54—				
	FINE GRADE	480	SF		—				
	RE-BAR	641	LBS			.12	77—		
	POUR FOUNDATION	15	CY	16	240—	17.	255—		
	MASONRY								
	12" CONC. BLK (1 COURSE)	370	EA.	.50	185—	.45	166—		
	8" CONC. BLK	9033	EA.	.50	4516—	.45	4065—		
	{ TOP COURSE UNDER								
	{ PURLINS								
	CEILING								
	{1X4 STRIPS @ 16" O.C.	3.3	MBF	150	495—	135	446—		
	OPTION{4" BATT INSULATION	11.5	1000 SF	90	1035—	60	690—		
	{½" PLYWOOD	12.1	MBF	110	1331—	130	1573—		
	OWENS INSULATION (SUSPENDED)							6800—	
	DOOR UNITS								
	12'X14' SLIDING	2	EA.		148—		970—	50—	
	3° X 6¾ EXTERIOR (METAL)	2	EA.	3	6—	90	270—		
	4'X4' WINDOWS	14	EA.	3	42—	24	336—		
	{PAINT CEILING (2 COATS)	11.5	1000 SF			100		1150—	
	TOTAL MATERIAL								6139—
	6% MATERIAL								362—
	TOTAL LABOR								5416—
	15% LABOR								812—
	TOTAL SUB								6850—
	TOTAL								19579—
	8% PROFIT								1566—
	GRAND TOTAL								21145—
	1.95/SF								
	*PLYWOOD CEILING · 7312 + PROFIT								

FIGURE 20–19
Time Ticket

| Name _____ ID No. _____ |
| Date _____ Regular Wage Rate _____ |

Order No.	Dept.	Time Started	Time Stopped	Time Elapsed

Source: From R. Lee Brummet and Jack C. Robertson, *Cost Accounting for Small Manufacturers*, 2d ed. (Washington, D.C.: Small Business Administration, 1972), Small Business Management Series, No. 9.

FIGURE 20–20
Job Cost Record

JOB COST RECORD

For _____ Order No. _____

Product _____ Quantity _____

Date Wanted _____ Date Started _____ Date Completed _____

Direct Materials			Direct Labor			Applied Overhead		
Date	Req. No.	Amount	Date	Time Card No.	Amount	Basis	Rate	Amount

Summary for Order No. _____

Direct Materials _____

Direct Labor _____

Applied Overhead _____

Total Factory Cost _____

Factory Cost per Unit _____

Source: From R. Lee Brummet and Jack C. Robertson, *Cost Accounting for Small Manufacturers*, 2d ed. (Washington, D.C.: Small Business Administration, 1972), Small Business Management Seires, No. 9.

FIGURE 20-21

Production Cost Summary by Customer Order

| Production Cost Summary for Month of _____ | | | | | | | | |
| For Department _____ | | | | | | | | |
Date Completed	Order No.	Product	Quantity	Direct Materials	Direct Labor	Applied Overhead	Total Cost	Cost per Unit

Source: From R. Lee Brummet and Jack C. Robertson, *Cost Accounting for Small Manufacturers,* 2d ed. (Washington, D.C.: Small Business Administration, 1972), Small Business Management Seires, No. 9.

FIGURE 20-22
Multipart Hospital Record

OUT PATIENT	DRUID CITY HOSPITAL TUSCALOOSA, ALABAMA				00100

PATIENT'S NAME		PHONE	SERVICE	CHARGE $
PATIENT'S HOME ADDRESS	AGE	DATE OF BIRTH		
PATIENT'S MAILING ADDRESS	SEX ☐ M ☐ F	RACE ☐ COLORED ☐ WHITE		
EMPLOYER		PHONE		
ADDRESS				
INSURED BY	POLICY No.	TYPE		
SUBSCRIBER OR RESPONSIBLE PARTY		PHONE		
ADDRESS				

DATE	HOUR M	DEPARTMENT	DISPOSITION	TYPE OF CASE	(1) MED. (2) SURG. (3) OB (4) ACCIDENT	COMPENSATION ☐ YES ☐ NO	

ATTENDING PHYSICIAN AND ADDRESS	DIAGNOSIS	TOTAL	$

NURSES NOTES AND TREATMENT

ACCIDENTS ONLY
NATURE & EXTENT OF INJURIES – (COMPLETE & SIGN BY DOCTOR)

_____M. D

PLACE OF ACCIDENT

BY WHOM INJURED | HOW BROUGHT TO HOSPITAL

WITNESSES

NOTIFICATION & TIME (POLICE, CORONER, FRIENDS, ETC.)

MEDICAL RECORDS COPY

chapter 21

Planning for a Profit

Profit should not be left to chance. However, all too often, that is what is done. It is assumed that historic relationships are fixed and that profits will therefore continue. However, because of the changing nature of our economic environment, only if all goods and services are priced for profit will there be an assurance of profit. This chapter will aid you in planning what profit you desire and in determining how you can achieve it.

HOW TO PLAN FOR PROFIT

When you study the profit-and-loss statement in Figure 19–2, you may tend to "read" it in the following manner: "The Sample Company received $231,574 in sales, expended $145,631 on goods sold, had $72,971 in other expenses, and had $12,972 left over as profit." Profit seems to be a "leftover."

Neither you nor Mr. Sample, owner-manager of The Sample Company, can do anything about the past. However, you can do something about the future. Since one of your goals is to make a profit, you should plan your operations so that you attain the profit you feel you should make from your business. The steps you need to take to achieve this goal during the coming year are:

1. Establish your profit goal.
2. Determine your planned volume of sales.
3. Estimate your expenses for the planned volume of sales.
4. Determine your estimated profit on the basis of the plans reached in (2) and (3).
5. Compare your estimated profit with your profit goal.

If you are satisfied with your plans, you can stop after completing Step 5. However, you may want to check further to determine whether improvements can be made—particularly if you are not happy with the

282

results of Step 5. The following steps may help you understand better how certain changes in your business activities may affect your profit. they are:

6. List possible alternatives which can be used to improve your profit position.
7. Determine how your costs vary with changes in sales volume.
8. Determine how your profits vary with changes in sales volume.
9. Analyze your alternatives from a profit standpoint.
10. Select changes in your plans, if any, and implement the changes through the use of budgets.

You should be realistic when going through these steps; otherwise you may not be able to attain your goals. You may feel that the future is too uncertain to make such plans, but the greater the uncertainty, the greater the need for planning.

The following material deals with the use of the above steps in The Sample Company. The details are shown in Figure 21-1.

Exhibit 58 of *The Dow Jones-Irwin Business Papers* will help you plan for your profits. You may either use it now or after you have completed these steps. We recommend that you use it as a checklist as you actually do the planning for your profits.

Place yourself in Mr. Sample's shoes as he plans for the coming year. He should start making his plans several months ahead of the time to put them into effect, say, starting in October for the coming calendar year. In order to present a systematic analysis, we will assume that he is planning for the first time. Actually, he should be planning for each month at least six months or a year ahead. This can be done by dropping the past month, adjusting the rest of the months in his prior plans, and adding the plans for another month. This planning will give him time to anticipate needed changes and do something about them.

STEP 1: ESTABLISHING YOUR PROFIT GOAL

Your desired profit must be a specific value which you set as a target. Since you are managing the business, you are paying yourself a reasonable salary. Also, as the owner, you should receive a return on your investment—both your initial investment and prior earnings left in the business. In order to determine your desired profit, you can consider what you would receive in salary by working for someone else, plus the income you would receive if you invested the same amount of money in a savings and loan association, house loans, bonds, or stocks.

Each of these investments provides a return with a certain degree of risk—and pleasure. If you could invest at, say, a 7 percent return with little risk, what do you feel the return on your business should be?

Originally Mr. Sample invested $80,000 in his company, and has left $20,000 of his previous profits in the business. He made about 10 percent on his investment this past year. He could make about 8 percent if he invested his money in a good grade of bonds. He judges that his return has been too low for the risk he is taking and feels that a return of about 15 percent is reasonable.

In Figure 21-1, Step 1, he enters his investment, his desired profit, and his estimate of income taxes (from the past and after consultation with his accountant), and determines he must make $20,000 before taxes, or a 20 percent return on his investment. Having set his goal, he next turns to the task of determining what his profit before taxes will be from his forecast of next year's plans.

FIGURE 21-1

THE SAMPLE COMPANY
Planning the Profit for the Year, 19 ——

Step	Description	Analysis	Comments
1.	*Establish your profit goals*		
	Equity invested in company	$ 80,000	
	Retained earnings	20,000	
	Owner's equity	$100,000	
	Returned desired	$ 15,000	15% x $100,000
	Estimated tax on profit	5,000	25%
	Profit needed before income taxes	$ 20,000	
2.	*Determine your planned volume of sales*		
	Mr. Sample's estimate of sales income	$250,000	8% increase over last year
3.	*Estimate your expenses for planned volume of sales*		

Item of Expense	Actual Last Year	Estimate 19___
Cost of goods	$145,631	$159,100
Salaries	41,569	44,000
Utilities	3,475	3,600
Depreciation	5,025	5,025
Rent	1,000	1,000
Building services	2,460	2,500
Insurance	2,000	2,000
Interest	1,323	1,500
Office expenses	2,775	2,900
Sales promotion	5,500	6,100
Taxes and licenses	3,240	3,400
Maintenance	805	850
Delivery	2,924	3,200
Miscellaneous	875	900
Total	$218,602	$236,075

Step	Description	Analysis
4.	*Determine your profit based on (2) and (3) plans*	
	Estimated sales income	$250,000
	Estimated expenses	236,075
	Estimated net profit before taxes	$ 13,925

FIGURE 21-1 (continued)

5. *Compare your estimated profit with your profit goal*

Estimated profit before taxes $13,925
Desired profit before taxes 20,000

Difference . . . . -$ 6,075

6. Some alternatives:
   a. Increase planned volume of units sold.
   b. Increase or decrease planned price of units.
   c. Decrease planned expenses.
   d. Add other products or services.
   e. Subcontract work.

7. *Determine how costs vary with changes in sales volume*

Item of Expense	Total Estimated Expenses	Fixed Expenses	Variable Expenses
Goods sold	$159,100		$159,100
Salaries	44,000	$20,000	24,000
Utilities	3,600	2,600	1,000
Depreciation	5,025	5,025	
Rent	1,000	1,000	
Building services	2,500	2,000	500
Insurance	2,000	2,000	
Interest	1,500		1,500
Office expenses	2,900	1,500	1,400
Sales promotion	6,100		6,100
Taxes and licenses	3,400	2,500	900
Maintenance	850	450	400
Delivery	3,200		3,200
Miscellaneous	900	900	
Total	$236,075	$37,975	$198,100

8. *Determine how profits vary with changes in sales volume*

Total marginal income = Sales income − variable expenses
= $250,000 − $198,100 = $51,900

Marginal income per dollar of sales income = $51,900 ÷ $250,000
= $0.208/$ of sales income

Estimated costs and profits at various sales volumes:

Sales Volume	Fixed Costs	Variable Costs		Profit
$175,000	$37,975	0.792 x 175,000 =	$138,600	-$ 1,575
200,000	37,975	0.792 x 200,000 =	158,400	3,625
225,000	37,975	0.792 x 225,000 =	178,200	8,825
250,000	37,975	0.792 x 250,000 =	198,100	13,925
275,000	37,975	0.792 x 275,000 =	217,800	19,225
300,000	37,975	0.792 x 300,000 =	237,600	24,425

A forecast of your sales for next year is based on your estimate of such factors as market conditions, the level of your sales promotion, your competitors' activities, and forecasts of business activity made by business managers, such magazines as *Business Week*, government specialists, and people specializing in forecasting. Talks with your banker, customers, vendors, and others provide added information.

Mr. Sample has been gathering this information and has been watching his company's sales trend. From these, he estimates that he can

**STEP 2:
DETERMINING YOUR
PLANNED VOLUME
OF SALES**

increase his sales about 8 percent. Thus, he enters $250,000 (1.08 X $231,574) in the figure as Step 2.

STEP 3:
ESTIMATING YOUR
EXPENSES FOR THE
PLANNED VOLUME
OF SALES

To estimate next year's expenses, you collect the company's costs for the past years. Mr. Sample has listed these for the past year in Step 3. (He also has them for the previous years if he needs to refer to them.) These expenses must be adjusted for the planned sales volume, for changes in economic conditions (including inflation), for changes in sales promotion and for improved methods of production.

Mr. Sample has figured that about 63 percent of his income is expended on materials and on the labor used directly on the goods he sells. He uses this figure (63 percent), adds a 1 percent increase in the unit costs for inflation and enters the result, $159,100, for cost of goods. He estimates the value of each of the other expenses, recognizing that some expenses vary directly with volume changes, that others do not change at all, and that still others change slightly. He enters each figure for expense in the appropriate place.

STEP 4:
DETERMINING
YOUR PROFIT FROM
STEPS 2 AND 3

In this step, he deducts the figure for his total expenses from the sales income, and adds the total of any other income, such as interest. Mr. Sample calculates this amount, and finds that his estimated profit before taxes is $13,925 ($250,000–$236,075). This amount is slightly better than the $12,972 made last year. (See Figure 19-2.) However, he had thought that the increased volume of sales would increase his profit more than $953.

STEP 5:
COMPARING YOUR
ESTIMATED PROFIT
WITH YOUR
PROFIT GOAL

Mr. Sample then compares his estimated profit with his desired profit. He enters the value for these profits in Figure 21-1, and finds that his plan will result in a profit figure which is $6,075 ($20,000–$13,925) lower than his goal. After pondering what he should do, he decides to follow the rest of the steps.

STEP 6:
LISTING POSSIBLE
ALTERNATIVES TO
IMPROVE YOUR
PROFITS

As shown in Figure 21-1, Step 6, a number of alternatives for improving profits are available to Mr. Sample. Some of these are:

1. Change the planned sales income by:
   a. Increasing the planned volume of units sold by increasing sales promotion, improving the quality produce or service, making the product more available, or finding new uses for the product.
   b. Increasing or decreasing the planned price of the units. The best price may not be the planned one. How will these changes affect the profit? Have there been price changes in the past, and if so,

286

what has happened? Have there been changes in the attitudes and economic status of the company's customers? Which products' prices should be changed?

    c.   Combining *(a)* and *(b)*. It has been observed, on occasion, that some independent business owners become too concerned with selling on the basis of price alone. Instead, you should price for profit and sell quality, better service, reliability, and integrity. Never be entrapped by the cliché, "I won't be undersold." Many businesses have failed because of this pricing strategy.

2.   Decrease planned expenses by:

    a.   Establishing a better control system. Money may be lost by having too many people operate the cash register, by poor scheduling, and by having too much money tied up in inventory. Expenses may be reduced if these areas are spotted and controls are established.

    b.   Increasing the productivity of people and machines by improving methods, developing proper motivators, and improving the types and use of machinery.

    c.   Redesigning the product. Research is constantly developing new materials, machines, and methods for improving products and reducing costs.

3.   Add other products or services:

Costs per unit can be reduced by adding a summer product to a winter line of products, selling as well as using parts made on machines with idle capacity, and making some parts customarily purchased.

4.   Subcontract work.

Having listed possible alternatives, Mr. Sample needs to evaluate each of them. Some may not be good choices now. Their evaluation can be delayed until after deciding on more favorable alternatives. An understanding of cost and volume relationships is important in evaluating the alternatives.

Mr. Sample planned for changes in his expenses with an increase in sales volume, as shown in Step 3 of Figure 21-1. He used a simple break-even chart, which is shown in Figure 21-2. Notice that as the volume of sales changes, the costs of doing business also change. Straight lines are used because costs are estimated and a straight line adequately approximates them.

Mr. Sample collected the figures for production volume and costs from his records of the past five years. Production figures and costs for such items as direct materials, depreciation, and office supplies which are shown in Table 21-1, are plotted in Figure 21-3. Note that when the cost of direct materials (A) is plotted in the figure, the cost increases in

STEP 7: DETERMINING HOW YOUR COSTS VARY WITH CHANGES IN SALES VOLUME

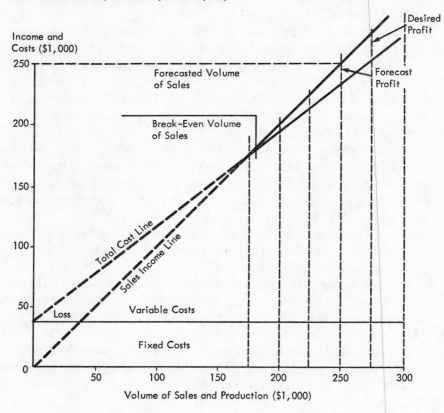

FIGURE 21-2
Break-Even Chart, The Sample Company

TABLE 21-1
Data Collected from The Sample Company Records

Year	Production Volume	Direct Materials	Depreciation	Office Supplies
1	$110,100	$45,900	$3,100	$2,150
2	139,000	52,900	3,100	2,500
3	165,200	60,700	3,800	1,900
4	205,000	74,800	4,400	2,800
5	231,600	85,100	5,025	2,800
19—*	250,000	92,000	5,025	2,900

*Estimated

direct proportion to sales volume, starting at zero cost and zero volume. This is to be expected, as materials used directly in manufacturing the product increase directly as the volume of products increases.

Depreciation (B) is the loss in value of the machinery and equipment as they are used and as they get older. Businesses usually deduct the estimated resale value of an item from its costs and divide the balance by the life of the item—in years—to obtain its annual depreciation cost.

FIGURE 21–3
Costs and Volume of Production

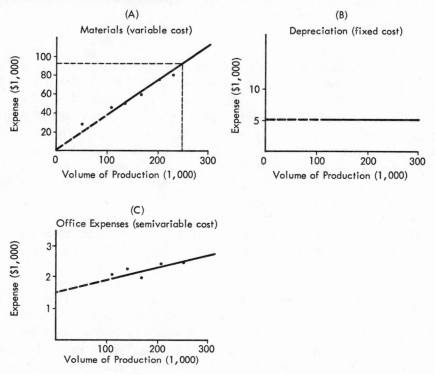

(A)
Materials (variable cost)

(B)
Depreciation (fixed cost)

(C)
Office Expenses (semivariable cost)

Depreciation is called a fixed cost because its cost per year does not change, regardless of the volume of output, until you buy or sell the fixed asset. Other fixed costs, such as rent, are paid each period.

The account office expenses (C) is shown to illustrate what is called a semivariable expense. When Mr. Sample plots this cost, the line starts at about $1,500 at zero sales volume, and increases from that amount as the sales volume increases. You can use the graphs to help you in your analysis, but be sure to recognize that:

1. The relationships exist only within limited changes in sales volume. Very high sales volumes may be obtained only by such measures as extraordinary sales promotion, added fixed costs for machinery, and increases in overtime. Low sales volumes result in extra costs of idle capacity, lost volume discounts, and so forth.

2. Past relationships may not continue in the future. Inflation or deflation, changing location of customers, new products, and other factors can cause changes in the costs per unit. Mr. Sample recognized a possible increase in the cost of goods sold for the next year, and increased his cost of goods.

Mr. Sample computed fixed and variable costs for each of his items of expense at his planned volume of sales, and entered the figures in Figure 21-1.

STEP 8: DETERMINING HOW YOUR PROFITS VARY WITH CHANGES IN SALES VOLUME

How much does profit increase when you increase sales by $1? Mr. Sample planned for $250,000 of sales and $236,075 of expenses. Therefore, each dollar of sales will incur a cost of $0.944 ($236,075 ÷ $250,000). However, if he increases his sales $1, the extra sales should not cost him $0.944. The fixed costs will stay constant, and only the variable costs should increase. So his cost should increase only by the variable portion. For $1 of sales increase, his cost should increase by only $0.792 ($198,100 ÷ $250,000). His increase in profit per dollar of increase in sales volume, often called *marginal income* (MI), is $0.208 ($1—$0.792). What do you think this means to Mr. Sample?

The marginal income (or gross profit) can be determined for each product, and tells you which product is the most profitable.

STEP 9: ANALYZING YOUR ALTERNATIVES FROM A PROFIT STANDPOINT

Mr. Sample can compute his cost and profit at several sales volumes in order to give him a picture of the changes in profit. This is shown in Step 8 of Figure 21-1, and is plotted as a graph in Figure 21-2. Note that the sales volume at which the company still makes no profit is close to $175,000, and that the company can make the desired profit only if sales increase to $275,000.

Mr. Sample can use marginal analyses to help him in his decision making, as follows:

1. How much can he reduce his price for a sale to bring in more sales volume? He must not reduce it more than 20.8 percent, for if he does he would be paying out more than the extra sales bring in. Any smaller reduction would contribute to reducing the fixed-cost charges, or increasing the profit.

2. Is it profitable to increase his advertising $2,000 which, Mr. Sample estimates, would increase his sales $15,000? He should obtain additional profits of $3,120 ($0.208 X $15,000) for the $2,000 he paid out. This would give him an added profit of $1,120 ($3,120—$2,000).

3. Is it profitable to increase the price 2 percent if he can expect a drop of 5 percent in sales? The price increase would result in a marginal income (MI) of about $0.228 ($0.208 + $0.02), and the profit would change to about $16,175 ($0.228 X 0.95 X $250,000—$37,975), which would be better than the present expected profit of $13,925.

4. What would a reduction of 5 percent in his variable costs do to profit? The MI should increase to $0.2476 ($1.00—$0.792 X .95), and the profit at $250,000 sales volume would be $23,925 ($250,000 X $0.2476 — $37,975). This looks very good if the means can be found to reduce the variable cost without hurting other operations.

5. Which product is the most profitable?

Having made these economic analyses, Mr. Sample is now ready to make his final plan for action.

STEP 10: SELECTING CHANGES IN YOUR PLANS

The selection of the changes, if any, depends on your judgment as to what would be most beneficial to your firm. The results of the analyses you have made in the prior steps provide the economic inputs. These must be evaluated along with your other goals. Cost reduction may result in laying off employees or in a reduction in service to your customers. But lowering prices may satisfy your goal for a larger volume of sales. Higher prices are risky.

Mr. Sample has just read this book, and has been studying some other management literature. He feels that he can reduce his cost of goods by 2 percent. Figure 21-4 shows a simplified statement of his planned income and outgo for the next year.

FIGURE 21-4

THE SAMPLE CO.
Planned Profit and Loss Statement
For the Year 19 ___

Sales income		$250,000
Less:		
Cost of goods sold	$155,900	
Other expenses	76,975	232,875
Net profit before taxes		$ 17,125
Return on investment		17.1%

DETERMINING WHETHER FULL EARNING POTENTIAL IS BEING MET

Profits do not just happen! Planning your operations improves your chances of achieving your profit goals. You can achieve more by knowing your goals, understanding your company's sales income to cost relationships, and determining the best operating plan. You should know where your break-even point is and what the effects of alternative plans would be.

However, though you may have considered the expected net income, and even calculated the net income to sales and net income to equity ratios, you may need to make a more detailed examination of your business in order to determine whether its full earning potential is being exploited. The form in Exhibit 59 of *The Dow Jones-Irwin Business Papers* can help you perform such an evaluation.

Before making your final plans, you need more information about the financial condition of your company. Chapter 22 provides you with some more tools for obtaining this information.

chapter 22

Maintaining Financial Control

This chapter places control in focus by providing you with sufficient information to understand its nature, its mechanics, and its objective. Specifically, you will become aware of some causes of poor performance, some characteristics of an effective control system, and some ways of setting up and operating a control system. In addition, the chapter discusses the design and use of budgets.

WHAT IS INVOLVED IN CONTROL?

Profit planning alone is not enough! After developing plans for generating a profit, you must design a system to help you carry out those plans. Then the system must be controlled to see that the plans are carried out.

As shown in Part Two, your managerial functions are planning, organizing, directing, and controlling. As shown in Chapter 7, planning provides the guides and standards used in performing the activities necessary to achieve your company's goals. A system of controls is essential if you are to make actual performance conform to your plans. Any deviation from the plans points to a need for change—usually in performance, but sometimes in the plans themselves.

Regardless of where it occurs, the process of control consists of these steps:

1. Set up standards of performance.
2. Measure actual performance.
3. Compare the actual performance with the standards.
4. Determine whether the deviations are excessive.
5. Determine the appropriate corrective action.

This chapter covers these five steps in detail.

292

Control systems should be timely, not overly costly, provide the accuracy needed, be quantifiable and measurable, show cause-and-effect relationships, and be the responsibility of one individual.

To keep them timely, checks should be made frequently and as soon as practical after they are needed. You cannot wait until the end of the year to find out what your sales are and whether they meet your plans. Some stores check their sales daily for indications that their performance is not meeting expectations. They make many small sales and a daily check helps indicate whether changes are needed. Since manufacturers handle fewer transactions on a less regular basis, they may find that weekly or monthly checks are sufficient.

Controls Should Be Timely

The collection of the totals of an activity, such as sales, takes time. Such data collection has been simplified through the use of cash registers with tapes, minicomputers, and other office machines.

A system for fast checks is valuable. The old adage "It is too late to lock the barn door after the cow has left" applies to your controls.

All controls require the time of a person or of some equipment. Often, paperwork is involved. The cost of the control system needs to be balanced against its value to you. It is not economical "to spend a nickel to save a penny." Therefore, you should try to reduce the time you and your employees spend in collecting information. A systematic inspection of what is on the shelves may give enough information for control without having a clerk provide a written or tabulated summary of what has been removed from the shelves. At selected times, however, extra costs may be justified to provide for more detailed controls.

Controls Should Be Economical

Inspection for control of quality can test every unit of product or only a sample of the units. Statistical techniques can be applied to many areas of control in order to reduce cost and improve quality. You can periodically check output per hour, the cleanliness of the stockroom, and the cost of material to obtain a good check of performance.

Controls Should Provide the Accuracy Needed

Performance can vary above as well as below standard. Also, part of the variance from standard cannot be controlled, while part can. But should you control the variance if you can? The correction of a variation of a few cents in a $10,000 figure may not be justified, whereas it may be very significant in a figure of $0.05 per unit.

The choice of measuring sticks for control is vital. Sales can be measured in dollars, pounds, tons, barrels, gallons, grams, kilograms, meters, or other units. Which will give you the information you want for

Controls Should Be Quantifiable

control? Which is the least costly? You should choose the unit that will give you the needed control for the least cost.

Controls Should Show Causes

A report that the costs of a manufactured product have risen, indicates the actual situation but does not explain it. On the other hand, a report that the cost per unit of purchased goods is higher than planned, shows the actual situation, and also identifies its source.

Controls Should Be Assigned to One Person

Because you do not have the time to control all activities yourself, you need to delegate the authority for such action to a subordinate. Give that person authority, provide him with the necessary resources, and then hold him responsible for accomplishments.

CAUSES OF POOR PERFORMANCE

Poor performance in a company can result from many factors. Some of these factors are:

1. Customers not buying the company's product.
2. Poor scheduling of production or purchases.
3. Theft or spoilage of products.
4. Too many people for the work to be performed.
5. Opportunities lost.
6. Too many free services or donations.

ESTABLISHING STANDARDS OF PERFORMANCE

Standards of performance are developed from many sources. These include:

1. Intuition.
2. Past performance.
3. Plans for desired accomplishment.
4. Careful measurement of activities.
5. Comparison with other standards or averages. (See Chapter 13 for a discussion of time standards.)

Once the standards of performance are determined, they may be communicated by means of policies, rules, procedures, statements, and budgets to the people who are to meet the standards.

Standards are norms, stated in writing, for employees to follow. They are usually stated in terms of units consumed or of prices paid or charged. Examples include standard hours per unit to produce a good or service, miles per gallon of gasoline used, and price per part for purchased goods. Standards inform the employee of the time in which he is to do a job, and measure how well he does it. They are valuable in locating sources of both efficient and inefficient performance.

Information on actual performance is obtained through some form of feedback. It can be obtained by observation, oral reports, written memos or reports, and other methods.

Observation will probably be most satisfying to you, as you are at the scene of action and have direct control over the situation. However, this method is time-consuming and you cannot be in all places at once. Observation is justified when your knowledge is needed, when your presence may improve the work, or when you are present for other purposes.

Oral reports are simple and less time-consuming, and provide two-way communications. They are the most prevalent type of control used in business.

Written reports are prepared when a record is needed and when many facts must be assembled for decision making. These reports are most costly unless they are the original records. A good record system, as discussed in Chapter 20, is a valuable aid, and, when the system is designed, the reports needed should be considered.

OBTAINING INFORMATION ON ACTUAL PERFORMANCE

Information about actual performance, obtained by feedback, is compared to standards to determine whether any changes are needed. This procedure will usually be simple, since informal controls exist for most of your decision making. The measures of performance are carried in your head; you make the comparison as you receive feedback; and you make your decisions accordingly. It must be emphasized, however, that such informal control follows the same steps as the more formal types of control. Control through the use of standards, discussed in Chapters 12 through 14, follows the same pattern as control through the use of budgets. The rest of this chapter will cover the design and use of budgets which are of most value to independent firms.

COMPARING ACTUAL PERFORMANCE WITH STANDARDS

As stated in Chapter 7, a budget can be defined as an itemized summary of probable expenditures and income for a given period of time, which embodies a systematic plan for meeting expenses. The budget system is based on your profit plans for the coming period. As each day, week, or month passes, checks are made to assure progress toward meeting your goals. If actual performance equals the budget, the company is meeting its goals. If it differs from the budget, decisions can be made about whether changes are needed. Thus, budgets provide:

THE DESIGN AND USE OF BUDGETS

1. Guideposts toward your goals.
2. Indications of where trouble exists.
3. Planned actions which need to be taken.
4. At planning time, evaluation of the feasibility of the plans.

An effective budget system would include close controls in the areas in which poor performance most affects your company. Other areas may be controlled less often. For example, the cost of goods sold by The Sample Company is planned for 63 percent of the sales dollar, and utilities cost 1.4 percent. The cost of goods sold might be divided into materials and labor and checked weekly. Utilities might be checked on a monthly basis.

The Sales Budget

The sales budget is the most basic one, for once sales are planned and budgeted, the other budgets can be prepared more easily.

This budget should be your responsibility or the responsibility of a sales manager. Let us assume that you have a sales manager. You and he should have worked up the sales plan for the coming year. Now, how much does the sales department need to sell each day? The plans for The Sample Company call for sales of $250,000 per year. If the firm plans for 203 sales days per year, it must average $1,230 ($250,000 ÷ 203) per sales day. But some sales days are good and some are poor. You may have noticed seasonal, monthly, and even daily patterns in the past. The daily average can be adjusted upward or downward for each day in the week or for the month.

Another method which can be used to obtain daily, weekly, or monthly sales is to modify the figures for the past year. If you think the pattern of sales for the coming year will be the same as that of the past year, merely change last year's daily sales by a given percentage. Mr. Sample planned to increase his sales by 8 percent, as shown in Step 2, Figure 21-1.

How often should you compare actual sales to the budget? A grocery store manager usually makes a daily check, for he finds that the daily sales vary considerably from his budget. This is to be expected, but they should be within range of the budget, and actual sales should range above the expected figure at least as often as below it. If they do not, you have a warning signal to do a more complete check or to take some corrective action. Weekly, monthly, and year-to-date summaries provide more stable relationships for control.

Companies may check at longer intervals and may use other types of checks. One owner watches the number and size of contracts at the end of each month. Others control by product line, by units of product sold, and by territory. The detail needed for control depends on the nature of the business.

For budgeting purposes, it may be adequate to tally sales in one column of a control pad, the budget in a second column, and the difference in a third column.

The Cash Budget

Cash planning is very important if a company is to meet its payments. Cash planning takes two forms: (1) the daily and weekly cash requirements for the normal operation of the business, and (2) the maintenance of the proper balance for all requirements.

The first form tends to be routine. For example, your company may have a fairly constant income and outgo. Policies can thus be established for the level of cash and a procedure set up to keep cash at that level. These operating demands represent a small part of the cash needed and tend to remain fairly constant.

The second form requires a budget for, say, each month of the year. Payments for rent, payroll, purchases, and services require a regular outflow of cash. Insurance and taxes may require large payments a number of times each year. A special purchase of, say, a truck, will place a heavy demand on cash. It takes planning to have the *right* amount of cash available at all times.

Figure 21-1 shows a cash budget for three months ahead. Each month is completed before the next month is shown. Lines 1-3 show estimated cash receipts. The Sample Company expects to receive 20 percent of its monthly sales in cash. A check of its accounts receivable budget (presented in the next section) can provide estimates of the expected cash receipts in January. Other income may be expected from interest on investments or the sale of surplus equipment.

Expected cash payments, lines 5-12, should include items for which the company pays cash. The Sample Company might list salaries and utilities separately, and combine advertising and selling expenses under sales promotion. Cash is often paid in the month after the service is performed. Examples are payments for electricity and for materials. Some cash payments can be made at any one of several times. For example, payments on a new insurance policy can be set when your other cash demands are low. The cash budget shows when payment is to be made.

The cash balance on the first of January, plus the month's receipts, less the month's cash payments, provides you with an expected cash balance. A negative balance will require an increase in cash receipts, a decrease in payments, or the floating of a loan. In addition, a company should have a certain amount of cash to take care of contingencies. Line 17 shows the amount needed as a minimum balance. Lines 18-22 show alternative means of maintaining a reasonable cash balance.

A three-month projection is probably the practical minimum for a cash budget. If your company is seasonal or you expect heavy demands on your cash balance, longer periods may be necessary. Also, as you approach the end of a month, your performance should be checked and a month added. In Figure 22-1, the budget for February and March is reviewed toward the end of January, and April is budgeted.

The cash budget is a technique for controlling your cash flow so that you can make needed payments and not maintain too high a cash balance. Many independent business people do not recognize the importance of moving money through their system as quickly, effectively, and efficiently as possible. Everything else being equal, the faster you can move your

FIGURE 22-1
The Sample Company Cash Budget Form

CASH BUDGET (for three months, ending March 31, 19__)	January		February		March	
	Budget	Actual	Budget	Actual	Budget	Actual
EXPECTED CASH RECEIPTS:						
1. Cash sales						
2. Collections on accounts receivable						
3. Other income						
4. Total cash receipts						
EXPECTED CASH PAYMENTS:						
5. Raw materials						
6. Payroll						
7. Other factory expenses (including maintenance) ...						
8. Advertising..............................						
9. Selling expense						
10. Administrative expense (including salary of owner–manager)............................						
11. New plant and equipment......................						
12. Other payments (taxes, including estimated income tax; repayment of loans; interest; etc.).....						
13. Total cash payments						
14. EXPECTED CASH BALANCE at beginning of the month						
15. Cash increase or decrease (item 4 minus item 13)...						
16. Expected cash balance at end of month (item 14 plus item 15).............................						
17. Desired working cash balance						
18. Short-term loans needed (item 17 minus item 16, if item 17 is larger)..........................						
19. Cash available for dividends, capital cash expenditures, and/or short-term investments (item 16 minus item 17, if item 16 is larger than item 17).............................						
CAPITAL CASH:						
20. Cash available (item 19 after deducting dividends, etc.).............................						
21. Desired capital cash (item 11, new plant equipment)						
22. Long-term loans needed (item 21 less item 20, if item 21 is larger than item 20)................						

money and turn it over in sales and income, the greater should be your profit. The form in Exhibit 60 of *The Dow Jones-Irwin Business Papers* should help you achieve a "quick" cash flow.

Credit, Collections, and Accounts Receivable

As previously stated, the extension of credit increases the potential for sales. In Chapter 21, you may have found that the amount in accounts receivable for The Sample Company was large relative to its credit sales. It can be dangerous to wait until the end of the year to find this out. Frequent checks should be made to identify slow-paying customers and to determine the reasons for the slow payments. It is believed that the average retailer loses more from slow accounts than from bad debts.

The best control of losses on accounts receivable starts with their prevention. You will enhance your position if you investigate the customer's ability and willingness to pay and provide clear statements of terms. Balance the level of risk against the gain from giving credit. Then, establish surveillance of past-due accounts each month so that a slow account will be followed up promptly. As time passes and an account is not paid, the probability of collection decreases. You can expect to collect only about one quarter of the accounts over two years old and none of the accounts over five years old.

A check should be made of the total amount of your accounts receivable. Chapter 19 discussed the ratios used to evaluate the amount of receivables to sales (collection period). Then a comparison of your planned figures and the actual amounts indicates whether the situation is satisfactory overall. Next, the accounts can be tabulated by their age. Thus, The Sample Company's accounts receivable might be something like the following:

Age of Accounts

	30 Days or less	60 Days or less	6 Months or Less	1 Year or Less	Over One Year	Total
Amount	$17,150	$8,102	$2,500	$990	$1,500	$30,240

Figure 22–2 shows one page of an actual analysis.

What should be done? Particular attention should be given first to accounts over 60 days past due, then to the 30–60 day accounts. Remember that most customers are honest, and that you want your customers to be willing and able to pay.

Mr. Sample's analysis may lead him to write off some accounts as bad debts and to provide some incentive for earlier payments by slow-paying customers. Bad-debt adjustments should be made at or near the end of the fiscal year. *Uncollectible accounts* receivable create a misstatement of income, and therefore an unjustified increase in your firm's income tax liability. Unless there is a reasonable expectation of collecting the account, a good rule of thumb is to write off all accounts six months old or older at tax time. Mr. Sample should examine next year's profit plans for the extra cost of bad debts and for a review of his credit policy.

The questionnaire in Exhibit 61 of *The Dow Jones-Irwin Business Papers* will help you set up policies and procedures for credit and accounts receivable which should provide you with the best balance between "gains" and "losses."

Other Budgets

Many other budgets can be used to control the activities and investments of your company. Each expense can increase gradually without your noticing the change. Have you noticed how fast the cash in your

FIGURE 22-2
Aging of Accounts Receivable

A/C Receivables
March 1973

		Over 30	Over 60	Over 90	Total
519	Lithograving, Inc.			115	115
818	Bell associates			116	116
125	Hummel Maid, Inc.			204	204
8	Western Electric			50	50
22	Robertson Rubber Products, Inc.	45			45
51	Pictronics, Inc.			2000	2000
226	Solomon Foods	934 ¹/₃₀	934		1868
23/33	Tanner's Grocery Store	721			721
128	Allied Securities Co	6360			6360
27	Star Electric Shop	213			213
1971	Ruth's Dashiki		345		345
731	Central Plastics, Inc.			66	66
126	Kellog Motors			2	2
129	Metal Specialties, Inc.		801		801
1227	Dependable Motors, Inc.			2	2
	The Powell Company	²/₉ 176	¹/₁₇ 2016	⁹/₁₉ 1016	3208
1229	Hofmann Paint Company			42	42
1970	La-Tex Casket, Inc.			155	155
	Drake Printers	²/₂₁ 495	¹/₃₀ 495		990
1023	Roberts Tire Service			2	2
	Martin's Clothes, Ltd.	2247		276	2523
29	University Cinemas	307			307
	Clearview Optics			1051	1051
	Reach-a-Lamp	134			134
1971	Anders Bakery			1000	1000
	The Stair-Chair			144	144
22	Ideal Sheen Cleaners	35			35
28	Panther Inn	2273			2273
1227	Metal Fabricators			26	26
1113	The National Insurance Co.			96	96
	The Son-in-Law	³/₂₁ 464	¹/₁₉ 41		505
	Shaffer's Drive Inns	1792		1927	3719
	The A-B Cleaning Corporation			⁵/₂₅ 305	305
	The Mother and Child Shop		1569	60	1629
	Graham's Pet Food	203	40		243
		16,399	5,896	9,000	31,295

pockets disappears? You know how hard it is to control this. Some call it being "nickeled and dimed to death." A company has similar problems. All sorts of situations may contribute to a creeping increase in your firm's costs—a clerk is hired to take care of added paperwork; a solicitor comes in for donations; a big customer wants a special delivery; employees use company stamps for personal letters. Such costs must be controlled if your firm is to survive.

The detailed control of inventory was discussed in Chapter 14. An inventory budget can be established for weekly or monthly checks, based on the level of your expected sales. Purchases may be budgeted on the basis of the demand for materials. The budget can then be coordinated with the inventory and cash budgets. Similar analyses can be performed for other expenses.

Control over current liabilities is tied to expense and cash plans. Fixed assets and long-term liabilities usually change on a fixed basis, except for infrequent changes of equipment and other needs. Capital stock changes are infrequent, and retained earnings change as a result of company operations. Budgets for fixed items can be maintained through quarterly financial statements.

Figure 22–3 illustrates a set of forms which can be used to make period-to-period comparisons for trend analyses, and Figure 22–4 illustrates a set for planning by months for one year ahead and then comparing plans and budgets with actual performance. You can use the form in Exhibit 62 of *The Dow-Jones-Irwin Business Papers* in conjunction with this figure to plan your financial operations. The form in Exhibit 63 is designed to present changes in your company's operations—or in the operations of a company you may be considering for purchase. Use it to help you compare what you have planned with what you have actually achieved.

FIGURE 22–3
Trend Analysis of Income and Costs

THE SAMPLE COMPANY Evaluation of Financial Performance 19 ___				
Item	Current Period	This Year to Date	Period Last Year	Last Year to Date
Sales Income				
Cost of Goods Sold				
Gross Profit				
Selling Expenses				
Administrative Expenses				
Operating Profit				
Other Income				
Other Outgo				
Net Profit before Taxes				
Income Taxes				
Net Income				

FIGURE 22-3 (continued)

Detail of Cost of Goods Sold

Item		Current Period	This Year to Date	Period Last Year	Last Year to Date
	Material				
140	Beginning Inventory				
305	Purchases				
	Available				
140	Ending Inventory				
	Material Cost				
405	Labor Cost				
	Overhead Cost				
	Total Production Cost				
142	Beginning Finished Goods Inventory				
	Cost of Available Unit				
142	Ending Finished Goods Inventory				
	Cost of Goods Sold				

Production Overhead 19___					
Item		Current Period	This Year to Date	Period Last Year	Last Year to Date
402	Salaries – Supervision				
405	Wages – Compounding				
408	Wages – Materials Handling				
409	Overtime – Excess Wages				
410	Repairs and Maintenance				
412	Plant Expense				
413	Machinery Rent				
414	Utilities				
415	Building Rent				
416	Taxes				
417	Insurance				
418	Depreciation				
419	Amortization				
430	Packing				
	Total Production Overhead				

FIGURE 22-3 (concluded)

Selling and Distribution Expenses
19___

Item		Current Period	This Year to Date	Period Last Year	Last Year to Date
803	Salaries				
815	Rent				
816	Taxes				
817	Insurance				
819	Amortization				
852	Telephone and Telegraph				
853	Dues and Subscriptions				
854	Professional				
860	Advertising				
861	Distributor Discount				
870	Living				
871	Travel				
872	Entertainment				
890	Miscellaneous				
809	Overtime				
	Total Selling Expenses				

Administrative Expenses
19___

Item		Current Period	This Year to Date	Period Last Year	Last Year to Date
901	Salaries – Officers				
903	Salaries – Clerical				
915	Rent				
916	Taxes				
917	Insurance				
918	Depreciation				
919	Amortization				
950	Office Supplies				
951	Stationery and Printing				
952	Telephone and Telegraph				
953	Dues and Subscriptions				
954	Legal and Professional				
955	Employee Relations				
970	Travel and Entertainment				
975	Interest				
990	Life Insurance				
991	Donations				
909	Overtime				
	Total Administrative Expenses				

FIGURE 22-4
Financial Income and Cost Plans and Controls

The Sample Company

Balance Sheet 19___

Assets

		January 31			February 28			December 31		
		Planned	Actual	Diff.	Planned	Actual	Diff.	Planned	Actual	Diff.
	CURRENT ASSETS:									
100	Petty Cash									
101	X Bank									
110	Notes Receivable – Officers									
111	Advance Payments									
120	Accounts Receivable – Trade									
121	Reserve for Bad Debts									
130	Accrued Interest Receivable									
140	Inventory – Raw Materials									
141	– Work in Process									
142	– Finished Goods									
144	– Packing Material									
150	Prepaid Insurance									
151	Prepaid Rent									
	TOTAL CURRENT ASSETS:									
	FIXED ASSETS:									
170	Plant Equipment									
171	Deprec. Reserve – Plant Equipment									
172	Office Equipment									
173	Office Furniture									
174	Deprec. Reserve									
	TOTAL FIXED ASSETS:									
	OTHER ASSETS:									
180	Cash Value of Life Insurance									
181	Advance Officers									
191	Group Insurance									
	TOTAL OTHER ASSETS:									
	TOTAL ASSETS:									

FIGURE 22-4 (continued)

		Balance Sheet 19___ Liabilities and Stockholders' Equity								
		January 31			February 28			December 31		
		Planned	Actual	Diff.	Planned	Actual	Diff.	Planned	Actual	Diff.
	LIABILITIES:									
201	Accounts Payable									
210	Notes Payable – Bank									
211	Loan Payable – Insurance									
212										
220	FICA Payable									
221	Federal Taxes Withheld									
222	State Taxes Withheld									
223	Unemployment Taxes Payable									
224	Georgia Sales Tax Collected									
230	Accrued Wages Payable									
232	Accrued Taxes Payable									
233	Accrued Royalty Payable									
234	Accrued Property Taxes									
235	Accrued Legal & Accounting									
	TOTAL LIABILITIES:									
	STOCKHOLDERS' EQUITY:									
250	Capital Stock									
255	Paid in Capital									
260	Retained Earnings									
	TOTAL STOCKHOLDERS' EQUITY:									
	TOTAL LIABILITIES & STOCKHOLDERS' EQUITY:									

FIGURE 22–4 (continued)

Evaluation of Financial Performance
19___

Item	January			February			December		
	Budget	Actual	Diff.	Budget	Actual	Diff.	Budget	Actual	Diff.
Sales Income									
Cost of Goods Sold									
Gross Profit									
Selling Expenses									
Administrative Expenses									
Operating Profit									
Other Income									
Other Outgo									
Net Profit before Taxes									
Income Taxes									
Net Income									

Detail of Cost of Goods Sold

Item	January			February			December		
	Budget	Actual	Diff.	Budget	Actual	Diff.	Budget	Actual	Diff.
Material									
140 Beginning Inventory									
305 Purchases									
Available									
140 Ending Inventory									
Material Cost									
405 Labor Cost									
Overhead Cost									
Total Production Cost									
142 Beginning Finished Goods Inventory									
Cost of Available Unit									
142 Ending Finished Goods Inventory									
Cost of Goods Sold									

FIGURE 22-4 (continued)

Production Overhead
19___

Item	January Budget	Actual	Diff.	February Budget	Actual	Diff.	March Budget	Actual	Diff.	December Budget	Actual	Diff.
402 Salaries – Supervision												
405 Wages – Compounding												
408 Wages – Materials Handling												
409 Overtime – Excess Wages												
410 Repairs and Maintenance												
412 Plant Expense												
413 Machinery Rent												
414 Utilities												
415 Building Rent												
416 Taxes												
417 Insurance												
418 Depreciation												
419 Amortization												
430 Packing												
Total Production Overhead												

Selling and Distribution Expenses 19___

Item	January Budget	Actual	Diff.	February Budget	Actual	Diff.	March Budget	Actual	Diff.	December Budget	Actual	Diff.
803 Salaries												
815 Rent												
816 Taxes												
817 Insurance												
819 Amortization												
852 Telephone and Telegraph												
853 Dues and Subscriptions												
854 Professional												
860 Advertising												
861 Distributor Discount												
870 Living												
871 Travel												
872 Entertainment												
890 Miscellaneous												
809 Overtime												
Total Selling Expenses												

FIGURE 22–4 (concluded)

	Administrative Expenses 19___								
	January			February			December		
Item	Budget	Actual	Diff.	Budget	Actual	Diff.	Budget	Actual	Diff.
901 Salaries – Officers									
903 Salaries – Clerical									
915 Rent									
916 Taxes									
917 Insurance									
918 Depreciation									
919 Amortization									
950 Office Supplies									
951 Stationery and Printing									
952 Telephone and Telegraph									
953 Dues and Subscriptions									
954 Legal and Professional									
955 Employee Relations									
970 Travel and Entertainment									
975 Interest									
990 Life Insurance									
991 Donations									
909 Overtime									
Total Administrative Expenses									

chapter 23

Safeguarding Your Assets

The final chapter on profit planning and control deals with the many risks you face in managing and operating your company. The more common risks are emphasized: fire hazards; flood, hurricane, and tornado losses; business interruptions; liability; loss of a key executive; business frauds; and crime.

Insurance provides one of the surest methods of safeguarding yourself against extremely large losses from these risks—with the possible exception of the last. In addition, there are many security measures that enable you to reduce further your chances—or at least the magnitude—of loss.

The first part of the chapter discusses how you can use insurance to minimize your losses. The second part looks at a security system you might use to deter losses from crime.

In deciding what to do about your business risks, you should ask yourself what would happen to your company if, without adequate insurance:

1. You die or suddenly become incapacitated?
2. A fire destroys your firm's building or inventories?
3. A customer is awarded a liability judgment for an accident?
4. There is pilferage by customers—or employees?
5. An employee embezzles company funds?
6. A robber "hits" your firm.

When these disasters occur in independent companies with inadequate insurance protection, the owners are often forced to the wall. Therefore, you need to understand as much as possible about how you can use insurance for your protection.

The Nature and Limitations of Insurance

Pure risk always exists when a loss is possible, but you do not know its possible extent. To illustrate, the consequences of a fire, the death of a key man, or a liability judgment cannot be determined with any degree of certainty. Yet it is probably impossible to handle the full burden of pure risks through insurance, because the premiums would be so great that they would leave you with little or nothing to operate your business.

Insurance reduces pure risk. In buying insurance, you trade a potentially large loss for a small but certain cost (the premium).

Insurance should not be used:

1. If the potential loss is trivial.
2. If the insurance premium is a substantial proportion of the value of the property. For example, if the annual premium for a $50 deductible automobile collision insurance policy is $35 greater than the premium for a $100 deductible, the insured would in effect be paying $35 for $50 additional coverage.

A well-designed insurance program not only provides for losses, but can also provide such other values as reduction of worry, freeing funds for investment, loss prevention, and easing of credit.

Alternatives to Commercial Insurance

Methods other than commercial insurance for dealing with risk include: noninsurance, loss prevention, risk transfer, and self-insurance. Perhaps you can reduce costs related to risks in your company by using one or more of these methods or by combining them with commercial insurance.

Most firms use *noninsurance*, for they must inevitably assume some risks. You should use this method only when the potential loss is low and for risks that are more or less predictable, preventable, or largely reducible.

Loss prevention programs reduce the probability of loss, say, from fire and burglary. Such programs usually result in reduced insurance premiums.

Risk transfer involves transferring the risk of loss to others, as in leasing an automobile under a contract whereby the lessor buys the accident insurance.

To consider *self-insurance*, you should have adequate finances and broadly diversified risks. Often, independent companies cannot meet these requirements. Self-insurance plans should be actuarially maintained, with a cash reserve to provide for losses.

Types of Coverage

Among the major types of insurance you should consider are:

1. Fire insurance.
2. Casualty insurance.
3. General liability.
4. Workers' compensation.
5. Business life insurance.
6. Fidelity and surety bonds.

310

The standard *fire insurance* policy, excluding endorsements, insures you only against fire, lightning, and losses due to the temporary removal of goods from your premises because of fire. In most instances, this basic policy should be supplemented with an extended-coverage endorsement which insures against windstorm, hail, explosion, riot, and aircraft, vehicle, and smoke damage. Business interruption coverage should also be provided through an endorsement, because the cost of "indirect" losses is frequently greater than that of direct losses. To illustrate, while rebuilding after a fire, you must continue to pay the salaries of key employees and such expenses as utilities, interest, and taxes.

Casualty insurance consists of collision and public liability automobile insurance, plus general liability, burglary, theft, robbery, plate glass, and health and accident insurance. Automobile liability insurance is necessary because firms are often legally liable for the use of vehicles, even though they do not own any. For example, if an employee uses his own car on behalf of the employer, the employer is liable in case of accident. Automobile physical-damage insurance, covering such perils as collision, fire, and theft, is also essential.

General liability insurance is particularly important because, in conducting your business, you are subject to common and statutory laws governing negligence to customers, employees, and anyone with whom you do business. One liability judgment could easily result in the liquidation of your business.

Workers' compensation and *employer liability* insurance are related to common-law requirements that an employer provide his employees a safe place to work, hire competent fellow employees, provide safe tools, and warn his employees of any existing danger. Damage suits may be brought by employees against employers for failing to perform these duties. State statutes govern the kinds of benefits payable under workers' compensation policies, which typically provide for medical care, lump sums for dismemberment and death, benefits for disablements by occupational disease, and income payments for a disabled worker or his dependents.

Business life insurance can be used in several ways in independent firms. A firm can buy, or help buy, group life insurance and health insurance policies for its employees (see Chapter 10).

Business owner's insurance:

1. Protects an owner or his dependents against losses from premature death, disability, or medical expenses.
2. Provides for the continuation of a business following the premature death of an owner.

Business continuation life insurance, which is related to (2), is used by sole proprietorships, partnerships, and closely held corporations. Advance planning involves provision for ample cash and its use. Life insurance often provides the cash, and a trust agreement, coupled with a purchase-and-sale plan, provides for its use. The cash can be used to retire the interest of a partner or sole proprietor, or to repurchase the stock of a closely held corporation. As for life insurance, partners or stockholders may buy sufficient insurance on one another's lives to retire one another's interest in case of death. Or the firm may buy the necessary insurance on the lives of its principal owners.

Fidelity and surety bonds guarantee to another firm that your employees and others with whom your company transacts business are honest and will fulfill their contractual obligations. Fidelity bonds are purchased for employees occupying positions which involve the handling of company funds in order to provide protection against their dishonesty. Surety bonds provide protection against the failure of others to fulfill contractual obligations.

The questionnaire in Exhibit 64 of *The Dow Jones-Irwin Business Papers* is a checklist designed to make you aware of your need for insurance.

Guides to Buying Insurance

In buying insurance, the two most important factors are:

1. The financial characteristics of the insurer and his flexibility in meeting your requirements.
2. The services rendered by the agent.

Financial Characteristics and Flexibility of the Insurer. The major types of insurers are: stock companies, mutual companies, reciprocals, and Lloyd's groups. While mutuals and reciprocals are cooperatively organized and sell insurance "at cost," in practice their costs may be no lower than those of profit-making companies. In comparing different types of insurers, you should use the following criteria:

1. Financial stability.
2. Specialization in types of coverage.
3. Flexibility in the offering of coverage.
4. The cost of protection.

Only after you are satisfied with 1, 2, and 3, should you consider 4.

While you ordinarily rely on your insurance agent to judge the financial stability of insurers, *Best's Insurance Reports* are reliable sources of financial ratings and analyses of insurers if you want to check for yourself.

Some insurers specialize in certain types of coverage and offer you the advantage of greater experience in these lines. For example, Lloyd's groups often underwrite "dangerous" risks which other insurers will not assume.

Some insurers offer you great flexibility by tailoring their policies to meet your needs. Tailoring can be accomplished by inserting special provisions in the contracts and by providing certain services to meet particular requirements.

In making cost comparisons, you should not confuse the *initial* premium with the *net* premium. Some insurers have a lower initial rate (deviated rate), while others have a higher initial rate but pay a dividend to the insured.

Valid comparisons of insurance costs are difficult to make, but insurance brokers, independent insurance advisers, or agents may assist you. In general, you should avoid an insurer who offers a low premium.

Services Rendered by Agent. You should decide which qualifications of agents are most important to you, and then inquire about agents among business friends and others who have had experience with them. In comparing agents, some of the things to look for are contacts among insurers, professionalism, degree of individual attention, quality of "extra" services, and help in time of loss.

You should determine whether the agent's contacts among insurers are broad enough to supply all the coverage you need without undue delay and at reasonable cost. Professionalism is indicated by the agent's possession of the Chartered Life Underwriter or Chartered Property and Casualty Underwriter designations. You want an agent who is willing and able to devote enough time to your individual problems to justify his commission, to survey your exposure to loss, to recommend adequate insurance and loss prevention programs, and to offer you alternative methods of insurance. He should also be known for serving his clients well in time of loss. The quality of the agent and of the companies he represents may be validated by checking with the insurance commissioner of your state or his representative.

The form in Exhibit 65 of *The Dow Jones-Irwin Business Papers* can help you develop appropriate records for insurance purposes.

SAFEGUARDING YOUR ASSETS WITH SECURITY SYSTEMS

In this era of high crime incidence, it is imperative that independent business owners be aware of crimes that may be committed against their businesses. Criminal acts have forced both small and large businesses into insolvency.

We will discuss the potential dangers, and make suggestions that will help you minimize them. We hope that through knowledge of the possibilities you will develop security systems that will deter the armed robber; the thief in the night; the pilfering customer, employee, or delivery person; the "con artist"; the white-collar thief; and others. You will note that we said "deter," not "prevent." In today's world, it seems impossible to have a security program that will prevent all criminal acts against your business. The best you can hope for is to minimize their occurrence and severity.

Armed Robbery

In recent years, armed robbery has increased significantly. An armed person—or persons—enters the premises with the intent of obtaining cash as quickly as possible and then departing. Since time is of the essence, locations that afford easy access by foot or car and relatively secure escape routes seem most vulnerable. Once the bandits are inside, access to the cash register, the safe, or the office area where cash receipts are held is vital, since they usually want to get out in three minutes or less in order to minimize the risk of identification or apprehension. The pressure of the situation tends to make the bandits "trigger-happy." The increase in drug consumption has encouraged addicts to fund their habit by robbery. This increases the danger of physical harm and lessens the likelihood of talking the culprits out of the act. Businesses that use the same person, schedule, and route to take cash deposits to and from the bank increase their vulnerability to armed robbery.

Armed robbery is not necessarily confined to cash. It may involve high-value merchandise, such as diamonds, watches, drugs, electronic components, finished products, television sets, digital computers, cameras, radios, and stereophonic and high-fidelity equipment.

We are becoming more aware of areas of high crime potential and high crime incidence. In such areas, crimes seem to follow a pattern. For example, there may be neighborhoods where armed robbery occurs frequently; others where pilferage is the major problem; and still others where both armed robbery and pilferage are problems. If you are a prospective business owner, you should evaluate potential sites with this problem in mind. If you own an existing firm, you may conclude that it is time to select another site.

Pilferage

Pilferage has become a serious problem for American business—for many reasons. People whose incomes have not kept abreast of inflation pilfer to maintain their standard of living. Many national merchandising businesses add a 2-3 percent pilferage cost to their prices, but even this may not be enough to compensate them for such losses. The recent high level of unemployment has resulted in increased pilferage. For some people, pilferage is a challenge—Can I get away with it?—and unfortunately, some pilferage is done to win peer approval.

Types of Pilferage. There are essentially two types of pilferage—pilferage by outsiders, which is usually called shoplifting, and pilferage by employees.

Shoplifting may be done by the novice, the kleptomaniac, or the professional.

The *novice* is someone who takes an item or two to see whether he can get away with it or because he is overwhelmed by desire for an item he cannot afford. The *kleptomaniac* is an individual with an uncontrollable urge to take things. The *professional* may wear specially prepared or large garments or carry a large box to accommodate stolen merchandise. Other professionals may ask you for an empty box or boxes, which they then use to facilitate their thefts. Still others may enter your store with an air

314

of confidence—giving the impression that they are delivery persons or clerks—pick up merchandise, and leave.

> A convenience food store was forced out of business by pilferage losses. Its customers concealed prepackaged cheese, luncheon meats, and high-value items in their pockets and handbags.
>
> Upon inspection, the large purse of a well-known matron was found to contain several prepackaged steaks and packages of luncheon meat. The store owner said, "I thought she was one of our good customers. She has been coming in here for years."

Employee pilferage ranges from the theft of a small item by an individual to the removal of truckloads by groups. The individual pilferer is often the person least likely to be suspected. He may take anything from an inconspicuous item to whatever he can get out the door.

Two or more employees may conspire to steal from their employer. Some merchants have thought that employees would be less likely to steal if they were required to purchase merchandise from other employees. In such instances, employees have sometimes conspired to reciprocate by inaccurately reporting the amount of the sale on the sales ticket.

Employees sometimes conspire with outsiders to steal from their employers. They may do this by charging a lower price or by placing additional merchandise in the package.

Special Areas. Among the areas needing special attention are the pilferage of construction materials, the pilferage of supplies and inventory, and white-collar crimes.

Construction materials may be pilfered by insiders or outsiders. Lack of controls, looseness of accountability, and minimal security at storage yards and job sites lead to this type of pilferage.

> Workers loaded material to take to a jobsite, but did not fill out a tally sheet identifying the quantity or kind of material. They detoured to unload some of the material at the site of a job they were doing after hours.

> Whole truckloads of materials have been removed from unattended job sites or storage areas on weekends.

The pilferage of supplies and inventory, such as raw materials, finished goods, maintenance supplies, tools, equipment, and parts, is common among employees of independent businesses.

> A fast-food restaurant lost $20,000 worth of chickens in six months. The chickens were stolen by the case—out the back door.

> A chemical compounder wrote off 50,000 pounds as inventory shrinkage in six months. He said, "It costs too much to take physical inventory each month."

"The take" for white-collar crime may be greater than that of all other categories combined. White-collar crime includes the removal of cash; accounting manipulations; computer manipulations; bribes of purchasing agents and other employees; unrecorded transactions; sales of proprietary information; and sabotage of new technology, new or old products, and customer relations.

Preventive Measures

Armed Robbery. Your chances of being robbed can be reduced by modifying the layout of your store, securing entrances, using dogs, varying your routine for making cash deposits, and redesigning the surrounding area.

Modifying Store Layout. Proper location of the cash register or cash is important in preventing armed robbery. If the perpetrators are not able to dash in, scoop up the cash, and dash out again within a very short time, they are less likely to attempt robbery. Visibility from the outside, or being able to see all over the customer area, is also important.

> A convenience food chain removed all material from its windows that would impair interior visibility. It encouraged crowds at all hours by using various gimmicks. It attracted police officers by giving them free coffee. The average annual "hit" dropped from ten per unit to one per unit.

Securing Entrances. Security of entrances and exits is extremely important in preventing robbery. Rear doors should be kept locked and barred. Windows should be secured by bars and locks. In high-crime neighborhoods, many businesses have found it advantageous to use tough, shock-resistant, transparent materials in place of glass in their windows. Many businesses now allow no more than one or two people access to the combination of the safe. It is not uncommon for a sign to be posted on or near the safe advising that the person on duty does not have access to the combination.

Dogs. You may obtain security dogs from companies that specially train dogs to attack on command. Such dogs have proved to be effective deterrents against armed robbers. The animals may be purchased or rented. It may be advisable to have the dogs run through a refresher course periodically to keep them effective. In some jurisdictions, health and sanitation regulations prevent the use of security dogs.

Varying Routine for Depositing Cash. Daily deposit of cash is highly recommended. Banks and other businesses are rigidly enforcing minimum cash rules for cash drawers. In order to reduce the loss in the event of an armed robbery, some business people have found it expedient to keep only minimum cash in cash drawers and to use safes with unobtrusive hiding places.

The schedule for making bank deposits should be varied frequently. Different people and different vehicles should be used to make the

316

deposit. A fixed routine and the use of easily recognized people and vehicles to make such deposits invite the would-be armed robber and make it easier for him to plan and carry out his crime.

Redesigning the Surroundings. Well-lighted parking lots help deter robbers. If possible, try to keep vehicles from parking too near the entrance of your business. Anything that reduces the convenience of access and creates the possibility of a foul-up reduces the probability of an armed robbery.

> A convenience food store parking lot has concrete precast bumper blocks so dispersed that they serve as a deterrent to fast entry and exit from the lot.

It is advisable for some businesses to use video cameras to photograph the crime in action from several different camera angles or to use video cameras linked to TV monitors in a security office.

Pilferage. A number of techniques can be used by retail establishments and construction firms to reduce pilferage.

Retail Merchanding Establishments. These firms have found the following measures effective in reducing pilferage.

1. *Wide-angle mirrors* places strategically about the store make it easier to observe employee or customer behavior that indicates pilferage.

2. *One-way mirrors* with secret passageways are used by some retail outlets to observe activities in various parts of the store. Not all locations are occupied for observation at one time.

3. *Electronic noise activators* are attached to merchandise. These gadgets activate an alarm if the merchandise is removed from the area without first detaching the warning device.

4. *TV cameras* are frequently linked to receivers so that one person can monitor a large portion of the store.

5. *Security people* are used. If your business is large enough and pilferage is serious enough, you may wish to employ a full-time security person. However, since such people are often poorly trained and ineffective, you may wish to obtain the services of an independent security organization. (Recent national publicity has charged that the employees of such organizations have received inadequate training.)

6. *Security audits* are effective. *Unannounced spot checks of cash register activity* may be advisable. Check to see whether appropriate amounts are being rung up. Be sure that correct change is returned and that all items are accounted for by the clerk or cashier.

Unannounced spot checks may be made of employees' packages, car trunks, lunch pails, or other personal effects, and of restrooms. Check garbage or waste disposal holding areas for camouflaged materials that may be removed later.

Visible security surveillance may be used. It is important to observe employees in their normal work activities for indications of criminal acts.

Monthly or quarterly physical inventory checks may be made. Experience indicates that this often serves as a deterrent. On occasion, it has been found necessary to conduct inventory checks on a weekly basis.

7. *Polygraph tests* may be used before and after hiring—if legal requirements are met. Although the use of the polygraph has been questioned by union spokesmen and others, many business people consider it an effective deterrent against employee pilferage. Some firms require that employees take such a test every three months, while others administer the test every six months. In certain circumstances, the test may be administered specially. It is also used, on occasion, in screening new employees. *A word of caution*—You should thoroughly investigate the background of the persons or organizations administering the tests. We would go one step further and suggest that you obtain the *counsel of your attorney* before asking them.

Construction Contractors and Home Builders.   These firms need to take special care to prevent—or minimize—pilferage.

Planning and control are important. You should develop a schedule of the materials needed for each job, including both a correct enumeration of materials and the time they will be used. This will facilitate ordering appropriate quantities and timing deliveries properly. Delivering materials far in advance of need increases the possibility of loss.

Ordering dimensioned lumber and other materials and determining the exact material requirements as specified in the "project plans" reduce waste in the construction process and make it more difficult to remove materials from the jobsite without detection. Such improved purchasing procedures also help you maintain more effective control over your costs.

Other security measures which you can take include:

1. *Fenced and well-lighted storage yards.* There should be a cleared area adjacent to the fence on all sides.

2. *Dogs to patrol construction areas.* Robbers sometimes use tranquilizer dart guns or live ammunition to neutralize the effectiveness of dogs. Nonetheless, dogs are one of the most effective and economical deterrents to after-hour losses.

3. *The use of your own security guards.* For small projects, you may want to procure the services of private security patrols. In recent years, the vandalism at residential project sites by children and adults and the removal of plumbing fixtures, lighting fixtures, carpeting, and so forth, have underscored the need for on-site security patrols.

4. *A combination of security dogs and security guards.*

5. *Locks that are difficult to "jimmy".* A visit to your locksmith or your building hardware dealer may provide you with the latest complementary lock systems. No system is foolproof, however, and some of these systems may discourage only amateurs.

6. The use of a *receiving clerk* or some other employee who is *sufficiently knowledgeable to assume the responsibility for checking material into the jobsite.* Unfortunately, too many people fail to recognize the

318

importance of this activity and deal with it haphazardly. They say, "put it over there, and when you've finished unloading, check back with me." Unannounced rotation of the person responsible for receiving material may deter collusion with the deliverer.

White-Collar Crime. Special measures must be taken to minimize crimes committed by white-collar personnel.

Purchasing agents take bribes, either in cash or in the form of gratuities. Audits of inventory levels and prices on a comparative basis may uncover such activity. This means a much more thorough and detailed audit in this area than is sometimes carried out.

Cashiers and disbursing agents have been known to *factor in bogus or forged invoices, purchase orders, receiving reports,* and so forth. Spot audits of documents and even actual receiving areas should help reduce this type of loss.

Sales adjustments should be handled by an officer of the company. Permitting salespersons to make such adjustments allows collusion and cash compromises to the advantage of the customer and the salesperson. Reports showing the adjustments made on each customer's account should aid in revealing such misdeeds.

Computer crimes are increasing in frequency and severity. If you use a computer in your business, you need the services of a CPA firm with computer security expertise. Your business is always vulnerable in this area.

You should be aware of your white-collar employees' work habits. You should ask yourself: Do they work nights regularly? Do they never take a day off? Do they forgo their usual vacation? Is their standard of living, dress, car, housing, entertainment, and travel out of line with their income?

Fraud. The cashing of bad checks, the use of stolen credit cards, and passing bogus trade documents also require special measures.

Check Cashing. The demand for proper identification, along with a device that takes pictures of the check and the person cashing it, tends to discourage "bad check artists." Proper identification procedures are effective in reducing bad check losses. Your bank may assist you in developing effective identification procedures.

Credit Cards. Since credit cards are frequently stolen, you or your cashier should require additional identification. You should be sure that the signature corresponds to the one on the card.

Trade Documents. Each year, millions of dollars are lost by business people through carelessly allowing others to palm off bogus docments on them. A careful check with the appropriate bank or company would have prevented many of these losses.

Warehouse Crimes. Many preventive measures may be employed to reduce warehouse crimes. A thorough check on the background of employees should aid you in weeding out undesirables. A thorough system of receiving and dispatching goods from the warehouse is also important.

Monthly or quarterly physical inventory checks will make you aware of any shortages and will discourage criminal acts against the warehouse. Doors and loading docks should be of material that affords security, with locks, pins, and bars where needed. Closed-circuit TV camera systems may be useful deterrents. Alarm systems that activate an exterior horn, bell, or the like may prove effective, though alarms alone seem to leave much to be desired. The professional may be able to effectively deactivate them, or the lag between the time the alarm is activated and the time that a meaningful response can be made may permit the burglars to escape. You may wish to have security dogs patrol the warehouse when it is closed. A combination of security personnel working with dogs seems to be effective.

The form in Exhibit 66 of *The Dow Jones-Irwin Business Papers* will enable you to evaluate the security status of your business and your physical facilities.

Document Security

Our recent experiences in working with independent businesses—as well as newspaper headlines in recent years—have made us aware of the importance of document security. *Information is a vital facet in the direction and control of business activity.* The proper management and maintenance of information is necessary to assure the perpetuation of a business. Since the lifeblood of a business is dependent on the appropriate recording of such information and on its transmission to the appropriate persons, it is essential to have a storage facility that will protect the information from unauthorized persons and from loss by fire or other hazards.

In the discussion that follows, the term *document security* will concern not only the physical document but the need to document information and to route documents to the appropriate persons in an organization.

The proprietary nature of business records and various documents makes it essential to protect them from unauthorized eyes and hands. The trade secrets and competitive advantage of a firm may be lost if business documents pass into the wrong hands.

In an effort to preserve the sanctity of information records and business documents, it may be necessary to process and store them in a restricted area. An unbending rule should be that *under no circumstances will you permit the removal of this material from the restricted area.* In some instances, business owners thought they could gain an economic advantage by permitting employees to work on such records at home after hours. The possibility of loss, the opportunity for access by unauthorized persons, and the risk of a charge for inadequate compensation make this practice a "no, no."

In order to minimize the space requirements for business records, it may be desirable to have older, inactive records transferred to microfilm

FIGURE 23–1
Logic Flowchart for Marketing Risk Decisions

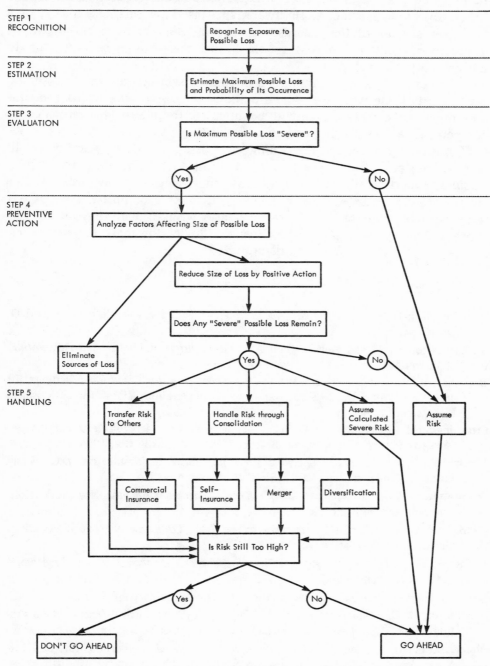

STEP 1
RECOGNITION

STEP 2
ESTIMATION

STEP 3
EVALUATION

STEP 4
PREVENTIVE
ACTION

STEP 5
HANDLING

Recognize Exposure to Possible Loss

Estimate Maximum Possible Loss and Probability of Its Occurrence

Is Maximum Possible Loss "Severe"?

Yes

No

Analyze Factors Affecting Size of Possible Loss

Reduce Size of Loss by Positive Action

Does Any "Severe" Possible Loss Remain?

Eliminate Sources of Loss

Yes

No

Transfer Risk to Others

Handle Risk through Consolidation

Assume Calculated Severe Risk

Assume Risk

Commercial Insurance

Self–Insurance

Merger

Diversification

Is Risk Still Too High?

Yes

No

DON'T GO AHEAD

GO AHEAD

or microfiche. This requires a classification and cataloging system that permits retrieval of the material for reference at the request of the IRS or other government agencies. Hardware, such as filing cabinets, a safe, or a vault for storage of the records, and checkwriters, is an essential part of your records system. Access to these facilities should be restricted to authorized personnel.

In designing and maintaining a document security system, you should make a list of the personnel who are allowed access to confidential records and documents. This list should be updated frequently and provided to the persons responsible for document security.

Another aspect of safeguarding your assets is care in granting credit and making collections. The form in Exhibit 67 of *The Dow Jones-Irwin Business Papers* should help you improve this aspect of your business.

The form in Exhibit 68 will help you make a complete audit of the risks faced by your business. You may also wish to analyze your risks in another manner by using Mark Greene's "logic flowchart for marketing risk decisions." This is shown in Figure 23-1.

WHERE TO LOOK FOR FURTHER INFORMATION

Anthony, Robert N. *Management Accounting,* 4th ed. Homewood, Ill.: Richard D. Irwin, Inc., 1970.

Anthony, Robert N., and Welsch, Glen A. *Fundamentals of Management Accounting.* Homewood, Ill.: Richard D. Irwin, Inc., 1974.

Brummet, R. L., and Robertson, J. C. *Cost Accounting for Small Manufacturers,* 2d ed. Washington, D.C.: Small Business Administration, 1974. (Small Business Management Series, No. 9.)

Crowningshield, Gerald R., and Gorman, Kenneth A. *Cost Accounting: Principles and Managerial Applications,* 3d ed. Boston: Houghton Mifflin Co., 1974.

Greene, Mark R. *Insurance Checklist for Small Business.* Washington, D.C.: Small Business Administration, 1971. (Small Marketers Aids, No. 148.)

Gruenwald, A. E., and Nemmers, E. E. *Basic Management Finance.* New York: Holt, Rinehart, and Winston, Inc., 1970.

Hedrick, F. G. *Purchasing Management in the Small Company.* New York: American Management Association, Inc., 1971.

Horngren, Charles T. *Cost Accounting: A Manager's Analysis,* 3d ed. Englewood Cliffs, N.J.: Prentice-Hall, Inc., 1972.

Katz, B. *Happiness or Misery.* Alexandria, Va.: Overlook Company, 1971.

Kreutzman, H. C. *Managing for Profits.* Washington, D.C.: Small Business Administration, 1968. (Management and Financial Control Series.)

Miller, D. E. *The Meaningful Interpretation of Financial Statements,* rev. ed. New York: American Management Association, Inc., 1972.

Mocker, Robert J. *The Management Control Process.* New York: Appleton-Century-Crifts, 1972.

Moran, Christopher J. *Preventing Embezzlement.* Washington, D.C.: Small Business Administration, 1973. (Small Marketers Aids, No. 151.)

Niswonger, C. Rollins, and Fess, Phillip E. *Accounting Principles,* 11th ed. Cincinnati, Ohio: South-Western Publishing Co., 1973.

Sanzo, Richard. *Ratio Analysis for Small Business,* 3d ed. Washington, D.C.: Small Business Administration, 1970.

Welsch, Glenn A. *Budgeting: Profit Planning and Control,* 3d ed. Englewood Cliffs, N.J.: Prentice-Hall, Inc. 1970.

Welsch, Glenn A., and Anthony, Robert N. *Fundamentals of Financial Accounting.* Homewood, Ill.: Richard D. Irwin, Inc., 1977.

Woelfel, B. L. *Financial Audits: A tool for Better Management.* Washington, D.C.: Small Business Administration, 1972. (Management Aids, No. 176.)

Zwick, Jack. *Handbook of Small Business Finance.* Washington, D.C.: Small Business Administration, 1965. (Small Business Management Series, No. 15.)

PART SEVEN

Some Special Considerations in Managing an Independent Business

Most of the general aspects of managing an independent business have been covered in the preceding parts. However, problems still need to be looked at.

First, there is the problem of whether you will operate your own business or a franchise. This problem is explored in Chapter 24.

Another problem is whether or not to operate a service station. This is taken up in Chapter 25.

Finally, there is the problem of providing for management succession. We have found that the vast majority of business owners do not want to talk about this problem. Yet if you want to assure the continuance of your firm to provide a going concern for your children to operate, you must look at this problem analytically. The material presented in Chapter 25 will help you do this.

chapter 24

Franchising

Franchising has existed for many generations. However, its structure, organization, characteristics, and operations have been evolving. In recent years, many new activities have begun to be franchised.

Our concern is to deal with franchising as it exists today, for that is where your interests lie. There are still many franchising opportunities, as you may see in the daily paper—the want ads, the business opportunity section, and so forth—and various business publications, including *Franchising* magazine. Yet the fact that such opportunities exist does not mean that your probability for success in each franchising situation is good, for the spectrum ranges from the "gyp" to almost guaranteed economic success. You should be cautious in dealing with franchisors who promise you a guaranteed return on your investment, particularly vending machine franchisors. Often, contracts with these elusive or vanishing organizations have proved worthless.

We want you to become aware of what it means to be a franchisee and of how you can best proceed in selecting the franchise that is right for you. Perhaps, after analyzing the matter, you will conclude that franchising is not for you.

THE IMPORTANCE OF FRANCHISING

Franchising has been one of the most rapidly expanding areas of business activity in recent years. The large percentage of new businesses that fall in this category explains its prominent treatment in this book. A discussion of the aspects of franchising considered to be most important to the prospective new franchisee is presented below.

Although service stations are considered a form of franchising, government documents separate service station franchises from other types. We also do this in our discussion.

Table 24-1 shows that there were 791 franchising companies in 1971. The average company had between 11 and 50 franchises. However, 39

TABLE 24-1

Franchising: Size Distribution by Number of Establishments—1971*

	Franchising Companies (number)	Establishments		Sales	
Size Groups		Number	Percent	Millions of Dollars	Percent
Total	791	175,549	100	$24,010	100
1,001 and greater	39	11,352	63	13,620	57
501 to 1,000	23	15,373	9	3,220	13
151 to 500	93	26,377	15	3,850	16
51 to 150	158	14,126	8	2,190	9
11 to 50	268	7,268	4	1,010	4
0 to 10	210	1,053	1	120	1

*Size group distribution not available for automobile and truck dealers, gasoline service stations, and soft drink bottlers.

Source: From *U.S. Industrial Outlook,* Department of Commerce.

companies had over 1,000 franchises, and these companies accounted for 63 percent of the establishments and 57 percent of the sales.

Franchise activities are growing, as is shown by Table 24-2. Sales increased 10 percent each year from 1971 to 1973. The number of establishments grew 3 percent from 1971 to 1972, and 5 percent from 1972 to 1973. In fact, it has been estimated that at least 60 percent of all U.S. businesses will be franchises by 1979.[1] It is also estimated that franchising accounts for about $177 billion in annual sales.[2]

WHAT CAN A FRANCHISE DO FOR YOU?

In our survey of the field, we have concluded that a franchise can take your money or make you financially independent—depending upon which franchise you choose. At this point, you should ask yourself: What can a franchise do for me that I cannot do for myself? In some instances, the answer may be, "Nothing," in other instances, the answer may be, "A great deal." The more successful franchisors tend to provide:

1. A training program that will equip you to manage your unit. (The more successful ones have special training schools—for example, McDonald's Hamburger University and Holiday Inn's Holiday Inn University.)

2. A standardized accounting and cost control system. These records are audited periodically by the franchisor's staff. In many instances, the franchisor requires standard monthly operating statements. The franchisor develops a set of standard performance figures, based on composite figures of reporting franchisees, and returns a comparative analysis to the franchisee as a managerial aid.

3. Financial assistance when minimum equity requirements are met by

[1] Charles Swayne and William Tucker, *The Effective Entrepreneur* (Morristown, N.J.: General Learning Press, 1973), p. 150.

[2] "Companies," *Business Week,* August 31, 1974, p. 75.

TABLE 24-2

Franchising: Trends and Projections, 1971–73 (in millions of dollars, except as noted)

	1971	1972*	Percent Increase 1971-1972	1973*	Percent Increase 1972-1973
Sales					
Total	$128,880	$141,450	10	$156,060	10
Franchisor	18,650	20,220	8	22,140	5
Franchisee	110,230	121,230	10	133,920	11
Establishments					
Total	431,169	443,815	3	466,049	5
Franchisor	74,721	77,408	4	80,662	4
Franchisee	356,448	366,407	3	383,387	5

*Based on estimates by respondents to recent survey by Bureau of Domestic Commerce.
Source: From *Y.S. Industrial Outlook*, Department of Commerce, p. 407.

the potential franchisee. This assistance covers land, building, equipment, inventory, and working capital.

4. Site selection and a "turnkey" facility. This includes the purchase of the site and the construction of a standardized structure which is identified as a part of the franchise's trademark.

5. Counsel and specifications for erecting and equipping the facility.

6. A local, regional, or national image.

7. Well-planned and implemented national or regional advertising programs that establish and maintain a uniform image.

8. A set of customer service standards. These are established by the franchisor and a professional staff whose members make regular inspection visits to assure compliance by the franchisee.

9. Continuing management assistance, training, and guidance.

10. Responsiveness to changing market opportunities. This responsiveness is illustrated by the success "fast-food" franchisors are achieving in the small-town market. In many instances, they have developed smaller units to accommodate this market.[3]

11. The possible buyer advantage of a larger corporation. (On this score, it is important to check franchisors on a comparative basis.)

12. An operations system that time has proved successful.

The above information to this point should enable you to choose whether to be independent or to operate a franchise. However, the form in Exhibit 69 of *The Dow Jones-Irwin Business Papers* can be of immeasurable assistance in helping you make this decision.

Recognizing that there are many categories of franchises, we have selected four whose track records make them worthy of your consideration: fast foods, motels, automotive, and convenience markets. We do not

SOME WORTHWHILE FRANCHISE CLASSIFICATIONS

---

[3] *Wall Street Journal,* April 26, 1976.

intend to imply that all franchises in these categories are worthy of selection. Nor do we wish to imply that they are the only categories worthy of consideration.

Fast Foods

Many factors account for the success of fast-food franchises. One factor is the demographic environment—the higher percentage of young people in the population; the large number of singles; the increasing percentage of working housewives; and the lack of available domestic help. Other factors are: a product that appeals to a significant segment of the market; fast service; a sanitary operation; and a structure with an easily recognizable trademark image.

Attributes that franchisors consider desirable are: a record of stability; a pleasant personality; a willingness to operate within an organizational framework; a track record of reasonable success; two years or more of college; and sufficient financial resources to satisfy the franchisor's minimum capital requirements. Generally, the franchisor is very public relations-oriented. The paramount interest of franchisors is to maintain a company image of quality service and product which contributes to the financial success of both the franchisor and the franchisee.

Motels

During the past three decades, the motel industry has grown phenomenally. Formerly an industry of "mom and pop" units with an often questionable image derived from the clientele it served, it has become an industry of large corporate complexes. These have both company-owned units and a franchise division operating units under the company trade name.

A pioneer in the change has been Holiday Inn. It set consistent standards for accommodations, service, and rates. Its success in providing a uniform image, complemented by its free Holidex reservation system, became a model for a new segment of the old hostelry industry. The advent of the interstate highway system and an affluent and mobile American public created a market with great potential. Almost every interstate highway interchange became a potential motel site. In the early years, success seemed assured.

The earlier successes may have been responsible in part for what became an industry with excess capacity. No one foresaw the "energy crisis" and its ultimate impact on gasoline prices and American life-styles. Nevertheless, the crisis came, along with changes in customers' views as to the amenities a motel should provide. As a result, we have suddenly discovered that the motel industry has achieved maturity. Many existing properties are now as obsolete as the "mom and pop" motels became with the coming of the national motels. The architecture, location, amenities offered, market, or finances of these properties make them unsuitable for modification. Instead, they will be phased out by the franchisor—so beware!

Evaluating Motel Opportunities. In considering the acquisition of an existing franchise motel property, you should make a careful determination of its status.

Traffic Information. You should study the current and projected traffic pattern and density. Identify the travelers and the types of accommodations they use. (State tourist bureaus or departments of transportation can often provide this information.)

Break-Even Consideration. You should investigate the occupancy rates for the past three years, looking for trends and their relationships to the break-even rate. In order to determine the break-even rate, you need to do some pencil pushing. Identify all of the cost factors: depreciation, maintenance, replacement and refurbishing, laundry, inventory, advertising in addition to the national franchisor's program, salaries and fringe benefits of officers and operating personnel, insurance, franchise license, various franchise costs (for example, percent of gross, room tax, advertising, signs, and reservation system), taxes, and so on. Such an analysis may reveal that the current rate structure is inadequate to cover all costs plus an adequate profit. We might note here that it is questionable whether very many economy motels can pass this type of analysis.

Status of Facilities. You should make a visual inspection of the exterior and the interior.

Interior. In each room, check such items as the wall covering, carpeting, furniture, bedding, television sets, lighting, heating, cooling, and plumbing. Check the laundry equipment and the linen inventory. Examine the lighting, cooling, heating, sound equipment, and acoustics of conference room facilities. Are partitions an adequate sound barrier? Is there sufficient conference space to accommodate the market? Inspect the food and beverage facilities. What is the quantity and condition of glassware, service accessories, china, pots, pans, fryers, ovens, dishwasher, sinks, ranges, mixers, blenders, tables and chairs, linen, draperies, carpeting, lighting, sound system, and other kitchen equipment. Inspect the lobby and office space equipment and furnishings.

Exterior. Inspect the state of the ramps, passageways, elevators, roofs and gutters, stairways, swimming pool and deck area, grounds and shrubbery, drainage, parking, and fire protection systems.

In the past, many properties have not always been adequately maintained. The owners have had a short-run objective of "Let's get as much as we can out of it and put as little as we can into it." This is less likely to occur with a franchised property, but it can happen, and the availability of the property for purchase may be a result of the franchisor's demands that the property be upgraded. (In recent months the better properties have come under heavier pressure. Some property owners have accused the franchisor of bringing pressure to bear in order to force the franchisee to sell to the parent organization.)

Trends in the Franchise Motel Business. There seems to be a consensus that the motel industry is overbuilt and that some properties are obsolete and should be phased out. This does not mean that new properties are not going to be developed. However, certain facts in the franchise motel business should be given careful consideration if you are interested in this field.

1. The number of units operated by the more reputable motel organizations will tend to remain constant.
2. New units will generally have 300-500 rooms.
3. Most new units will be constructed in metropolitan locations, designed to serve a segment of the convention market.
4. Some major motel companies will increase the percentage of units that will be owned and operated by the company.
5. Opportunities still exist for new franchisees to develop new properties that will be good revenue producers. However, greater care must be exercised in site selection than was needed in the past.

Automotive Franchises

Historically, automotive franchises have been retail outlets for parts and accessories. Some units have been affiliated with nationally known tire manufacturers, others with national automotive parts manufacturers. A comparatively recent entry into the automotive franchise field has been specialty service shops. These include shops specializing in transmission repairs and parts and in muffler and shock absorber repairs and parts; speed shops that provide technical assistance, modification, and specialized parts; and diagnostic centers with sophisticated electronic and computerized diagnostic equipment.

Automotive franchisors seek qualities that are significantly different from those desired by other franchisors. They prefer that the wife and family not be associated with the business. They consider a high school education adequate. (We think that technical school training should be required for the diagnostic centers and that some college engineering training would be desirable.) They do not consider friendliness essential. Since their greatest concern seems to be the ability of the franchisee to pay his bills and carry a sufficient inventory, they consider adequate personal finances and financial stability to be very important.

In general, the capital requirements of the automotive franchise are less than those for some fast-food and motel franchises. However, most automotive franchises give little help in terms of management assistance, site location, financial assistance, or training. Product line and national advertising may offer an advantage. Each situation should be carefully considered on its own merits. With this class of franchises, as with others, it is important to perform a cost-revenue analysis.

Convenience Markets

Although the term *convenience market* is usually associated with food outlets, it may in fact cover a variety of specialty shops. The latter assemble merchandise or materials into a single location, making selection and purchase convenient. Examples include Craft Shack and Radio Shack.

The questions in Exhibit 70 of *The Dow Jones-Irwin Business Papers* should help you to screen these franchise opportunities and to determine whether one of them is right for you. The exhibit should be used in conjunction with the following material. Let us again urge you to "push the pencil" on a cost-revenue analysis. However, this does not mean that the questionnaire should not be completed if you do the cost-revenue analysis.

WHAT FRANCHISE FOR YOU?

The material that follows will aid you in selecting the *right* franchise—the one that will help you achieve your objectives without jeopardizing your resources.

Some Questions to Ask

Many franchise situations are loaded with pitfalls. Some of these dangers were pointed out in a Small Business Administration press release.[4] of a study done for the U.S. Senate Select Committee on Small Business. Such franchises have left hundreds of disillusioned people in the aftermath of their onslaught. Unfortunately, many people have naively placed their life savings in ventures that were doomed to failure from the start. There has been a broad array of such activities, ranging from gum-vending machines, candy machines, and stamp machines to fast-food establishments (fried chicken, specialty items, soft custard, and hamburgers), motels, coin-operated laundries, ice cream parlors, and so forth.

A well-known radio-TV entertainer became involved with a fried chicken franchise. After a lot of fanfare a public stock offering was made. The fine print on the front page of the prospectus revealed more "padding" of assets than real value. From the outset, the franchisor did a poor job in assisting the franchisees. Consequently, they went down along with the company's stockholders.

A flurry of activity in mobile homes sales and home park franchises led many people to invest in the stock of the companies and buy their franchises. Many "fast-buck" operators rode to the pinnacle of paper success, but most investors lost substantial sums when the house of paper came crashing down.

In viewing a franchise possibility, you should probably question the objectives of the franchisor. Here is a simple list of questions you might want to investigate before "putting your money on the barrelhead."

---

[4]See Urban B. Ozanne and Shelby D. Hunt, *The Economic Effects of Franchising* (Washington, D.C.: Small Business Administration, 1971), especially pp. 1–2.

1. What's in it for me?
   a. Return on investment.
   b. Salary I can reasonably expect.
2. Is the franchisor just unloading a "white elephant"?

   One franchisor tried to sell home swimming pools by requiring the franchisee to purchase a display model at a price comparable to the standard retail price.

3. What services does the franchisor provide the franchisee? Are the services priced at a discount or priced above the benefits they offer?
4. Are the existing franchisors trying to "unload," or are they happy with the results?
5. What do my banker, CPA, Better Business Bureau, chamber of commerce, and community think of the franchisor and existing franchisees?
6. Is there a clause in the franchise contract that permits the franchisor to purchase the franchise at will on terms favoring the franchisor?

SOME CONCLUSIONS CONCERNING FRANCHISING

Even in the best franchise situations, the franchisor tends to hold an advantage. Usually, this relates to operating standards, supply and materials purchasing agreements, and agreements relating to the repurchase of the franchise. However, franchise operations may offer you an opportunity to derive a satisfactory income from your investment and efforts.

A large number of court cases relating to franchise activities are now being adjudicated. Among the issues involved are the territorial rights held by the franchisor and the franchisee, and the right of the franchisor to require the franchisee to purchase supplies and inventory from the franchisor. The decisions indicate that the franchisee may acquire some advantages and lose others from these legal actions.

This chapter has placed greater emphasis on fast-food and motel franchises than on automotive and convenience market franchises. Our basis for doing this is the significant and continuing growth in fast-food franchises and the growth and size of the motel industry. In both of these categories there are franchises which provide solid opportunities. These operations seem to provide a standard by which you may judge others.

chapter 25

Operating a Service Station

The "energy crisis" has created an atmosphere of uncertainty around the "service station industry." The stronger "dealer-operated" company stations have been under pressure. The relative shortage of gasoline has had a major impact on the volume of other service stations products and activities.

Until the petroleum industry achieves stability as to direction, product volume, retailing methods, and pricing, you should be cautious about venturing into this type of business. This chapter will help you decide whether or not to do so.

One should not confuse service station operations with other forms of franchises. The local distributor and petroleum company screen applicants for individual locations. In addition, the type of location and the type and size of inventory determine the investment you must make to enter this type of business.

During "normal" times, a station operating 12 hours a day with two or three pump islands usually averaged around 40,000 to 50,000 gallons of gasoline per month, supported by a good volume of TBA (tires, batteries, and accessories). Fast, high-quality, friendly, dependable service is the requisite for building a successful business in this highly competitive field.

Stations operating around the clock on interstate highways tend to have a diversity of drink- and snack-vending machines. These can provide a significant monthly income.

The mortality rate in the service station industry is very high due to these factors:

1. Changes in traffic patterns produced by such activities as neighborhood transitions, the opening of new shopping centers, and the construction of streets, expressways, and interstate highways.

THE NATURE OF SERVICE STATION OPERATIONS

2. Poor service and dirty facilities.
3. Using open-account credit rather than requiring cash or company credit cards.
4. Stocking excessive inventory, including items that have little demand.
5. Poor-quality employees.
6. Pilferage by customers and employees.
7. Poor merchandising, which does not assure adequate volume of TBA.
8. In times of shortages, the lack of products to assure an adequate volume of sales.

Many major petroleum companies provide training schools for incoming dealers. In some instances, the quality or effectiveness of these programs is questionable. A number of companies provide in-house advisory services to their dealers.

In the 1960s, petroleum companies overbuilt service stations in the United States in an attempt to protect their share of the market.[1] Many individuals were selected as dealers who did not have their suppliers' confidence. Until the early 1970s, dealer turnover was about 30 percent annually.

APPRAISING SERVICE STATION OPPORTUNITIES

In appraising the potential for independent dealers in the mid-1970s, you should consider a host of factors, such as the number of new stations, remodeling of existing stations, deactivations, sales volume, average sales per station, the proportion of dealers meeting payroll, the use of computer models by companies, self-service stations and other specialized stations, company-operated stations, dealer turnover, federal government legislation and regulation state franchise laws, the provision of company training and assistance, the amount of investment, the amount of equity, and rental or lease payments to companies.

The Number of New Stations

The number of new stations constructed from 1970-75 was:

1970 2,508	1973 971
1971 2,068	1974 191
1972 1,689	1975 266

During this period, remodeling of existing stations having potential for higher volume was popular because new zoning permits were not required.

The Number of Closings

Generally, deactivation, or permanently closing facilities, increased during the same period:

---

[1] The material in this chapter was developed from secondary research in the *National Petroleum News* and from interviews with major oil company marketing executives.

		1970 3,586	1973 7,479
		1971 3,630	1974 4,443
		1972 3,498	1975 4,500

Some companies even withdrew from broad geographic areas.

For these same years, the total dollar volume of service station sales **Volume** and the average sales per station were:

	Number of Stations	Sales Volume (in billions)	Average Sales per Station (in thousands)
1970	222,000	$27.9	$126.1
1971	220.000	$29.2	$132.7
1972	226,459	$33.7	$148.8
1973	215,880	$34.4	$159.6
1974	196,130	$41.0	$209.8
1975	193,000	$43.0	$222.8

Thus, while the number of stations declined about 15 percent after 1972, the average sales volume per station rose around 76.7 percent.

In 1972, the number of dealers meeting their payrolls was 183,385, or about 81 percent of the total.

Many major petroleum companies have been using computer models which accurately specify the potentials of given markets and indicate where service stations should be located.

THE CHANGING NATURE OF THE INDUSTRY

In the early 1970s, some oil industry observers were predicting that one half of the 222,000 outlets would be eliminated during this decade. Others disagreed, arguing that the pendulum would swing to self-service and then back to full service before 1980, due to the convenience of the conventional neighborhood service station.

The Increase in Self-Service

In 1975, there were 13,000 self-service stations. During the year there was a big surge in split-island self-serves. Six states prohibited self-service stations. In addition to self-service stations, a number of other types of specialized stations were being developed, including front-end specialty shops, tire-retailing centers, tune-up work centers, convenience store combinations, bicycle sales and repairs, combination car-wash, do-it-yourself repairs, and retail auto parts and service. Some observers predicted the rebirth of diagnostic centers. Convenience store combination operations were taking away considerable volume from conventional outlets.

The Increase in Company Ownership

Company-operated stations have been increasing in number. More self-service outlets would probably be company-owned were it not for Federal Energy Administration (FEA) allocations, which will be described later. Past allocations for some stations were too low for petroleum companies to be interested in them. Attrition—retirements, deaths, or incapacitations—could be expected to provide many opportunities for establishing company-owned stations. Mutual cancellations of dealer franchises with companies were also possible. Some predicted that 25 percent of service stations would become company-owned.

By 1974, dealer turnover had declined from 30 percent to 8 percent. An important reason for this decline was that marginal dealers became successful because of gasoline shortages and increasing prices. Furthermore, such dealers were sometimes "overprotected" by FEA regulations. The turnover percentage was expected to increase as competition reentered the industry. Too many dealers erred in lowering their prices in attempting to hold their volume. Many dealers had serious financial problems.

The Increase in Legislation

In 1975, franchise laws were pending—or on the books—in 11 states. Two issues usually covered by these laws were:

1. The right of the oil company to cancel or refuse to renew a lease without giving a reason for its action.
2. The right of the lessee to contest the oil company's action in court.

Top managers of the major oil companies were opposed to such legislation because they claimed that it would prevent them from exercising control over people who were using their trademarks and selling their products. Thus, they would be unable to replace inefficient dealers. Representatives of retail dealers' associations disputed these claims, arguing that companies could still terminate dealers for just cause. To them, the legislation required that companies set forth the causes for termination, give dealers adequate notice, and justify their actions. Some legislation prohibited major companies from operating their stations without a lessee dealer. Other legislation banned the construction of self-service stations because of the threat to lessee dealers. Pending bills required major oil companies to even withdraw from the retailing of gasoline. Companies were lobbying against this legislation at the state and national levels in 1977.

Some oil industry spokesmen believed that because of increasing rack prices, the gasoline dealers of major companies would fare better than independent dealers. Others disagreed on the ground that small refineries were exempted from the FEA's entitlement program. The exemption created a price advantage for the small refineries at the expense of the large, crude-sufficient refineries.

Effects of the FEA and the EPA

Regulations of the FEA and the Environmental Protection Agency (EPA) have had important effects on the petroleum industry.

Effects of the FEA. In early 1974, service station shutdowns—weekend closings—were prescribed. Refineries decreased gasoline production in order to divert petroleum to the production of heating oil. Suppliers had to service the customers they had in 1972 unless bad credit or some other valid reason existed for not doing so. Suppliers saw that priority customers, for example, hospitals and schools, obtained the products to which they were entitled. They allocated the supplies on hand, set a base percentage figure for their accounts, and advised their accounts of their monthly allocations.

The FEA attempted to equalize the quantity of oil available to refineries by taking oil from the big ones and offering oil to the small ones. Some oil industry representatives declared that "the control of petroleum product supply had moved out of the hands of industry and into those of the federal government." FEA regulations also specified to whom a company could sell, in what quantities, and at what price.

From 1972 to 1976, most oil companies did not accept any new business. However, by 1976 it appeared that the FEA officials would favor some new outlets and dealers. It seemed that there might even be a relaxation of regulations which made it difficult for a new operator to obtain a sufficient allocation. Some observers believed that the situation would improve for the independent dealer because new outlets were needed in order to serve various areas more adequately.

Effects of the EPA. The EPA's regulations were also affecting the oil industry. The EPA ordered a reduction of lead in all grades of gasoline. Also, since the Clear Air Act of 1970 specified the control of hydrocarbon emissions from service station pumps and storage tanks, the EPA required the installation of pump nozzles which would prevent these emissions when gasoline was pumped.

THE ROLE OF INDEPENDENTS

The independent dealer should continue to dominate the retailing segment of the oil industry for some time to come. Although there has always been room for successful independent operators, the oil companies are now becoming more selective in choosing dealers. As the number of outlets has declined, dealers have tended to become more qualified, and this trend should continue.

What Is Required for Success?

Prospective dealers should be willing to work long hours in establishing their stations. They should understand that service stations, like drugstores, must be open for business when everyone else is off from work—that is, before normal working hours, after hours, and on weekends and holidays. The dealer should have the approval of an understanding spouse. Companies should stress to prospective dealers that they will face a "starvation period" before their business is successful. The greater flexibility of the independent dealer, as opposed to the company employee, who is not usually expected to work such long hours, will help assure his or her success. The dealer should have better knowledge of the local market than the oil companies usually do. Good opportunities exist for the properly motivated, capitalized, and adaptable dealer.

The Role of the Oil Company

Most oil companies offer financial advice, training schools, and training stations to dealers. Company sales representatives, who serve as the liaison between the companies and the dealers, have undergone comprehensive training programs to enable them to provide effective assistance to dealers. Not all dealers seek the advice of these representatives—and not all follow their advice.

Most customer complaints to oil companies tend to concern the practices of unsuccessful dealers.

The Investment Required

The amount of investment by independent dealers depends on several factors. Does the dealer lease and operate someone else's facility, or does he or she own the facility? Where is the facility located? Does he have a 2-3 bay station that does tune-ups and front-end work and sells tires, batteries, and accessories?

The amount of investment varies among companies, but it tends to be around $10,000–$15,000—at a minimum. If leased, a full-service, high-volume outlet with considerable equipment and merchandise located at a major intersection will probably require a $50,000–$100,000 investment. If the dealer invests in the real estate and owns all the facilities (and is paid a rental by the supplier), the investment will be around $150,000 to $500,000. A minimum dealer equity of 25–30 percent is usually required.

The Lease Agreement

Dealers' rental or lease payments to companies can be either flat basis or on a combination flat and gallonage basis. For example, a $600 a month flat guarantee with a rental of 1-3/4 cents per gallon of gasoline might be used. Or lease payments might be 15–18 percent of gross profits or 4 percent of sales. Ideally, the oil companies want to obtain an adequate return from each of their properties.

chapter 26

Providing for Management Succession

In Chapter 1, two potential problems were pointed out. One was the possibility of failure. The material up to this point has been based on the assumption that you were going to be successful. However, if your business has not been totally successful, or if you suspect that you are not doing as well as you would like to, you might want to consider going out of business. If for any reason you feel that you would like to determine the feasibility of liquidating your business, the questionnaire in Exhibit 71 of *The Dow Jones-Irwin Business Papers* should help you.

The second potential problem mentioned in Chapter 1 was having your organization grow too rapidly. This may be a good time for you to evaluate your operations to see whether you are avoiding excessively rapid growth. The questionnaire in Exhibit 72 should help you recognize pitfalls and provide some guidelines for you to follow.

If you are not facing either of these problems, you may soon be facing a third, the need to provide for management succession.

In most independent firms, the development of managerial personnel and provision for management succession are often neglected until it is too late to do anything about them. Therefore, now that your firm is operating successfully, you should answer these questions: Who will take my place so that I can retire when I choose? If my business is a proprietorship, do I want my spouse or children to manage it when I leave? If it is a partnership and I leave it, do I want my spouse or children to be partners? How will my death or incapacity affect my firm?

You should realize that many relatives do not have the capabilities—or the interest—to manage your firm. Also, you need to be exceedingly competent to either judge their managerial talent or provide management training.

MANAGING A FAMILY-OWNED BUSINESS

When close relatives work together in a business, emotions often interfere with business decisions. Conflicts sometimes arise because relatives look at the business from different viewpoints. For example, relatives who are furnishing the capital—the "moneymen"—may consider only income. Relatives engaged in the daily operations may be concerned primarily with production, sales, and personnel.[1]

The firm's top manager should recognize the emotions involved and make objective decisions. It is often hard for the manager and other relatives to make rational decisions about one another's skills and abilities. Also, quarrels and ill feelings among relatives may spread to nonfamily employees or interfere with the firm's operations. The manager should not permit the business to be divided into factions.

Some family-owned companies are handicapped by high turnover among their most capable nonfamily employees. Relatives are sometimes responsible, for they may resent outside talent and make things unpleasant for nonfamily managers. Or, key managers may resign because the lines of promotion are closed to them. A troublesome relative may be discharged (with difficulty), assisted in starting another business in a noncompeting line, exiled to a branch office, or assisted in obtaining a job elsewhere.

Another problem is the family member who has occupied one job after another without being successful in any of them. But now this person has a job, a title, and a salary—with you. A "ghost," or a lesser manager who knows the job and knows how to perform it, is doing work for which the family member is getting credit. If the business is incorporated, perhaps the "floater" cannot be discharged because of a major stockholder's complaints. One out is to shift the useless family member to some newly created position with title and salary, but with no actual job to perform, and to give the ghost proper recognition.

Perhaps the manager is "in a bind" because he must clear routine matters with family members who will not let him forget past mistakes—particularly if the manager is young, an in-law, or a distant relative. Another difficulty may be that relatives indulge in excessive family talk during working hours. The manager should insist this not be done.

If the company can afford it, one way to obtain objective control in such a situation is to hire an outside professional manager to handle day-to-day operations. Definite lines of authority and responsibility are an absolute necessity. The responsibilities of family members should be specified, and the extent of their authority should be clearly stated. The nonfamily employee should be high enough in the organization to be involved in operations and assist in smoothing out any emotional family decisions. The manager's authority to suspend or discharge flagrant violators of company rules should also be specified. Control is weakened if the manager must make special allowances for "family employees."

---

[1] Robert E. Levinson, *Problems in Managing a Family-Owned Business* (Washington, D.C.: Small Business Administration, 1971), Management Aids for Small Manufacturers, No. 208.

A relative can demoralize an organization by loafing, taking special privileges, or making snide remarks. The manager should assign such a relative to a job involving minimum contact with other employees and requiring no important decisions.

A situation in which a family member "spies" on other employees can also be very demoralizing.

> In a retail clothing store, the aunt of the owner-president makes life miserable for other workers, especially females. She "sneaks" into the ladies' room and reports anyone found smoking. The employees always look behind clothing racks to see whether she is listening before they say anything about the family. They refer to her as "the Gestapo." Needless to say, morale is low and turnover is far greater than that for comparable stores.

Often the owner-manager may believe an expenditure is needed in order to improve efficiency; yet other family members may oppose the outlay because they consider it to be only money out of their pockets. To overcome this tendency, the manager might base arguments for the expenditure on information provided by nonfamily employees. Outside business advisers—including bankers, accountants, attorney, or consultants—might help the manager convince his relatives.

When some relatives in a family-owned business grow older, they frequently develop a desire to maintain the status quo. They can block company growth. Such relatives might be given an opportunity to convert their common stock to preferred stock or to sell some stock to younger relatives. Perhaps they could be "gradually retired" through salary reductions and induced to relinquish some of their interest in the firm.

Provisions for paying family members and dividing the profits equitably among them can also be difficult. In a corporation, stock dividends may be appropriate. The salaries of family members should be competitive with those paid others of comparable rank and ability in the same area. Fringe benefits—such as deferred profit-sharing plans, pension plans, insurance programs, and stock purchase programs—can be useful in dividing profits equitably.

If you manage a family-owned business, you are not alone. You should exchange ideas with other individuals managing family companies in the same community and learn how they solved problems similar to yours. Also, if you manage an independent corporation, having outsiders on the board of directors can be of benefit to you.

PROBLEMS WITH MANAGERS

You will have many problems with your managers, whether or not they are members of the family. You should be familiar with three staffing problems, which are particularly difficult in independent firms: (1) the manager who thinks only in terms of "the past," (2) the manager who "makes work," and (3) the manager guilty of work duplication.

The first refuses to learn and adopt new methods of management, regardless of how necessary they are. Dismissal or transfer is appropriate in this case.

The make-work manager may have been hired to perform a job that is no longer needed. Dismissal or transfer to a more productive position may be appropriate.

Work duplication may exist because two managers are both supervising the same project. Their duties should be reappraised.

If you are faced with similar staffing problems in your company, you should start with one or two changes at a time and see how they work out. You should also try to make changes before they become a dire necessity.

You may be faced with another type of staffing problem if one of your key executives leaves. Some dislocation will inevitably occur, but you usually have some latitutde in the kind of replacement you seek. You could consider reorganizing your management, redistributing the present assignments, and using present managers more effectively. The job specifications for a new manager could be written less narrowly, and the range of choice broadened. Your managers should participate in this planning because if they feel that they have contributed to the decision they will accept the newcomer more readily.

Often, your managers will prefer that an individual from within the firm replace a key manager who has left. This attitude usually appears both in the manager who expects to be promoted and in other employees. If you decide upon an outsider, you should discuss the reasons with the manager who expected the promotion and with your other managers.

If you recruit someone from the outside, you should have your people who will be working with the new manager meet and talk with candidates. You should observe their reactions and ask for their evaluations. You should seek answers to these important questions: Will the prospective manager fit into the community? Will his or her family be able to make the adjustment? You should give the prospective manager ample opportunity to consider your situation carefully.

You can appraise a prospective manager's ability by considering records of past performance, personal statements, and evaluations by others. Perhaps a prospective sales manager provides data which show a 60 percent increase in sales volume over the last five years while the sales force rose only 20 percent. The candidate's personal statements may reflect an interest in high-quality, custom-built products with low volume and high margin. You should determine whether there are inconsistencies in the candidate's statements. If you have doubts, you should ask more questions. You should not automatically reject the prospect because of a poor reference. This may result from a situation which does not affect the prospect's suitability for your company.

In determining compensation, you should review the remuneration of your present managers to see whether it is adequate and equitable, whether it is properly related to their contributions to the firm, and whether it is comparable to that of the new manager. You should probably have a five-year compensation plan in mind for a new manager. Keep in mind that if your offer is too high now you may limit your ability to increase rewards for improved performance in the future. However, you should not drive too hard a bargain. To help make the new manager's interests coincide with yours, you should consider offering a share of ownership in your firm.

When you hire a manager you should discuss with him or her how the relationship can be terminated. There should be some penalty for termination, but it should not be so great that you keep an unsatisfactory manager rather than pay the penalty. You also want to avoid giving the manager a bonus for taking a better job elsewhere. You should not conceal any unpleasant conditions that must be confronted soon after the new manager reports for work.

Some turnover in your middle management group can be beneficial. If a young manager with ability and ambition should desire to move, you should offer help in finding a better position. This assistance is preferable to his or her job-hunting without your knowledge.

Replacing a manager can sometimes benefit you. For example, suppose that a production manager who has excelled in plant layout, tooling, and production methods leaves you. In replacing this person, you might want a manager with a different mix of skills—perhaps including labor relations, employee productivity, and quality of supervision.

What preparations should you make when you are planning to retire, acquire another business, or otherwise turn your business over to someone else? Too often, an independent company suffers under these circumstances. Sales may decrease, or production may lag. These difficulties can be prevented by making available to your successor the specialized knowledge which you have accumulated over the years.

You should create a reference source for the new manager by making an inventory of the various kinds of information used to manage and operate your business. The inventory should consist of information about:

1. The general administration of the company.
2. The firm's finances.
3. Operation and technical aspects.

Examples of these inventories are presented in the appendix of this chapter. Such inventories should also help you evaluate your firm at any time.

You should set down some information about the goals and objectives you hope to see your company reach, both before and after you leave. This program should be supplemented with profit-and-loss and cash flow projections.

PREPARING FOR YOUR SUCCESSOR

In order to facilitate a smooth transition, you should bring in the new manager as early as possible. The length of the transition period may vary from three to five years, depending on your plans, your type of business, the new manager's experience and knowledge, whether the new manager is a relative or a hired outsider, and the size of your firm.

Ultimately, the moment arrives when you must turn over the business you have created to someone else. If you have built well, the business will survive as testimony of your creativity.

The questionnaire in Exhibit 73 of *The Dow Jones-Irwin Business Papers* should be of great help to you in determining whether you are adequately providing for management succession in your company.

A Management Self-Audit

At this point you are probably asking yourself, "How well am I doing?" All of us like to know how we are doing. Since you can answer this question best, we have provided two forms for your use. The questionnnaire in Exhibit 74 will enable you to evaluate the general management of your organization. The questionnaire in Exhibit 75 will help you look at the functional aspects of your business.

Since Exhibit 75 is *roughly* arranged according to the material in this text, you should be able to refer to the text in doing the self-analysis. The second part of the questionnaire in Exhibit 75 is designed to be completed by retailers only, while the third part is designed for manufacturers. We wish you "good luck" as you do this analysis. We hope you "pass."

APPENDIX: INVENTORY OF INFORMATION USED TO MANAGE AND OPERATE YOUR COMPANY[2]

Inventory of facts about general administration

Company history:	Date organized, key founders, and major events.
	Clippings of stories from newspapers and trade journals concerning your company.
	Brochures concerning new products, processes, sales personnel, and so on.
Company organization:	Organization chart.
	Job specifications.
	Description of key employees, including your evaluation of their potential.
	Report of studies on your company made by your employees or by outside consultants.

---

[2] Source: Frederick E. Halstead, *Preparing for New Management* (Washington, D.C.: Small Business Administration, 1972), Management Aids for Small Manufacturers, No. 183.

Policies:	Information on credit and selling terms, vacations, retirement plans, employee loans and advances, and so on.
Legal matters:	Patents, licenses, and royalty agreements. Information on where each formal document is filed. Employment and labor agreements. Leases. Contracts with suppliers and customers. Outcome of past lawsuits and information on pending suits.
Outside services:	List and brief description of outside professional people who work with your company, including bankers, accountants, insurance agents, advertising agencies, consultants, and so on.

Inventory of financial data

Profit-and-loss statements for past ten years.

Copy of most recent balance sheet.

Copy of most recent budget.

Brief description of company's working capital turnover trends, return on investment trends, operating ratios, and so on.

List of current bank accounts, including average balances and name of bank employee who handles accounts.

List of prior banking connections, indicating the line of credit and bank officers who arranged it.

List of paid tax bills.

List of insurance policies, including a description of coverages and premiums and name of agent.

Copies of your financial and control reports, with notation about frequency of preparation and distribution.

Copies of procedures or procedure manuals.

Inventory of operating and technical information

Marketing:

List of company's products or services, and notes concerning customer acceptance, profitability, and future potential.

List of geographic areas in which each product is sold, types of customers, and the largest customers.

List of distribution channels.

Brief outline of advertising program, including how it is coordinated with other sales efforts.

Brief descriptions of sales training programs.

Brief description of how prices are set for current and new products.

Brief description of competitors, including a list of their products, the location and size of their plants, their share of the market, pricing policies, and channels of distribution.

Production:

List of major pieces of equipment. Brief appraisal of efficiency of the plant and equipment.

List of product and manufacturing specifications and process procedures.

List of studies made to improve layout and quality control, replace existing equipment, and so on.

Brief description of how production is scheduled and controlled (orders on hand or for stock).

Brief description of standards used for measuring performance and methods for eliminating waste.

Purchasing:

Lists concerning: (1) major materials purchased; (2) names of suppliers; (3) present contracts with suppliers; and (4) procedures for buying, including kind of approval needed for various types of purchases.

Other areas:

Inventory of knowledge in special areas, including research and development, engineering, quality control, and so on.

WHERE TO LOOK FOR FURTHER INFORMATION

Halstead, E. Frederick. *Preparing for New Management.* Washington, D.C.: Small Business Administration, 1972. (Management Aids for Small Manufacturers, No. 183.)

Levinson, Robert E. *Problems in Managing a Family-Owned Business.* Washington, D.C.: Small Business Administration, 1970. (Management Aids for Small Manufacturers, No. 208.)

Robinson, Joseph A. *How to Find a Likely Successor.* Washington, D.C.: Small Business Administration, 1968. (Management Aids for Small Manufacturers, No. 198.)

PART EIGHT

Special Forms

This part contains some special forms to help you determine the licenses you must obtain and the taxes you must pay, and a sample to help you prepare a calendar that tells you when to pay your taxes.

This itemized list will aid you in identifying tax, license, permit, and regulatory requirements that determine your right to do business. Many business owners are not aware of all the items that apply to them. Consequently, they encounter difficulties and sometimes incur significant additional costs.

We recognize that the regulations vary among jurisdictions, that is, among cities, counties, and states, as well as among various types of businesses. You should check with the appropriate authorities for detailed information. In addition, you should obtain an employers tax bulletin and a Small Business Tax Guide from the Internal Revenue Service.

FORM VIII-1
Tax, License, Permit Checklist

Item	Applies to My business	Date for Filing/Making Application/Payment

A. Local (city/county)
  1. Zoning (selected location zoned for my type business)
  2. Building permit
  3. Business license
    a. General
    b. Special
      (1) Application
      (2) Advertising
      (3) Hearing
    c. Permits
      (1) Beverage
      (2) Food
      (3) Agricultural
      (4) Other:

      ————————
      ————————
      ————————

  4. Business taxes
    a. General
      (1) Declaration
      (2) Date due
    b. Special
      (1) Declaration
      (2) Date due
    c. Ad valorem
      (1) Declaration
      (2) Date due
    d. Inventory Tax
      (1) Reporting
      (2) Date due
    e. Sales tax
      (1) Reporting
      (2) Date due
    f. Real estate
      (1) Declaration
      (2) Date due
    g. Income tax
      (1) Return filed
      (2) Date due

FORM VIII–1 (continued)

Item	Applies to My business	Date for Filing/Making Application/Payment
B. State		
1. Sales tax number		
2. Corporation tax		
3. Sales tax		
a. Report		
b. Payment		
4. Unemployment tax		
5. Income tax		
a. Estimated income		
b. Quarterly income estimate payment		
c. Annual income tax return		
d. Payment dates for income tax		
C. Federal		
1. Employer identification number		
2. Depositing withheld income tax and social security (FICA) taxes		
3. Quarterly return of withheld income tax and social security (FICA) taxes		
4. Paying federal unemployment tax		
5. Report of withheld income tax		
6. Federal excise taxes (see IRS schedule)		
7. Federal income tax		
a. Filing estimated return		
b. Quarterly estimate payment		
c. Filing annual return		
d. Payment dates		
8. Occupation tax		
9. Federal use tax		

FORM VIII–2
Sample Tax Calendar

			november			
s	**m**	**t**	**w**	**t**	**f**	**s**
	1 Employers file Form 941 for income tax withheld and social security taxes.	2	3	4	5	6
7	8	9	10 Employees receiving cash tips of $20 or more in October report them.	11	12	13
14	15 Deposit employee withholding income tax and FICA taxes.	16	17	18	19	20
21	22	23	24	25	26	27
28	29	30 Suppliers of communication or air transportation service file tax.				

PART NINE

The Language of Business

Glossary of the Most Frequently Used Business Terms*

The following glossaries should help you understand the terms used in the text and the exhibits.

ABC inventory control. An inventory classification system which breaks down the inventory into similar unit values.

Absolute liability Liability for injury resulting to another where no account is taken of the standard care exercised. Liability of a principal as distinguished from that of a guarantor.

Accelerated depreciation Depreciation expense which offers an allowance for the wear and tear (including an allowance for obsolescence) of tangible property used in business or held for the production of income.

Accruals Continually recurring short-term liabilities, such as accrued wages, accrued taxes, and accrued interest.

"Affirmative action" Guidelines of the Office of Federal Contract Compliance state that contractors take "affirmative action" to avoid unlawful discrimination in employment by actively recruiting members of minority groups being under-utilized.

Agent A business unit which negotiates purchases and/or sales but does not take title of the goods in which it deals.

Amortize To liquidate on an installment basis. An amortized loan is one in which the principal amount of the loan is repaid in installments during the life of the loan.

Annuity A series of payments of a fixed amount for a specified number of years.

Balloon payment When a debt is not fully amortized, the final payment is larger than the preceding payments.

Better Business Bureau A community organization which is sponsored by the local businessmen which acts to police unfair business practices.

Bill of lading A written acknowledgment by a carrier of the receipt of goods described therein and an agreement to transport them to the place specified therein and deliver them to the person specified therein.

Bond A long-term debt instrument used to provide external funds for business.

*Prepared by Frank White, University of Georgia.

Bonding An obligation made binding by a money forefeiture, such as an insurance agreemnt pledging security for financial loss caused by an act or default of a person or by some contingency.

Book value The accounting value of an asset.

Break-even analysis An analytic technique for studying the relation between fixed cost, variable cost, and profit.

Broker An agent who negotiates contracts of purchase or sale but does not take control of the goods.

Bureaucracy A form of organization which has many of the characteristics of the classical organizational design; i.e., it is highly structured and centralized, with narrow spans of control.

Business cycle A definable pattern of changes in business activity which is periodically repeated. Particular cycles do not correspond to any accounting period.

Capital See Owners' equity.

Capital asset An asset with a life of more than one year that is not bought and sold in the ordinary course of business.

Capital budgeting The process of planning expenditures on assets whose returns are expected to extend beyond one year.

Capital gains Profits on the sale of capital assets held for six months or more.

Capitalization rate A discount rate used to find the present value of a series of future cash receipts. Sometimes called the discount rate.

Carrying costs Costs associated with holding inventory, such as interest charges or funds invested in inventory. Storage costs and costs of storage devaluation due to physical change, obsolescence, or market changes.

Cash A broad classification of easily transferred negotiable assets, such as coin, paper money, checks, money orders, and money on deposit in banks.

Cash cycle The length of time between the purchase of raw materials and the collection of accounts receivable generated in the sale of the final product.

Caveat emptor "Let the buyer beware." A maxim of common law expressing the rule that the buyer purchases at his peril. Implied warranties in the sale of personal property are exceptions to this rule.

Caveat vendor "Let the seller beware." This means that it is the seller's duty to do what the ordinary man would do in a similar situation.

Chattel mortgage A mortgage on personal property (not real estate), such as a mortgage on equipment.

Civil Rights Act of 1964 Federal law that was passed to eliminate job discrimination based on race, color, religion, sex, or national origin, and to insure due process and equal protection under the law.

Clayton Act Prohibits certain practices in commerce if they might substantially lessen competition or tend to create a monopoly. It also exempts labor unions and farm cooperatives from the provisions of the Sherman Antitrust Act.

Commercial bank An ordinary bank of deposit and discount, with checking accounts, as distinguished from a savings bank.

Compensating balance A required minimum checking account balance that a firm must maintain with a commercial bank. The required balance is generally equal to 15 to 20 percent of the amount of loans outstanding. Compensating balances can raise the effective rate of interest on bank loans.

Conditional sales contract A method of financing new equipment by paying it off in installments over a one- to five-year period. The seller retains title to the equipment until payment has been completed.

Consideration One of the prerequisites for a contract which makes it clear from the contract's terms that each party has incurred a detriment in exchange for the other party's doing so also. Something given in exchange for a promise.

Consumer Product Safety Commission This commission has primary responsibility for establishing mandatory product safety standards where appropriate, to reduce the risk of injury to consumers from consumer products. It can also ban consumer products found to present an unreasonable risk of injury.

Cooperative The joining together of independent producers, wholesalers, retailers, consumers, or a combination thereof to act collectively in buying or selling or both.

Cost-benefit analysis An analytic technique of weighing the specified costs of a project or investment against the benefits derived from the project or investment.

Credit union An organization, usually by labor groups, to provide financial services for employees. Credit unions offer low-cost loans and sometimes cooperative buying power to employees who participate by buying stock in them.

Debenture A long-term instrument that is not secured by a mortgage on specific property.

Decentralization A method of organizing a business so that separate parts are designated as divisions or organized as subsidiaries of the parent company. Thus, each division or subsidiary will function almost *autonomously* under conditions of controlled competition among the groupings. Each is responsible for its production, procurement, personnel, and other needs as they fit into the overall picture of company profits. Decentralization also provides an improved opportunity for manager development.

Depreciation The accounting procedure for apportioning the cost of fixed assets as a part of the expense of each period. Thus, the cost is amortized over a defined period of time.

Depression The bottom of the overall business cycle, marked by a low level of production, a widespread unemployment of resources, especially labor, and a sharp drop in price levels due to decreased demand. (See Recession.)

Detail man A company's salesperson who is responsible for direct selling of products to retailers or to the ultimate consumer without the use of an agent. Often he is responsible for setting up point-of-purchase displays and other special promotional materials.

Disposable income Personal income remaining after the deduction of taxes on personal income and compulsory payment, such as social security levies.

Dow-Jones industrial average An unweighted arithmetic average of 30 stock prices, adjusted for splits, which represented, in 1970, approximately one third of the value of all stock on the New York Stock Exchange.

Drop shipment The delivery of goods directly from a producer to the consumer, while the sale is handled by an agent for the producer, such as a middleman or a company representative.

Dun and Bradstreet A mercantile agency which offers credit ratings, financial analysis, and other financial services, usually on a contractual basis. A well-respected source of credit information about businesses and businessmen in the United States and elsewhere.

EBIT Abbreviation for earnings before interest and taxes.

EEOC (Equal Employment Opportunity Commission) The federal administrative agency which is responsible for enforcing the provisions of the Civil Rights Act of 1964 and promoting voluntary action programs to put equal employment opportunities into actual operation.

Employee turnover The rate at which employees are hired and terminated. It is usually represented as the percentage of the total work force which is hired on payroll and later taken off payroll within a year.

EOQ Economical ordering quantity, or the optimum (lowest cost) quantity of merchandise which should be purchased.

EPA (Environmental Protection Agency) An administrative agency set up to protect and improve the quality of the environment. Most of its work has been in the area of air and water pollution.

EPS Abbreviation for net earnings per share of stock after interest and taxes are provided for. It is computed by dividing the number of shares outstanding into the net earnings.

Equity The net worth of a business, consisting of capital stocks, capital (or paid-in) surplus, earned surplus (or retained earnings), and occasionally, certain net worth reserves.

Escrow Placing in the hands of a third party the property, money, or assets of a firm which are to be released to a grantee only upon the fulfillment of a condition.

Excise tax A tax on the manufacture, sale, or consumption of specified commodities.

Factoring A method of financing accounts receivable under which a firm sells its accounts receivable (generally without recourse) to a financial institution (the factor).

Fair Labor Standards Act of 1938 This act (commonly called the Wage and Hour Law) was the original wage and hour law. It and its amendments cover minimum wages, maximum working hours per week, payment of overtime, and restrictions on child labor.

Fair Trade Act An amendment to the Federal Trade Commission Act which permits minimum price levels for products for resale in states with fair-trade laws, without violating any antitrust laws.

FDA (Food and Drug Administration) A part of the Department of Health, Education, and Welfare which acts to protect the nation against impure and unsafe foods, drugs and cosmetics, and other potential hazards.

Federal Reserve Bank The national banking system which acts as a reserve and discount for affiliated banks in its 12-member system. Its purpose is to provide an elastic currency, to afford a means of rediscounting commercial paper, and to establish a more effective supervision of banking in the United States.

Field warehousing A method of financing inventories in which a "warehouse" is established at the place of business of the borrowing firm.

Fixed assets Assets of a business which are of a relatively permanent nature and are necessary for the functioning of the firm, such as buildings, furniture, equipment. See Capital Assets.

Fixed costs   Costs which do not vary with changes in output, such as interest on long-term loans, rents, or overhead.

Franchise   An agreement by a retailer to sell only the produce manufactured or distributed by the seller.

FOB (free-on-board)   This refers to the point at which the title of goods transfers from the producer to the buyer. "FOB-origin" means that the title is transferred upon leaving the loading dock of the producer and that the shipping costs are paid by the buyer.

FTC (Federal Trade Commission)   This commission is an independent administrative agency that assists in the enforcement of the Clayton Act and other laws for maintaining free competitive enterprise as the keystone of the American economic system.

Good faith   Acting with a sincere belief that the accomplishment intended is not unlawful or harmful to another. The antithesis of fraud and deceit.

Goods-in-process   Goods in the midst of production or manufacture such that they are neither in a raw materials state nor finished and ready for sale.

Goodwill   Intangible assets of a firm established by the excess of the price paid for the going concern over its book value.

Gross national product (GNP)   A measure of the economic performance of the economy as a whole.

Holding Company   A corporation operated for the purpose of owning the common stock of other companies.

Hurdle rate   The effective capitalization rate which must be met or exceeded before a project or investment will be made. Any rate of return on assets above this rate assures that a profit is being made.

Implied warranty   A guarantee arising from contract law which implies that goods for sale are reasonably fit for their ordinary and intended purpose or are fit for a particular purpose.

Inflation   The injection of more money into the economy relative to the volume of goods and services. It results in generally rising prices for goods and factors of production.

Intrinsic value   The value which, in the mind of the analyst, is justified by the facts. It is often distinguished from the asset's current market price.

Inventory   The total of items of tangible personal property which (1) are held for sale in the ordinary course of business, (2) are in process of production for sale, or (3) are to be currently consumed in the production of goods and services to be available for sale.

Investment tax credit   A credit from federal income taxes that is computed as a percentage of the initial cost of certain capital assets.

IRR (internal rate of return)   The rate of return on an asset investment. This return is calculated by finding the discount rate that equates the present value of future cash flows to the cost of investment.

Jobber   A synonym for wholesaler or distributor.

Job cost   The aggregate cost of direct labor, material costs, and indirect Manufacturing expenses associated with a specific order or job.

Leverage   The use of external funds (as opposed to equity) to generate profits. For example, borrowing funds at 8 percent and making a net return on the funds of 12 percent constitute a use of leverage.

Line of credit   An arrangement whereby a financial institution commits itself to lend up to a specified maximum amount of funds during a specified period.

Line and staff   A descriptive term which defines the structure of an organization. Line refers to jobs or roles which have direct authority and responsibility for output. Staff personnel contribute indirectly to production. Usually they advise line personnel.

Liquidity   Refers to a firm's cash position and its ability to meet maturing obligations.

Loss leader   A product of known or accepted quality priced at a loss or no profit for the purpose of attracting patronage to a store.

Management by Objective (MBO)   A management technique of defining attainable goals for subordinates through an agreement of the supervisor and the subordinate. It offers continual feedback to subordinates in terms of their contribution to the organization's total performance.

Manufacturer's agent   An agent who generally operates on an extended contractual basis, often sells within an exclusive territory, handles noncompeting but related lines of goods and possesses limited authority with regard to prices and terms of sales. He or she may be authorized to sell a definite portion of the principal's output.

Marginal contribution   The contribution by an additional unit of production sold to the fixed and/or variable cost of a firm.

Marginal cost   The cost of an additional unit. In production, it is the cost of producing one additional unit.

Marginal revenue   The additional gross revenue produced by selling one additional unit of output.

Markdown   A reduction in selling price. An item priced at $1 would have a 20 percent markdown if it were discounted to a special price of 80 cents.

Market segmentation   A marketing strategy consciously developed to produce a product or service that embodies characteristics preferred by a small part of the total market for the product or service—for example, compact autos.

Markup   The percentage change in price from the purchase price or the cost of goods sold to the selling price. An item costing 80 cents to produce and sell would have a 25 percent markup if it sold for $1.

Merchant   A business unit that buys, takes title to, and resells merchandise. Both retailers and wholesalers are considered middlemen or merchants.

Missionary salesman   A salesman employed by a manufacturer to call on customers of his distributors, usually to develop goodwill and stimulate demand, to help or induce them to promote the sale of his employer's goods, to help them train their salesmen to do so, and often to take orders for delivery by such distributors. Also used to introduce a new product or service.

Motivation   The inner state that activates or moves, including inner strivings, such as drives, desires, and motives.

National brand A manufacturer's or producer's brand, usually enjoying wide territorial distribution.

NLRB (National Labor Relations Board) An administrative board set up to protect labor's right to organize and bargain collectively and thereby encourage the "friendly adjustment of industrial disputes" by restoring equality in workers' bargaining positions with employers.

Pledging accounts receivable Short-term borrowing from financial institutions where the loan is secured by accounts receivable. The lender may physically take the accounts receivable but typically has recourse to the borrower.

Price/earnings ratio The ratio of price per share to earnings per share. Most growing firms have higher P/E ratios.

Private brand A brand sponsored by a merchant or agent as distinguished from brands sponsored by manufacturers or producers.

Product line A group of products that are closely related because they satisfy a class of needs, are used together, are sold to the same customer groups, are marketed through the same type of outlet, or fall within given price ranges.

Progressive tax A tax that requires a higher percentage payment on higher incomes.

Promotion A blend of the three following sales activities: (1) mass, impersonal selling efforts (advertising); (2) personal sales; and (3) other activities, such as point-of-purchase displays, shows or exhibits, and other nonrecurring sales efforts.

Proxy A document giving one the authority or power to act for another.

Purchasing power The amount of goods and/or services which money can purchase. During times of inflation, the purchasing power of money declines.

National Retail Credit Corporation The world's largest consumer credit rating service. It provides credit investigations on a contractual basis for anyone having a legitimate business need.

Opportunity cost The rate of return on the best investment *alternative*. It is the highest return which will *not* be earned if the funds are invested in a given project.

OSHA (Occupational Safety and Health Act) This act established specific safety standards requiring the installment of safety appliances by employers and the use of safety equipment by employees. It develops and issues regulations and conducts investigations and inspections to determine the status of compliance.

Owners' equity Those assets left over after all creditors have been paid off. The two sources of equity are owner investment and prior earnings from profitable operations.

OTC Stocks which are sold over the counter rather than through an organized stock exchange.

Overhead All the costs of business other than direct labor and materials. Overhead costs include such items as maintenance, supervision, utility costs, and depreciation.

Payback period The length of time required for the net revenues of an investment to return the cost of the investment.

PERT/CPM Management aids that place the separate activities of a project on a schematic network to view the interrelationships of each project. The technqiue is used to cut costs by planning, scheduling and monitoring, and control of the overall project.

Peter Principle   A humorous book by L. J. Peter and R. Hull which examines the "Peter Principle" in hierarchical organizations. The principle states: "In a hierarchy every employee tends to rise to his own level of incompetence."

Rack jobber   A wholesaling business unit that markets specialized lines of merchandise to certain types of retail stores and provides the special services of selective brand and item merchandising and arrangement, maintenance, and stocking of display racks. Usually rack jobbers place merchandise in a store on a consignment basis.

Recession   The downturn or a fluctuation in the aggregate business cycle recognized by a decrease in the growth in GNP for two successive quarters. It is characterized by changes in inventory levels, increased unemployment, changes in government spending, and attempts by the Federal Reserve Board to control inflation by tightening credit.

Retailer   A merchant or agent whose main business is to buy goods for resale to the ultimate consumer.

Robinson-Patman Act   The Robinson-Patman amendment to the Clayton Act gave the FTC jurisdiction to eliminate quantity discounts and to forbid brokerage allowances, except to independent brokers, and to prohibit promotional allowances, except on the equal basis. Any discrimination of this kind has to be based upon a cost justification.

Salary   A fixed compensation paid regularly for services.

Salvage value   The value of a capital asset at the end of a specified period. It is the current market price of an asset being considered for replacement.

Savings and loan bank   A bank which accepts and pays interest on deposit savings, subject to whatever conditions may be prescribed as to the time such savings remain on deposit. Chartered by the Federal Home Loan Bank Board to encourage thrift and promote home ownership by making loans for home financing.

Sherman Antitrust Act   The first law passed by the U.S. Congress to preserve competition in the "free-market" system. It outlawed monopolies and all combinations to restrain trade or commerce.

Soldiering   A term which was used during the scientific management era to refer to the observed practice of output restriction. Thus, employees were observed to be producing at a lower than expected rate.

Standard   The basic limits or grade ranges in the form of uniform specifications to which particular manufactured goods may conform, and uniform classes into which the products of agriculture and extractive industries may or must be sorted or assigned. The expected employee performance upon which product costing and employee pay are determined.

Stock dividend   A dividend paid in additional shares of stock rather than in cash. It involves a transfer from earned surplus to the capital stock account; therefore, stock dividends are limited by the amount of earned surplus.

Stock-out   A situation in which the supply of an item in a firm's inventory is found to be used up. This is usually the consequence of poor inventory management.

Stock split   An accounting action to increase the number of shares outstanding. This action involves no transfer from surplus to the capital account.

Stock turnover   The rate at which the minimum order quantity purchased is sold. It may be calculated by dividing the cost of goods sold by the average inventory for the accounting period.

Surtax A tax levied in addition to the normal tax. The normal corporate tax rate is 22 percent, but a surtax of 26 percent is added to the normal tax on all corporate income exceeding $25,000.

Target market The segment of the total market which is selected for a concentration of promotional effort.

Theory X A set of assumptions about the nature of man which, according to Douglas McGregor, underlies classical management theory. The assumptions stress the indolence of man.

Theory Y An approach to management which is based on precepts exactly opposite to those of Theory X. They are: (1) workers do not inherently dislike work; (2) workers do not want to be controlled and threatened; (3) workers under proper working conditions seek out additional responsibility; and (4) workers desire to satisfy other needs besides those related to job security.

Time-motion study The process of determining the appropriate elapsed time for the completion of a task or job. This was a technique used by scientific managers to determine a fair day's work.

Trade association An organization formed to benefit members of the same trade. Nationally it works to inform its members of issues and developments within the organization and about how changes outside the organization will affect the members.

Trade credit Interfirm debt arising through credit sales and recorded as an account receivable by the seller and as an account payable by the buyer.

Trademark A brand or part of a brand that is given legal protection because it is capable of exclusive appropriation; because it is used in a manner sufficiently fanciful, distinctive, and arbitrary; because it is affixed to the product when sold; or because it otherwise satisfies the requirements set up by law.

Uniform commercial code A comprehensive code of practices drawn up by various legal and commercial associations to simplify, clarify, and modernize the law governing commercial transactions; to permit the continued expansion of commercial practices through custom, usage, and agreement of the parties; and to make uniform the law among the various jurisdictions.

Value added The part of the value of a product or a service to the consumer or user which results from the change from one form to another, for example, the conversion of a raw material into a *finished* product for sale.

Voluntary group A group of retailers, each of whom owns and operates his own store and is associated with a wholesale organization or manufacturer to carry on joint merchandising activities, and who are characterized by some degree of group identity and uniformity of operation. Such joint activities have been largely of two kinds: cooperative advertising and group control of store operation.

Wages A payment usually of money for labor or services, usually according to contract, and on an hourly, daily, or piecework rate.

Wholesaler A business unit which buys and resells merchandise to retailers and other merchants and/or to industrial, institutional, and commercial users but which does not sell in significant amounts to ultimate consumers.

Working capital Refers to a firm's investment in short-term assets—cash, short-term securities, accounts receivable, and inventories.

REFERENCES

American Marketing Association. *Marketing Definitions: A Glossary of Marketing Terms.* Chicago: American Marketing Association, 1960, pp. 9-23.

Bach, G. L. *Economics: An Introduction to Analysis and Policy,* 2d ed. Englewood Cliffs, N.J.: Prentice-Hall, Inc., 1957.

Ballentine, J. A. *Ballentine's Law Dictionary,* 3d ed. San Francisco: Bancroft-Whitney Company, 1969.

Corley, R. N., and **Black, R. L.** *The Legal Environment of Business,* 3d ed. New York: McGraw-Hill Book Company, 1973.

Donnelly, J. H.; Gibson, J. L.; and **Ivancevich, J. M.** *Fundamentals of Management.* Austin: Business Publications, Inc., 1971.

Gist, R. R. *Marketing and Society.* New York: Holt, Rinehart, and Winston, Inc., 1971.

Gross, Harry. *Financing for Small and Medium-Sized Business.* Englewood Cliffs, N.J.: Prentice-Hall, Inc., 1969.

Meigs, W. B., and **Johnson, C. E.** *Accounting: The Basis for Business Decisions,* 2d ed. New York: McGraw-Hill Book Company, 1967.

Myer, J. N. *Accounting for Non-Accountants.* New York: New York University Press, 1957.

Samuelson, P. *Economics,* 8th ed. New York: McGraw-Hill Book Company, 1970.

Still, J. W. *A Guide to Managerial Accounting in Small Companies.* Englewood Cliffs, N.J.: Prentice-Hall, Inc., 1969.

Weston, J. F., and **Brigham-Holt, E. F.** *Essentials of Managerial Finance.* New York: Holt, Rinehart, and Winston, Inc., 1968.

Whiteside, C. D. *Accounting Systems for the Small and Medium-Sized Business.* Englewood Cliffs, N.J.: Prentice-Hall, Inc., 1961.

SBA Glossary *

Active Corps of Executives (ACE) Volunteers not retired, recruited from local and national associatons, service clubs, companies, educational institutions, and civic groups to supplement the talent and expertise in the SCORE group. Both SCORE and ACE perform a service by helping borrowers who are in need of management assistance.

Accounts Payable Business accounts of the borrower representing obligations to pay for goods and services received.

Accounts Receivable Business accounts of the borrower representing moneys due for goods sold or services rendered, attested by notes, statements, invoices, or other written evidence of a present obligation.

Advances Disbursements to contractors or grantees to provide working capital required in performing contract or grant requirements. The advance is an outlay but not an obligation. Advances are also used internally (e.g., travel and transportation).

Adverse change An alteration in the borrower's collateral or financial or business condition which materially increases the risk of a loan's collectibility.

Advisory Councils Provide communication between SBA and the public in their respective areas of the country. They report on independent business needs and on the effects of SBA programs in each community as well as nationally.

Amortization The gradual reduction of debt by periodic payment sufficient to pay current interest and to eliminate the principal at maturity.

Appraisal The act of placing a value upon property, either real or personal.

Assumption The undertaking or adoption of debts or obligations.

Auction A public sale in which goods are sold to the highest bidder.

Bankruptcy A proceeding in which the property of a debtor in taken over by a receiver or trustee in bankruptcy for the benefit of the creditors. This act is performed under the jurisdiction of the courts as prescribed by the National Bankruptcy Act or state insolvency laws.

---

*Extracted from *SBA Glossary* (Washington, D.C.: Small Business Administration, 1973).

Break-even analysis   The break-even point in any business is that point at which the volume of sales or revenues exactly equals total expenses—the point at which there is neither a profit nor a loss—under varying levels of capacity. The break-even point tells the manager what level of output or activity is required before the firm can make a profit; it reflects the relationship between costs, volume, and profits.

Business Loan and Investment Fund (BLIF)   This fund finances regular business loans, displaced business loans, and prime contracting operations under Sections 7(*a*), 7(*b*)(3), 7(*e*), 7(*g*) (handicapped), and 8(*a*), respectively, of the Small Business Act; economic opportunity loans under Title IV of the Economic Opportunity Act of 1964; and state and local devlopment company loans and small business investment company debenture purchases (loans) under Titles V and III, respectively of the Small Business Investment Act of 1958.

Business loans   7(*a*), economic opportunity, development company, and displaced business loans.

Call contracts (406)   SBA contracts with private consultants to provide management and technical assistance to small businessmen on call by SBA.

Canceled loan   The annulment or rescission of an approved loan prior to disbursement.

Cash flow   Projections based on analysis of past operating experience, payment of obligations, and collection of receivables. This experience is applied to budgeted sales and costs for a future period in order to allow for repayments of loan obligations and to assure adequate working capital from earned income. Cash flow forecasts provide a fundamental financial-management tool for planning cash needs and ensuring adequate liquidity.

Certificate of Competency (COC)   SBA certification of the technical and financial ability of an independent business to perform a specific government contract (see Procurement assistance).

Charge-off   A bookkeeping transaction removing the unpaid balance of a loan from the active receivable accounts.

Charged-off loan   An uncollectible loan the principal and accrued interest of which were removed from the loan accounting records. Referral of an account to DOJ is based on the presumption of collectibility.

Closed loan   Any loan for which an initial disbursement has been paid.

Closing   Actions and procedures required to effect the documentation and disbursement of loan funds after the application has been approved.

Collateral   Something of value pledged to ensure the fulfillment of an obligation.

Colpur   Abbreviation for collateral purchased, referring to borrower's pledged assets, usually acquired through a foreclosure sale.

Concession   Lease of government-owned property to socially or economically disadvantaged businessmen (under the 8[*a*] program) to operate a business providing goods or services for the benefit of government employees and others.

Contingent liability   An obligation that may be incurred, depending upon the occurrence of a future event, e.g., a legal obligation that depends on the outcome of pending litigation.

Contracts

   Negotiated   Agreement between two or more persons consisting of an offer and acceptance supported by consideration.

Fixed price Proposal to SBA by cost element plus proposed profit (fixed price), or fee (cost-type).

Costs Money obligated for goods and services received during a given period of time, regardless of when ordered or whether paid for. Includes the SBA share of loans disbursed, exclusive of guaranteed loan disbursements by lending institutions.

Counseling Management advice and assistance given by SBA employees and volunteers on problems concerning marketing, accounting, production analysis and methods, financial forecasts and analysis, etc.

Credit rating A grade assigned to a business concern to denote the net worth and credit standing to which the concern is entitled in the opinion of the rating agency.

Debenture A debt instrument evidencing the holder's right to receive interest and principal installments from the named obligor. Applies to all forms of unsecured long-term debt evidenced by a certificate of debt.

Debt financing The provision of long-term loans to independent business concerns in exchange for debt securities or a note.

Declined application An application for financial or management assistance the approval of which was denied.

Defaults Loans for which an installment remains unpaid 30 days or more after its due date. From 30 to 60 days is classified as "past due" and 60 days and over is classified as "delinquent." A loan is deemed to be "current" if the installment remains unpaid for less than 30 days subsequent to the due date. Defaults also occur in rent payments under lease guaranty and/or failing to complete contracts guaranteed by a surety bond program.

Deferred loan Loans whose principal installments are postponed for a specified period of time.

Deprived area (01) Program category classification covering all assistance designed to stimulate independent business in major geographic areas designated by SBA and other agencies for special attention in the application of resources (e.g., persistent labor surplus areas, major poverty areas, SBA target cities, and HUD model cities).

Development company loans (DCL) Loans under Sections 502 and 501 to local or state development companies for use in implementing the planned economic growth of communities by promoting and assisting the growth and development of business concerns in the area under Section 502. SBA may lend up to $350,000 for up to 25 years for each independent business to be assisted by a development company project.

Direct loan Loan made solely by SBA utilizing government funds. 7(*a*) limited administratively to $100,000 (by statute $350,000); EOL limited by statute to $50,000.

Disaster loan Low-interest loans made to victims of disasters to repair physical damage or overcome economic injury.

1. *Physical damage loans* Loans made to repair, rehabilitate, or replace property destroyed as a result of storms, floods, earthquakes, or other catastrophes. Generally, the amount of the loan may not administratively exceed $55,000 for repair or replacement of homes, household goods, and personal property, and $500,000 for the rehabilitation of a business, regardless of size. Both home and business disaster loans may be made for any period up to 30

years. SBA may also make long-term loans to commercial or industrial enterprises which are major sources of employment in stricken areas. There is no limitation on the size of the loan for physical or economic injury to these enterprises.

2. *Economic injury loans (EIDL)* Loans made to small firms suffering damage as a result of disasters, as determined by the president, the SBA administrator, or the secretary of agriculture, to provide working capital and pay financial obligations.

3. *Product disaster loans (PDL)* Loans made to independent firms that have suffered substantial economic injury through inability to process or market a product for human consumption because of disease or toxicity of the product.

4. *Health and safety loans* Loans made to independent businesses for alterations or additions to equipment, facilities, and methods of operation considered necessary to meet the requirements imposed by the Coal Mine and Occupational Safety and Health acts.

5. *Consumer protection loans (CPL)* Loans made to independent business concerns likely to suffer substantial economic injury from its required change of equipment, facilities, and operations so as to meet requirements imposed by the Egg Products Inspection Act, Wholesome Poultry Products Act, and the Wholesome Meat Act of 1967.

6. *Regulatory economic injury loans* Loans made to independent businesses seriously affected by (1) federal action limiting the development of strategic arms, or (2) water pollution control requirements.

Disaster Loan Fund (DLF) This fund finances physical disaster loans to repair or replace property damaged or destroyed by "natural" disasters, and economic injury disaster loans resulting from plant and facility requirements imposed by various consumer protection and regulatory acts as authorized in Sections 7(*b*) (1), (2), (4), (5), (6), (7), and 7(*c*) (2), and 7(*g*) (water pollution) of the Small Business Act.

Discrimination As used by SBA means discourtesy, failure to assist, or failure to employ or promote because of the race, color, creed, sex, or national origin of an individual. The term includes the residual effects of past discrimination in cases where there is such effect even though discrimination is not currently practiced.

Displaced business loans Loans made to relocate or reestablish small firms which suffered substantial economic injury as a result of being displaced or by their proximity to federally aided urban renewal highway, low-rent public housing, and other construction projects.

Divestitures Conversion of ownership and/or control of a business from a majority to disadvantaged persons. In SBIC parlance, divestiture ordinarily refers to the required dispossession of certain portfolio investments.

Earning power The ability of a business to employ its capital profitably over a period of time. When a concern's profits show a reasonable return on invested capital and are sufficient to provide for a high standard of maintenance of property, planned expansion, and servicing of debt, the concern is said to have a demonstrated earning power. Demonstrated earning power is the foremost test of the business risk in passing upon an application for a loan.

Economic growth (03) Program category classification covering all assistance designed to promote the independent business contribution to economic growth and a competitive environment. All assistance which does not fall into the (01), (02), and (04) categories.

Economic opportunity loans (EOLs)   Loans to socially or economically disadvantaged existing or prospective independent businessmen. The maximum amount of an EOL is $50,000 for up to 15 years.

Economically or socially disadvantaged   Whether one is economically or socially disadvantaged is based on the composite of several factors including whether the person is a member of a disadvantaged race, has special handicaps, or is located in a depressed area, which, because of reasons beyond the person's control, severely limit his or her ability to develop and maintain a profitable business enterprise.

8(a) contract   A subcontract awarded by SBA to a socially or economically disadvantaged independent business concern. A contract is entered into by SBA with other federal agencies for supplies, services, construction, etc. SBA then arranges for the performance of such contracts by negotiating subcontracts with disadvantaged independent business concerns.

Equity financing   The provision of funds for capital or operating expenses in exchange for capital stock, stock purchase warrants, and options in the business financed. Equity financing includes long-term subordinated securities containing stock options and/or warrants.

Escrow accounts   Funds placed in trust by a borrower for a specific purpose and to be delivered to him only upon the fulfillment of certain conditions.

Federal Register   A daily publication providing a uniform system for making available to the public regulations and legal notices issued by the executive branch of the federal government. These include presidential proclamations and executive orders, federal agency documents having general applicability and legal effect, documents required to be published by act of Congress, and federal agency documents of public interest. Rules and regulations are incorporated annually in the Code of Federal Regulations (Title 13, chapter 1).

Final action   The decision to approve or decline an application for financial assistance.

Financing   The provision of operating funds to a business (by either loans or purchase of debt securities or capital stock).

Fiscal year   The government's budgetary and fiscal account period. It begins on July 1 and runs through June 30 of the following year. Is designated by the calendar year in which it ends; e.g., FY 1973 runs from July 1, 1972, through June 30, 1973.

Foreclosure   The act of the mortgage, upon default in the payment of interest or principal of a mortgage, of enforcing payment of the debt by selling the underlying security.

Forgiveness credit   Allowable credit applied against the principal balance of a disaster loan borrower who qualifies under applicable legislation—Sections 7(b)(1), (2), and (4).

Franchising   A continuing relationship in which the franchisor provides a licensed privilege to the franchisee to do business, plus assistance in organizing, training, merchandising, marketing, and management, in return for a consideration. Franchising is a form of business by which the owner (franchisor) of a product, service, or method obtains distribution through affiliated dealers (franchisees). The product, method, or service being marketed is usually identified by the franchisor's brand name, and the holder of the privilege (franchise) is often given exclusive access to a defined geographic area.

Guaranteed loan A loan made and serviced by a lending institution under an agreement that SBA will purchase the guaranteed portion if the borrower defaults. Also includes SBA guarantees of debentures issued by Small Business Investment Companies.

Hazard insurance Insurance required and made payable to SBA covering certain risks on real and personal property used for securing the loan.

Immediate participation loan (IP) SBA and a private lending institution each put up part of the funds immediately. SBA's share administratively may not exceed $150,000 for 7(a) (the statutory limitation is $350,000).

Insolvency The inability of a borrower to meet his financial obligations as they mature.

Institutional investors Institutions whose investment of funds is important to their operations but which are formed principally for purposes other than investment, e.g., insurance companies, eleemosynary institutions, and pension trusts.

Insufficiency appropriations Appropriations to permit trustor (SBA) to pay trustee, Government National Mortgage Association (GNMA), the amount by which required payments of interest and principal on outstanding certificates for SBA exceed collections on pooled loans serving as "collateral" for the certificates.

Actually, such insufficiencies have arisen in respect to interest only because the trust agreement requires SBA to replace delinquent loans; and with limited exceptions all loans pledged by SBA are amortized monthly. With a 5 percent overpledge involved, principal collections have always been adequate to meet principal payments on the certificates.

Interest An amount paid for the use of funds.

Inverse order of maturity When payments are received from borrowers that are larger than the authorized repayment schedules, the overpayment is credited to the final installments of the principal. This reduces the maturity of the loan and does not affect the original repayment schedule.

Investment banks Businesses specializing in the formation of new capital. This is done by outright purchase and sales of securities offered by the issuer, standby underwriting, or "best-efforts selling."

Investment company SBICs (Small Business Investment Companies) and MESBICs (Minority Enterprise Small Business Investment Companies) are SBA-licensed, privately owned and operated investment companies which provide equity capital and long-term loans to independent business concerns. A MESBIC, organized under Section 301(d) of the Small Business Investment Act of 1958, invests only in independent business concerns having at least 50 percent ownership by minorities. MESBICs are also referred to as a limited SBICs.

Judgment Judicial determination of the existence of an indebtedness.

Lease A contract between the owner (lessor) and the tenant (lessee) stating the conditions under which the tenant may occupy or use a property.

Lease guaranty An insurance policy issued on behalf of an independent businessman guaranteeing to his landlord that rent payments will be made. The policies may be underwritten directly by SBA or by private insurance companies backed by SBA reinsurance agreements.

Legal rate of interest The maximum rate of interest fixed by the laws of the various states which a lender may charge a borrower for the use of money.

Lending institution Any institution, including commercial banks, savings and loan associations, and commercial finance companies, qualified to participate with SBA in the making of loans.

Lien A charge upon or security interest in real or personal property maintained to ensure the satisfaction of a debt or duty ordinarily arising by operation of law.

Line of credit The amount which a person or concern is entitled to borrow at any given time. It constitutes the total potential credit balance at the disposal of a borrower.

Liquidating value The net value realizable in the sale (ordinarily a forced sale) of a business or a particular asset.

Loan receivable SBA share of outstanding loan balances in SBA portfolio.

Loss verification An estimate prepared by an SBA appraiser verifying damage to real and personal property as the result of a physical disaster.

Management ability evaluation An analysis of the applicant's management abilities in terms of his prospects for becoming a successful businessman.

Management assistance plan A plan setting forth the proper assistance and guidance to be furnished to the applicant so as to achieve successful business operation.

Maturity extensions Extensions beyond the allowable period for repayment of a loan (maturity) in cases involving severe financial hardship, especially for loans approved for physical disasters.

Merger A combination of two or more corporations wherein the dominant unit absorbs the passive ones, the former usually continuing operation under the same name. In a consolidation, two units combine and are succeeded by a new corporation, usually with a new title.

Minority (02) Program category classification covering all assistance of any type made to promote minority entrepreneurship (independent businesses or Local Development Companies [LDCs]), with 50 percent or more ownership by minorities). Minority classifications include blacks, Puerto Ricans, American Indians, Spanish-Americans, Asians, and Eskimos/Aleuts.

Minority vendor system The provision to major private corporations of a service which matches the private company's needs with an inventory of minority suppliers. The system also provides a means of identifying new business venture opportunities for the minority business community.

Mortgage A deed given to secure the repayment of a loan made by the mortgagee (lender). In legal contemplation there are two types: (1) title theory—operates as a transfer of the legal title of the property to the mortgage; and (2) lien theory—creates a lien upon the property in favor of the mortgagee.

Net worth Property owned (assets) minus debts and obligations (liabilities) is the owner's equity (net worth).

New or existing business For 7(*a*), EOL, and DCL, a new business is one in operation for 180 days or less, regardless of former ownership. The acquisition of a business which has already been in existence over 180 days constitutes an "existing" business.

Notes and accounts receivable Secured or unsecured receivables evidenced by notes or open accounts arising from activities involving liquidation and disposal of loan collateral.

Obligations · Liabilities incurred. Technically defined as "amount of orders placed, contracts awarded, services received, and similar transactions during a given period which will require payments during the same or a future period." This includes the SBA share of loans approved, ignoring for the purposes of this particular definition the fact that guaranteed loans are "funded" at less than 100 percent of the SBA share and that for the annual certification under Sections 1311 of the Supplemental Appropriations Act, 1955, valid loan obligations include only those in which a loan agreement has been executed.

Optical character recognition (OCR) Machine identification of printed characters through the use of light-sensitive devices utilized for transferring data into a computer system directly from source documents.

Outlays Net disbursements (cash payments in excess of cash receipts) for administrative expenses and for loans and related costs and expenses (i.e., gross disbursements for loans and expenses minus loan repayments, interest and fee income collected, and reimbursements received for services performed for other agencies).

Participation certificates Debt instruments evidencing the holders' beneficial interest or participation in a pool of loan obligations and in the right to receive interest and principal collections therefrom.

 The sale of participations (certificates) was authorized in the Participation Sales Act of 1966 as a technique for obtaining the financing of government agency loan portfolios by the private sector. Initially the transactions were recorded and reported under a concept that defined them as a "sale of loans." Subsequently the concept was changed to recognize them as "borrowings," which they actually are, with the pledge loans as collateral therefor.

 An agency can "sell" certificates only to the extent of authorization in an appropriation act. SBA was authorized to sell a total of $1,350,000,000— $350,000,000 was authorized in FY 1966; $850,000,000 in 1967; and $150,000,000 in 1968.

Partnership A legal relationship existing between two or more persons contractually associated as joint principals in a business.

Pool loans Loans made to corporations formed and capitalized by groups of independent business companies for purchasing raw materials, equipment, inventory, or supplies to use in their individual businesses, and also obtain the benefit of research and development.

Prime contracts Contracts and purchases awarded by the federal government to private enterprise for the provisions of supplies and services.

Private sector participation That part of an SBA-approved participation loan disbursed by the participating institution; i.e., the "bank's" share of the principal on an immediate participation loan, and the total principal on a guaranteed loan.

Problem loan An intensively serviced loan which contemplates potential problems. Such loans warrant constant attention and follow-up to ensure that any difficulties arising are fully understood and readily resolved by appropriate assistance.

Procurement assistance SBA assistance provided to independent concerns to help them obtain government prime and related subcontracts. Activities include directing the independent businessman to federal agencies and private companies that buy the products and services they supply, helping them get their names on bidders' lists, and ensuring that, where applicable, purchases and contracts of government agencies are set aside for exclusive independent business bidding. Also, if the independent firm is a low bidder and is denied contract because of the government agency's determination that the independent firm lacks the technical capacity and/or credit to perform, SBA will make an on-site review of the firm at its request. If it is found to be capable of performing the contract successfully, SBA will issue a certificate of competency which requires the federal agency to award the contract to the firm.

Procurement source program   A uniform method of receiving and responding to requests for potential independent business sources to meet the needs of SBA's prime and subcontract requirements.

Program category structure   Consists of groupings of major SBA program objectives and provides the basic method used to plan, program, and budget SBA resources. The program category structure is represented by a six-digit code. The first two digits represent the main program object categories (e.g., 01, Stimulation of Small Business in Deprived Areas). The second two digits represent subcategories which contribute to the accomplishment of main program objectives (e.g., 01, Facilitating Access to Capital and Credit). The third two digits represent "elements" which focus on specific agency program outputs (e.g., 01, Regular Business Loans). The complete SBA program category structure is set forth in SOP 20 20.

Proposed rule making   Proposed SBA rules and regulations and changes thereto are published in the *Federal Register*, notifying the public that consideration is being given to an addition or amendment to the Code of Federal Regulations. By publication, in addition to notice, interested persons are given an opportunity to comment or otherwise participate in developing the final rules and regulations.

Ratio   Denotes the relationships of items within and between financial statements, e.g., current ratio, quick ratio, inventory turnover ratio, and debt/net worth ratios.

Receiver   A person appointed by a court to take custody of the property of the debtor and to preserve the business for the benefit of creditors under court supervision.

Reconsideration   Request, based upon new or additional information for reevaluation and redetermination of a previously declined loan application.

Revolving fund   A fund account in the Treasury and an accounting unit established on the books of SBA for assuring that the revenues and other assets thereof are applied only to authorized financial transactions. Distinguished from other fund accounts in that it is established to finance a continuing cycle of business-type operations and is credited with repayments and revenues collected. The total resources of a revolving fund, represented, for example, by capital appropriations and repayments and revenues earned, are available for obligation, but only in accord with the budgetary plan approved by Congress in an annual (or supplemental) appropriation act, and the apportionment plan approved by OMB. SBA finances its various loan and lease and surety bond guarantee programs from three revolving funds:

1. Business Loan and Investment Fund (BLIF).
2. Disaster Loan Fund (DLF). These two are authorized by Section 4(*c*)(1) of the Small Business Act.

3. Lease and Surety Bond Guarantees Revolving Fund. Programs and funds authorized by Title IV of the Small Business Investment Act of 1958.

Rules and Regulations When adopted and published in the *Federal Register,* SBA regulations are presumed to be within the constructive knowledge of all affected by them and the courts will take judicial notice thereof. All regulations and amendments are compiled in the Code of Federal Regulations (CFR) annually.

SBA share That portion of approved loans in which SBA has actual or potential loss exposure—represented by the total amount of direct loans, the SBA share of immediate participation loans, and the SBA share of guaranteed loans.

Screening A review of a loan application by a loan officer to determine whether the application is acceptable (adequacy of documentation and pertinent information) prior to processing.

Seasoned loan A loan either (1) on which for more than two years after regular scheduled installments of principal and interest commenced, all such payments have been made as scheduled in the note without any deferments or lateness exceeding 30 days; or (2) the principal balance of which has been reduced to 50 percent of the original balance, and all payments as required by the note have been made for the past year without deferment or lateness exceeding 30 days. In either case, the collateral must be deemed adequate and the account satisfactory in all other respects.

Secondary market That portion of a guaranteed loan sold by the original lender to a secondary participant, such as other banks, institutional investors, insurance companies, credit unions, and pension funds.

Service Corps of Retired Executives (SCORE) Normally retired successful business-men who volunteer to render assistance in counseling and guiding struggling independent businesses.

Servicing office The SBA office responsible for all administrative and clerical functions incident to the administration and liquidation of all loans under its jurisdiction. Organizationally the servicing offices of SBA are grouped in ten separate regions for administrative direction and control.

Set-asides Federal procurement of supplies and services which are restricted for exclusive bidding by independent business.

7(a) business loans Loans to finance construction, expansion, and the acquisition of equipment, machinery, and supplies; and to supply working capital.

Sole proprietorship A business entity privately owned and managed by a single individual.

Standard Industrial Classification (SIC) The classification covers the entire field of economic activities and is a classification of establishments by the type of activity in which they are engaged. This classification by codes facilitates the collection, tabulation, and presentation of data used by government and state agencies, trade associations, and private research organizations.

Standard operating procedure (SOP) SOPS are administrative publications issued for the use of employees in conducting agency business. They are the main source of information about SBA's internal operations and contain all mandatory instructions—including agency policies (preferred outcomes or objectives) and procedures (required activities and functions).

State Development Company loans (SDCs) Loans to state development companies operating pursuant to special enabling legislation for use in implementing economic growth throughout the state by promoting and assisting the growth and development of independent business concerns. SBA loans under Section 501 may be for as long as 20 (administrative limitation) years in an amount matching the borrowings of the state development company from all other sources.

Statutory limitations Ceilings imposed by Congress—Section 4(*c*)(4) of the Small Business Act—on the amount outstanding at any one time for loans receivable, guaranteed loans, and undisbursed loan commitments under each loan program, other than those financed from the Disaster Loan Fund, and under the Section 8(*a*) prime contracting program.

As last amended by PL 92-320 approved June 27, 1972, these ceiling amounts are:

1. $4,300,000,000 for business loans and commitments under Sections 7(*a*), 7(*b*)(3), 7(*e*), and 7(*g*) (handdicapped loans) of the Small Business Act; business loans and commitments (not to exceed $350,000,000) under Title IV of the Economic Opportunity Act; and prime contracts under Section 8(*a*) of the Small Business Act.
2. $500,000,000 for Small Business Investment Company debentures, loans, and preferred securities under Title III of the Small Business Investment Act.
3. $500,000,000 for development company loans and commitments under Title V of the Small Business Investment Act.

In determining amounts chargeable against these ceilings, guaranteed loans are included at the full SBA share amount thereof, in contrast to the financing of such loans at a percentage (10 percent or 40 percent) representing an estimate of the proportion of guarantees that SBA will probably be required to purchase.

Subcontract A contract award made by a prime (or original) contractor to a second (or lower tier) contractor of a portion of a government contract received by the prime contractor.

Subordination agreements Agreements between SBA and lienholders under which the priority of paying off claims is structured.

Surety bond guarantee An SBA reinsurance/indemnification agreement with a private surety company issued on behalf of an independent businessman bidding on a contract to assure performance in accordance with his bid.

Technology utilization The dissemination of information on technological advances to independent manufacturers to assist them in applying relevant innovations, in processes, techniques, and materials.

Ten percent contingency The amount authorized in the S&E appropriation language each year for transfer from the three revolving funds for administrative activities that cannot be projected and provided for in the estimates. Currently considered available only for disaster loan expenses which cannot be projected.

327 actions All modifications of loan terms and conditions or administrative actions on specific loan accounts are accomplished by use of SBA Form 327.

Total loans outstanding (portfolio) The outstanding principal amount of all active loans containing a principal balance (current, past due, delinquent, and in liquidation) owed to SBA and participating banks. This includes guaranteed loans. Depending on use, can be expressed in terms of the total amount or of the SBA share. Ordinarily, the term *portfolio* refers only to the SBA share (loss exposure) of outstanding loans.

Trouble loans   A loan in liquidation status or on which repayment is 60 or more days past due.

Undelivered orders   The amount of orders for goods and services outstanding for which the liability has not yet accrued. For practical purposes, represents obligations incurred for which goods have not been delivered or services have not been performed.

Uniform Commercial Code (UCC)   Codification of uniform laws concerning commercial transactions. In SBA parlance, generally refers to a uniform method of recording and enforcing a security interest or charge upon real or personal property that exists or is to be acquired.

Unobligated (uncommitted) balance of fund   As of any date, the balance of a fund which is available for additional loans and/or expenses.

Withdrawn application   The revocation or recall of a loan application by the applicant prior to SBA's approval or declination.

INDEX

Index

Mental abilities, 21
Meshing of objectives, 14
Middlemen, agent, 215-20
Money-purchase pension plan, 116; *see also* Wages and salaries
Morality, 190
Motion study, 150
Motivating, 78; *see also* Managing your business
Motives
    Herzberg's motivators and maintenance factors, 11
    of independent owner-managers, 11-12
    of independently owned businesses, 12-14
    Maslow's needs hierarchy, 10

N

National Alliance of Businessmen (NAB), 113
National Apprenticeship Act of 1937, 113; *see also* Training and developing
National Institute of Occupational Safety and Health, 126
National Labor Relations Act of 1935 (NLRA), 123
National Labor Relations Board (NLRB), 123, 127, 128
National Safety Council, 126
Needs, physical plant; *see also* New business
    buy or lease, 48
    location, 47-48
Net income
    to investment ratio, 39
    to sales ratio, 39
New business; *see also* Economic environment
    concept of entering, 24
    how to establish, 44-55
        determining a timetable, 44-45
        determining personnel requirements, 47; *see also* Employees
        determining physical plant needs, 47-48
        establishing business objectives, 45; *see also* Objectives
        implementing plans, 55
        locating sources of funds, 51-55
        planning approach to market, 48-49
        preparing budgets, 50-51
        setting up organizational structure, 45-46
    planning and organizing, 23-83
    starting a, 33-34
        reasons against, 34
        reasons for, 34

O

Objectives
    establishing business, 45
    of independent owner-managers, 11-12
    of independently owned businesses, 12-14
        growth, 13
        profit, 13
        service, 12-13
        social, 13
        subsidiary, 14
    meshing of, 14
    personal, 10-12
Occupational Safety and Health Act of 1970 (OSHA), 42, 125-27
Office of Business Economics, 30
On-the-job training, 112
Operating
    budget, 50
    process chart, 139-40
Operation sheet, 142

Operations, 133; *see also* Changing inputs to outputs
Organization
    chart, 71-72
    forms of
        functional, 70
        informal, 71
        line, 71
        line and staff, 71
Organizational structure, 45-46; *see also* New business
Orientation, employee, 10
Outputs; *see* Changing inputs to outputs
Outside training, 112

P

Partnership, 62-64; *see also* Training and developing
    rights of partners, 64
    tests of, 64
    types of, 63
Pension plan, 116
Pension Reform Act, 116-18
Performance, appraising employees', 121
Personal
    analysis
        attitudes, 21-22
        mental abilities, 21
        philosophy of life, types of, 19-20
    selling, 191
Personnel requirements, 47; *see also* New business
Petty cash slip, 275
Philosophy of life; *see* Personal analysis
Physical examination, 102
Piece-work, 116
Planning, 56-74; *see also* New business
    administrative structure, 68-75
        forms of organization, 70-71
        growth, 68-69
        organization chart, preparing, 71-73
        organizational problems, 73-74
        organizing, ways of, 71
        principles and practices, 69-70
        strategies, planning, 74-75
    barriers to, 59
    financial structure, determining, 65-68
        corporation, 66-68
        partnership, 66
        proprietorship, 66
    functions of, 59-62
    how to plan, 56-57
    legal form, determining, 62-68
        corporation, 64-65
        holding company, 65
        partnership, 62-64
        proprietorship, 62
        trust, 65
    levels of, 57-58
    and organizing a new business, 23-83
    types of, 59-62
    to use time wisely, 58
Plant needs; *see also* New business
    buy or lease, 48
    location, 47-48
Policies, marketing, 190-95
Preferred stock, 67
Pricing; *see* New business *and* Sales forecasting, pricing, and promoting policies